THE JESUS MOVEMENT AND ITS EXPANSION

The Jesus Movement and Its Expansion

Meaning and Mission

Seán Freyne

WILLIAM B. EERDMANS PUBLISHING COMPANY

GRAND RAPIDS, MICHIGAN / CAMBRIDGE, U.K.

Published 2014 by

Wm. B. Eerdmans Publishing Co.

2140 Oak Industrial Drive N.E., Grand Rapids, Michigan 49505 /

P.O. Box 163, Cambridge CB3 9PU U.K.

Printed in the United States of America

20 19 18 17 16 15 14   7 6 5 4 3 2 1

Library of Congress Cataloging-in-Publication Data

Freyne, Seán.

The Jesus movement and its expansion: meaning and mission / Seán Freyne.

pages   cm

Includes index.

ISBN 978-0-8028-6786-5 (pbk.: alk. paper)

1. Church history — Primitive and early church, ca. 30-600.

I. Title.

BR165.F77   2014

270.1 — dc23

2014009422

www.eerdmans.com

Contents

Contents

Preface

Several people should be mentioned as facilitators and encouragers as this account of early Christian history and expansion took shape over the past several years.

As always I want to thank my family — my wife Gail and my daughters Bridget and Sarah — for their support and interest in the project. This included travels together at various times to Israel, Jordan, Syria, Lebanon, and Turkey. These journeys will always hold happy memories for me, and hopefully for them also.

I owe a deep debt of gratitude to my doctoral student and colleague Dr. Margaret Daly Denton for her careful reading of the manuscript, despite her own busy schedule. Her recommendations and corrections were invaluable and have ensured that the text reads much more fluently than would otherwise have been the case. Her own excellent knowledge of the field of early Christianity has meant that her suggestions about various topics were invaluable and gladly received. I take full authorial responsibility for any mistakes of fact or style that may have survived her watchful eye.

I must also thank sincerely Mr. Allen Myers, commissioning editor with William B. Eerdmans publishing house. He has been most encouraging about the project from the outset but also embarrassingly patient as various deadlines for the receipt of the manuscript were not met.

Finally, I want to thank Dean Harry Attridge and his colleagues at Yale Divinity School, especially Professors John and Adela Collins, for the warm hospitality I received when delivering the Shaffer lectures at the University in 2010. As I mention in the Introduction it was that experience that encouraged me to pursue further some of the issues having to do with Christian origins that arose then and that, hopefully, have received a more satisfactory treatment here.

Abbreviations

AASOR	*Annual of the American Schools of Oriental Research*
Ant	Josephus, *Jewish Antiquities*
BA	*Biblical Archaeologist*
BAR	*Biblical Archaeology Review*
BASOR	*Bulletin of the American Schools of Oriental Research*
BTB	*Biblical Theology Bulletin*
BZ	*Biblische Zeitschrift*
CBQ	*Catholic Biblical Quarterly*
CRINT	Compendia Rerum Iudaicarum ad Novum Testamentum
FRLANT	Forschungen zur Religion und Literatur des Alten und Neuen Testaments
H.E.	Eusebius, *Historia Ecclesiastica*
HTR	*Harvard Theological Review*
IAA	Israel Antiquities Authority
IEJ	*Israel Exploration Journal*
INJ	*Israel Numismatic Journal*
JAAR	*Journal of the American Academy of Religion*
JBL	*Journal of Biblical Literature*
JR	*Journal of Religion*
JRA	*Journal of Roman Archaeology*
JRS	*Journal of Roman Studies*
JSJ	*Journal for the Study of Judaism*
JSNTSS	*Journal for the Study of the New Testament* Supplement Series
JSOT	*Journal for the Study of the Old Testament*
JSOTSS	*Journal for the Study of the Old Testament* Supplement Series
LXX	Septuagint

NEAHL	E. Stern, ed., *The New Encyclopedia of Archaeological Excavations in the Holy Land* (Jerusalem: Simon and Schuster, 1993; Supplementary Vol., 2008)
NovT	*Novum Testamentum*
NTS	*New Testament Studies*
Q	Q Source
RB	*Revue Biblique*
RHPR	*Revue d'histoire et de philosophie religieuses*
SNTSMS	Studiorum Novi Testamenti Societas, Monograph Series
TSAJ	Texte und Studien zum antiken Judentum
War	Josephus, *Jewish War*
WUNT	Wissenschaftliche Untersuchungen zum Neuen Testament
ZDPV	Zeitschrift des deutschen Palästina-Vereins
ZNW	*Zeitschrift für die Neutestamentliche Wissenschaft*

Introduction

I have long wanted to develop my views on the rise and expansion of Early Christianity within the ambience of the Greco-Roman world. The invitation to publish the Schafer lectures, which I delivered at Yale in the Fall of 2010, provided me with the challenge to develop further various ideas and trajectories that I have entertained for a long time. I am very grateful to Dean Harry Attridge and his Divinity School colleagues, especially John and Adela Collins, for the warmth of their hospitality during my stay. The reception that my talks received was encouraging and persuaded me to persist with presenting a fuller account of my ideas.

When I set about preparing the lectures for publication, however, I quickly realized that they required considerable reworking. The spoken and the written word make different demands. What was originally a set of three lectures on the historical Jesus in his setting has mushroomed considerably to include a fuller treatment of the *matrix* that was Greco-Roman Palestine (chs. 1-3) and four further chapters on the *mission* and expansion of the Jesus movement in Palestine and beyond during the first hundred years of its development (chs. 5-8). The central chapter dealing with the *ministry* of Jesus (ch. 4) expands and develops some of my earlier writing on the topic, especially on his relationship with Jerusalem and his ideas about the future.

It is my belief that the emphasis on Galilee in recent writing on the historical Jesus, while important in giving a specific location for the public ministry, is in danger of distorting the picture, by appearing to set up an opposition between Galilee and Jerusalem. Clearly there were differences, partly those that pertain to the relationship of a religious capital with its more remote hinterland, and partly because of the economic and social

1

demands that the central shrine of Jewish practice and belief could make on the goodwill of all the adherents of its symbolic system. However, to magnify these differences to the point of speaking about Galilean Judaism in opposition to its Judean counterpart, as though they were hostile neighbors, flies in the face of what we know about the situation from literary, historical, and archaeological sources.

My hoped-for readership is not just academics, who may or may not be interested in my "take" on certain methodological issues arising from an enterprise such as this, though, of course, it is always encouraging when one's insights are deemed worthwhile by one's peers in the field of New Testament studies. In writing, however, I have a broader readership in mind, that of the interested layperson who is looking for a more informed view on Jesus and his message through a better understanding of his Jewish upbringing and practice as well as the possible impact of Greco-Roman values and lifestyles on him and his followers.

I have included a number of lengthier than usual footnotes at various points in the text. These are intended to provide information about various aspects of Jewish life and other topics with which the average reader may not be familiar. I have also included some pictorial evidence, since I wish to share with readers my own experience of what firsthand knowledge of the landscape of ancient Palestine can bring to the reading and interpretation of the texts. Maps and time lines will hopefully assist readers in following the sequence of persons, places, and events.

Over the past forty years, there has been an explosion in the amount of archaeological evidence from various regions and sites, all of which adds to our understanding of the social conditions and cultural affiliations of the inhabitants of Hellenistic and Roman Palestine. Ceramic objects, such as pots, pans, and jugs for water and wine tell us about cooking and dietary practices. Vine and olive installations are pointers to the ways in which local produce was harvested and prepared for both domestic and religious use as well as for export. Boats, harbors and other fishing objects are indicators of the importance of the fish industry in the lake region. Building techniques, imported artifacts, decorative aspects such as stuccoed walls and mosaic ornamentation help to distinguish between the rich and powerful and the poor and the oppressed. Milestones and remains of ancient roads tell us about the movements of people for trading and other engagements, as well as the routes taken by ancient armies and pilgrims alike. Coins serve to illustrate the propaganda slogans and images of the ruling elites, as well as provide some indications of the levels of trade and commerce that took place. Tombs tell their own story of regional burial customs and different beliefs about the afterlife. Dedicatory inscriptions can provide important information about the purpose of various public buildings and the particular deities that were worshipped. Stepped pools and public buildings with benches suggest respect for Jewish rituals and religious gatherings away from Jerusalem and the temple. Regional surveys can provide information about demographic changes at different periods. . . . The list is endless, but constantly fascinating for the ancient historian and the modern traveler alike.

While my account falls into three distinct parts — matrix, ministry, and mission — my hope is that the reader will make the connections between them. As the story unfolds, there is a considerable amount of back-referencing in order to remind the reader that we are still dealing with the matrix in which Jesus and his first followers operated. It has been my experience as a teacher that very often the information imparted in standard introductions is forgotten or left aside as interesting but largely irrelevant information when it comes to reading the texts. Background is just that, background, and therefore does not claim our constant attention as readers. It is for this reason that I use the term "matrix" rather than "background," since for me it implies a living, dynamic environment that is constantly interacting with the various levels of human life and activity that are taking place. It assists us in envisaging and being attentive to a complex set of relationships that are operative and at play as the various actors go about their daily chores.

For this first part of the study I have taken three epigraphs, mentioned in passing in Mark's account of Jesus' ministry, as opening hints about the world in which the story is being plotted. As modern readers we can easily pass over these as embellishment or mere local color of little direct impact on the meaning of the story being told. Yet once they are kept in mind as pointers to the matrix of first-century Palestinian life they can help to open windows on processes at work within the narratives that would otherwise go unnoticed.

The first example is Mark's description of Jesus' meeting with the Syro-Phoenician woman (Mark 7:24-30). Alone of the Evangelists in giving her ethnic origins (Syro-Phoenician), Mark also mentions that she is "Greek," an indication that her cultural world was that of a Hellenized resident of one of the Phoenician cities. This vignette points to a long history of the presence of Greek culture in the region as a whole, dating back to Alexander the Great's conquest of the Persian Empire in the fourth century

B.C.E. Tyre and Sidon, the two most important Phoenician cities of the region in the first century, are mentioned subsequently, once in relation to the provenance of those who followed Jesus (Mark 3:8), and a second time in a description of the peripheral territories that Jesus traversed (7:31). This suggests that for the Evangelist this larger world of Greek culture was of significance for Jesus himself, and even more so subsequently for his followers.

One wonders in what language Mark supposed Jesus conversed with the woman — in Greek or in a Semitic one, Aramaic or Phoenician? What were the relations between Galilean Jews and Syro-Phoenicians at this period, given the often fraught conditions that had existed between the two peoples reaching back to Israelite times? In other words, what were the linguistic habits of the region, and how well was Jesus himself equipped to participate in that larger world of Greek culture of the eastern Mediterranean?

My two other examples from Mark's gospel also illustrate in different ways the Roman presence in Palestine. In the first century B.C.E. Herod the Great had aggressively propagated the Greek heritage there, and after his death his sons and grandsons continued the same policy in the divided kingdom: Archelaus in Judea, Antipas in Galilee and Perea, and Philip in the northern Transjordan region. Mark's narrative is strangely silent about the Herodian presence in Galilee, however. Antipas intrudes on the story line briefly, but the account of his birthday celebration surrounded by, among others, "the leading men of Galilee" (Mark 6:14-29) serves merely to highlight the dissolute and dismissive ethos in which the elite treated their subjects. Subsequently, when Jesus is instructing his disciples regarding the exercise of authority in his community, he contrasts the way they are to behave with that of "those who seek to rule over the nations" by "lording over" and "oppressing" their subjects (10:42-45), a veiled allusion, no doubt, to the contemporary situation in Herodian Galilee and Judea.

Two stories in the Jerusalem section of the gospel remind us of the ubiquity of Rome's presence in the land as reflected by the coins in circulation. It should be recalled that in the ancient world all money was minted, not printed, and had a propaganda purpose as well as a commercial value. Jesus is confronted with the conundrum of whether it was lawful to pay tribute to Caesar and replies by asking to see a *denarius*. He was obviously aware that it bore the image and name of the emperor (probably that of Tiberius), but he forces the questioners not only to mention Caesar's name but also to acknowledge that by possessing such a coin they have already implicitly accepted Caesar's authority in the land (Mark 12:13-17).

A second story dealing with coins is that of the Jerusalem widow who casts her two mites *(lepta)* into the temple treasury, a sum, Mark tells us, that was the equivalent of a small Roman coin, a *quadrans* (Mark 12:42). Once again the reader is reminded how Roman control reached down to the lives of even the poorest of the poor. Jesus recognizes the reality of the widow's situation and acknowledges her generosity of spirit, giving up "her whole livelihood." The story illustrates the gulf between rich and poor within Jerusalem society and highlights the issue of social inequality in Roman Judea, even though the levirate law dealing with family responsibility for the wife of a dead brother, was specifically intended to protect Jewish widows (Deut 25:5-10). The Jerusalem community of Jesus-followers whose interests Paul had in mind in making a collection for the poor in Jerusalem (Gal 2:10) may well have come from circles similar to those of this poor widow.

These three examples from Mark's Gospel illustrate the way in which a writer can hint at the larger matrix of life within which his story is taking place but leaves it to the readers to fill in the gaps if they wish to understand fully the processes at work in the lives of the characters. In the opening three chapters of this study I seek to fill out those snapshots more fully.

As just mentioned, the first three chapters of this book are concerned to establish the *matrix* in which the Jesus movement was to emerge and develop in various directions. Chapter 1 deals with the process of Hellenization, that is the encounter between Greek culture and the Semitic world of the East after Alexander the Great's defeat of the Persian king, Darius, in 323 B.C.E. This might appear to be a rather distant point of departure as far as the first-century situation is concerned, yet it must be remembered that the process that had begun with Alexander became even more intense in the Roman period. Hellenization took on a somewhat sinister aspect in the middle of the second century B.C.E. when one of Alexander's successors, the Syrian King Antiochus IV, attempted to replace the worship of Yahweh, the Jewish God, with that of Zeus, the head of the Greek pantheon, with some support from Hellenized Judeans. The response of the loyal Judeans was daring and determined, but the episode left its mark on subsequent relations with the surrounding cities where Greek culture continued to be fostered and celebrated.

Chapter 2 deals with the history of Roman presence in Judea from the middle of the first century B.C.E. up to the two revolts against Rome, 66-70 and 132-35 C.E. The focus here is mainly on the effect of the Herodians on Judean life, especially the support of its most celebrated figure, Herod the Great (king of the Jews 40-4 B.C.E.), for the newly established sole ruler of the Roman Empire, Octavian Augustus. Herod's ambivalent character, Idumean by race but born of a Judean mother, was demonstrated in his active propagation of the cult of Augustus as a divine figure and at the same time his efforts to placate Judean sensitivities by his magnificent expansion of the temple precincts and his rebuilding of the sanctuary itself. On his death, his kingdom was divided among his three surviving sons, one of whom, Antipas, who was assigned to Galilee, was an important figure during Jesus' ministry.

Chapter 3 explores the social and economic situation that developed in Judea from the Hellenistic to the Roman period, in order to understand better the situation that prevailed for ordinary people when Jesus began his public ministry in Galilee after the death of John the Baptist. The results of archaeological explorations are drawn on here for documenting these changes and helping to produce a more accurate profile of conditions in Jerusalem and Galilee in particular. Various different scenarios have been proposed in recent scholarship, particularly with regard to the quest for the historical Jesus, often with quite different if not conflicting views of the situation. To some extent, these differing pictures are due to an over-rigid use of different models for interpreting ancient agrarian societies. The dangers of allowing the model to dictate the resultant picture are very real, especially in the absence of all the relevant data. My own procedure is not to rely on any one model but to combine both a deductive approach based on actual evidence with an inductive application of various theoretical scenarios, in the hope of arriving at the best fit between evidence and social theory in our present state of knowledge.

Chapter 4 is the central chapter of the book, dealing with the *ministry* of the historical Jesus, despite all the attendant obstacles that our sources impose on such an enterprise. The focus here is not substantially different from that of my *Jesus, a Jewish Galilean: A New Reading of the Jesus Story*,[1] even though I have revised and expanded several aspects from the earlier work. That study emphasized Jesus' indebtedness to his own Judean and Israelite heritage, especially that of the Sabbath and Jubilee years, and the importance of the landscape in shaping his responses to the situations he encountered. Josephus's account of Jesus' ministry of word and work in his teaching and healing ministry provides the framework for examining his activity in both these spheres and evaluating its significance. The choice of the Twelve as his permanent retinue places his whole ministry under the banner of Israelite/Judean restoration hopes, and his excursions to what

---

1. Edinburgh: Clark / New York: Continuum, 2005.

may have been deemed as Gentile territory can also be explained within the framework of what may be called "the geography of restoration." This was based on the information about the ideal boundaries for the land as — these continued to be recalled in various circles over the centuries. Chapter 4 concludes with a consideration of Jesus' understanding of the future, including the admission of Gentiles and the circumstances of his death by crucifixion.

The final four chapters deal with the *Mission and Expansion* of the new movement. Chapter 5 focuses on the importance of Jerusalem as center, beginning with a discussion of the significance of the resurrection for Jesus' Galilean followers. Luke's portrayal of the Jerusalem community is discussed, especially the distinction between the Hebrews and the Hellenists, with particular emphasis on their understanding of the mission to the Gentiles. The possibility of Jesus-followers in Samaria is examined, and in addition, the role of James, the brother of the Lord, is assessed in view of his significance for different strands of the Jesus movement in the second century. Chapter 6 then seeks to discover traces of Palestinian Jesus-followers in Galilee and its environs, as seen through the lens of the various sayings sources that are available, especially the Q source, the *Gospel of Thomas* and the *Didache*.

Chapter 7 adopts a similar approach to the narrative gospels, especially Mark and Matthew, both read against the backdrop of the worsening political situation in Judea prior to the first revolt of 66-70 C.E. and its immediate aftermath. Finally, Chapter 8 seeks to trace the transition from the earlier, "New Testament" period to later generations as the Christian movement began to acquire a much higher profile, but also greater diversity, in the second century. Issues of orthodoxy and heresy, the ongoing relationship with the Jewish world, and the need to negotiate the case for being a *religio licita*, not a *nova superstitio*, within the Roman world, are the topics that suggest themselves as most pressing in order to explore developing Christian identity more adequately.

No account of Christian mission and expansion would be complete without a proper treatment of Paul and his journeys across the Mediterranean world. However, thanks to Luke as author of Acts, as well as Paul himself, that story has been told and retold many times. Unfortunately, we do not have such "firsthand" information about the missionaries who brought the message north and east from Jerusalem. It is for this reason that Paul gets rather less treatment in this study than might be expected. Luke's account in Acts has somewhat distorted our understanding of the

Christian mission as a whole. After his Damascus Road experience, Paul shared the horizons of the Hellenists, adopting a strategy of being "a Jew to the Jews" and "to those outside the law as one outside the law" (1 Cor 9:19-23). Thus his success as a missionary was undoubtedly due to his Diaspora Jewish background as a participant in two cultures. However, even though he repeatedly insisted on his Jewish identity when he came under attack from fellow Jewish followers of Jesus (Gal 1:13-17; Rom 9:1-5; 2 Cor 11:21-29; Phil 3:3-6), he was never able to win the full confidence of his Palestinian coreligionist Jesus-followers. Increasingly, it would seem, he saw his mission as that of "apostle to the Gentiles" (1 Cor 9:1-2), in contrast to that of Peter, who was sent to "the circumcised" (Gal 2:7-10), while both sought to maintain their links with Jerusalem.

I have become increasingly convinced of the need to understand the ways in which various issues and trends that were present, but often latent in the first century, came to the surface and had to be dealt with in the second, and thereby to identify features that would become essential hallmarks of the Christian religion subsequently. In this regard one is reminded of the insight of Jewish scholar Jacob Neusner, who has claimed that the fourth century was the real "first century" as far as later Judaism was concerned. This seeming paradox was meant to highlight the fact that rabbinic Judaism was fashioned in the increasingly Christian world of the post-Constantinian accommodation of church and state, whereby Christianity became the religion of the empire. Inevitably, that circumstance was to determine ways that were taken by the parent Judaism and explains why other options, equally valid from the perspective of an earlier diversity, were abandoned.

"Second-century" Christianity was faced with a similar dilemma. Mindful of the fact that terms such as "first" and "second" century are at best very rough approximations of different and distinguishable periods in the life of the early Christians, they are, nevertheless, useful as indicators of shifting patterns and concerns that emerge as new generations of adherents, often from different social and cultural backgrounds to those of the earlier periods, come on the stage. Max Weber's notion of "the routinization of charism" was meant to describe a regular pattern of development in all adventist movements, such as early Christianity; namely, the replacement of the free-flowing charism of the founder by the development of institutional systems of governance that were concerned with order and discipline. One can indeed recognize elements of this pattern in the proposals of various scholars for the Pauline and Johannine trajectories. Yet other external factors came into play, especially in Palestine, where the destruction of the Jerusalem temple and the ongoing tensions with Rome up to the Bar Kokhba war in 132 C.E. left a dissident Jewish movement with messianic claims increasingly vulnerable, caught as it was in a double bind. On the one hand, it was no longer possible to seek refuge in the legal protection that Roman law had granted to the Jews in previous generations. At the same time, Christian Jews living in the land were under pressure to share in the aspirations of Jewish nationalism, the militancy of which was totally counter to the example and memory of Jesus.

Inevitably this situation would give rise to serious anti-Jewish attitudes among Christians of Gentile background. The success of Marcion's preaching in Rome and eventually throughout the eastern Mediterranean can be traced, in part at least, to this growing gulf between the parent Judaism and the Christian offspring by the mid–second century. Marcion eventually solved the dilemma of the Jewish question by his espousal of two gods, the creator and law-giver of the Hebrew Bible and the god who was Father of Jesus Christ. In order to propagate his ideas, Marcion produced his own canon of Scripture, one which rejected the Hebrew Bible entirely and opted for one gospel only, that of Luke. In addition he edited Paul's letters to suit his own theological position, and this meant that the "apostle to the Gentiles," who had played such an important role in the development and expansion of the new movement in the first century, was somewhat ignored by the emerging great church in the second.

The outcome of Marcion's popularity was a growing interest in developing clear lines of demarcation between so-called orthodoxy and heresy, as various apologists for what would eventually become the dominant strand within the new movement came to the fore. The apologists, Justin Martyr, Irenaeus, Hippolytus, and Tertullian, all mounted a vigorous defense of what they perceived to be the true doctrine handed down from apostolic times. The need for a canon, or list of authoritative writings, was a priority, especially in view of Marcion's flawed and seriously truncated collection, which had achieved widespread diffusion. This involved engagement with Jewish lists and their Greek translations on the one hand, and on the other a declaration of those gospels, letters, and other writings from the Jesus movement itself that were deemed authoritative on the basis of apostolic authorship. The fact that there were uncertainties about some of the works that eventually became part of the canon shows that the process of canonization was itself "political," not the result of any divinely inspired revelation received from on high.

In addition to this development of what were deemed to be author-itative Scriptures, another major issue had to be dealt with by the defin-ers and defenders of orthodoxy. This was the presence and attraction of the "gnostics, so-called," as Irenaeus rather disparagingly described them. The discovery of the Nag Hammadi writings in Egypt in 1945 has gradually given rise to renewed interest in this branch of early Christianity, which had been effectively written out of the history ever since the second-century heresiologists employed their rhetorical powers so successfully to vilify them. The fact that the Nag Hammadi writings have come to us in fourth-century Coptic translations rather than in their original Greek versions has meant that study of this material has until recently been the preserve of a few specialists. However, as individual works are edited and studied more carefully, it is becoming increasingly clear that the orthodox charges against the gnostics, especially their alleged lack of any ethical concern, is a serious distortion of the reality. Nor is it correct to categorize all these writings un-der the single label of "gnostic." Various trends that are quite different, often associated with different teachers, have been identified. These often reflect different philosophical positions then current, showing how their authors were engaged in a process of inculturation within the larger intellectual ferment of the time. No account of the development and spread of Chris-tianity is complete unless these documents and the theological positions they represent are also given a hearing, independently of their "orthodox" detractors, ancient and modern.

THE JESUS MOVEMENT AND ITS EXPANSION

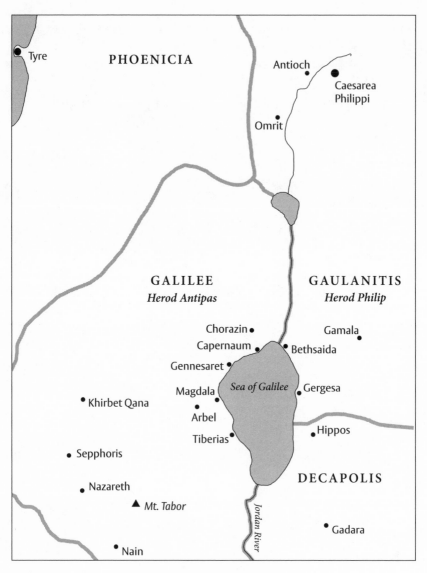

Galilee in the First Century C.E.

CHAPTER ONE

"Galilee of the Gentiles"?

The woman was of Syro-Phoenician origin, a Greek.

(MARK 7:26)

Hellenization is usually understood as the spread of the Greek way of life in the East after Alexander the Great's defeat of the Persian king Darius in 333 B.C.E. The process has often been interpreted as one of suppression and replacement of the much older cultures of the Orient, however. Its impact on Jewish belief and practice has, therefore, been couched in terms of two implacably opposing forces, labeled *Hellenismos* and *Ioudaismos*. These terms appear for the first time in the highly apologetic account in 2 Maccabees, which, together with 1 Maccabees, describes the bravery of Jewish resistance to the Syrian king Antiochus IV Epiphanes. He saw himself as the new Alexander and sought to unite under single rule the vast territory that in the Persian period had been known as "Beyond the River," a province that included both Syria and Egypt.

Hellenistic Reform and Judean Resistance

As part of his overall policy, Antiochus had set out in the mid–second century B.C.E. to transform the Jerusalem cult center into a shrine of Zeus, the head of the Greek pantheon. This action provoked strong resistance from pious Jews, such as the Maccabean family, who were country priests, and others known as the *Hasidim* or pious ones, the forerunners of the later Essenes and Pharisees. The Jerusalem high priestly family had already begun to adapt to Greek ways, however. "The vile Jason," as the author of 2 Maccabees describes one incumbent of the office, had established a *gymnasion* in Jerusalem, where young males were introduced to Greek education, and a *palaestra*, where they could take part in wrestling and other athletic pursuits typical of the Greek lifestyle (2 Macc 4:7-17).

Jason is vilified by the author for having "destroyed the lawful ways of living" and for "showing irreverence for the divine laws," yet the sequel suggests that even the most Hellenized of the Jerusalem elite drew the line when it came to full participation in pagan worship, as Antiochus had demanded. On the occasion of the quadrennial games at Tyre, Jason sent a delegation, described as "the Antiochian citizens from Jerusalem," with an offering of three hundred silver drachmas to honor the patron god of the games, Herakles. However, on arrival in Tyre, the delegation decided that such use of the money was inappropriate and instead allowed it to be used for the building of triremes, thus boosting Tyrian sea power. Religious belief, participation in aspects of Greek culture and economic considerations all intermingle in this incident (2 Macc 4:18-20). It is noteworthy that despite the way in which the delegation is given a decidedly Greek profile by the author, they demur at engaging directly in the worship of the pagan god.

In the century and a half prior to Antiochus's attempt to transform the Jerusalem sanctuary the Jews, like other indigenous peoples of the Near East, had learned to adapt to and indeed benefit from the sweeping changes that followed in the wake of Alexander's defeat of Darius in 333 B.C.E. These changes influenced every aspect of life: commercial, political, and cultural. In the case of the Jews, in particular, their distinctive belief in and worship of Yahweh as the only God, as expressed in the daily prayer, the *Shema* (Deut 6:4-9), received formal endorsement from Antiochus III, the predecessor and father of Antiochus IV. His so-called "Charter for Jerusalem" outlines the privileges and permissions that he was prepared to accord to the Jews of Palestine. He thereby effectively constituted a temple state within the larger kingdom, granting tax exemptions, restoring the temple, and forbidding any foreigner to violate the purity laws associated with the temple and the city (*Ant* 12.138-44). These concessions were due to the fact that the Judeans had supported the Syrian Seleucids in their ongoing struggle with the Egyptian Ptolemies for control of the country, a struggle that had given rise to at least four wars over a protracted period.[1]

---

1. The Seleucids and Ptolemies take their names from two of Alexander's generals who, after his death, came to power in the eastern part of his vast empire. Seleucus controlled

Josephus preserves what is probably a later legend when he recounts how Alexander, on his way to the East to conquer the Persian forces, visited Jerusalem and was met by the High Priest dressed in ceremonial attire and accompanied by the priests and people outside the city. Alexander proceeded to offer sacrifice to the Jewish God under the guidance of the High Priest, having acknowledged that he had already seen him in a vision in Macedonia and had been encouraged by a voice to set out on this campaign. Alexander not only gave the Judeans permission to follow their ancestral laws, including the right to observe the Sabbath year exemption from tax, but also extended this privilege to their kinsmen in Babylonia (*Ant* 11.329-39). The probability is that in fact Alexander never actually visited Jerusalem, such was his eagerness to confront Darius. However, the story neatly underlines the idea that there was no inherent opposition between Greek culture and Jewish religion. The Jewish Diaspora in Egypt had come to this realization earlier still, as the story of the translation of the Torah into Greek at the request of the Ptolemaic ruler illustrates.[2]

Participation in aspects of Greek culture combined with worship of their own God is characteristic of the relationships that continued to prevail in the homeland into the first century B.C.E., despite the brief hiatus caused by Antiochus Epiphanes. Even those who might have benefited from the new possibilities of the Greek world and were prepared to participate in certain aspects of the new cultural situation drew the line when it came to worshipping a god other than Yahweh. It is now generally recognized that Antiochus's attempt to abolish the Jerusalem cult was a brief but shocking interlude in Jewish history, one that created great sensitivity with regard to the temple and its sanctity thereafter, as we shall see. With the gradual demise of the Seleucid regime in the late second century B.C.E., the Maccabean brothers gradually won more independence from their Syrian over-

---

Syria and Ptolemy controlled Egypt, with their respective capitals at Antioch and Alexandria. Throughout the third century B.C.E. their successors fought several wars for control of Palestine, with the Seleucids eventually winning out at the battle of Paneion in Upper Galilee in 198 B.C.E.

2. LXX is the Roman numeral for 70, the number of those who were said to be engaged in the translation of the Bible from Hebrew into Greek; hence the name Septuagint (Greek for seventy) for the translation. The story of the Egyptian king asking to have copies of the sacred books of the Jews available in Alexandria is found in a work entitled the *Letter of Aristeas,* dated to the second century B.C.E., though the Septuagint itself is usually dated to a century earlier. According to the letter's (legendary) account, when the seventy translators arrived from Jerusalem, each was put to work separately. Yet when the work was completed their translations were miraculously identical, thereby assuring its authenticity for Greek-speaking Jews.

lords. Territories such as Galilee and Samaria in the north and Idumea in the south were reclaimed as part of what were deemed to be the ancestral lands on the basis of ancient Israelite traditions (1 Macc 15:33). Thus a new state, known as the Hasmonean state, emerged, and it retained its independent status for almost 100 years, until the arrival of Rome in the person of Pompey the Great, in the middle of the first century B.C.E.[3]

Judeans in Galilee

At the outset it is important to clarify what precisely is meant by the terms "Jew," "Judean," and "Jewish" in this context. Some scholars have recently argued that the term "Jew" is too general, indeed anachronistic for the period of the Second Temple. The claim is that in the sources for that period it carried an essentially geographic connotation, referring to the inhabitants of Judea in the strict sense. Accordingly, *Ioudaios/oi* should always be translated as "Judean(s)," referring to the inhabitants of the former tribal territory of Judah, which was more or less coterminous with the Persian province of Yehud. Josephus appears to endorse this when he declares that the name *Ioudaioi* was applied for the first time to those who returned in 515 B.C.E. from the Babylonian exile (*Ant* 11.173). However, to restrict its range of reference to the purely territorial is to ignore the fact that these first returnees were motivated mainly by their attachment to the Jerusalem temple and the restoration of the cult there after its destruction by the Babylonians in 589 B.C.E. As the Diaspora expanded in the Hellenistic and Roman periods, the name *Ioudaios* came to be associated with those who worshipped in and were supporters of the Jerusalem sanctuary, irrespective of where they were born or resided. Loyalty to the temple and acceptance of the customs, rituals, and practices associated with this worship were the primary criteria for being named a *Ioudaios*. Thus, I do not see any reason to abandon the English terms "Jew" and "Jewish" when referring to such people, while obviously employing "Judean" when it is clear that one is talking about an inhabitant of Judea, as in the case of internal immigration to Galilee from the south.[4]

3. According to the Jewish historian Josephus (*Ant* 12.263), the name "Hasmonean" is derived from the name of the great-grandfather of Mattathias, the father of the Maccabee brothers.

4. S. J. D. Cohen, *The Beginnings of Jewishness: Boundaries, Varieties, Uncertainties* (Berkeley: University of California Press, 1999), claims that before the Hasmonean period the term *Ioudaios* should always be translated as "Judean." He discerns the shift from the

The later Hasmoneans espoused a combination of Greek technical expertise in building, warfare, and commerce with a display of Jewish piety. Thus, they would definitely have thought of themselves as *Ioudaioi* in the full sense of that term — natives of Judea, but also attached to the restoration of the Jewish worship after the desecration of the temple by Antiochus, which had lasted for three and a half years. Their coins were aniconic with legends in Greek and Hebrew, announcing the *Hever ha Yehudim* ("the assembly of the Jews") and claiming the title *Cohen gadol* ("High Priest").[5] This latter claim angered the more pious Jews, who on one occasion in the reign of John Hyrcanus, a second-generation Hasmonean, protested during the Feast of Tabernacles that it was sufficient for him to be king and that he should relinquish the high priesthood (*Ant* 13.288-92). As we shall discuss later, the Hasmoneans' palaces combined luxurious living with definite signs of observing ritual purity.[6] Other indigenous peoples such as the Itureans in the north and the Idumeans and Nabateans in the south and east who had infiltrated the traditionally Jewish lands over several centuries were forced either to convert or to emigrate.

This was the political and religious context in which "Galilee of the Gentiles" was incorporated into the Judean state. That particular epithet for the region went back to the eighth-century Jerusalem prophet Isaiah, who promised that salvation would also come in the future to the whole northern region of the Promised Land, Israelite and non-Israelite alike (Isa 8:23[9:1]). This designation for Galilee was alluded to later by the author of 1 Maccabees to describe the beleaguered condition of the few Jews living in Galilee at the time of Antiochus's attack on the temple (1 Macc 5:15). As we shall see, it also plays an important role in early Christian claims about Jesus' ministry in Galilee. Some modern scholars have made use of the description to suggest that Galilee continued to have a pagan or at least non-Jewish population, even at the time of Jesus.[7] It must be remembered,

---

ethno-geographic to the religious significance of the term in 2 Macc 6:6 and 9:17. See also J. Ashton, "The Identity and Function of the IOUDAIOI in the Fourth Gospel," *NovT* 27 (1985), 40-75, for a detailed discussion of the different proposals for translating the term in the New Testament.

5. U. Rappaport, "The Hellenization of the Hasmoneans," in M. Mor, ed., *Jewish Assimilation, Acculturation and Accommodation* (Lanham: University Press of America, 1989), 2-13, especially 5-6.

6. E. Regev, "Royal Ideology in the Hasmonean Palaces of Jericho," *BASOR* 363 (2011), 45-72.

7. R. Horsley in his important study *Galilee: History, Politics, People* (Valley Forge:

however, that while the Judean expansion to the north by the Hasmoneans involved Greek military strategy and even the use of foreign mercenaries, its stated aim was to reclaim "ancestral lands" (1 Macc 15:33). In this regard, archaeological evidence can help to fill the gaps left by the literary sources.

It emerges from cumulative evidence that from the time of the Hasmonean conquests onward there was a steady growth in the number of settlements in Galilee with a distinctly Judean ethos. These developments more or less coincided with the disappearance of sites that clearly were of non-Jewish character. Thus the important Persian-Greek cultic site Har Mispey Yamim, situated in the center of Upper Galilee, shows signs of deliberate destruction.[8] At other, smaller settlements, the pottery and other remains point to a non-Jewish population in the late Persian and early Hellenistic period. These too begin to disappear by the mid-second century B.C.E.[9] At

---

Trinity, 1995), argues that there was a residue of old Israelite stock living in Galilee who had developed their own customs and practices over the centuries and that the arrival of the Judeans was a colonizing imposition on them from the south. In this he is partly following a position adopted much earlier by A. Alt, who also argued that the Assyrian conquest of the north in the eighth century B.C.E. did not involve wholesale depopulation of the region: "Die Assyrische Provinz Megiddo und ihr Späteres Schicksal," in *Kleine Schriften zur Geschichte des Volkes Israels* (Munich: Beck, 1953-64), 2.374-84. Unlike Horsley, however, Alt sees the incorporation of Galilee into the Judean state as a natural and peaceful transition. However, recent studies of the Assyrian records as well as archaeological surveys in Galilee do not support their assumption of the continuity of the Israelite population of Galilee after the Assyrian invasion. Cf. S. Freyne, *Jesus, a Jewish Galilean: A New Reading of the Jesus Story* (New York: Continuum, 2005), 16, 61-63.

8. In his account of the finds at the site, consisting of a *temenos* or sacred precinct with several adjoining rooms, R. Frankel describes the signs of deliberate destruction of images of the Egyptian triad Osiris, Isis, and Horus. Images of other Egyptian deities were also discovered among the destruction layers. The site's name, literally "the mountain of the two seas," suggests a sacred "high place" from which both the Mediterranean and the Sea of Galilee could be seen. The shrine dates from the Persian period, and its destruction and abandonment took place in the Hellenistic period, a date that coincides with the Judean advances in the north. R. Frankel and R. Ventura, "The Mispey Yamim Bronzes," *BASOR* 311 (1998), 39-55.

9. A number of detailed surveys of various sub-regions of Galilee have been conducted in recent times. While the results are for the most part dependent on pottery sherds and other items found at surface levels and are therefore provisional, a clear pattern seems to be emerging, namely, that some sites were inhabited in the Persian and early Hellenistic periods and were abandoned and not inhabited thereafter, whereas the number of new sites with clear evidence of Judean-style material remains continues to increase from the second century B.C.E. to the Byzantine period. Cf. R. Frankel, et al., *Settlement Dynamics and Regional Diversity in Ancient Upper Galilee* (Jerusalem: IAA, 2001), and U. Leibner, *Settlement and History in Hellenistic, Roman and Byzantine Galilee* (TSAJ 127, Tübingen: Mohr Siebeck, 2009).

the same time a number of new settlements, especially in eastern Galilee and the Golan, start to appear. On the basis of various identity markers, it is assumed that these were established by people of Judean origins, the result of immigration from the south. According to several surveys conducted in the region as a whole the number of these sites continued to increase into the late Roman period.[10] While surface surveys alone can be unreliable, wherever detailed excavations have taken place a consistent pattern emerges with regard to the presence of stone vessels, oil lamps, and household pottery, similar to those found in Jerusalem and Judea.

The presence of stepped pools, usually identified as *miqva'oth* or ritual baths, at various village sites and in domestic settings, as well as the distinctive modes of burial common in Judea, all point to the fact that these settlers were indeed of Judean origin.[11] Until quite recently, few traces of synagogue buildings from the pre-70 C.E. period had been found. However, the discovery of a large public building at Khirbet Qana that has provisionally been identified as a synagogue, as well as one at Magdala, have begun to change the picture.[12] The presumption must be that future excavations at Galilean village sites will

---

10. M. Aviam, "Distribution Maps of Archaeological Data from the Galilee: An Attempt to Establish Zones Indicative of Ethnicity and Religious Affiliation," in J. Zangenberg, et al., eds., *Religion, Ethnicity and Identity in Ancient Galilee* (WUNT 210, Tübingen: Mohr Siebeck, 2007), 115-32.

11. J. Reed, "The Identity of the Galileans: Ethnic and Religious Considerations," in Reed, *Archaeology and the Galilean Jesus: A Re-Examination of the Evidence* (Harrisburg: Trinity, 2000), 23-61, has gathered the evidence from archaeological sites in Galilee for clear links with Judea. D. Adan-Bayewitz, "Preferential Distribution of Lamps from the Jerusalem Area in the Late Second Temple Period (Late First Century B.C.E.–70 C.E.)," *BASOR* 350 (2008), 37-85, shows the preponderance of oil lamps produced in Jerusalem at Galilean Jewish sites, in comparison with sites in the general area where the population was mixed. This is one indicator from archaeology of Galilean pilgrims in Jerusalem, since these lamps had religious significance for the Sabbath celebrations.

12. Khirbet Qana (as distinct from Kefr Cana, which is close to Nazareth) is situated across the Bet Netofa valley to the north. Recent excavations conducted at the site by the late Douglas Edwards and his team have uncovered the foundations of a public building that is provisionally interpreted as the remains of an early synagogue. Reports on the IAA website from Magdala (modern Migdal, on the shore of the Sea of Galilee) confirm the discovery of a table with various decorative reliefs, including a menorah, carved on its side. Stone benches on three sides of the building resemble those at the Gamla synagogue. Cf. D. Edwards, "Khirbet Qana: From Jewish Village to Christian Pilgrim Site," in J. H. Humphrey, ed., *The Roman and Byzantine Near East* (JRA Supplement Series 49, Portsmouth: Journal of Roman Archaeology, 2002), 101-32, especially 113-14; J. Zangenberg, "Archaeological News from the Galilee: Tiberias, Magdala and Rural Galilee," *Early Christianity* 3 (2010), 471-84, especially 475-77 for Magdala.

uncover similar evidence for the earlier period. Furthermore, evidence from sites such as Capernaum, Meiron, and Gischala, where synagogues from a later period have been excavated, shows that these were erected over the ruins of earlier buildings. These early Galilean synagogues closely resemble ones found in Judea from the same period. Rectangular in shape and with stone benches on three sides, they suggest a communal style of interaction. They lack such standard items from later periods as a fixed *bema* or lectern for Torah reading and a shrine for the Torah scroll. However, *miqva'oth* are found in close proximity to such earlier synagogues as the one at Gamla in the Golan and Qiriath Sefer in Judea.[13]

Despite loyalty to their cultural background and its symbol system, comprising of temple, land and Torah, the recent arrivals into Galilee seem to have made use of the possibilities that their new environment had to offer. These opportunities involved harvesting the benefits of the natural resources of Galilee's soil, water, and climate and finding ways of marketing their produce in other regions, such as Tyre and the Dekapolis. In a word they made use of the increased opportunities that the Hellenization process represented, while still remaining staunchly loyal to their Judean roots in terms of observing the customs and practices associated with Judea and the temple. This meant that some at least of the population acquired a certain facility in the Greek language, yet the older Aramaic, which had held sway as the lingua franca since Persian times, would have remained so for the majority of the population.

If these new arrivals were unlikely to embrace all aspects of pagan culture, were they reconnecting with their Israelite cousins from previous centuries, as Alt suggested?[14] Judeans in various Diaspora settings had been able to adapt without renouncing their heritage, as the Egyptian experience, already alluded to, illustrates. For Judeans moving to Galilee the experience was somewhat different. There was a sense that this was indeed part of their inherited land, inhabited in the distant past by the tribes of Zebulon, Naphtali, Asher, and Dan, as the books of Joshua and Judges attested. The unity that the monarchy of David and Solomon had imposed on the loose tribal confederacy that preceded it was a relatively short-lived experience in the tenth century B.C.E. The schism initiated by Solomon's successor Jeroboam

---

13. Y. Magen, "Khirbet Badd 'Isa-Qiryat Sefer," in Y. Magen, et al., eds., *The Land of Benjamin* (Judea and Samaria Publications 6, Jerusalem: IAA, 2008), 179-242.

14. A. Alt, "Die Umgestaltung Galiläas durch die Hasmonäer," *Kleine Schriften,* 2.407-23.

meant that thereafter there were two distinct kingdoms, Judah in the south and Israel in the north, with their capitals at Jerusalem and Shechem/Samaria respectively.

After the Assyrian depopulation of the northern kingdom's territory in the eighth century, the Galilean tribal territories were sparsely inhabited for some time, and a non-Israelite people were planted in Samaria. Yet, Isaiah's prophecy of restoration for the whole northern region, previously alluded to, had promised a redemption that would include all those dwelling in different Assyrian provinces: "The way of the sea," "The land beyond the Jordan," and "Galilee of the Gentiles" (Isa 8:23[9:1]). Hopes of restoration were always kept alive, especially in Judea/Jerusalem because of the promise to David, announced by the prophet Nathan, that his descendants would have Yahweh's special protection and rule for ever (2 Sam 7:4-16). It was this prehistory, remembered and celebrated, that inspired Judeans to settle in Galilee and in some instances at least to see their presence there as a sign that messianic times were imminent.[15]

These ancient stories must have generated a sense of belonging and reassurance, yet the fact remained that Galilee was encircled by Greek cities, each with its own territory, typical of the Greek *polis* system of governance. These cities were expected to function as nuclei of Greek culture in the oriental world that had been the Persian Empire. Yet the reality was somewhat different, depending on the background of different places and their prior cultural and cultic allegiances. Mark's description of the Syro-Phoenician woman, a Greek, whom Jesus encountered on the borders of Tyre, used as the epigraph for this chapter, is typical. In an important article dealing with the nature of the Hellenization process in the Phoenician cities, Oxford historian Fergus Millar pointed out that, because of their extensive seafaring exploits in the Mediterranean, the Phoenicians had a long acquaintance with the Greek world prior to Alexander's campaigns in the East. This meant that in the case of the Greco-Phoenician territories cultural change associated with the process was one of translation rather than wholesale disruption of older patterns of life. These city-territories bordered on the Galilean hinterland, and inevitably this must have led to commercial and other exchanges, despite Josephus's disavowal of any such contact.[16]

15. S. Freyne, "The Geography of Restoration: Galilee-Jerusalem Relations in Early Jewish and Christian Experience," *NTS* 47 (2001), 289-311, especially 292-97, where the relevant literature dealing with Judean hopes of restoration is discussed.

16. In his study *The Roman Near East 31 BC–AD 337* (Cambridge: Harvard University Press, 1993), Fergus Millar has given a detailed account, region by region, of the ways in which

As suggested previously, Greek began to replace Aramaic as the lingua franca of trade, commerce, and administration throughout the eastern Mediterranean from the third century B.C.E., gradually acquiring the status of a prestige language among the elite. In the Jewish world, colloquial or vernacular Hebrew, as distinct from literary Hebrew, also continued to be used, as is clear from the editing in Sepphoris in Galilee of the great Jewish law book the Mishnah, as late as 200 C.E. While lack of sufficient evidence for linguistic practices makes definitive judgments difficult, the question is not so much which languages were spoken, since there is some evidence for all three, Hebrew, Aramaic, and Greek, even in the secluded setting of the Essenes at Qumran.[17]

The real issues are: Which of these languages was most frequently used? By whom? In what circumstances? And what religious and cultural changes does such usage point to? The question previously posed in the Introduction with regard to which language Jesus might have used in speaking with the Syro-Phoenician woman can assist in addressing these broader questions. We might suppose that he was able to converse to some extent in Greek, while Aramaic and/or Hebrew were likely to have been his mother-tongue(s). On the other hand, as culturally Greek but of Semitic origin, she may well have been proficient in several of the languages then in use. An anecdote about an early-first-century B.C.E. Greek poet from Gadara, Meleager, may be relevant in the woman's case also. He considered himself a cosmopolitan and declared: "If you are Syrian, I say *Salam*. If you are Phoenician, *Adonis*. If you are Greek, then *Chaire*." Familiarity with the Greek language alone need not imply wholesale abandonment of one's older heritage, however. As with all immigrants, that would certainly have been true for Judeans of strong nationalistic leanings settling in Galilee. The role that the Greek cities played in the circle of Galilee may well shed further light on these questions.

Greek culture and Roman presence related to the older cultures of the Near East. His discussion of the Phoenician cities is on pages 285-95.

17. For a recent useful discussion of the language situation in Palestine see W. Smelik, "The Languages of Roman Palestine," in C. Hezser, ed., *The Oxford Handbook of Jewish Daily Life in Roman Palestine* (Oxford: Oxford University Press, 2010), 122-44.

Encircled by Greek Cities

Archaeology has shown that the earliest traces of an Israelite presence are in the central mountainous region of Upper Galilee. There the Israelites were indeed "encircled" by such Canaanite cities as Megiddo and Hazor, with whom they had less than cordial relations. It has been suggested that the name "Galilee," meaning "circle," may have originated in those circumstances, and it was no accident that it should reappear in the Hellenistic age as a territorial indicator also. Did this occur because the same experience of being surrounded by centers of an alien culture obtained once again? It is in the sphere of religious dedications and observances that the most obvious signs of Greek influence can be discerned. Even here, however, there is need for caution in estimating the impact of the changes that were occurring. The native gods were often given Greek names, but without changing their basic character, or, as in the case of Samaria, ongoing belief in and worship of Yahweh continued in close proximity to the Hellenized cult in the principal cities there, namely Sichem (ancient Shechem) and Samaria/Sebaste.

Paneas/Caesarea Philippi

On the northern border of the land at the ancient Israelite cult site of Dan, a bilingual inscription (Greek and Aramaic) has been found. It is dedicated "to the God who is in Dan," by one Zoilos. The fact that no name is given for this god suggests to some people that it was the Israelite God, still honored there in the Hellenistic period. Yet the dedicant, Zoilos, has a Greek, not a Semitic, name, and it has been suggested that this god should be identified with Pan, whose shrine is located at nearby Paneion. Pan was the Greek god of hunting and was associated with the outdoors, particularly caves and groves. In Greece he was also associated with protection of soldiers, often patrolling rocky and isolated terrain. His worship consisted of music and merrymaking, so he is sometimes represented, together with Dionysus the god of wine, playing his pipes. His shrine at Paneion consisted of a natural pool at the foot of a deep escarpment in the foothills of Mount Hermon, and it is likely that it was the Ptolemies who introduced his cult to this region bordering on the rival Seleucid territory. However, in their struggle to retain control of Palestine they lost a decisive battle at Paneion in 198 B.C.E. The name Pan is, of course, the same as the Greek word for "all" and in the Hellenistic age Pan took on universal traits. It is no surprise therefore, that the Jerusalem scribe Ben Sira, writing a few decades after the battle of Paneion, appropriated this name for Yahweh, when he writes of the Jewish God as follows: "We could say more, but could never say enough. Let the final word be: He is the All" (Sir 43:27).

Later, Paneion was renamed Caesarea Philippi by Philip, the son of Herod the Great, and it was by that name that the place would have been known in Jesus' day. Yet the older association with Pan was not forgotten, as is evident from the coins of the city. It is noteworthy, however, that it was the *villages* of Caesarea Philippi, not the city itself, that Jesus is said to have visited according to Mark 8:27. There are several possible reasons for Jesus to have visited this region, which will be discussed in a later chapter. However, it should be noted here that there may well be a subtle allusion to Pan and Dionysus in Jesus' contrast between his own open and joyful disposition and that of the ascetic John the Baptist: "We *piped* to you and you would not *dance*, we sang dirges for you and you would not mourn." It was because of this joyful attitude to life that Jesus was labeled by his enemies as "a wine drinker and a glutton," that is, as the leader of a Dionysiac association, a charge that we shall discuss further later in this chapter (Q Matt 11:16-19; Luke 7:31-35).

According to Josephus, it was also believed that one of the headstreams of the Jordan River flowed from the pool of Pan, creating a spring close by and delivering water that was "sweet to the taste and excellent to drink" to the Sea of Galilee (*War* 3.506). This place had become an oracular center for those in search of healing and remained active as a healing sanctuary well into the fourth century C.E. The church historian Eusebius claims that Jesus' healing of the woman with the issue of blood (Mark 5:25-34) took place in this city and that he himself had seen a plant there with miraculous healing properties. This had grown up at the feet of the statue of a man dressed in a comely robe and with his hand stretched out to a suppliant woman kneeling before him. "This," they said, "bore the likeness of Jesus" (*H.E.* 7.18). In the Markan sequence (ch. 8), Jesus' journey to the region takes place somewhat later and is not associated with this particular cure, which Mark reports at an earlier point in his narrative (5:25-34). It may well be that this example of Jesus as healer became associated later with Paneion as a form of early Christian competition with the pagan healing activity associated with Pan's pool.[18]

18. According to Eusebius of Caesarea, a Christian holy man (late third century C.E.) eventually brought the shrine to an end by disproving the miracle that was said to take place

Grotto of Pan at Paneion, renamed Caesarea Philippi by the son of Herod the Great. The site remained a healing sanctuary in Jesus' day.
(Todd Bolen/BiblePlaces.com)

While there are many shrines and inscriptions to pagan gods in the region of Hermon, the place was also important in Israelite lore. According to the psalmist, dew from Hermon would water Zion (Ps 133:3), a reference that suggests more than the physical water that the melting snows from the mountain provided for the whole country. It is quite probable that Hermon was attractive to Jews and pagans alike, since it was by far the highest mountain in the region and was a natural site for belief in a numinous presence associated with high places generally. Indeed an inscription found high up in the mountain range as long ago as 1870, though usually interpreted as a reference to the head of the pagan pantheon, could equally well be understood as a reference to the God of the Israelites. It reads: *theos megistos kai hagios:* "the most high and holy God."

The Jewish apocryphal book *1 Enoch* is a composite work that includes a number of independent segments. One of these is known as "The Book of

there. On a certain festival day a sacrificial animal was cast into the pool and if it did not reemerge at the spring lower down, this was a sign that a healing would take place. However the holy man's prayer was effective and the animal was seen floating on the water, and so, Eusebius claims, the cult fell into disrepute (*H.E.* 7.17).

the Watchers," (chs. 1–36 of *1 Enoch*), dealing, as it does, with a group whose wicked deeds meant that the Most High had passed a sentence of condemnation against them. Enoch, who is described repeatedly as "a scribe of righteousness" and who is charged with announcing the message of condemnation against the watchers, is asked by them to intercede on their behalf. We are told that "they were no longer able to speak or lift their eyes to heaven out of shame for their deeds" (*1 Enoch* 13.5). Enoch, having gone to "the waters of Dan southwest of Hermon" (13.7), prepares himself spiritually before entering a deep sleep and is transposed in a dream vision to the divine throne room. There he encounters "the Great Glory, whose cloak was like the appearance of the Sun and *whiter* than much snow" (14.20). The Great One reassures Enoch, and his role as intercessor on behalf of "those who should have been interceding on behalf of men" is acknowledged. But the judgment against the watchers must stand, since "they have abandoned the high, holy and eternal heaven, and slept with women and defiled themselves with daughters of the people, taking wives and acting like the children of the earth, and begetting giant sons" (15.2-4).[19]

The significance of this episode is the possibility that the Mount Hermon region, whose geography is so precisely marked in *1 Enoch,* was home to a visionary form of Jewish practice that was highly critical of the Jerusalem temple authorities, thinly disguised as the watchers. At least the sacred mountain of the north had been chosen as the most suitable location for this stinging criticism of Jerusalem and its temple personnel. Was Jesus himself and/or the Evangelists aware of this tradition? Mark was the first to locate the Transfiguration story in the immediate context of his journey to the villages of Caesarea Philippi (Mark 9:2-8). Moreover, he stresses the *whiteness* of Jesus' changed apparel in terms very similar to Enoch's description of the Great Glory cited above.

As we shall see in the next chapter, this same region was home to one of the three temples built by Herod the Great to Roma and Augustus,

---

19. The book combines a number of traditions that had developed around this enigmatic figure from the pre-flood period. He is said to have "walked with God, and he was no more" (Gen 5:24). The background to the episode in the Book of the Watchers is the Genesis story, about the sons of God having intercourse with the daughters of men, thereby adding to the evil of the world (Gen 6:1-4). For a development of the suggestion that the Enoch story may have played a part in Mark's account see G. Nickelsburg, "Enoch, Levi and Peter: Recipients of Revelation in Upper Galilee," *JBL* 100 (1981), 575-600. Cf. also Nickelsburg's comprehensive work, *A Commentary on I Enoch Chapters 1–36, 81–108* (Hermeneia; Minneapolis: Fortress, 2001).

celebrating the emergence of Augustus as sole Roman ruler as the arrival of a new age for humanity. There would appear to be more than mere coincidence to the fact that it was here, under the shadow of Hermon, that Jesus' followers proclaimed him as Messiah (Mark 8:29). In that event, not merely was Mark hinting at severe criticism of the Jerusalem religious elite on the part of Jesus and his movement, but the power and prestige of Rome were being confronted with another vision of the new age, one that would not merely proclaim peace and justice but actually seek to have these values implemented through revolutionary praxis.

Tyre, Sidon, and Ptolemais/Acco

To the west the Phoenician cities and their territories separated Galilee from the Mediterranean coast, prompting Josephus to write — a little chagrined it would appear — that "the Jews were not a maritime people" and had "no interest in commerce nor the intercourse with the outside world that it promotes" (*Ag. Ap.* 1.60). The founder god of Tyre, Melqart, was given the name of Herakles (Latin Hercules), the Greek hero who had achieved the Olympian status of the gods through his heroic deeds ("The Labors of Hercules"). He was also celebrated as the founder and patron of cities and was therefore a suitable equivalent of Melqart. Similarly, Eshmun who had a healing sanctuary in Sidon became Asklepius, the Greek god of healing. Nearby was another temple dedicated to the Semitic female goddess Astarte, who is mentioned together with both Melqart and Eshmun even prior to the Greek period and is celebrated as "the one who listens."[20] In both instances the process of renaming the city gods took care to respect their original Semitic character while giving them Greek identities. In other words, Hellenization could be a two-way process and did not always involve the destruction of the older culture, but rather its translation into a Greek idiom.

While Tyre and Sidon were likely to have impinged directly on Up-

---

20. S. Freyne, "Galilean Studies: Old Issues and New Questions," in Zangenberg, et al., eds., *Religion, Ethnicity and Identity*, 13-32, especially 16-19, with a discussion of some of the cult objects recovered from Har Mispey Yamim and Qadesh. Of greatest interest is a *situla* or ritual drinking cup which was originally engraved with an image of a dedicant making offerings to a number of Egyptian gods, identified in hieroglyphs. Around the rim an inscription in Phoenician has been incised secondarily that reads: "Aqbar son of Bod-Eshmun for Astarte because she listens to my voice."

per Galilee, Ptolemais/Acco was, according to Josephus, directly opposite Lower Galilee. Its adjoining territory, the Plain of Acco, rich in vitreous sand, was surrounded on all sides by mountains (*War* 2.187-91). Its harbor offered easy access to the interior for commercial operations, as in the case of Zenon's tour of inspection of the Ptolemaic royal estates in the region.[21] Several military sorties were also launched against Galilee from Ptolemais, especially in the Roman period when it was raised to the status of a Roman *colonia* by the emperor Nero. This meant that Roman veterans were permanently settled in the territory with the purpose of maintaining Roman peace in the region. In fact, one of the city coins features the emperor plowing with an ox and a cow as part of the foundation ceremony of the colony, with standards of four different Roman legions in the background.

Ptolemais was founded in 261 B.C.E., the only city in the region that maintained its dynastic name over the centuries and also the first to mint its own city coins. Many of these coins, though dated to the Roman imperial period, reflect aspects of the mythology of the city's gods: Perseus with the Medusa's head; a wounded Herakles receiving a medicinal plant from the river Belus, with Tyche seated on a rock; a boat inside the harbor of the city, the only such representation of a harbor on a coin from Palestine; a nude Aphrodite standing in her bath; a sacred tree with two guardian serpents; a statue of Zeus Heliopolites, the patron god of the city, standing in a portable shrine with his thunderbolt.[22]

While these coins give an insight into the official mythology of the city, two inscriptions found in the territory dated almost six centuries apart can tell us more about individual beliefs. Despite the difference in time between them, they also demonstrate the persistence of particular divinities in the region, and their relationship with other cult sites in the east. The earlier of the two, to be dated probably to the mid–third century B.C.E., not long after the founding of the city by Ptolemy Philadelphus, reads as follows:

21. See V. Tcherikover's study *Palestine under the Ptolemies: A Contribution to the Study of the Zenon Papyri. Mizraim I-IV* (New York: Stechert, 1937) for an important study of this papyrus archive from Alexandria dealing with Zenon's tour of Ptolemaic Palestine on behalf of the finance minister Apollonius. In his magisterial study of Jesus' parable of the wicked tenants (Mark 12:1-12) John S. Kloppenborg presents the text in Greek with an English translation of fifty-five Zenon papyri dealing with viticulture: *The Tenants in the Vineyard* (WUNT 195; Tübingen: Mohr Siebeck, 2006), Appendix I, 355-543.

22. Y. Meshorer, *City Coins of Eretz-Israel and the Dekapolis in the Roman Period* (Jerusalem: The Israel Museum, 1985), 12-15 and 110-11, numbers 1-53 in the catalogue.

To Hadad and Atargatis,
the gods who listen,
Diodoros the son of Neopolemos
on behalf of himself and Philistia
his wife and the children
(has dedicated) the altar
in fulfillment of a vow.

As the eminent Israeli scholar Michael Avi-Yonah, who published both inscriptions, notes, this early one has three interesting features: the dedicants are Greeks on the basis of their names, yet they retain the Semitic names of the gods they wish to honor without any attempt to offer a Greek equivalent; the deities are described as "the gods who listen."[23] Hadad and his consort Atargatis were ancient Syrian deities with a long and checkered history. Hadad was deemed to be the equivalent of the old Canaanite deity Baal Shamem, Lord of the Heavens, and was worshipped on high mountains. The thunderbolt was one of his symbols, thus making his assimilation to Zeus among the Greeks natural. However, he was also identified with the Sun God and so was worshipped at the great sanctuary Baalbek/Heliopolis in the Lebanon.[24]

It is this connection that makes the second inscription interesting also. It reads:

To Heliopolitan Zeus, (god of) Carmel,
Gaius Iulius Eutyches, colonist of Caesarea . . .

This inscription is from a plinth with a foot belonging to a larger than life statue attached. The dedicant in this instance has a Latin name and is a

23. M. Avi-Yonah discusses both inscriptions: "Mount Carmel and the God of Baalbeck," *IEJ* 2 (1951), 118-24; "Syrian Gods in Ptolemais/Akko," *IEJ* 9 (1959), 1-12.

24. The cult of Atargatis had spread widely both in the Near East and the Mediterranean, including Greece, eventually arriving in Rome, where a temple to the goddess was established and she was known as Dea Syria, the Syrian Goddess. Unusually for a consort deity, Atargatis kept her own name and identity better than Hadad, and she was extremely popular with Syrian merchants, slaves, and military personnel, who were probably responsible for the wide diffusion of her cult. It had its primary seat at a Syrian city called Hierapolis, close to the Euphrates River. A water ceremony that attracted devotees from all over Syria was the main activity at her shrine, and in the procession her image preceded that of Hadad, according to Lucian of Samosata, a second-century c.e. Greek writer who had traveled through Syria and described the various shrines he visited.

colonist of Caesarea, not Ptolemais as we might have expected. What is particularly interesting is that Zeus of Heliopolis (i.e., Baal Shamem/Hadad) is identified with the god of Mount Carmel, where the inscription was found. This god (Baal/Lord) is known from the famous episode involving the Hebrew prophet Elijah that is told in 1 Kings 18. Elijah engages in a power struggle with the priests of the god of Carmel, whose worship was being propagated by the royal house of Samaria. Writing in the early second century C.E., the Roman historian Tacitus knows of a god of Carmel, presumably the same god that Elijah encountered. However, Tacitus declares that there was no image or temple of the Baal of Carmel, "an altar only and reverence" (*Histories* 2.78).

These two inscriptions illustrate the persistent attraction of the Semitic gods for Greeks and Romans who find themselves in the East. The explanation for this phenomenon would seem to be the belief that, unlike the aloof Olympians of the Greek pantheon, about whose very existence Greek philosophy was beginning to raise serious questions, the eastern deities were deemed to be interested in the fate of humans. The description of Hadad and Atargatis as *hypekooi,* that is, "listening gods," and the fact that the god of Carmel was seen as an oracular deity who cared for the needs of suppliants, suggest that it was this caring aspect that made them attractive. It also explains the popularity of the Jewish God among Greco-Roman pagans, as can be seen in the various mentions of "God-fearers" in inscriptions in Jewish synagogues and elsewhere such as, for example, the famous one from Aphrodisias in Asia Minor.[25] This should be seen as one of the factors that brought about the rapid spread of Christianity also. Not merely did the Christians proclaim a God who listens, but they now also had a "new god," the risen Jesus, who differed from the newer gods of paganism like Dionysus and Herakles in being a real human person of history, as the biographical dimension of the gospels attests.

Despite this attraction there would appear to have been little contact, commercial or cultural, between the Judeans of Galilee and Ptolemais. Per-

---

25. A. Chaniotis, "Godfearers in the City of Love," *BAR* 36 (2010), 32-44. The term "God-fearer" or "worshipper" occurs most frequently in the Acts of the Apostles, where it is used of Gentiles who are in close association with Jewish synagogues and are receptive to Peter and Paul, in contrast to Jews who reject their preaching. Several inscriptions, especially from Asia Minor, refer to them also, but without necessarily implying anything more than Gentiles who had good relations with their Jewish neighbors and assisted them in certain civic undertakings. They differ from Gentiles who had, in fact, fully converted to Jewish faith and practice and were known as proselytes.

haps memory of the antipathy between Elijah and the priests of Carmel's god played some part in the animosity that continued to exist both for the Maccabean brothers and the Hasmoneans (1 Macc 5:21-23; 10:46-48) and for the Galilean Jews of the first century C.E. (*War* 2.457-60, 477-80). Evidence of trading between the two regions in terms of city coins of Ptolemais being found at nearby excavated Galilean sites such as Jotapata and Sepphoris, is minimal, once the Judean expansion to the north had taken place. A little vignette from Josephus is illustrative. Just prior to the outbreak of the first revolt in 66 C.E., the Roman legate of Syria, Cestius Gallus, advanced on Galilee from Ptolemais. On arriving at the Judean border village Chabulon, he found that all the inhabitants had fled. Nevertheless, he reluctantly sacked the village, even though he admired the beauty of the houses that had been built in the Phoenician style (*War* 2.503-4). Clearly, architectural borrowings did not signify cultural exchange or religious tolerance. It is interesting also to note that even though there is some evidence in the tradition that Jesus' ministry was inspired by the prophet Elijah, he is not said to have traveled in this region nor to have visited Carmel, as we might have expected.

The Cities of the Dekapolis

As one of the regions visited by Jesus, Mark also mentions the territory of the Dekapolis (literally "the ten cities"), situated east of the Sea of Galilee. These cities formed a loose federation, which the Roman general Pompey the Great had established as part of Rome's strategy in the eastern Mediterranean region in the mid–first century B.C.E. This fact continued to be remembered on the coins of these cities in subsequent centuries, all of them adopting the Pompeian era in their dating. Two of these cities, Hippos and Gadara, overlooked the Sea of Galilee from the eastern side and were therefore close neighbors but also potential rivals of the various Jewish towns along the western shore of the lake such as Capernaum, Bethsaida, Magdala, and later Tiberias. Both Hippos and Gadara had suffered at the hands of the Hasmonean Alexander Jannaeus as he expanded the Judean territory in the early first century B.C.E.

Despite Pompey's restoration of their autonomy, strained relations between the inhabitants of these cities and their Judean neighbors were to continue into the first century C.E. During the reign of Herod the Great they sought independence directly from Augustus by diplomatic means, but these efforts failed (*Ant* 15.315, 354-58). Both cities and their territories were transferred to Agrippa II in 56 C.E. by the emperor Nero. A decade later, immediately prior to the Jewish revolt of 66 C.E., we hear from Josephus of the burning of some of the villages of Gadara and Hippos by people from Tiberias, led by an important citizen whom we shall meet later, Justus of Tiberias (*Life* 42). We must assume, therefore, that earlier, in the thirties of the first century, a Judean prophet/healer coming into their territory from Galilee would not have been very welcome. Furthermore, the profiles of both places that can be drawn from archaeology and scattered literary sources indicates that a strong Greek ethos prevailed.

Hippos/Susita: Herakles and His Deeds

Recent excavations at Hippos/Susita have uncovered the remains of a thriving city that was destroyed by an earthquake in 749 C.E. The city was founded in the early Hellenistic period, but reached its heyday in later Roman and Byzantine times when it was an important ecclesiastical center with several churches. One of these was built on the ruins of a pagan temple from the Hellenistic period that had been destroyed, probably by the Judean king Alexander Jannaeus as he sought to conquer and "cleanse" the ancestral land of its pagan symbols between 83 and 80 B.C.E. (*Ant* 13.394-97). Pompey restored it some 20 years later, however, and Hippos/Susita continued to thrive thereafter, as can be seen today from the paved streets, an aqueduct, Corinthian columns, an agora, and an open-air temple that probably housed a statue of the reigning emperor.[26]

One find is particularly interesting, namely the discovery of a stuccoed head of Hercules, beautifully crafted, emphasizing his indomitable spirit and strength. The discovery was made in the ruins of the bath-house, which itself can be dated to the mid–second century B.C.E. Presumably this head adorned the entrance, just as a statue of Aphrodite adorned the entrance to the bath-house in Ptolemais/Acco, according to the Mishnah, prompting a clever reply from Rabbi Gamaliel when asked why he would

26. At the time of writing, the excavations are still in progress at this site. Three popular articles by the excavators as well as a report from the first five seasons at the site are the most up-to-date accounts so far. A. Segal and M. Eisenberg, "The Spade Hits Sussita," *BAR* 32 (2006), 40-51, 78; "What's Luck Got to Do with It?" *BAR* 36 (2010), 24, 70; "Hercules in Galilee," *BAR* 37 (2011), 50-51; *Hippos-Sussita: Fifth Season of Excavations and Summaries of All Five Seasons (2000-2004)* (Haifa: University of Haifa, Zinman Institute of Archaeology, 2004).

Decumanus maximus at Hippos, a Hellenized
town of the Dekapolis east of the Sea of Galilee.
(Image courtesy of www.HolyLandPhotos.org)

enter a bathhouse with a statue of a pagan goddess.[27] Hercules, we have
seen, was the patron god of Tyre, but clearly his popularity was not confined
to any one place, given his bravery in completing the labors that the gods
had imposed on him as punishment for his irascible nature. His story was
extremely popular throughout the whole Mediterranean region, raising the
question whether the emphasis on Jesus' mighty deeds in the various gospels may have been intended to challenge the Greek hero's popularity. We
shall return to this question in a later chapter.

Gadara: Meleager and Wisdom, Asklepius and Healing

The second city of the Dekapolis that overlooked Galilee was Gadara,
whose territory Jesus probably visited, despite the variant reading at Mark

27. Rabban Gamaliel's reply to the question why he was bathing in a bathhouse that
had a statue of Aphrodite displayed was: "I did not enter her domain, but she entered mine"
(Abodah Zara 3.4). This reply suggests that the famous rabbi was not in favor of pagan symbols in the land of Israel but had found a way to accept what he could not change without
compromising his beliefs.

5:1.[28] This city (modern Um Qais in Jordan) is particularly interesting. Not only did it have a thriving Greek cultural ethos that is better documented than in other places, but it was also famous as a healing center in antiquity.[29] We already encountered (p. 22) one of its citizens when discussing the issue of languages, the cosmopolitan Meleager (first century B.C.E.), who could converse in three different tongues and whose poetry was tinged with a satirical tone. He is one of four poets/philosophers from this city mentioned by the first-century C.E. historian and geographer Strabo. One of the others, Menippus, a satiric poet had lived 200 years earlier and is mentioned as Meleager's inspiration in one of his epigrams. In this brief four-line poem Meleager also mentions Gadara as "the new Athens in Assyria," even though he had later studied in Tyre and lived on the island of Cos in his old age. Clearly, the city had a proud literary history throughout the Hellenistic period, and Meleager, in fact, is said to have claimed that Homer, the father of Greek poetry, was a native of the region also. Meleager is just one of several poets from this city who, inspired by Menippus's work, displayed a mastery of several genres — satire, parody, epigram, and love poetry. It is this virtuosity that has prompted some modern scholars to suggest that Gadara was home to the Cynic philosophy, which at a popular level was countercultural and dismissive of conventional values.[30]

Some recent discussions of Jesus' pithy and proverbial sayings, as well as his itinerant lifestyle, have suggested that the Cynic philosophy had taken root in Galilee also, and that he too was influenced by its worldview.[31] However, this suggestion is most unlikely for several reasons, not least the strained relations historically between Jewish Galilee and the Dekapolis. Furthermore, the worldview of Meleager and his ilk is very

---

28. In opting for the Matthean reading "Gadarenes" (Matt 8:28) rather than "Gerasenes" (Mark 5:1 and Luke 8:26) I am swayed by the geographic descriptions that the story presumes, that is, close to the lake with a steep incline, despite the text-critical view that "Gerasenes" was the original.

29. Thomas M. Weber, "Gadara and Galilee," in Zangenberg, et al., eds., *Religion, Ethnicity and Identity in Ancient Galilee,* 449-76, for a summary of his detailed study of Gadara. See n. 32 below for more publications on Gadara by this scholar.

30. See M. Hengel, *Judaism and Hellenism* (Philadelphia: Fortress, 1974), 1:83-87, on Gadara's literary history.

31. G. F. Downing, *Christ and the Cynics: Jesus and Other Radical Preachers in First Century Tradition* (Sheffield: Sheffield Academic, 1988); John Dominic Crossan, *The Historical Jesus: The Life of a Mediterranean Jewish Peasant* (Edinburgh: Clark, 1993). Cf. critique by Hans Dieter Betz, "Jesus and the Cynics: Survey and Analysis of an Hypothesis," *JR* 74 (1994), 453-75.

different from that of Jesus, whose hopes for a new age stem from Jewish apocalyptic and messianic aspirations. Meleager, despite his pride in his native city, traveled widely, but did not find a true home and did not return to Gadara, despite his admiration for its culture. The tradition of parody and satire challenged the norms of the dominant Stoic philosophy, which viewed the *kosmos* as an ordered whole, based on the model of the ideal Greek city. "Chaos has created death for all," he writes, even as he announces his ability to speak different languages as a citizen of the world. His universal outlook would seem not to have brought him any more assurance about life's meaning.

Jesus' association with Gadarean Cynics or familiarity with their teachings would appear to be somewhat unlikely, therefore. Nor is there any great probability that the Cynics would have been welcome in the Judean towns and villages of Galilee. The healing practices associated with the Gadara region would appear to be a more likely attraction for people to cross cultural and ethnic boundaries. The Syro-Phoenician woman who was prepared to approach the Jewish healer Jesus on behalf of her daughter is illustrative of such flexibility when it came to issues of life and death.

A first-century B.C.E. Greek papyrus containing an incantation formula against all kinds of inflammation is attributed to a Syrian woman from Gadara. This would suggest that the healing arts were associated with the city from quite early in the Greek period. It was during the reign of Emperor Antoninus Pius in the second century C.E. that clear evidence of a health spa emerges. The site is some 7 kilometers from Gadara, in the gorge of the river Yarmuk at a place called Emmatha/Hamat Gader. Due to the volcanic nature of the rock in the whole rift valley from Banias in the north to Kalirhoe near the Dead Sea in the south, a number of such mineral-rich hot springs were known in antiquity. The healing properties of these springs were recognized, but their locations also functioned over time as recreational centers for elites as well as centers for philosophical discussion. Herod the Great, for example, developed such a center at Kalirhoe, and visited the site shortly before his death in the hope of being healed (*Ant* 17.171-81). In time Hammath Gader was to develop into a very important center, as can be seen today from the architectural remains of the main building. This consisted of an impressive oval-shaped hall of fountains, where bathers could experience water at different temperatures, arriving eventually at the *clibanus* or oven-like spring in which the water was 51 degrees C. In addition a number of other rooms offered privacy for those who were taking part in the special incubation ritual associated with the healing god Asklepius.[32]

Originally, Apollo, the son of Zeus, was known for his healing powers as well as his other attributes within the Greek pantheon. However, the need for a more individual and personalized form of religion began to emerge, something that was accentuated by the greater mobility of people in the Hellenistic Age. Sickness and healing, like life and death, were deemed to be in the hands of the gods, and consequently the art of healing became closely associated with religious observances of various kinds. In addition to the ancient remedies that had been handed down through the generations, study of the human body and the beginnings of scientific medical knowledge also made an appearance in this period. This was the context in which Asklepius, who was a human hero in Homer's *Iliad*, achieved divine status as Apollo's son. He appealed more directly to the needs of individuals than the lofty Olympian gods, and records of his popularity can still be seen today at such famous centers as Epidauros in Greece, Pergamon in Asia Minor, and the island of Cos. The many votive offerings and inscriptions at these shrines give us an insight into the thoughts and hopes of wealthy suppliants who came to the shrines in search of healing.[33]

Inevitably, the cult of Asklepius spread quickly to the east. The transformation of the Sidonian god Eshmun to Asklepius, already mentioned, is another example of how the accommodation of a Greek god with a Semitic original could occur. The name Eshmun is derived from the word for oil (Hebrew *Sheman*), which was in frequent supply in Upper Galilee and was deemed to have healing properties as well as being used in food preparation. The evidence from the Gadara region comprises statues of Asklepius from the city itself as well as from other cities of the Dekapolis such as Pella, Jerash, and Philadelphia/Amman. An altar relief from Gadara (now sadly missing) depicts the god in military dress but with a mild expression. The military dress seems to be a local feature, since he appears in similar guise

32. The most detailed archaeologically based study of Gadara is that of Thomas M. Weber, *Gadara Decapolitana. Untersuchungen zur Topographie, Geschichte, Architectur und Bilden Kunst einer "Polis Hellenis" im Ostjordanland* (Wiesbaden: Harrassowitz, 1993). Cf. also his "Thermalquellen und Heilgötter des Ostjordanlandes in römischer und byzantinischer Zeit," *Damaszener Mitteilungen* 11 (1999), 433-51 and table 57-60, especially 442-46 on Hamath Gader.

33. Aelius Aristides, a second-century C.E. Greek writer and native of Asia Minor, spent a considerable amount of time in the *Asklepeion* at Pergamum and has left us a detailed account of his dreams and revelations from Asklepius in a work entitled *The Sacred Teachings*.

in two other reliefs found in the Golan. He holds a spear in his right hand, and the serpent that is a constant in all depictions of him is coiled around the spear. Sometimes also he is represented with his daughter *Hygeia* (the Greek term for health) with a thoughtful and kindly gaze. She appears on her own also on several coins from Tiberias, seated on a rock and feeding the snake.[34]

Some of the details in Mark's story of Jesus' visit to the region of the Gadarenes take on an added significance when read with an awareness of their city's popularity as a healing center in mind. The people Jesus encounters in the story are from the territory, the *chōra*, not from the city itself. It is safe to say that already in the first century C.E. hot springs had been developed at Hamath Gader similar to those at Hamath Tiberias across the lake. We might ask why a remedy was not sought there, rather than the rather crude form of restraining the possessed man by chains. Clearly there are two different clienteles in question, namely, the elite who could avail themselves of the medicinal and therapeutic facilities of the health spa and the country peasants who would not be in a position to frequent such places and had to rely on folk healers or magical formulas.

Another comparison is worth making at this point also, one to which we will return in a later chapter. Among the techniques associated with the cult of Asklepius was incubation, a ritual sleep in order to obtain a dream with regard to healing. We have an interesting account, albeit from a much later period, of what was involved in a visit to a shrine of Asklepius. An anonymous Christian pilgrim to the Holy Land from Piacenza in Italy describes a visit to Hamath Gader in 570 C.E. as follows:

> We went to a city called Gadara, and three miles from the city there are hot springs called the baths of Elijah. Lepers are cleansed there, and have their meals from the inn at the public expense. The baths fill in the evening. In front of the basin is a large tank. When it is full, all the gates are closed and they are sent in through a small door with lights and incense, and sit in the tank all night. They fall asleep, and the person who is going to be cured sees a vision. When he has told it the springs do not flow for one week.

34. Snakes were regarded as guardians in antiquity, possibly because of their habitat in crevices and underground caves. As such they became associated with various gods, especially Demeter, whose daughter Persephone had been snatched by Hades and brought to the underworld. During a plague the Romans brought the snake of Asklepius from Epidauros, and the snake chose the island in the Tiber as its Roman home.

This description and the techniques involved differ pointedly from the Gospels' accounts of Jesus' healings. True, Mark does mention the use of spittle and touching in two accounts (Mark 7:33; 8:23). But even then, in the first of these instances where the actions would appear to border on the magical, Jesus utters a cry as he looks to heaven, suggesting reliance on divine power rather than on any human technique. In terms of some recent discussions of medical anthropology, Jesus could be said to range between the categories of the popular healer and the folk healer, rather than being a professional healer. While the borders between the first two categories are often blurred, the third is clearly well defined in terms of acquaintance with medical knowledge, as this had been developed in the Greek world, especially in the Hippocratic corpus. Shrines of Asklepius would appear to have combined all three categories, but clearly only the elite were able to enjoy the luxuries of access to professional healers associated with such places.

Scythopolis and the Wine God

A third member of the Dekapolis group of cities that bordered Galilee was Scythopolis, situated near an old crossing of the Jordan. Of all the cities of the Dekapolis, Bethshan/Scythopolis had by far the oldest profile, dating back to chalcolithic times. In the early Israelite period it was an Egyptian outpost, before being incorporated into the kingdoms of Saul and David. The visitor to the site today first encounters a highly impressive Roman town with bathhouse, a theater, a colonnaded street, and a hippodrome nearby. These buildings reflect the developments of a later period before the city's destruction in the earthquake of 749 C.E. Behind the Roman town stands the impressive Tel Beth Shean, where as many as seventeen strata of occupation have been uncovered.

The city received its new Greek name in the early third century B.C.E., when a Scythian military colony was stationed there. A century or so later it received the added name Nysa, which appears on the city's coins thereafter. This was based on a legend claiming that Nysa, the nurse of the young Dionysus, was buried there. A later (141-42 C.E.) inscription from a hexagonal altar with Dionysiac motifs on each side proclaimed "the Lord Dionysus, the founder of the city."[35] The city suffered at the hands of the Hasmoneans,

---

35. For the coins of Scythopolis in addition to Meshorer (n. 22 above, pp. 39-42) cf. Rachel Barcay, *The Coinage of Nysa-Scythopolis* (Jerusalem: Israel Numismatic Society and

but was restored by Pompey, and, like the other cities of the Dekapolis, dates its era from the Roman general's rearrangement of the Judean territory in 63 B.C.E. It is the only one of the ten cities that is situated on the western side of the Jordan, and consequently it would seem to have had a different relationship with Judeans. Pilgrims from Galilee to Jerusalem who did not wish to travel over the central hill country through hostile Samaritan territory would cross the Jordan close to Scythopolis and travel south through Perea as far as Jericho before making the *aliah* or ascent to the Holy City.

The connection of Scythopolis with the wine god Dionysus is of special interest for our understanding of the ways in which the Greek culture penetrated Judean society, especially in Galilee. Unlike others of the newer gods in the Greek pantheon, Dionysus was not confined to any one country or place, but, in the words of the Roman historian Tacitus, "he conquered the Orient." Alexander the Great was deemed by his earliest biographers to have emulated Dionysus's journeys to the East, where, according to the legend, the god had taught the Indians how to cultivate the vine and how to conduct their worship of the gods, including Dionysus himself, with wine. The historian Arrian makes the connection explicit when he writes of Alexander's visit to Nysa as follows: "He [Alexander] had already reached the point where the god [Dionysus] reached, and would go even further" (*Anabasis* 5.1.5-7). Alexander's successors inevitably continued the tradition of the links with the god, and it comes as little surprise that, as well as introducing Zeus to the Jerusalem temple, Antiochus IV insisted on Jews wearing ivy wreaths as they processed on the feast day of Dionysus (2 Macc 6:7; cf. 14:33).

Dionysus was honored as the discoverer of the delights of the grape, an event that was celebrated every year at Tyre. Thereafter, the Phoenicians introduced the gift to Greece and ultimately to Rome, where the god was known as Bacchus. Jews, too, could integrate aspects of Dionysus worship into their celebration at the Jerusalem temple. On the occasion of the rededication after its three-year profanation by Antiochus, they are said to have carried *thyrsi,* the sacred staffs that were symbols of Dionysus worshippers, and worn ivy wreaths on their heads (2 Macc 10:7). The book of Judith, a first-century B.C.E. tale of Jewish triumph over their enemies

---

Bar Ilan University, 2003), especially 112-33 for images of Dionysus on the city coins. The inscription declaring him "founder" of the city has been studied by Leah di Segni, "A Dated Inscription from Beth Shean and the cult of Dionysos *Ktistes* in Roman Scythopolis," *Studia Classica Israelitica* 16 (1997), 139-61.

through the intervention of a woman, concludes with a triumphant victory dance led by Judith and the other women of Israel as they approached the temple in Jerusalem. They are said to have carried *thyrsi* and are garlanded with olive wreaths (Jdt 15:12-13). This scene is uncannily similar to those of dancing women celebrating aspects of Dionysiac worship as this is known to us from Greek literature and from various mosaics and pottery decorations. Yet Judith and her companions are celebrating the God of Israel rather than Dionysus.

These adaptations of aspects of Dionysiac worship within Judean ritual were possible because of the long association of Yahweh, the Jewish god, with the gift of wine as well as other bounties of nature. In Isaiah's description of the banquet that Yahweh will prepare for all peoples, wine features prominently: "fine wines" and "fine strained wines" are prepared (Isa 25:6). The same prophet likens Israel to a vineyard that he cares for in a special way, and, despite Israel having become a wasteland and suffering judgment for a time (5:1-25), the image recurs as part of the description of restoration to come: "That day, sing of the vineyard of wine! I, Yahweh am its keeper; every moment I water it for fear its leaves should fall; night and day I watch over it" (27:2-3). Indeed the perceived affinity between the Jewish god and the Greek Dionysus was such that Plutarch, the Roman writer, believed that the Jewish feast of Tabernacles was a Dionysiac festival (*Quaestiones Conviviales* 6.1). Tacitus, too, was aware of the identification but dismissed it, contrasting the joyful rites of Dionysus with the "sordid and absurd customs of the Jews" (*Histories* 5.5.5).

As is well known, women were given a restricted place in the Jerusalem temple, not being allowed to pass beyond the women's court, because of the strict purity laws concerning menstruation. Thus the image of Judith and her female companions preceding the males as they dance their way into the Temple in a manner that mirrors a Dionysiac procession is striking, even subversive. This theme of female devotion to Dionysus had been famously developed already in the fifth century B.C.E. by the Greek tragedian Euripides. His play *The Bacchae* deals with the rejection of Dionysus by the city of Thebes, even though Dionysus's mother Semele was a Theban princess. He has his revenge by bringing about a state of madness in the women, including the king's mother, and prompting them to worship him in a wine-induced orgy on the mountains. When the king spies on the celebration, he is mistakenly believed to be a wild animal and is torn to pieces by the women. His own mother carries his head triumphantly back to Thebes, only to discover when her frenzy subsides that she has killed her own son.

The play explores the vengeful power of the divine in Greek mythology and the tragic consequences of emotions run wild. Despite Euripides' critique of the excesses of the Dionysiac worship, it continued to prosper as a mystery cult for initiates, which also included men in the Roman period. Eventually the Roman Senate intervened and banned the worship in Italy as early as 186 B.C.E.

The worship of Dionysus continued to prosper in the East also well into the Christian era. A magnificent floor mosaic discovered in a wealthy villa at Sepphoris, dated to the early third century C.E., gives a unique view of how a more domesticated form of the worship of Dionysus continued to have particular appeal, dare one say in a Jewish city, or at least in a city where Jews still had a prominent role in civic and religious life.[36] The mosaic consists of a central panel depicting Dionysus and Herakles engaged in what has been described as a drinking contest, though it is more likely intended to suggest that Herakles was a member of a Dionysiac association. A number of separate scenes depicting episodes from the Dionysus legend surround the central panel, each with a Greek label. These display a detailed knowledge of the mythology concerning Dionysus and his experiences. An outer panel depicts a procession approaching the god with gift-bearers, flute players, and the flora and fauna associated with the god of the vine and other vegetation. A medallion of a beautiful lady at one side of the mosaic recalls the popularity of the god with female devotees, possibly suggesting that the house of this wealthy matron was the center of a Dionysiac cult group.

The Sepphoris mosaic is dated to the early third century C.E., but the popularity of Dionysus was undoubtedly well established in the Palestinian region as elsewhere in the East much earlier. While there is evidence of males playing some role in Dionysiac celebrations later, the special appeal for female devotees is well documented. In the past this phenomenon has often been explained in terms of "the emotional needs of women" or the association of Dionysus with fertility. However, modern feminists rightly resist such "explanations," pointing instead to the complex social and political situation of women in ancient societies, no less than in many modern societies. Their ascribed roles of child-bearing and performance of domes-

---

36. Eric M. Meyers, Ehud Netzer, and Carol L. Meyers, "Artistry in Stone: The Mosaics of Ancient Sepphoris," *Biblical Archaeology* 50 (1987), 223-27; *Sepphoris* (Winona Lake: Eisenbrauns, 1992); R. Talgam and Z. Weiss, *The Mosaics of the House of Dionysus at Sepphoris* (Qedem 44; Jerusalem: Institute of Archaeology, Hebrew University, 2004).

tic chores such as cooking and weaving were taken for granted. Success in these roles did not earn the same status as that accruing to males who excelled in the public spheres of warfare, hunting, agriculture, commerce, and the like. This imbalance in status recognition required some remedial outlet, and participation in the Dionysus cult would appear to have provided such a safeguard for many women in the Mediterranean world.[37]

The devotees of Dionysus were known as maenads, that is, women possessed by a divine spirit of the god, and this phenomenon, however induced, freed them from any responsibility for their actions. That they would "return to normality" was recognized and accepted by the males in the society, and social stability was thus assured rather than threatened by their actions. These involved a deliberate inversion of "normal" activity, for example, child bearing, in order to engage in activities such as hunting that properly belonged in the male sphere. Judean society was no more tolerant of females who deviated from the accepted social norms than any other in the ancient world. Yet the story of Judith who, while using her female charms, beheaded the wicked Holofernes and then engaged in joyful celebration with the other women of Israel, clearly merited acclaim in the tradition. The mother of the Maccabean martyrs is another example of a woman displaying the bravery associated with males in recommending death to her seven sons rather than betrayal of their ancestral values (2 Macc 7:1-41).

The issue of Dionysiac influences among Jesus' first followers has been discussed mainly in terms of the wine-making miracle at Cana (John 2:2-10). This story is certainly quite different from all the other accounts of miracles and signs in both the Synoptic Gospels and the Fourth Gospel. However, the argument that the author had in mind a competition between Dionysus and Jesus is not wholly convincing. In particular the alleged parallels between the Johannine story and one from a later period dealing with a Dionysus festival at Tyre celebrating the god's gift of wine are by no means as clear as some have claimed.[38] But this does not remove Jesus' Galilean

37. Ross M. Kramer, "Ecstasy and Possession: The Attraction of Women to the Cult of Dionysus," *HTR* 72 (1979), 55-80.

38. M. Smith, "The Wine God in Palestine: Gen 18, Jn 2 and Achilles Tatius," in *Salo M. Baron Jubilee Volume* (Jerusalem: Israel Academy of the Sciences, 1975), 815-29, includes a description of a Phoenician wine festival by a Greek writer of romances, Achilles Tatius. Smith seeks to give an early date to this writer's work and claims the passage in question as a contemporary parallel to the Cana story of John 2. Not everybody agrees with this dating, and the parallels between the two stories are not as obvious as Smith claims. The Cana story belongs to the miracle genre, dealing with the changing of water into wine, whereas the

ministry from the sphere of the Dionysus cult. The response to those in his audience who rejected both John the Baptist and Jesus himself would appear to offer a more promising starting point.[39]

In the early Q saying mentioned previously, Jesus accuses his audience of neither responding to John's doleful message nor to his own joyful one in terms that seem to presuppose the Dionysus cult in the background:

> To what then will I compare the people of this generation? They are like children sitting in the market place and calling to one another, "We played the flute for you and you did not dance; we wailed and you did not mourn." For John has come eating no bread and drinking no wine, and you say, "He has a demon." The Son of Man has come eating and drinking and you say, "Look a glutton and a drunkard, a friend of tax collectors and sinners." Yet Wisdom is justified by her deeds. (Luke 7:31-35; Matt 11:16-19)

Mention of flute playing and dancing recalls the Dionysiac orgies, but also Pan with his pipes. Jesus' message proclaimed the joy and peace of messianic times, but his opponents refused to listen. Neither did they take heed to John's message of repentance. Instead, they vilified Jesus as a wine drinker/ *oinopotēs* (and a glutton). The Greek term *oinopotēs* is quite rare, but it does suggest the excesses that were usual among the devotees of Dionysus. Furthermore, the charge of being a "friend of tax collectors and sinners" has equally negative connotations in terms of Jesus' association with the representatives of foreign power and with prostitutes.[40] In all probability this charge was provoked by the presence of women as well as men in Jesus' permanent retinue. His ultra-conservative opponents seek to label him as a Dionysiac, but he responds by aligning himself with Lady Wisdom, who invites all, both wise and foolish, to come and partake of her wine and eat of her bread (Prov 9:1-6), symbols that will later become important in early Christian worship.

Achilles story is aetiological, explaining the origins of a wine festival. P. Wick, "Jesus gegen Dionysos? Ein Beitrag zur Kontextualisierung des Johannesevangeliums" *Biblica* 85 (2004), 179-98; W. Eisele, "Jesus und Dionysos. Göttliche Konkurrenz bei der Hochzeit zu Kana (Joh 2, 1-11)," *ZNW* 109 (2009), 1-25.

39. S. Freyne, "Dionysos and Herakles in Galilee: The Sepphoris Mosaic in Context," in D. R. Edwards, ed., *Religion and Society in Roman Palestine: Old Questions, New Approaches* (New York: Routledge, 2004), 56-69.

40. S. Freyne, "Jesus the Wine Drinker, Friend of Women," in *Galilee and Gospel: Collected Essays* (WUNT 125; Tübingen: Mohr Siebeck, 2000), 271-86.

Samaria

The likelihood of Samaria, either as region or as city, having any major influence on Galilean life in the Hellenistic-Roman period is minimal. Two episodes from the first century C.E. illustrate the point. The Evangelist Luke tells us that the Samaritans rejected Jesus' emissaries because "his face was set toward Jerusalem" (Luke 9:53). Josephus is even more explicit in describing the harassment that Galilean pilgrims were likely to experience as they traveled through Samaritan territory on their way to Jerusalem for the festivals.

During the reign of Claudius (c. 48 C.E.), a group of Galilean pilgrims was attacked and one pilgrim *(War;* or "a multitude" in *Ant)* was killed, giving rise to open hostilities. The Jerusalem authorities attempted to pacify the Galileans who had already arrived in the city, but failed to prevent them engaging a brigand chief to lay waste some Samaritan villages, causing the procurator Cumanus to intervene. Eventually the governor of Syria was called in, and, having dispatched the leaders on both sides, he sent the others who were involved, including the Jewish High Priest, the temple captain, and Cumanus to Rome in chains, there to explain the whole affair to the emperor (*War* 2.232-47; *Ant* 20.118-36; cf. Tacitus *Annals* 12.54). Little wonder that the Samaritan woman was more than a little surprised, when, according to the Fourth Gospel, the Galilean Jewish prophet Jesus, returning from Jerusalem, asked her for a drink as he rested at Jacob's well near Sychar in Samaria. The Johannine author explains: "Jews do not associate with Samaritans" (John 4:7-9).

Such regional hostilities had a long prehistory, dating back to the Assyrian conquest of the north in the eighth century B.C.E. Archaeological investigation indicates that Galilee and Samaria were both devastated by different Assyrian kings, Galilee by Tiglathpileser III in 733 B.C.E. and Samaria by Shalmaneser I in 721 B.C.E. However, while there is no mention of Galilee being repopulated, people of a non-Yahwistic background were planted in Samaria according to 2 Kgs 17:24. Josephus, who as a member of the Jerusalem high priestly circles had his own axe to grind against the Samaritans of his day, seeks to date the schism between the two religious centers to this event, claiming that the new settlers were Cuthean foreigners of devious and unfaithful character, as reflected in their religious rites "up to this day" (*Ant* 11.290).[41]

---

41. S. Freyne, "Behind the Names: Galileans, Samaritans, *Ioudaioi,*" in E. Meyers,

However, there are serious problems, both historical and archaeological, concerning such claims. There is independent evidence that the Samaritans continued to understand themselves as Israelites as late as the second century B.C.E. At some point, probably already in the Persian period, that is, the fifth to fourth century B.C.E., they had built a temple on their sacred mountain, Gerizim, close to the old Israelite center of Shechem.[42] It was there that Joshua had renewed the Mosaic covenant in a solemn ceremony involving the twelve tribes of Israel immediately after the conquest of the land in the tenth century B.C.E. (Joshua 24). The Samaritan temple features in an incident in Egypt that occurred during the reign of Ptolemy Philometer (180-45 B.C.E.) that is highly informative. Shortly after the Judean High Priest, Onias IV, the incumbent when Antiochus Epiphanes had intervened, had been ousted, he received permission from the Ptolemaic ruler to build a temple for Yahweh worshippers in Egypt (*Ant* 13.66). Soon afterward Judeans and Samaritans appeared before the king debating as to whether offerings should be sent to the temple in Jerusalem or to that on Mount Gerizim, as the authentic Mosaic shrine (*Ant* 13.74; cf. 12.10). While the king favored the former group and the leaders of the Samaritans were executed, the episode clearly indicates that they also regarded themselves as Yahweh worshippers, even if they did not subscribe to the Yahweh-alone party's claim that it was only in Jerusalem that the God of Israel could be worshipped. There is further evidence from the Samaritan diaspora, this time from the island of Delos, where a first-century B.C.E. inscription mentions "the Israelites who make their offerings to holy Argarizim."[43]

In the light of this evidence one is tempted to ask why the Samaritan animosity toward the Galileans if, as Alt and later Horsley have claimed, they were descendants of the Israelites? Indeed in the period of the divided kingdom from the time of Jeroboam's secession from the Davidic/Solomonic kingdom in the ninth century B.C.E., the inhabitants of Samaria

---

ed., *Galilee through the Centuries: Confluence of Cultures* (Winona Lake: Eisenbrauns, 1999), 39-56.

42. The date of the building of the temple is disputed, partly due to the difficulty of interpreting Josephus's account in *Ant* 11.302-46. Cf. J. Zangenberg, *Samareia. Antike Quellen zur Geschichte und Kultur der Samaritanerin deutscher Übersetzung* (Munich: Franke, 1994), 59-64; R. Marcus, *Josephus, Jewish Antiquities*, VI (Loeb Classical Library, Cambridge: Harvard University Press, 1966), Appendix C: "Alexander the Great and the Jews," 513-32.

43. P. Bruneau, "Les Israelites de Délos et la Juivriie Délienne," *Bulletin de correspondence hellénique* 106 (1982), 465-504; A. T. Krabel, "New Evidence for the Samaritan Diaspora Has Been Found on Delos," *BA* 47 (1994), 44-46.

and Galilee belonged together in the northern kingdom of Israel, separated from the southern kingdom of Judah. The hostility toward the Jerusalem priestly class can be dated to the period of the immediate return from the Babylonian exile of some Judeans in 515 B.C.E. These returnees refused the offer of assistance from the Samaritans in rebuilding the temple in Jerusalem. It is possible that it was this that prompted the Samaritans' building of a separate temple on Gerizim, a mountain that also had its own biblical warrant as a holy mountain (Deut 27:11-16; cf. 11:29-30). Its first High Priest was a Judean, Manasses, who had married the daughter of the governor of Samaria, Sanballat, and was ostracized by his coreligionists for taking a foreigner as wife. It is against this background that the Judeans who inhabited Galilee after the Hasmonean conquest of the north were seen by the Samaritans not as fellow Israelites but as hostile Judeans who were unwelcome in Samaritan territory.

The Hellenistic period exacerbated the strained relationships further, as Greek influences were more pronounced in the region. Many commentators accept the information that it was at the time of Alexander the Great that the Gerizim temple was built, as an account in Josephus claims (*Ant* 11.306-12). However, this may well be a further example of the Jerusalem author's bias against the alternative temple in the land, suggesting that it was an illegitimate foundation from the outset.[44] Unlike the strong Judean resistance to Antiochus Epiphanes in his attempt to impose the worship of Zeus in Jerusalem, Josephus claims that the Samaritans had asked Antiochus to introduce the cult of Zeus "the friend of strangers," even though the author of 2 Maccabees suggests that it was imposed on the Samaritan cult-center by Antiochus (*Ant* 12.257-64; cf. 2 Macc 6:2).

At all events the Samaritans were the first to bear the brunt of the Hasmonean backlash. John Hyrcanus, the father of the dynasty, sacked the city of Samaria after a year-long siege, probably in 108-107 B.C.E., having previously (113-112 B.C.E.) destroyed the Gerizim temple and the nearby city of Shechem (*Ant* 13.254-56, 275-81; *War* 1.63-65). A colony of Sidonians had been settled there, presumably for commercial reasons associated with this fertile region. Not unlike the role of Jason and his followers in Jerusalem in the same period, these Phoenician settlers may have been responsible for the Hellenistic ethos of the city and the shrine. Despite these changes the majority of the inhabitants of the region, especially those living in the coun-

---

44. R. J. Coggins, *Samaritans and Jews: The Origins of Samaritanism Reconsidered* (Oxford: Blackwell, 1985), 96-97, 103-6.

tryside of Samaria, continued to be Yahweh worshippers, as the story of the Alexandrine Samaritans and the Delos inscription testifies.[45]

The Gerizim temple was never rebuilt, but the mountain remained holy for the Yahweh worshippers there. It was among these that the Samaritan Pentateuch came to be established as their sacred text over time, and there is archaeological evidence to suggest that the purity laws were practiced and synagogue gatherings held in the region also.[46] Yet the rift with Jerusalem was never healed. The city of Samaria recovered under the Romans, having been made the capital of the district by Pompey's successor Gabinius in 57 B.C.E. (*Ant* 14.88). Some decades later in 28 B.C.E. the newly installed emperor, Octavian/Augustus, bequeathed Samaria and its territory to Herod the Great, who immediately renamed it Sebaste, to honor his patron. Herod also planted 6000 veterans in the fertile region of the city and built the first of his three temples to Roma and Augustus there as part of his effort to promote the cult of the newly established sole ruler of the Roman world, a topic that will be dealt with in the next chapter.

Conclusion

In this chapter we have traced the Hellenization process as it impacted on the Judeans, following the leads from the literature of the period and from archaeological evidence from both Galilee and Jerusalem. The aim of the chapter has been to focus on those aspects of the situation that touch on the story of Jesus as this is told in the Gospels, especially that of Mark. It has emerged that despite the trauma brought about by Antiochus IV's desecration of the Jerusalem temple and the strong resistance mounted by the Maccabees and their successors, Jews in both Galilee and Jerusalem did not wholly turn their back on the Greek world. Rather, many availed themselves of the opportunities that were on offer within the larger context while resisting any easy assimilation to that culture, especially its religion.

45. Y. Magen, "Qedumim — A Samaritan Site of the Roman-Byzantine Period," "Ritual Baths *(miqva'oth)* at Qedumim and the Observance of Ritual Purity among the Samaritans," and "Samaritan Synagogues," in F. Manns and E. Alliata, eds., *Early Christianity in Context* (Jerusalem: Franciscan, 1993), 167-80, 181-92, and 193-30.

46. R. Pummer, "Samaritan Pentateuch," in J. J. Collins and D. C. Harlow, eds., *The Eerdmans Dictionary of Early Judaism* (Grand Rapids: Eerdmans, 2010), 1189-90, who claims on the basis of comparison with some Dead Sea Scrolls texts that the origins of the Samaritan Pentateuch can be dated to the second or first century B.C.E.

A strong Judean presence emerged in Galilee, but with a long lasting and deep attachment to the symbols of Jerusalem and its temple. This confirms the view that, despite some scholarly claims, the epithet "Galilee of the Gentiles" was not an appropriate description of the population of the region from at least 100 B.C.E. The discussion of the Greek cities that formed a virtual circle around the province opened windows on that larger culture, particularly its gods and their worship. These provide interesting and important points of comparison with Jesus and his movement as it spread in all directions during the first to the fourth centuries C.E. We shall return to these issues in subsequent chapters, but next it is necessary to explore the Roman presence in Palestine.

The story of the gradual expansion of Rome's influence in the East began already in 190 B.C.E. with the defeat of the Seleucid king, Antiochus III at the battle of Magnesium in Greece. The growing importance of their expansion for the indigenous peoples of the eastern Mediterranean was quickly recognized by Judas Maccabeus, who sent a delegation to Rome requesting a treaty of friendship between the Romans and the Judeans (1 Maccabees 8). The leader of the delegation, Eupolemus, was in all probability the same person who wrote a history of the Jews in Greek, fragments of which are still extant. This exercise in *realpolitik* on the part of Judas was quite significant subsequently. As his name suggests, Eupolemus was a Hellenist, and he could therefore reassure the Roman Senate that, despite their stand against Antiochus's attack on their native religion, the Jews were not averse to all aspects of Greek culture, so popular among elite Romans. Julius Caesar would recognize the long-standing relationships between the two peoples and reaffirmed the treaty between them. It was only in the first century C.E. that the relationship became strained to the breaking point as Judean nationalism began to reassert itself in ways that could not easily be reconciled with Roman imperialism.

Table One: Important Hellenistic Rulers and Events

333 B.C.E.	Alexander the Great, the Macedonian king, defeats Persian King Darius at Ipsus in Syria and is crowned king of Persia, but dies suddenly in 323. Even though Greek influences in the East predate these events, the beginning of the Hellenistic Age proper is associated with Alexander's campaigns.
323-301	Period of the *Diadochi* or Successors, as Alexander's generals vied for power. Eventually the Seleucids in Syria and the Ptolemies in Egypt

are successful, but there is an ongoing conflict between these two ruling houses throughout the third century B.C.E. Palestine, or Coele-Syria, as it was also called, was often the theater for these wars.

300-198   The Ptolemies were in control of Palestine and introduced many aspects of Hellenistic culture, administration, and commercial expertise to the country. Alexandria was the new capital of Egypt and a large Jewish Diaspora was quickly established there. The Hebrew Bible was translated into Greek in Alexandria sometime in the mid–third century B.C.E. It is known as the Septuagint ("seventy," or LXX) because of the legend surrounding its translation by seventy men as told in the later *Letter of Aristeas*. This Greek Bible was used by the early Christians subsequently, giving rise to disputes with Jewish opponents about translations of various important passages.

259   Tour of inspection of various estates in Palestine by Zenon, a high official of the Ptolemaic regime, who had introduced landowning patterns similar to those in Egypt. Zenon's reports are preserved in the *Zenon Papyri* and are a precious snapshot of conditions in Palestine at the time, indicating the extensive trading patterns that operated between the two countries. They reveal a highly organized local bureaucracy of estate managers, tax officials, border guards, and peasant serfs, who were not always amenable to centralized control.

198   After several unsuccessful attempts the Seleucid king, Antiochus III (223-187), was victorious at the battle of Paneion (later Caesarea Philippi) in Upper Galilee. He was assisted by the Jews in having the Ptolemaic garrison removed from Jerusalem, and he granted them generous tax concessions.

190   Antiochus, who had been active in Asia Minor was defeated at the battle of Magnesium, resulting in a large war indemnity being imposed on the Seleucid regime by the Romans, who had now begun to move eastward.

175-64   Antiochus IV Epiphanes, who succeeded his father, had ambitions to be another Alexander. However, the war indemnity to Rome was a major problem. In 169 he plundered the Jerusalem temple on his way to Egypt. In 167 he issued a decree outlawing the Jewish religion and imposing Zeus worship on the Jews as a way of uniting all the peoples of his realm. This gave rise to the Maccabean uprising, which would eventually win political autonomy for the Jews. As a first step the temple was rededicated in 164 B.C.E., a victory that the book of Daniel anticipates. The Seleucid dynasty waned after Antiochus's death as internecine disputes took over, allowing various indigenous peoples, including the Jews and the Itureans, to emerge. Rome would eventually establish the province of Syria to fill the political vacuum left by the demise of the Seleucids.

Table Two: The Maccabees and the Hasmoneans

164 B.C.E.	The Jerusalem temple is rededicated after the victories of Judas Maccabeus over the Seleucid generals.
152	Jonathan, Judas's brother, accepts the High Priesthood, thereby possibly ousting the legitimate successor, who has been identified with the Teacher of Righteousness, the reputed founder of the Qumran community.
142	Simon, the third Maccabean brother, is confirmed as religious and secular leader of the Jews and gains tax concessions from Seleucids.
134	The beginnings of the independent Hasmonean state, with John Hyrcanus, son of Jonathan, as ruler. The Jewish philosophies are first mentioned: Sadducees, Pharisees, and Essenes. The Essenes may have been the same as the Hasideans mentioned in 1 Macc 2:29.
104	Aristobulos I, John Hyrcanus's son, takes the title "King of the Jews." Internal emigration of Judeans to Galilee takes place.
103-76	Alexander Jannaeus takes over from his brother Aristobulos. He attacks Hellenistic cities in Palestine, including Samaria, and wins more of the "ancestral lands" east of the Jordan. He encounters internal opposition from the Pharisees, however.
76-67	Alexandra, wife of Alexander, is queen regent. Pharisees begin to play an important role in political life.
67	Pompey, the Roman general, intervenes in Judean politics because of civil war between the two sons of Alexander, Hyrcanus II and his brother Aristobulos II. Pompey enters the Jerusalem temple, an offensive act for pious Jews who long for a just king (*Psalms of Solomon* 17–18).
63	The Roman governor of Syria, Gabinius, dismantles the Hasmonean state and establishes five different local councils, one of which is centered at Sepphoris in Galilee.
47	The young Herod is appointed as governor in Galilee but runs afoul of the Jewish Sanhedrin by executing a local leader without seeking permission in Jerusalem.

40-37   Antigonus II, a Hasmonean prince, with the assistance of the Parthians, Rome's opponents in the East, declares himself king of the Jews. Herod the Great is appointed "king of the Jews" by the Roman Senate, giving rise to a bitter civil war, which Herod eventually wins. He purges Judea of Hasmonean nobles, even though he has married the Hasmonean princess Mariamne, whom he subsequently also murders with her sons. He also takes control of the High Priesthood and introduces appointees from the Diaspora.

CHAPTER TWO

The Roman Presence

Is it lawful to pay taxes to Caesar or not?

(MARK 12:14)

Mark's gospel, we have seen, is strangely reticent about the Roman presence in Jesus' Galilee. Yet in the episodes dealing with the coin of the tribute and the widow's mite we catch a glimpse of the controversial nature of that presence, but also a hint of its social implications for the poor and the marginalized. This chapter will concentrate on the scale and nature of the Roman presence in both Galilee and Judea. Insofar as Jesus' ministry took place in Galilee, as narrated in the Synoptic Gospels, his likely encounter with Rome was mediated through the Herodian presence of Antipas and his administration as a client ruler on behalf of Rome. It was in Judea that Jesus would come face to face with direct Roman rule in the person of the procurator, with his power to suppress peremptorily any movement that might challenge Rome's belief that it was destined to rule the world.

Herod the Great and the Imperial Ideology

Jesus' career coincided with the first decades of what has come to be called "the Augustan Age." After a period of civil war when various alliances of military commanders sought to seize power, Octavian, the adopted son of Julius Caesar, had become the sole ruler of the far-flung territories, east and west, that constituted the Roman Empire. Defeat of the other contender,

Mark Antony, in the battle of Actium in 31 B.C.E. led to his being hailed as both *Imperator* or sole ruler and *Augustus* by the Roman senate. This latter honorific title suggested a divine aura for the ruler. Its Greek equivalent, *Sebastos,* expresses more clearly a status that called for reverence toward the person of the emperor on the part of his subjects. Such an understanding was based on a much older oriental notion of the divine origins of the ruler, who could be described as "a son of god," suggesting divine paternity. Roman poets Horace and Virgil, historian Livy, and client kings such as Herod the Great sought to celebrate the new age that had dawned and Rome's rightful position as the center of the world. The provincial council of Asia declared that "the birthday of the most divine Caesar should serve as the same new year's day for all the citizens." Records of Augustus's achievements, the *Res Gestae Divi Augusti,* were carved in stone and erected in the provinces, and cities competed for the honor of being declared *neokorate,* that is, given the right to celebrate the imperial cult annually.[1]

It is important to emphasize that the arrival of Rome in the East in no way halted the promotion of Greek culture. If anything, there was an intensification of the process of Hellenization. "Captured Greece conquered the arms of its capturers" is how one Roman poet described the fascination of the Romans with Greek culture in every sphere — literature, architecture, art, sculpture, and language. As far as Judea/Palestine was concerned, there is a contrast between the ways in which the Hasmonean elites and the Herodian elites embraced aspects of the Greek way of life. It has been said that while the former "acted Greek without becoming Greek," the latter "embraced Greek culture with enthusiasm and alacrity."[2] As client kings of Rome, the Herodian house was very much dependent on imperial favor and consequently followed the trends that were set at the center. Indeed some of Herod's descendents were educated in the imperial household in Rome. Herod himself was a lavish benefactor of many projects in Syria, Rhodes,

---

1. S. R. F. Price's study *Rituals and Power: The Roman Imperial Cult in Asia Minor* (Cambridge: Cambridge University Press, 1984) has been highly influential in discussions of what was involved. For him, the cult must be seen within the network of power relations between the center and the periphery of the Roman Empire. It involved, therefore, a two-way process, namely a public display of Rome's claim to universal rule and a grateful recognition by subject peoples that they accepted the implications of such a claim.

2. B. McGing, "Hellenism, Judaism and the Hasmoneans," *Simbolos. Scritti di Storia Antica* 1 (1995), 57-74; T. Rajak, *The Jewish Dialogue with Greece and Rome: Studies in Social and Cultural Interaction* (Leiden: Brill, 2002), especially 61-80 dealing with the Hasmonean uses of Hellenism.

and Asia Minor. In Greece he contributed to the renewal of the Olympic games, which had fallen into disrepute, and was appointed president of the games for life because of his munificence (*Ant* 16.149).

Nothing exemplifies better the unquestioned acceptance by Herod and his successors of the Roman imperial ideology than the manner in which the imperial/ruler cult was enthusiastically embraced. In 28 B.C.E., within a year of Octavian being declared Augustus by the Roman senate, Herod planned a lavish celebration in Jerusalem to honor him (*Ant* 15.267-79). These celebrations consisted of athletic and theatrical events, chariot races, gladiatorial contests, and the dreaded *venationes,* which involved humans fighting with wild beasts. Inevitably there was an outcry from some of the Jerusalem populace, particularly the charge that Herod had introduced idolatrous images into the holy city. It should be recalled that Judaism had a strong aniconic tradition, whereby no image of the divine was tolerated, in accordance with the second command of the Decalogue received at Sinai. In the Greek world, on the other hand, athletic contests had a strong religious significance. Those who excelled either in athletics or the more aesthetic contests were deemed to have been endowed with a special divine gift, thereby manifesting further the power of the "divine" emperor in whose honor games were being celebrated.

From the outset, therefore, there was the potential for a clash between worship of the only God as enjoined in the Torah and recognition of the emperor as divine. The destruction of the Jerusalem temple by the Romans in 70 C.E. must be seen as the inevitable outcome of the clash between these two opposing worldviews. Worship of the emperor was later to become a problem for Christians also when they developed an understanding of Jesus' divine origins and were confronted with the choice of publicly recognizing the emperor's status or accepting martyrdom. A famous letter from the governor of Bithynia, Pliny, to the emperor Trajan in 112 C.E. illustrates the tension perfectly. On the one hand the Christians sang "hymns to Christ as to a god" when they assembled for their sacred meal, whereas Pliny required that they offer incense to the statue of the emperor under pain of arrest and execution (*Letters* 10.96).

Missing from Herod's Jerusalem celebration in 28 B.C.E. were such cultic rituals as sacrificial offerings, a sacred meal, prayers, and a procession of a cult statue. All or some of these features were important in the celebrations elsewhere, especially in Asia Minor, as we learn from various sources. Even then living emperors were reticent in having such public recognition of their divine status, especially in Italy, according to the Roman historian

Dio Cassius (*History* 51.20.6-8). In order to circumvent the problem, it was usual to combine the goddess Roma with the emperor as his patron and protectress in the dedication of temples, altars, and shrines. However, the emperors Gaius Caligula (37-41 C.E.) and Nero (54-68 C.E.) showed no such reticence, the former insisting that a golden statue of himself be erected in the Jerusalem temple and the latter initiating in 64 C.E. a pogrom against Roman Christians, including Peter and Paul, presumably because they were the recognized leaders of a group that had refused to recognize the emperor's status suitably.

Herod had won the trust of Augustus and was duly rewarded by several increases of territory, so that his kingdom eventually was practically as extensive as that of King David in the ninth century B.C.E. In recognition of this generosity and in order not to antagonize his Jewish subjects further, he had three temples built in the newly acquired, largely pagan territories, all dedicated to Roma and Augustus: one at Samaria, renamed Sebaste (from Greek *Sebastos,* venerable or august) in honor of the emperor, in 26 B.C.E.; a second at Caesarea Maritima, where the temple overlooked the magnificent harbor that Herod had constructed there in 20 B.C.E., and a third at Caesarea Philippi/Banias, near the pool of Pan and the sources of the Jordan.[3] Each of the three was constructed on a raised podium and built to a definite plan modeled on a temple to the goddess Venus Genetrix, which Herod would have seen on his first visit to Rome.

As a convinced Hellene, Herod participated fully in the Roman exploitation of the idea of one world. Several centuries earlier the Stoic philosopher Zeno had declared that the whole world was "like a city-state where law reigns supreme," thereby supplying Rome with a Greek philosophical underpinning for its political ambitions. Yet an important trend in recent scholarly portraits of this enigmatic character, Herod, suggests that his concerns for his Jewish subjects were also real. It has been suggested that he may in fact even have seen himself as a second Solomon because of his decision to rebuild the Jerusalem temple on a grander scale than before (cf.

---

3. Recent excavations at Omrit, 2 km south of the Pool of Pan have uncovered a temple complex that has definite Herodian features. It seems to follow the plan of the temples at Sebaste and Caesarea Maritima, as these can be reconstructed from the ruins at both sites. See E. Netzer, *The Architecture of Herod the Great Builder* (Grand Rapids: Baker, 2008), 85-89 and 103-6. The archaeological report from Omrit does not claim definitively that the site is that of Herod's temple, yet, *faute de mieux,* the evidence seems to point in that direction. Cf. J. A. Overman and D. N. Schowalter, eds., *The Roman Temple Complex at Horvat Omrit* (BAR International Series 2205; Oxford: Oxford University Press, 2011).

Ant 15.385).[4] The speech that he is said to have delivered to the Jewish people at the announcement of this project is clearly Josephus's composition. Yet, it should be remembered that in the first century C.E. there was a lively expectation among many pious Jews that an ideal king, who would introduce peace and justice to Israel, would soon appear.

There was no question of Herod claiming to fill that role, since he had been appointed "king of the Jews" by the Roman senate, nor could he claim full Jewish parentage, being the son of an Idumean father. Yet the ideals associated with the messianic king in Judaism, many of them articulated by the prophet Isaiah in the eighth century B.C.E. and repeated later in such works as the *Psalms of Solomon,* were not dissimilar to the blessings that the Roman poets were attributing to the Augustan age.[5] Peace in terms of an end to warfare, harmony in nature, and justice among peoples were standard themes. Could it be that the astute Herod sought to tap into those Jewish hopes in order to legitimate his espousal of Augustan aspirations for more personal ends? Herod, the great builder, seized the opportunity to deliver one of the hopes associated with the messianic king, namely, to build a new temple where Yahweh would be pleased to make his name to dwell, as the *Temple Scroll* from Qumran expresses it (11QTemple 51). Yet, ironically, the completed construction was an architectural combination of a Semitic-style inner sanctuary and a Roman colonnaded agora.[6]

Antipas and Philip: Architecture, Coinage, and Cult

Herod's architectural legacy was in place by the time Jesus was an adult, and Mark highlights the awe his Galilean disciples experienced on seeing the temple complex on their arrival in Jerusalem (Mark 13:1-2). As mentioned previously, Jesus and his retinue could scarcely have been unaware of the

---

4. P. Richardson, *Herod, King of the Jews and Friend of the Romans* (Columbia: University of South Carolina Press, 1996); S. Rocca, *Herod's Judaea* (TSAJ; Tübingen: Mohr Siebeck, 2008).

5. S. Freyne, "The Herodian Period," in M. Bockmuehl and J. Carlton Paget, eds., *Redemption and Resistance: The Messianic Hopes of Jews and Christians in Antiquity* (London: Continuum, 2007), 29-43.

6. D. W. Roller, *The Building Program of Herod the Great* (Berkeley: University of California Press, 1998), claims that in building the stoas around the temple Herod was imitating the porticoes that were common in Rome at the time (p. 216). For details, see Netzer, *The Architecture of Herod,* 137-78.

temples to Roma and Augustus, especially the one at Caesarea Philippi in the north. Herod may have been dead, but his monuments continued to speak the language of empire. While his son Herod Antipas had hoped to succeed him as "king of the Jews," Augustus decided to divide the realm between the three contenders: Archelaus received Judea (which included Samaria and Idumea), Philip received Transjordan (the territories of Paneas and Batanea, Auranitis, and Trachonitis), and Antipas received Galilee and Perea (which was east of the lower Jordan). None of them received the title "king," but rather that of "tetrarch," that is, "ruler of a section." This introduced a degree of competition between the three half-brothers in terms of displaying their allegiance to Rome, yet none of them was blessed with the same political skills as their father.

In Judea, Archelaus soon overstepped the mark as far as Rome was concerned and was banished in 6 C.E. He was replaced by a Roman procurator, who was under the oversight of the governor of Syria. This meant that while there was no Roman legion stationed permanently in Judea until after the first revolt in 70 C.E., the procurator would have an auxiliary force made up of non-Jewish personnel. He resided at Caesarea Maritima on the coast, leaving Jerusalem to be the religious capital. This arrangement weakened further the political influence of the High Priest, whose office had already been diminished by Herod the Great's imposition of his own appointees from abroad to a position that was meant to be hereditary.

Even though the procurator was subordinate to the governor of Syria, he did have responsibility for military matters, the administration of justice, and control of financial affairs. In fact, the title procurator derives from the office of imperial finance officer. Given the fact that the "Jewish people" *(ethnos tōn Ioudaiōn)* had a long-standing treaty of friendship with Rome, the procurator's powers were in theory limited. Thus in military affairs he was allowed to have an auxiliary force composed of cohorts of infantry and *alae* or wings of cavalry, named after the ethnic groups from which they had been recruited.[7] These could be deployed to quell various disturbances, serve as bodyguards of the procurator in Caesarea, and provide garrisons at other towns in the region. A permanent cohort was stationed in Jerusalem, which was augmented to police the crowds during Jewish festivals, when nationalistic sentiments would be running high. These were stationed

---

7. Thus we hear of the *Sebastenoi* (*War* 2.52, 58, 63) who would have been recruited in the region of Samaria around Sebaste, and the *Kaisareis* from Caesarea, who were, in fact, of Syrian extraction (*War* 2.266-68) and were often hostile to Judeans.

in the Arx Antonia, overlooking the temple area, while the procurator resided in Herod's palace on the Western Hill. It was there rather than in the Antonia that the trial of Jesus would have taken place. In matters of legal administration the Judeans were allowed to administer their own ancestral laws under the supervision of the High Priest and the Sanhedrin, but the *ius gladii*, "the right to execute," was retained by the procurator, as in the case of Jesus' crucifixion.

The third area of the procurator's responsibility was that of oversight of the finances of the region. The census under Quirinius mentioned by Luke (Luke 2:2) was held in 6-7 C.E. for the purpose of implementing the Roman tax system. Since he was the governor of Syria, Quirinius had responsibility for overseeing matters in Judea as well, even though a procurator, Coponius, had also been appointed there. Josephus tells us that this census was "an assessment of the property" of the Jews (*Ant* 18.1-2). This would suggest that it was only the *tributum soli,* that is, the land tax, that was intended. It was not, therefore, a census of the people, as is sometimes supposed because of Luke's account of Joseph having to register in Judea though resident in Galilee (Luke 2:4).[8] Judeans were not expected to pay the second Roman tax that applied elsewhere, namely the *tributum capitis*, or personal tax, at least initially. However, a later digest of laws refers to the fact that on making Caesarea Maritima a Roman *Colonia* in 70 C.E. Vespasian gave a remission of the *tributum capitis* to the citizens. If this applied generally, this tax would have been paid in cash, as elsewhere in the empire. Since, however, there is no mention of a personal census as distinct from a property census in Judea between 6 and 66 C.E., perhaps the Romans acknowledged that the Judeans were already paying a head tax in terms of the annual half shekel offering for the temple, and did not demand that they pay a second one until after 70. The *tributum soli* was paid in kind, it would seem, even if we do not know the exact percentage of the produce that was demanded, and this arrangement continued up to the outbreak of the revolt in 66 C.E. (Josephus, *Ant* 18.272-75; *Life* 70-73). There is no clear evidence as to how the tax in kind was collected, but mention of "the imperial corn that was stored in the villages of upper Galilee" (*Life* 71) suggests that there were collection depots in the different

8. It is generally recognized that Luke's notice of this census, which he says was for the whole world (Luke 2:1-2), is incorrect on several points. He links the census with the birth of Jesus, which he assumes took place while Herod the Great was still alive, i.e., 6-4 B.C.E. For a thorough discussion see E. Schürer, *The History of the Jewish People in the Age of Jesus Christ,* revised edition ed. G. Vermes, F. Millar, and M. Black (Edinburgh: Clark, 1973-84), 1:399-427.

administrative districts. It was only after the destruction of the temple in 70 C.E. that the annual half shekel offering that all male Jews were expected to pay to the temple was transformed into a head tax payable by all Jews to the Roman treasury.

Despite this concession on the part of Rome, the census signaled the emergence of a radical anti-Roman movement "with a passion for freedom" that Josephus calls "the Fourth Philosophy" (*Ant* 18.23-25). In the *Jewish War* account, a man named Judas chides his fellow countrymen for paying tribute to Rome, thereby submitting themselves to mortal masters (*War* 2.118). While there are some discrepancies between Josephus's two accounts, both agree that it was the census that sparked this radical call to arms and equally that the reason for resistance was the rebels' belief that God alone was their Lord.[9] In all probability, the protest arose from the Pentateuchal claim that the land was Yahweh's gift to Israel, the very pledge of his fidelity to the Mosaic covenant. This fundamental belief of Israel's existence and destiny was now being openly challenged by Rome's imposition of a *tributum soli.* An alternative system was in place whereby a tithe of the fruits of the land was offered to the Jewish God in his temple in Jerusalem. At this very moment, therefore, the inevitable seeds of an ideological clash were sown, one that would continue to threaten over the next several decades, leading up to the first revolt in 66 C.E. The priest/ apologist Josephus repeatedly recognizes this situation as he describes the various manifestations of protest that occurred, making the connection with Judas the Galilean and his family several times throughout his major works, *War* and *Antiquities.*[10]

There were two distinct phases of procuratorial rule in Judea. The first one lasted from 6 to 39 C.E., during which seven procurators were appointed to Judea. We know very little about any of them except the penultimate one, Pontius Pilate, who ruled from 26 to 36 C.E. His role as the governor of Judea who sanctioned the crucifixion of Jesus is well docu-

9. Thus in *Ant* Judas is described as a Galilean and is aided by a Pharisee Saddok, whereas in *War* he is said to come from Gamala in Gaulanitis. Also in *War* Judas's sect has nothing in common with the other three, the Essenes, the Pharisees, and the Sadducees, whereas in *Ant* it is put on a par with the others by being described as the Fourth Philosophy and is said to agree with the Pharisees in all matters except for its passion for liberty.

10. For an excellent summary of these protest movements, including the Fourth Philosophy, see James McLaren, "Resistance Movements," in J. J. Collins and D. Harlow, eds., *The Eerdmans Dictionary of Early Judaism* (Grand Rapids: Eerdmans, 2010), 1135-40, especially 1136-37.

mented in the Gospels, where he is presented, on the whole, as indecisive and weak. However, both Josephus and the Jewish apologist Philo of Alexandria present a very different and probably truer picture of a man whom Philo describes as harsh and obdurate in discharging his duties, driven by greed, vindictiveness, and cruelty (*Embassy* 38). Josephus recounts several incidents of insensitivity to Jewish customs, including Pilate being deliberately provocative in bringing Roman military standards into Jerusalem and daring to rob the temple treasury in order to build an aqueduct for the city (*War* 2.169-77; *Ant* 18.55-62).

Antipas and Philip were faced with rather different issues in their respective territories, especially as far as honoring Rome was concerned. Antipas had to deal with a largely Jewish population, especially in Lower Galilee, as we saw in the previous chapter. This restricted him somewhat as to how he could show open support for Roman imperial ideology. Philip's area on the other hand was mainly pagan, giving him the freedom to recognize and celebrate the imperial rule. As a show of his independence, he was the first Herodian to have his own image engraved on his coins in contravention of Jewish law but in best Hellenistic fashion.

Our attention to the propaganda dimension of Roman coinage was prompted by the use of an imperial image on a denarius. When Jesus' opponents raised the issue of his attitude to paying the imperial tax, he cleverly turned the tables on them: their being in possession of a coin with an imperial image was already indicative of their acquiescence in the reality of empire. However, his further utterance, "Render to Caesar what is Caesar's and to God what is God's" (Mark 12:17), would appear to be deliberately ambiguous. Is "render to God what is God's" merely calling for temple taxes to be paid as well? Or is Jesus juxtaposing the authority of Caesar and the supreme authority of God, suggesting that in his view there is no equivalence between the two? Whatever our judgment on this conundrum, it is clear that the political dimension of coins was a live issue in Roman Palestine. The fact that Jews minted their own coins during the two revolts against Rome (66-70 C.E. and 132-35 C.E.), with appropriate non-human symbolism and Hebrew legends, underlines their importance as statements of independence by a subject people.

During a long reign (4 B.C.E. to 39 C.E.) Antipas issued relatively few series of coins, five in all, and then only bronze ones and not in great quantities. For the purpose of evaluating their propaganda value, the iconography that is chosen and the legends used are more important than the size, worth, or even the number of the coins minted. His earliest issue was in year four of his reign, namely 1 C.E.[11] Only one small copy of this issue has been found so far. It features a grain of barley or wheat and an abbreviation of the words "tetrarch" and "Herod" in Greek lettering. On the reverse, a palm tree with seven branches could possibly be an imitation of a menorah, and again the abbreviated name "Herod." If, in fact, the reverse image is intended as a menorah, it may well have been chosen in order to placate Antipas's Jewish subjects. There had been an outbreak of violence by Jewish nationalists at Sepphoris on the death of Herod the Great, an incident that prompted swift retaliation from the Roman general Varus, who sacked the city. Later Antipas restored it "making it the ornament of all Galilee" according to Josephus.[12] At the same time he sought to placate Roman sensibilities by adding the epithet AUTOKRATORIDA, that is, "sole ruler" to the city's name, a clear reference to the nature of the Augustan rule.

A second series of coins dated to 19 C.E. (Antipas's twenty-fourth regnal year) in several denominations, clearly coincided with his founding of Tiberias on the lakefront to honor the new emperor. The coins have the Greek legend "Of Herod the Tetrarch" and a plant, which has been variously interpreted as a reed or a palm branch on the obverse. The reverse has *TIBERIAC* surrounded by a laurel wreath. This symbolism and dating are quite important. Clearly, Antipas wanted to celebrate the foundation of a new city as an expression of his desire to honor Tiberius, lately become sole ruler after his co-regency with his step-father Augustus. This may explain the wreath (a symbol of victory) on the reverse. The unusual plant on the obverse has attracted some attention because of Jesus' use of the image of the reed in making a deliberate contrast between John the Baptist and Antipas: John was a strong and forceful prophet in contrast to Antipas, who resembled "a reed shaking in the wind" (Matt 11:7; Luke 7:24). This judgment on Antipas matches Josephus's comment that he was an indolent character in contrast to other offspring of Herod the Great (*Ant* 18.245).[13]

---

11. M. Jensen, *Herod Antipas in Galilee* (WUNT 215; Tübingen: Mohr Siebeck, 2006), 187-220, especially 203-13 and figures 21-29 on pp. 297-300.

12. L. Feldman's translation of Josephus's work in the Loeb series renders the Greek description as "he fortified Sepphoris to be the *ornament* of all Galilee" (*Ant* 18.27). "Ornament" has tended to suggest magnificent Roman buildings. However, the excavations at the site do not support that claim for the first century. The more elaborate buildings in the lower city are from a later period. However the word *proschēma* can also mean "fortification" or "rampart," but in fact no trace of Varus's destruction or Josephus's walls have so far been discovered.

13. G. Theissen, "The 'Shaken Reed' in Mt 11, 7 and the Foundation Coins of Tiberias,"

Of the three other series of coins issued by Antipas, those of the years 28-29, 33, and 38-39 C.E., the last, issued shortly before his banishment, is the most significant. For the first time the name of an emperor appears on a coin of Antipas, that of the new emperor, Gaius Caligula, who succeeded Tiberius in 37 C.E. Gaius befriended Antipas's nephew and brother-in-law Agrippa, appointing him as king over Philip's territory to the north in 37 C.E. Obviously, this stirred Antipas to honor belatedly the new emperor also. The obverse on this series has a palm tree and the name "Herod the Tetrarch" in Greek, and the legend on the reverse reads in Greek "to Gaius Caesar Germanicus" surrounded by a wreath. In one variant the epithet *Sebastos* is also added. Despite this show of support for the new emperor, Gaius banished Antipas when, at the instigation of his wife Herodias (the sister of Agrippa), he appeared in Rome seeking to be honored with the title king. Agrippa now had Galilee added to the territory he had already inherited on the death of Philip and soon afterward was given Judea also, so that for the short period of his reign (41-44 C.E.) he ruled over a territory as large as that of his grandfather, Herod the Great.

A brief comparison of the coins of Antipas with those of Philip is interesting. As mentioned already, Philip had no hesitation in having his own image engraved on the earliest of his eight coin issues. He appears bare-headed and without a crown, with the Greek legend "Of Philip the Tetrarch." The reverse shows the facade of a tetrastyle temple, generally regarded as a representation of Herod the Great's temple to Roma and Augustus, which was situated in Philip's territory. This image appears on all subsequent issues of his coins, a much more explicit acknowledgment of the imperial cult than anything on the coins of Antipas.[14]

A further development in Philip's coins is the inclusion of the female members of the imperial household. Livia, later named Iulia (to signify her inclusion into the family of Julius Caesar), the wife of Augustus and mother of Tiberius, features prominently. She had a highly influential, if checkered career in Roman political life, especially during the fifteen years in which she outlived Augustus. She is represented as Demeter/Ceres, the goddess of plenty on a coin of Philip, dated to the year 30 C.E. The obverse depicts her in simple

---

in Theissen, *The Gospels in Context: Social and Political History in the Synoptic Tradition* (Edinburgh: Clark, 1992), 25-42.

14. For a discussion of the coins of Philip, see F. Strichert, "Coins of Philip," in R. Arav, et al., eds., *Bethsaida: A City by the North Shore of the Sea of Galilee* (Kirksville: Truman State University, 1999-2007), 1:165-92; A. Kindler, "The Coins of the Tetrarch Philip and Bethsaida," in *Bethsaida*, 2:245-68; Jensen, *Herod Antipas*, 198-200.

fashion, facing right, draped and unveiled, with a distinctive hairstyle. The legend reads *IOULIA SEBASTE*, thus extending the imperial honorific title to the emperor's wife also. The reverse has the legend *KARPOPHOROS*, that is, "fruit bearer," a clear reference to the goddess of bounty. With this iconography Philip is thought to emulate a similar coin issued by Pilate, the Roman procurator of Judea, in the previous year. Both coins have three stalks of grain tied together on the obverse. But on Pilate's coin the two outer stalks are drooping, a signal, it is thought, of Iulia's death in that year. In Philip's coin on the other hand all three stalks are standing upright, celebrating, it would seem, the abundance that the imperial rule had brought to the world, for which Iulia, now assimilated with the goddess of plenty, continued to be responsible.[15]

Clearly, Philip was much more explicit in his celebration of the Augustan age than was Antipas, on the basis of their respective coins. While Herod the Great had established a temple to Roma and Augustus in the north of his kingdom, Philip actually developed a new foundation close to the pool of Pan, with its official name Caesarea Panias intended to honor the descendants of Julius Caesar. He was thereby emulating his father's foundation of the other Caesarea (Maritima) on the coast. On a coin dated to the year 29-30 C.E. a Greek abbreviation is added to the legend "Under Philip the Tetrarch," giving him the title of "founder" *(ktistēs)*. This clearly refers not only to his founding of Caesarea Philippi but also to his upgrading of the fishing village of Bethsaida, the home of Jesus' first permanent followers (Jn 1:44; cf. Mark 1:16-20), to Bethsaida Iulias, as Josephus informs us *(Ant* 18.28). This was a somewhat presumptuous self-description by a client king, possibly seeking to assert himself over the Roman procurator Pilate by emphasizing his right to rename a city in honor of the empress.

Recent excavations at what is generally deemed to be the site of ancient Bethsaida (et Tell) have discovered various indications of Rome's presence, but not in the abundance some would have hoped for if, in fact, this is the correct location of the town that had been upgraded by Philip. However, the outline of a first-century building that resembles that of the Herodian temples to Roma and Augustus has been reported. This discovery gives rise to the possibility that Philip had actually dedicated a temple to Iulia/Demeter there and that it is this temple that is depicted on his coins, not that of Herod the Great.[16]

15. F. Strichert, "The First Woman to Be Portrayed on a Jewish Coin: Julia Sebaste," *JSJ* 33 (2002), 65-91.

16. Continuous excavations at the site of et Tell, 2 km north of the current shore of the

As mentioned previously, Antipas too had shown his loyalty to Rome by giving the restored Sepphoris the epithet *AUTOKRATORIDA,* that is, sole ruler. He had also honored Iulia by naming Bethramphtha, a town in Perea (the other part of his territory), as Livias, which was subsequently changed to Iulias, after she had been accepted into the Julian clan in accordance with Augustus's will (*Ant* 18.27). Antipas was, as we saw, more cautious in his championing of the Roman imperial presence, especially on his coins. This was no doubt determined by the fact that there was a strong Jewish presence in Lower Galilee that he did not wish to alienate. Archaeological exploration of Sepphoris has revealed plenty of evidence of Rome's presence there, but much of this, especially in the lower city, comes from later centuries. Thus far, nothing that might suggest a royal palace has been discovered for the early Roman period, giving rise to the suspicion that Antipas may never have taken up permanent residence there.

Since his first wife was the daughter of the Nabatean king Aretas, it may well be that Antipas originally resided at Machaerus, a well-fortified fortress east of the Dead Sea in Perea but close to the borders of the Nabatean kingdom. It is there that Josephus locates the imprisonment and death of John the Baptist, an event which Mark also reports but with no indication of where it took place (*Ant* 18.119; Mark 6:17-29). Archaeological investigations at Machaerus have confirmed Josephus's account that Herod the Great had fortified the place and erected a palace there before it came into possession of Antipas after his father's death (*War* 7.171-77).[17]

The war that ensued over Antipas's divorce of Aretas's daughter may have influenced the former to establish a new residence in more salubrious surroundings. Tiberias had a much more Roman feel to it from the outset. The layout was typically Roman with a monumental gate and *cardo,* or main street, leading into the city. It had public basilical buildings, a stadium, and

---

Sea of Galilee, have practically confirmed that this was the site of ancient Bethsaida/Julias, even though some still query this conclusion. The major objections to the identification have to do with the distance from the lakeshore and the lack of monumental buildings consonant with a Roman city. However, neither objection is decisive. Explorations have shown that seismic activity in the region has brought about major changes to the shoreline, which has receded considerably over the centuries. Ongoing excavations confirm a strong Roman presence, as well as providing evidence of both the fishing industry and wine-making in the Roman period. See Arav, et al., *Bethsaida,* for detailed reports of various aspects of the excavations by scholars working at the site.

17. M. Piccirillo, "Machaerus," in E. M. Meyers, ed., *The Oxford Encylopedia of Archaeology in the Near East* (New York: Oxford University Press, 1997), 3:39-93.

a theater, mentioned by Josephus and confirmed by recent excavations there. It also had a royal palace with animal decorations and imported fine furniture (*Life* 65.68), at least at the outbreak of the first revolt in 66 C.E. In his account of the location of the city Josephus links it closely with the hot sulphur baths close by, which were a major attraction for those accustomed to an elite Roman lifestyle.[18]

The population was mixed from the outset, comprising local officials, people who were forced to take up residence there from both Galilee and Perea, and poor people who were given housing and plots of land as enticement to reside there (*Ant* 18.36-38). This picture of a socially mixed population is confirmed by Josephus's account of the various factions within the city when he came to Galilee in 66 C.E.: Herodians with landed property across the Jordan, those with a good Hellenistic education like Justus, and Jesus the son of Sapphias, the leader of the sailors and the destitute classes, a rabid anti-Roman zealot (*Life* 33-37.66). The administration, too, was on the lines of a Greek *polis*. It had a council *(boulē)*, a general assembly of citizens *(dēmos)*, a chief magistrate *(archōn)*, and a group of leading men *(prōtoi)*. In addition, Justus, Josephus's great rival, was said to be familiar with Greek education *(paideia)* and wrote a history of the kings, as well as an account of the revolt in Galilee (*Life* 40.336-37), suggesting at least the presence of a *gymnasion* in the city. Presumably this would not have been unlike the one established by Jason in Jerusalem two centuries earlier, that is, combining an education in Greek culture with Jewish learning.

Perhaps not all these developments were there in Antipas's day, but he certainly had sown the seeds of a Greco-Roman ethos from the beginning. In particular, the combination of a stadium and a theater suggests that perhaps games, similar to those which Herod the Great had celebrated in honor of the emperor in Jerusalem, were held there also, though our sources are silent on this particular aspect of life in Tiberias. Jesus' remark that "those dressed in fine garments belong in royal palaces" (Matt 11:8) fits admirably with what we can reconstruct about the elite of Tiberias. Furthermore, Jesus' and his Galilean audience's familiarity with the behavior of absentee landlords, as assumed in such parables as Mark 12:1-10 or Matt 20:1-16, may well be based on their experience of the Herodian upper class who lived in luxury at the expense of Galilean peasants and day laborers.

The fact that Tiberias was built on burial tombs in contravention of

---

18. Z. Weiss, "Josephus and Archaeology on the Cities of Galilee," in Z. Rodgers, ed., *Making History: Josephus and Historical Method* (Leiden: Brill, 2007), 385-414.

Jewish purity laws would appear to run counter to Antipas's cautious attitude toward his Jewish subjects, as reflected in his coins. This may explain
Josephus's reference to people having been compelled to live there (*Ant*
18.38). Indeed, forty years later, on the eve of the first revolt in 66 C.E., the
rebel party in Tiberias sacked the royal palace that Antipas had built under
the pretext that the Jewish ban on images had been violated there. They also
seized the opportunity to carry off some of the unminted silver stored in the
palace and were aided in this escapade by "some Galileans," that is, people
from the surrounding countryside (*Life* 66-68).

Toward the First Jewish Revolt and Its Immediate Aftermath

Comparisons of the manner in which Antipas and Philip promoted the
Roman imperial ideology in the north are, as we shall see later, highly significant in terms of our understanding of Jesus' ministry and movements.
Their combined territories represented, more or less, the area allegedly occupied by the Israelite tribes of old. Another traditional claim that featured
in Jewish restoration hopes extended the northern border of the Promised
Land into Syria, and this too may have been a motivation in the movements
northward as far as Antioch and Damascus of the early Jesus-followers in
the latter part of the first century C.E. At the same time, the political climate
in this whole area was changing also. Agrippa I (41-44 C.E.) and his son
Agrippa II (56-92 C.E.) continued to act as client kings of Rome under the
emperors Claudius (40-54 C.E.) and Nero (54-68 C.E.), interspersed with
a second period of Roman provincial rule that involved not just Judea but
part of Galilee also.[19] Their coins and overall demeanor continued the more
open approach of Philip rather than that of Antipas. Yet, as far as Rome was
concerned, they were brokers of the Jewish people's aspirations.

Agrippa I appears to have been an ambivalent character. He is celebrated in Jewish sources as pious in terms of ancestral practices. This may
also explain his hostility to the early Christians. His laying of "violent hands

19. As was discussed in the last chapter, Ptolemais/Acco was made a Roman *colonia* c.
56 C.E., marking a further upgrading of its role from Hellenistic times as watchdog over the
Galilean hinterland. Nero also partitioned Lower Galilee by granting Tiberias and Tarichea
and their districts, together with those of Hippos and Gadara, to Agrippa II in 56 C.E. There is
also a suggestion in Tacitus (*Annals* 12.54) that Rome appointed separate overseers for Galilee
and Judea in the wake of disturbances that occurred when Samaritans attacked and murdered
Galilean pilgrims on the way to Jerusalem during the procuratorship of Felix (52-60 C.E.).

on some who belonged to the church" (Acts 12:1) is an important indicator that only a decade after the crucifixion Jesus' Jerusalem-based followers were sufficiently noteworthy to be seen as dissidents and therefore as a threat to peace within the city. Agrippa also played an important role in averting a major crisis when the emperor Gaius Caligula sought to have his statue erected in the Jerusalem temple. This episode recalled the earlier desecration by Antiochus Epiphanes that gave rise to the nationalistic reaction of the Maccabean freedom fighters, the memory of which had been kept alive by the annual festival of Rededication. Now, however, it was not the statue of Zeus, but that of the divine emperor that was the threat to the sanctity of the Jerusalem temple.[20]

Gaius died before his wishes could be realized, and the crisis was temporarily averted. There was, however, a noticeable rise in Jewish nationalistic movements in the subsequent decades leading up to the first revolt of 66 C.E. Agrippa I is regarded as a hero in some Jewish sources, yet he is also described on an inscription from Transjordan as "friend of Caesar and friend of Rome." He sponsored games in honor of the emperor at Caesarea Maritima and at Berytus in Syria, following the patterns set by his grandfather Herod the Great (*Ant* 19.335-37). His coins are also indicative of the double role that he played. On the one hand he had a bronze coin of small value (the *prutah*) minted in Jerusalem in large quantities, with the legend "Agrippa the King" and a canopy on the reverse, and ears of grain on the obverse, presumably signifying the fertility of the land. Coins minted elsewhere continued the pattern of honoring the emperor and even representing some aspects of Roman history and mythology.[21]

On Agrippa the elder's sudden death in 44 C.E., the emperor Claudius did not immediately appoint his son, the future Agrippa II, to his father's kingdom, even though he had been educated in Rome. This may be due to the fact that, despite celebrating the emperor suitably, Agrippa I had also appeared somewhat unreliable in Roman eyes by calling a meeting of a number of client kings from the Near Eastern region at Tiberias. On hearing of that gathering, the governor of Syria quickly gave orders for the kings to disperse, and Agrippa the elder had to reaffirm his loyalty to Rome (*Ant* 19.338-42). Eventually, Claudius gave the younger Agrippa control of his uncle's kingdom of Chalcis in the Lebanon. Somewhat later, probably in 54

---

20. For a discussion of Agrippa's role in solving the affair of Gaius's statue in the temple, see the study by D. Schwartz, *Agrippa I* (TSAJ 23; Tübingen: Mohr Siebeck, 1980), 80-82.

21. Jensen, *Herod Antipas*, 201-2.

C.E., the new emperor, Nero, exchanged Chalcis for the tetrarchy of Agrippa's granduncle Philip and increased Agrippa's territory further by partitioning Galilee and adding Tiberias and Tarichea and their territories to his kingdom (*Ant* 20.159). In recognition of these favors, coins minted at Caesarea Philippi continued the tradition of honoring the imperial wives and daughters by representing them in the form of female goddesses such as Tyche/Fortuna and Demeter/Ceres. For a brief period also Caesarea's name was changed to Caesarea Neronias on Agrippa II's coins, only to revert to Caesarea Panias after Nero's flight and suicide in 68 C.E.[22]

While both Agrippas (I and II) continued the tradition of Herod the Great, celebrating imperial games at home and abroad and displaying their acceptance of the imperial ideology on their coins, they also sought to play an important role in the affairs of Jerusalem and the Jews. The refurbishment of the temple was only completed during the reign of Agrippa II, and, while he refused a request to have the outer portico on the eastern side raised higher, he did allow for the paving of the city with white stone (*Ant* 20.219-22). Ironically, the issue of another wall in the temple compound involved Agrippa himself and gave rise to a delegation being sent to Rome to plead the case with Nero. Agrippa had built a chamber in the royal palace from which he was able to see the whole city, including activity within the temple complex. The leading men of the Jews objected to this as contrary to their traditions and so erected a high wall around the inner temple building. Nero, on the pleading of his wife Poppea, who, as a God-fearer, was sympathetic to the Jews, agreed that the wall should be allowed to stand (*Ant* 20.189-96).

In addition to these matters to do with the architecture of the Holy Place, the Herods had continued to meddle in the affairs of the High Priests. This was also a sensitive issue, since historically the office of High Priest was hereditary, and the incumbent was a highly influential figure, as the trial and crucifixion of Jesus illustrates. However, Herod the Great had violated the hereditary principle early in his reign, and his successors continued in the same tradition (*Ant* 20.247-51). As a young man in Rome, Agrippa the younger had used his influence at the court of Claudius in assisting a Jewish delegation who were pleading to retain possession of the high priestly garment (which was worn on ceremonial occasions), while the then procurator sought to have it kept in Roman possession at the Arx Antonia close to the temple mount. This action was tantamount to a direct interference

---

22. Ya'akov Meshorer, *City Coins of Eretz Israel and the Decapolis in the Roman Period* (Jerusalem: Israel Museum, 1985), 67-69.

in Jewish religious affairs by the Romans and was likely to have caused serious disturbances. However, Claudius granted the delegation's wishes and allowed the Jews to retain possession of the precious garment (*Ant* 20.6-15). Nevertheless, Agrippa, having received the authority, previously invested in his uncle (Herod of Chalcis), "over the temple, the holy vessels, and the selection of the high priest" repeatedly used his prerogative to remove a High Priest and replace him with some other candidate, virtually at will.[23]

Roman politics and Jewish religious traditions had become inextricably intertwined in this network of power relations. The second period of procurators in Judea proper (44-66 C.E.), which also now included western Galilee, was no more accommodating of Jewish sensitivities than were those in the earlier period. Those appointed to Judea were of the equestrian order and could be described in Roman terms as "new rich" who saw their term of appointment as an opportunity for self-promotion and self-enrichment. Understanding of Judean sensibilities was not to be expected, especially since there was a considerable amount of anti-Jewish feeling in Rome itself. Strangely, we hear nothing of a second census for Galilee, once it was included in the provincial structure, presumably after the death of Agrippa I. A census must have taken place, however, since we hear that in 66 C.E. Josephus had to deal with the imperial corn stored in Upper Galilee, presumably for shipment to Rome, which one of the native Galilean aristocracy, John of Gischala, wanted to confiscate (*Life* 71). This would suggest that a land tax *(tributum soli)* was in operation in Galilee also, thus necessitating a census similar to the one held in Judea earlier.

There is more than a little rhetorical self-pity in Josephus's account in *Antiquities* (20.160-66, 252-58), written later in Rome under Flavian patronage, of the reigns of terror conducted by the last of the procurators, Felix, (52-60 C.E.), Albinus (62-64) and Gessius Florus (64-66). Yet the overall picture concurs with what he had written much earlier in *Jewish War* (2.252-65, 271-77). Furthermore, this unsatisfactory state of affairs is corroborated by Tacitus, who speaks of the endurance of the Jews continuing until the time of Gessius Florus, despite the fact that Felix "practiced every kind of cruelty and lust, wielding the powers of a king with all the instincts of a slave" (*Histories* 5.9-10). The overall picture that is given is one of complete breakdown of law and order, with urban and rural banditry giving rise to a reign of terror throughout the land. It comes as little surprise, therefore, to hear that in 66 C.E. the revolutionary party in Jerusalem refused to pay

---

23. *Ant* 20.16 (Cantheras), 196 (Joseph), 203 (Ananus), 222 (Jesus, son of Gamaliel).

the annual tribute to Rome and put an end to the "loyal sacrifices," the daily offerings in the temple on behalf of the emperor (*War* 2.409). Subsequently, they invaded the temple and appointed a new High Priest by lots, a country peasant who knew nothing about the office or its duties (*War* 4.147, 152-54). They thereby threw down the gauntlet, both to Rome and to the Judean elite. The outcome was disaster for the Jewish people, the destruction of their temple in 70 C.E. and the effective end of sacrifice, priesthood, and pilgrimage, the very center of the Mosaic dispensation.

After failing to dissuade the Jews from revolting, Agrippa II supported the Romans, supplying an auxiliary force to Vespasian, the general appointed by Nero to conduct the war against the Jews. In his lengthy account in the *Jewish War*, Josephus puts a dramatic speech on Agrippa's lips seeking to persuade the Jerusalem populace of the madness of their actions (*War* 2.345-401). Like all such speeches in ancient literature, it contains what the author thought was appropriate to the occasion rather than the actual words of Agrippa. Nevertheless, it gives some intimation of what upper-class Jews were thinking. After listing the various peoples east and west who had tried to resist Rome's advance and failed, he concludes that the Jews could not even hope for divine assistance, "since without God's aid, so vast an empire could never have been built up" (*War* 2.390). The Augustan ideology of Rome's right to universal rule had spectacularly triumphed, even among the Judean priestly elite, among whom Josephus counted himself.

Within a year, Titus had succeeded his father as general in charge of the Judean campaign, since Vespasian had been acclaimed as the new emperor by the legions in the east following the flight and subsequent death of Nero in 68 C.E. With Vespasian's elevation, the Julio-Claudian line of emperors, dating back to Octavian/Augustus, came to an end and a new dynasty, the Flavians, emerged to replace it. For this transition of power to run smoothly, it was important that the victory over the Jews be celebrated in as lavish a manner as possible. Agrippa II accompanied Titus to Rome, there to celebrate with an official triumph, an event memorialized in the famous Arch of Titus, still standing close to the Coliseum in Rome (*War* 7.132-62). Josephus also contributed handsomely to the embellishment of the Flavians' victory by his account, emphasizing as he does the magnitude of the war and the military skill and foresight of the Romans. The introduction to the *Jewish War* sets the tone for what follows: "The war of the Jews against the Romans — the greatest, not only of the wars of our own time, but so far as accounts have reached us, well nigh of all that ever broke out between cities and nations" (*War* 1.1).

As a result of his appointment by the revolutionary council Josephus had become embroiled in the revolt in 66, taking charge of affairs in Galilee. Despite his special pleading about his own role, he nonetheless gives valuable snapshots of the conditions in the province on the eve of the revolt. There are differences of emphasis, if not downright contradictions between his *Jewish War* and his *Life*. Yet we do get an inside picture of the factions and tensions that had bedeviled Judean politics throughout the first century C.E. This was the century in which the Jesus movement was emerging within the region, yet reading the gospels, some of them contemporaneous with Josephus's writings, we only catch the merest glimpse of the situation in both Galilee and Jerusalem. The appointment by the revolutionary council in Jerusalem of somebody from the upper, priestly class "of the first rank," reflects continuing Jerusalem concerns about Galilee. Where did Galilean loyalties lie? Were they at one with the aristocracy's views of the revolt, which for some at least involved containment rather than aggression? Or were they with the zealots, or possibly even with the Romans?

This unease by the Jerusalem ruling elite with regard to their influence in Galilee on matters both religious and political would appear to have been endemic. Scribes from Jerusalem had arrived in Galilee on two different occasions in order to challenge Jesus of Nazareth and his new movement according to the Evangelist Mark (Mark 3:22; 7:1-2). Another delegation came from Jerusalem in order to remove Josephus from his office, but they failed because, he claims, his popularity with the Galileans saved him (*Life* 195-98). This delegation was also comprised of people of priestly background, suggesting that the aristocracy was divided. Indeed Josephus's appointment and subsequent role in the revolt in Galilee raises the further question of how complicit in the revolt the Jerusalem elite actually was, even when calling for restraint. After his capture at the siege of Jotapata, Josephus had a "conversion" to the Roman cause, blaming the revolt on a small but reckless group of militant dissidents and seeking to exonerate himself and his class from the charge of any complicity in the events.

It is the inner-Galilean tensions that Josephus's narratives illumine best. Of the two chief cities, Sepphoris and Tiberias, the former was pro-Rome, having actually appealed to the governor of Syria for military protection, which the city duly received (*War* 3.4-8, 30-34). Josephus chides its residents for their disloyalty to the Jewish cause, failing as they did "to come to the aid of the temple which is common to us all" (*Life* 346-48). In fact, Sepphoris felt bold enough to issue a city coin in 68 C.E. with the legend "of Nero, Claudius, Caesar" on the obverse, and on the reverse "under

Vespasian, city of peace" *(eirēnopolis)*.[24] This was an astute move by Sepphoris, proclaiming its non-participation in the revolt while also echoing the imperial rhetoric about the *pax Romana*. It was to benefit greatly from this stance in the post-revolt period.

In Tiberias, on the other hand, there were several factions, one of them strongly anti-Roman. While the city was part of Agrippa II's territory, he was not able to pacify it, but Vespasian subsequently brought it and the neighboring Tarichea (Magdala) under control. After a protracted siege, he had earlier reduced Jotapata, where many of the Galilean rebels were holed up. It was there also that he obtained the surrender of Josephus, whom he kept captive in his retinue subsequently. Eventually, Vespasian repaired with some of his troops to Agrippa's capital, Caesarea Philippi, there to celebrate the victories already achieved. The festivities, which lasted for twenty days, included, presumably, imperial games as well as "giving thank offerings to god for the successes achieved" (*War* 3.444).

It was left to Vespasian's son Titus to complete operations in Judea. Once Jerusalem and its temple had fallen in 70 C.E., Titus too embarked on a celebratory tour of the region, eventually going as far as Antioch in Syria. Just as his father had done two years earlier, Titus visited Caesarea Philippi, spending a considerable amount of time there as guest of Agrippa II. According to Josephus, who as a captive of the Romans must have actually been present, the celebrations included all kinds of spectacles, including *venationes* in which prisoners were thrown to wild beasts (*War* 7.23-25, 39). At this point, Vespasian had already been acclaimed emperor and the new dynasty needed to affirm its continuity with the Augustan era and its project.

It is interesting to note the role that Caesarea Philippi played in the movements of the two Roman generals in the wake of their respective campaigns. Vespasian offered thanks to the god (unspecified) there, and Titus celebrated Roman-style games after his victory. One can understand the importance of Caesarea Maritima because of its prime location and as

24. This coin contrasts starkly with one minted a year later at Gamla in the Golan, a staunchly Jewish outpost that put up a brave resistance to the Roman general Vespasian. It eventually had to yield to superior power, and its wall was breached, followed by wholesale slaughter of the inhabitants and refugees from the neighboring villages (*War* 4.1-53, 62-83). The Gamla silver coin was struck locally and the legend, written in paleo-Hebrew script, reads "For the freedom of Zion" on the obverse and "Jerusalem the holy" on the reverse. Cf. D. Syon, "Gamla: City of Refuge," in A. Berlin and A. Overman, eds., *The First Jewish Revolt: Archaeology, History and Ideology* (London: Routledge, 2002), 134-53.

the seat of the Roman procurator. But Caesarea Philippi might appear to be of little strategic consequence, being well outside the inhabited Jewish territory and seemingly situated off the main north-south thoroughfare. It should be remembered, however, that Augustus had bequeathed this whole region to Herod the Great, precisely in order to control Batanea, Auranitis, and Trachonitis, territories that previously had been inhabited by Iturean Arabs in Transjordan, who were less than helpful as far as Rome's ambitions were concerned. A short time later, on the death of Zenodorus, the city territories of Ulatha and Paneas were also given to Herod, and it was then presumably that the temple to Roma and Augustus was erected.

Recent archaeological discoveries at Omrit, 2 km south of modern Banias, have uncovered a significant temple complex that the excavators have tentatively identified with Herod's temple to Roma and Augustus. The discovery of the temple at precisely this location, however, has helped to clarify the strategic importance of this region as far as Rome's policies in the East were concerned. In antiquity the site was close to the main east-west road leading from Tyre to Damascus and beyond. Andrew Overman develops a persuasive argument that Omrit's location at precisely that place was due to the fact that it signaled Rome's determination to control the important corridor to the east that ran nearby.

The Parthians continued to pose a serious threat across the Euphrates, one that had led to an ill-fated campaign in 53 B.C.E. by Crassus, the proconsul of Syria, who lost his life as well as the Roman standards. Later Mark Antony sought in vain to retrieve them, hoping thereby to win some acclaim in Rome. Some time later still, Augustus, with the assistance of Herod, succeeded in restoring Roman pride by negotiating a peaceful restoration of the standards. While this whole episode might appear to be relatively trivial, it should be recalled that the standards were the symbols of both Roman military prowess and the invincibility of the divine *imperator* as their leader.[25] Against that background, Vespasian and Titus recognized the need to visit this center also, thereby identifying themselves with the restoration of Roman pride, to which they had now also contributed by their victories over the rebellious Jews. Once again it was the duty of a client king, this time Agrippa II, to facilitate that acknowledgment of Rome's right to rule the world.

---

25. A. Overman, "Between Rome and Parthia: Galilee and the Implications of Empire," in Z. Rodgers, et al., eds., *A Wandering Galilean: Essays in Honour of Sean Freyne* (Leiden: Brill, 2009), 279-300.

Aerial view of the temple complex at Omrit, one of the few examples
of Roman imperial presence and rule in Israel, tentatively
identified with Herod's temple to Roma and Augustus.
(J. Andrew Overman)

The Palestinian Jesus-Followers and the Fall of Jerusalem

Josephus was not the only Jewish writer concerned about the historical
events of the Roman period leading up to 70 C.E. Others, too, adopting
both the rhetoric and logic of the apocalyptic worldview, were less accepting than Josephus in their judgment of Rome and its presence. The book of
Daniel, written at the height of the crisis generated by Antiochus Epiphanes,
was the prototype of the genre, one feature of which is the manner in which
oracles dealing with one historical crisis can equally well serve in similar
circumstances subsequently. Another aspect of the apocalyptic genre is the
couching of the message in symbolic language which calls for an "insider's"
appreciation of what is being communicated. As Mark pointedly states in
what has often been called the "little apocalypse," namely, ch. 13 of the gospel, "Let the reader understand." This notice to the reader/hearer, as well as
the repeated admonition "Beware" (vv. 5, 9, and 33) and warnings such as
"Do not be led astray" (v. 21), "Be alert" (v. 23), and "Learn the lesson of the

fig tree" (v. 28), all point to a secretive atmosphere where covert warnings are being addressed to a group whom the author wants to protect from being led astray by "false messiahs" and "false prophets."

As we have seen, any suggestion of a threat to the Jerusalem temple and its sanctity was likely to become a particular flash point. Events such as the usurpation of the high priesthood by the Hasmoneans, Pompey's entry into the Jerusalem temple, Gaius Caligula's demand to have his statue erected in the inner sanctum of the temple, and, of course, the final destruction of the temple in 70 c.e., all gave rise to veiled but serious condemnation of Rome and the Judean ruling elite in such works as the *Assumption of Moses, 4 Esdras,* and the *Psalms of Solomon.* The early Jesus-followers were heirs to this tradition also, and they, like others, must have been shocked by the destruction of the temple and the events that led up to it. Indeed, as we shall argue in later chapters, this event functioned as a catalyst for the early Christian gospel writings, just as it did for the development of the rabbinic movement for other Jews in the post-war period.

Of the gospel writers, Luke is the one who is most aware of the impact of these events and can speak about them freely. It is generally accepted that in writing his gospel Luke used Mark's earlier account as one of his primary sources. One of the most significant changes he made occurs in Jesus' farewell discourse before the passion narrative. As already alluded to, Jesus in Mark's account warns his hearers in words that are a combination of apocalyptic-style admonitions and practical advice for a coming crisis:

> When you see the desolating sacrilege set up where it ought not to be — let the reader understand — then let those in Judea flee to the mountains; the one on the housetop must not go down to take anything away; the one in the field must not go back to get a coat. Woe to those who are pregnant or nursing infants in those days! Pray that it may not be in winter. (Mark 13:14-18)

The desolating sacrilege (literally "the abomination that desolates") mentioned here is a direct allusion to the book of Daniel, recalling for the attentive reader the specter of Antiochus's desecration of the temple in 165 b.c.e., an event which Daniel refers to three times (Dan 9:27; 11:31; 12:11; cf. 1 Macc 1:54). Mark is recycling the Danielic expression but expecting his own readers to make the connection between what is happening (or about to happen) in the temple with the most heinous desecration in Jewish memory since the Second Temple had been restored after the Babylonian exile in 515 B.C.E. For some reason, perhaps because of his closeness to the event or because the final destruction had not yet taken place, Mark does not feel free to make an explicit statement of what he has in mind, choosing instead to draw on apocalyptic symbolism. However, the instructions not to seek to retrieve any personal items but rather to flee to remote places is a clear indication of the imminent danger in which the inhabitants of Jerusalem and Judea now find themselves. Clearly, Mark wants his readers to get away from the threat of capture and enslavement.

Luke's rewriting of this warning runs as follows:

> When you see *Jerusalem surrounded by armies, then know that its desolation has come near.* Then those in Judea must flee to the mountains and *those inside the city must leave it,* and those out in the country must not enter it, *for these are the days of vengeance, as a fulfillment of all that is written.* Woe to those who are pregnant and to those who are nursing infants in those days! *For there will be great distress on the earth and wrath against this people; they will fall by the edge of the sword and be taken away as captives among all nations; and Jerusalem will be trampled on by the Gentiles until the times of the Gentiles are fulfilled.* (Luke 21:20-24)

The italics in the quotation above indicate Luke's virtual rewriting of his Markan source. Three notable changes occur, all pointing directly to the events that had taken place in Jerusalem. The symbolic "desolating sacrifice" of Mark has been given a clear historical reference, namely "Jerusalem surrounded by armies." There is reference to "those inside the city" who must leave, with the ominous statements about vengeance and the fulfillment of the Scriptures. The plight of those fleeing is signaled in terms of wrath against the Judean population and the fact that many will perish and others will be sold into slavery. It is as though Luke had read Josephus's account of the last days of Jerusalem and the suffering of the Jewish people in the aftermath of the destruction and rewrote Mark's end-time scenario with that information in mind. Even the reference to the fact that all this was foretold "in what was written" need not be read as Christian polemic against the Jews because of the rejection of Jesus, as some later Christian apologists were to claim. Josephus had already come to the conclusion, without any reference to the Christian story, that God had favored the Romans and that it was foolhardy in the extreme to resist not just Rome's might but, even more importantly, the divine will. The Roman imperial ideology had indeed infiltrated the ranks of the Jerusalem aristocracy, as represented by Josephus.

Luke was clearly writing at a moment when the Christian mission to the Gentiles was in progress and the events in Judea were past history, perhaps as late as 100 C.E. or even later still.[26] By then the Pauline churches had been established and the Evangelist's task was not to mourn the fall of Jerusalem but to emphasize the central and unifying role that it was meant to play in the divine plan as the Christians embarked on a mission "to the end of the earth." In Luke's perspective, Jesus had journeyed from Galilee to Jerusalem, and now his followers must "begin from Jerusalem" (Luke 24:47) and journey to Rome and beyond in fulfillment of Isaiah's promise that the light of salvation should reach the end of the earth (Isa 49:6; cf. Acts 1:8; 13:47).

The narrative of that journey in his second volume, the Acts of the Apostles, is constructed around two central figures, Peter and Paul, with James the brother of Jesus playing a mediating role at a critical juncture (Acts 15:13-21; 21:17-24). The Paul of Acts is less independent and more deferential to the Jerusalem temple authorities than the several self-portraits in his letters would have it. Luke reserves the title "apostle" for the members of the Twelve, even though Paul had vigorously claimed it for himself also (1 Cor 9:1-2; 15:8-11). According to Luke, it was Peter, not Paul, who opened the mission to non-Jews by receiving into the community the Roman centurion and his household in Caesarea, as a result of a vision that he had received (Acts 10:1-48). The importance of this event for Luke is demonstrated by the fact that it is retold at two other points in his narrative when Peter justifies his decision for admitting non-Jews to the new movement (11:1-18; 15:7-12).

This portrayal undoubtedly has to do with in-house disputes among different strands of Christians in the early second century C.E. While addressing this issue in his two-volume work, Luke is deeply conscious of the Roman world within which early Christianity had to operate and compete. His accounts of Paul's missionary journeys in Asia and in Greece reflect an intimate knowledge of the culture, administration, and commercial life of the empire. Paul has to contend with religious competition in terms of magicians in Cyprus (Acts 13:4-12). He and Barnabas are hailed as embodi-

26. Precise dating of the Gospels is not easy. There is fairly general agreement on the order of their appearance: Mark, the earliest, followed by Matthew and Luke in that order, and John as the latest. But the absolute dates are more difficult to determine. Of late some scholars have argued for a very late date for Luke, as late as 150 C.E., but this would be a minority opinion. Cf. J. Tyson, *Marcion and Luke-Acts: A Defining Struggle* (Columbia: University of South Carolina Press, 2006).

ments of Greek gods (Zeus and Hermes) because of the healings they have performed at Lystra and Derbe, and the people want to offer sacrifice to them (14:8-18). This incident shows how in the Greek world the identification of humans with different deities could be readily accepted at a popular level. It also helps explain the widespread acceptance of the imperial cult, especially in Asia Minor. At Athens Luke has Paul utter a philosophical speech that captures the ethos of that city (17:20-34). On the other hand Paul runs foul of the silversmiths of Ephesus, who see their trade in effigies of the great mother Artemis threatened by Paul's popularity (19:23-41).

Luke is also well informed on the legal situation in Judea, with his descriptions of Paul's arrest and trials before the Roman governors Felix and Festus in Caesarea in the presence of the Herodians Agrippa II and his sister Bernice (Acts 23–26). The fact that Paul could claim his right as a Roman citizen to appeal to Caesar means that Luke's narrative brings us eventually to Rome, allowing him to show his virtuosity as a writer in his description of the sea journey and shipwreck. Unfortunately, his account ends rather abruptly with Paul under house arrest in Rome but proclaiming the gospel nonetheless. We would very much have liked to hear about the end of Paul's life and whether he fulfilled his ambition to go as far as Spain (Rom 15:28).

Unfortunately, we do not have any comparable account of the journey that the early Christian missionaries took from Jerusalem via Galilee to the north. Luke's very brief notice at Acts 9:31 about the church living in peace and growing in numbers in Judea, Galilee, and Samaria is not based on any accurate knowledge of the movement's travails throughout the turbulent years leading up to and immediately following the first revolt in 66-70 C.E. Yet there is clear evidence that the route north to Antioch and east to Damascus had already been taken at a very early stage. Indeed it is Paul who informs us about his desire to arraign the followers of Jesus in Damascus and also about the presence of the Christian community in Antioch (Acts 9:1-25; 11:19-21).

What stance did Jesus' followers in Galilee and Judea take with regard to the revolt against Rome? How did the new arrangements that Rome introduced after the fall of Jerusalem affect them? These are questions about which we have very little knowledge. We have one tantalizing piece of information from the fourth-century C.E. historian Eusebius. He claims that the Christian community in Jerusalem decided on the basis of an "oracle to approved men" to depart from the city "before the war" and settled in Pella in Transjordan. This was one of the cities of the Dekapolis, close to Gadara and itself also a healing spa (H.E. 3.5.3). What, if any, information can we glean from the gospels of Mark and Matthew, for example, that might shed light on this "hidden period" of the early Jesus movement? Did the destruction of the temple raise social and political issues as well as theological issues for them? These questions will be addressed in later chapters, but first it is important to trace briefly the story of Jews and Christians (as the Jesus-followers soon came to be called, first in Antioch) into the second century within the larger context of Roman imperial ambitions in the East.

Rome and Judea between the Revolts (70-135 C.E.)

Rome's post-war policy was (1) to give Judea the status of an independent province, consequently appointing a governor of senatorial rank, and (2) to strengthen the role of the cities in the region. Both moves stemmed directly from the experience of the first revolt. The surrounding cities did not offer any succor to the Jewish rebels, and within Judean territory itself, as we have seen, Sepphoris refused to support the revolt and Tiberias was halfhearted. With the appointment of a governor to the enlarged province, a Roman legion could now be stationed close to the flash points within Judea itself. The experience of moving several legions from Antioch was cumbersome and meant that the Jewish rebels were able to organize themselves with little resistance from the auxiliary forces that were stationed in Jerusalem and Caesarea. Augustus had organized the army into a stable and efficient organization, and subsequent emperors relied heavily on its support for accession to power, as in the case of Vespasian in 69 C.E. After the destruction of Jerusalem, the *Legio X Fretensis* was immediately stationed there. Subsequently a second legion, the *VI Ferrata* was located at Kefar 'Othnay/Legio in the plain of Esdraelon following the Bar Kokhba revolt in 135 C.E. Colonies of Roman veterans, such as those at Sebaste, Gaba, and Ptolemais from the pre-70 period, had already signaled Rome's concern in controlling what was deemed to be a troublesome region.

This increased presence of legionaries, auxiliaries, and veterans after the first revolt functioned as a symbol of imperial control and power throughout Palestine-Syria. The military shield had more than once proved a flash point for Judean-Roman relations, since it carried the image of the emperor as well as the Roman eagle. The explicit connection between the emperor and the army became much more pronounced after 70 C.E. also. Whereas in the first century C.E., only two emperors (Augustus and Vespasian) had visited the East, all the second- and third-century emperors visited Syria, often for military purposes. The extension of this intimate relationship between emperor and army can be seen in the fact that from the end of the first century C.E. emperors were consistently portrayed as Roman generals. Thus Trajan and Hadrian, and later Septimius Severus, took personal command of major campaigns, thereby enhancing their image in the eyes of both the legionaries and the provincials as protectors and saviors of the *Pax Romana*. A cuirassed statue of Hadrian with mythological representations on the breastplate, found close to Scythopolis in the Jordan valley, probably celebrates the successful end of the Bar Kokhba revolt under his leadership. A milestone found near Jerusalem has the names of both Vespasian and Titus and mentions that the work was completed by the *Legio X Fretensis*, thereby informing even the casual passer-by who was in charge of the country.[27]

As regards the increased role that cities could play in the administration of the province, those in Galilee seem to have fared better. The destruction of Jerusalem was almost total, and it became the campsite for the tenth legion. Only the fortresses of Herodion and Masada, both of which were occupied by zealots who had fled from Jerusalem, held out for a time, but they too were eventually reduced by 74 C.E. In Galilee, Sepphoris benefited from its pacific stance during the revolt. The metropolitan area was greatly extended, as can be seen in the archaeological remains from lower Sepphoris today, with the development of a colonnaded Roman street layout, a large basilica-style public building, a temple, and the use of Roman-inspired frescoes and mosaic floors in private houses and shops lining the cardo.[28] The administrative district that Sepphoris controlled on behalf of Rome was also greatly expanded to cover much of Lower Galilee. Early in the second century, during the reign of Trajan (98-117 C.E.), the city was issuing coins after the fashion of a Greek city, inscribed "Of the Sepphoreans." While the

27. W. Eck, *Rom und Judea* (Tübingen: Mohr Siebeck, 2007), 76-78 and 141-42; cf. also K. Fittchen, "Zur Panzerstatue aus Samaria Sebaste," in L. Rutgers, ed., *What Has Athens to Do with Jerusalem? Essays in Honour of Gideon Foerster* (Leuven: Peeters, 2002), 9-17; J. Pollini, "Gods and Emperors in the East: Images of Power and the Power of Intolerance," in Y. Eliav, E. Friedland, and S. Herbert, eds., *The Sculptural Environment of the Roman Near East: Reflections on Culture, Ideology and Power* (Leuven: Peeters, 2008), 165-94.

28. Z. Weiss, "Sepphoris," in E. Stern, ed., *NEAHL* Supplementary Volume, 2029-35; C. Thomas McCollough, "Monumental Change: Architecture and Culture in Late Roman and Early Byzantine Sepphoris," in D. Edwards and C. T. McCollough, eds., *The Archaeology of Difference: Gender, Ethnicity, Class and the "Other" in Antiquity, Studies in Honor of Eric Meyers* (AASOR 60/61; Boston: American Schools of Oriental Research, 2007), 267-78.

image of the emperor's head is on the obverse, the reverse has typical Jewish symbols such as a palm tree, a caduceus, and ears of barleycorn, but no ostensibly pagan symbol.[29] There are no coins from the reign of Hadrian (117-38 C.E.), possibly due to the fact that there was a Jewish revolt in North Africa in 115-18, followed by the Bar Kokhba revolt of 132-35. Minting at Sepphoris began again in 138 during the reign of Antoninus Pius (138-61). The name of the city was by that time Diocaesarea, "Of the divine Caesar/Zeus Caesar," while it also proclaimed itself as "sacred, inviolate, and autonomous" after the fashion of much older Phoenician cities.[30]

The coin profile of Tiberias is not as clear or as impressive as that of Sepphoris. This may be due to the fact that some of its citizens had played a part in the first revolt and that, therefore, the city was not allowed to mint coins until the second century, when there are several coins of Trajan from 100 and 109 C.E. The emperor's bust is on the obverse with the usual imperial titles, and on the reverse are images of Hygeia seated on a rock feeding a snake from a bowl (a clear reference to the city's hot springs and the health spa associated with them, mentioned previously), another coin has the city goddess Tyche standing on the rudder of a boat, and still another just an anchor, emphasizing the maritime location of the city. We learn from the fourth-century Christian writer Epiphanius that there was a temple of Hadrian at Tiberias, and indeed one of the coins from the city, dated to the year 120 C.E., does have a bust of Hadrian on the obverse and a temple on the reverse with a seated figure of Zeus/Hadrian.[31]

The third Galilean site where signs of Rome's increased presence into the second century might be seen is Banias/Caesarea Philippi. Whether the site of Herod's temple to Roma and Augustus is to be located directly in front of the cave of Pan or at the Omrit site two km away, the fact is that this latter site experienced significant changes in the late first century C.E.[32]

29. However, the appearance of the word *edoken,* "gave" or "permitted," suggests that they were allowed to issue coins of a Jewish-Roman kind by the grace of the emperor only.

30. Y. Meshorer, "Coins of Sepphoris," in R. Martin Nagy, et al., eds., *Sepphoris in Galilee: Crosscurrents of Culture* (Raleigh: North Carolina Museum of Art, 1996), 195-200, at p. 197; M. Chancey, "City Coins and Roman Power in Palestine from Pompey to the Great Revolt," in D. Edwards, ed., *Religion and Society in Roman Palestine: Old Questions and New Approaches* (London: Routledge, 2004), 103-12.

31. Later coins from the reigns of Caracalla and Elagabalus have representations of Hygeia also, but this time the epithet *colonia* appears, reflecting an anecdote from the Talmud of a conversation between Antoninus and Rabbi Judah about the status of the city (Palestinian Talmud Abodah Zara 10.71). Cf. Meshorer, *City Coins,* 34-35, 112-13.

32. Z. Uri Maoz, *Baniyas in the Greco-Roman Period: A History Based on the Excava-*

The building identified as Temple One was enlarged and embellished, being surrounded on three sides by Corinthian columns and with an enlarged *pronaos* or entrance colonnade, fronted with six Corinthian columns also. The interior of what the excavators are calling Temple Two was developed also with a raised *cella* that presumably housed the statues associated with the cult.[33] Could it be that this development was a monument to the new imperial house that had found this area congenial for celebrating their victory, but also important as far as Rome's future plans in the East were concerned?

The destruction of the Jerusalem temple was a traumatic experience for Jews everywhere, but especially for the inhabitants of the Holy City. Neither Antiochus Epiphanes' desecration nor Pompey the Great's entry into the Holy Place, serious though these incidents were, could be compared with the devastation caused by Titus's army once they had breached the walls after a three-month siege. The destruction involved the city as well as the temple complex, as the inhabitants fled or were captured by the Romans to be used in the triumphal parade in Rome or sold into slavery. Just as serious as the physical devastation was the impact on the religious psyche of the nation.

The first temple had been destroyed by the Babylonians in 589 B.C.E. but was restored some 75 years later, when Cyrus, the Persian ruler who replaced the Babylonians as masters of the East, allowed the conquered peoples and their gods, including the Judeans, to return to their respective homelands. The situation with the Romans was different. It had become increasingly clear throughout the first century C.E. that the Jewish symbol system which proclaimed that Yahweh was the only god, that the land was his gift to Israel, and that his temple should be in Jerusalem could not live easily with the ideology associated with the emperor as divine, especially when that claim was pushed to its limits as in the case of Gaius (Caligula) and Nero. Admittedly, for some time the Pharisaic movement had developed a system of religious practice whereby the symbolism of the temple's holiness could be observed away from the temple in homes and villages.

---

tions (Qazrin: Archostyle, 2007), is of the opinion that the temple stood directly in front of the entrance to the pool of Pan, whereas Netzer, *Herod the Great Builder*, 218-22, believes it was located on a ledge to the left of the entrance, where evidence of Roman *opus reticulatum* building style has been found. See also A. Berlin, "The Archaeology of Ritual: The Sanctuary of Pan at Banias/Caesarea Philippi," *BASOR* 315 (1999), 27-46.

33. M. Nelson, "A Preliminary Review of the Architecture of Omrit," in Overman and Schowalter, eds., *The Roman Temple Complex*, 27-44, at p. 40.

But the fact that Yahweh had appeared to abandon his own people in favor of the Romans, as even the priest apologist Josephus had declared, was a serious blow to Judean self-understanding.

Vespasian and Titus had conducted a clever campaign in Judea. While he was awaiting the outcome of the imperial succession in Rome and before launching the siege on the city, Vespasian made sure that he had secured the surrounding towns and the countryside, Lydda and Jamnia on the coast, Emmaus to the west, where he stationed the fifth legion, Samaria and Neapolis in the north, and finally Jericho to the east. Meanwhile within the city itself anarchy reigned, as various factions fought for control, one of them led by John of Gischala in Galilee, who had fled to Jerusalem with a crowd of followers following the defeat of the Galilean rebels at Jotapata. Supplies to the city were severely limited and the granaries had actually been burned down by some of the rebels. John and his group were in control of the temple area and were so unpopular that the High Priest invited one Simon bar Giora, a leader of a bandit group who had been plundering southern Palestine, to come to the aid of the citizens. However, matters only got worse, as there were now two rival factions vying for control of the revolt.[34]

Vespasian, therefore, decided to mount a second campaign in Judea and took control of several other places, while awaiting developments both in Jerusalem and in Rome. He was declared emperor by the legions in Egypt in July 69, and the legions in Palestine and Syria immediately followed suit. He was further encouraged by messages of support from various cities, first from Antioch and then from Alexandria, but he did not immediately go to Rome. Word arrived that Vitellius, who had replaced the murdered Galba, was himself murdered in late 69. Vespasian finally went to Rome in the early summer of 70 and was formally honored with a triumph by the senate.

The campaign against Jerusalem was now in the hands of Titus, who besieged the city, erecting ramps that would allow the siege engines to attack the well-fortified city. There had been stout resistance from the rebels as the tenth legion dug in. Eventually the first and second walls that surrounded the western part of the city were breached, but the temple area and the Arx Antonia, located on the eastern spur, proved more difficult. The temple, surrounded by Herod's colonnaded wall, was a virtual fortress and had been occupied by the rebels, even though the daily sacrifices continued

---

34. For a useful summary of Josephus's presentation of these factions and their leaders, see D. Rhoads, *Israel in Revolution, 6-74 C.E.: A Political History Based on the Writings of Josephus* (Philadelphia: Fortress, 1976), 94-149.

to be offered, according to Josephus (*War* 6.94). The final breach of the temple fortress took place after several repulses, according to Josephus's graphic account, torn as he is between heroizing the Judean rebels and lauding the bravery and astuteness of Titus and the Romans. A Roman soldier threw a firebrand into the temple chamber, and, in the confusion that followed, Titus's instruction to have it extinguished were ignored. The Romans stormed through, butchering all whom they encountered and erecting their standards in the outer court as a declaration of victory.[35]

There was, of course, much consolidation to be done before Titus could embark on his triumphal journey around the country, already alluded to. In order to understand the uncharacteristic ferocity of the Roman response to the revolt, especially the destruction of the national shrine, it should be emphasized that at the outbreak of the revolt the Judeans had actually established an independent state. This was an unprecedented action by a subject people, one that prided itself on its long-standing treaty of friendship with Rome. Local governors were appointed throughout the land, such as Josephus's assignment in Galilee. Even more impressive was the production of silver coins of excellent quality celebrating the freedom and the holiness of Jerusalem. The dating of these coins was from year one to five of the revolt, suggesting that a new era had dawned, and the symbols on them recalled Jewish festivals, especially those that celebrated the emancipation from slavery under Moses.[36]

While some of the inhabitants may have fled the city before the final onslaught, including Jewish followers of Jesus taking to heart the advice of Mark 13, there was undoubtedly wholesale slaughter. Titus declared that the priests should die with the temple that they served, and others of the aristocracy were imprisoned to be taken as trophies to Rome or sold into slavery. Lands were confiscated and sold to the highest bidder (*War* 7.216) or used to repay loyalty to Rome, as in the case of Josephus, who received lands in the Plain in exchange for his lands in Judea, which were now required to provision the legion in Jerusalem. Presumably this was by way of recompense for his contribution to Roman strategy once he had surrendered at Jotapata (*Life* 422).

A later rabbinic legend tells the story of Yohanan ben Zakkai, a highly

---

35. Schürer, *History of the Jewish People*, 1:496-513 recounts the details following Josephus's account.

36. M. Goodman, *The Ruling Class of Judea: The Origins of the Jewish Revolt against Rome, A.D. 66-70* (Cambridge: Cambridge University Press, 1987), 176-97.

respected sage, emerging from the city, emaciated and weak, having fasted continuously in the hope that God might avert the destruction. He was allowed by Titus to establish a school with others of his circle at Jamnia on the coast, and a second school was established at Lydda. It was these schools and their pronouncements that made it possible for some elements of Jewish religious life to continue for those who survived the final purge. Their rulings determined the calendar for the observance of various festivals without the temple, and it was they who decided which rituals formerly associated with the cult should now be performed and which should be put in abeyance.[37] There was no question of worship continuing at the temple, even though some may have hoped for its restoration one day, following the precedent of the rebuilding of the first temple some seventy years after its destruction by the Babylonians.

Unfortunately, we do not have a Josephus to describe the second Jewish revolt, the Bar Kokhba War of 132-35 C.E. Some brief mention in ancient writings and discoveries of caves, coins and letters in the Judean desert and the Shephelah have assisted in filling in some of the picture. One of the letters comes from the leader, Simon bar Kosiba, and is written in Greek, because he did not feel competent to write in the Hebrew language. His name was changed to Simon bar Kokhba, with reference to a "star," suggesting that he may have adopted a messianic status or had one ascribed to him. There are no traces, archaeological or literary, of the revolt reaching Galilee, but the fact that the names of as many as seven legions appear in inscriptions relating to the war is indicative of how seriously Rome took this second revolt. Undoubtedly, the uprising would seem to be the result of "unfinished business" of the descendants of those Judeans who had suffered so much in the wake of the first revolt. In particular, the fact that a Roman legion with all its symbolic and political significance was now located in the holy city of Jerusalem was an ongoing irritant, as far as Judeans were concerned. According to the Roman historian Dio Cassius, one of the reasons for the revolt was the upgrading of the city to a Roman *colonia,* with a new name, Aelia Capitolina. Presumably, this meant the introduction of images of the Capitoline triad, Jupiter, Juno, and Minerva, on the ruined site of the Jerusalem temple.[38]

37. J. Neusner, "Studies in the *Taqqanoth* of Yavneh," *HTR* 63 (1970), 183-98; "The History of a Biography: Yohanan ben Zakkai in the Canonical Literature of Formative Judaism," in *Formative Judaism: Religious, Historical and Literary Studies* (Brown Judaic Studies 91; Chico: Scholars, 1985), 79-96.

38. For a useful summary of both the war and the letters, see H. Eshel, "Bar Kochba

Jewish religious life had to find another way, and somewhat ironically, it was in Galilee that that would take place. It was there that the rabbinic movement eventually took root and a new program for life without the temple was fashioned, one that put sage and Torah, rather than priest and temple, at the center of Jewish life.[39] The new charter for Judaism, the Mishna and its commentary, the Palestinian Talmud, were produced in Sepphoris and Tiberias between 200 and 450. And there were other centers of study, the *bātēy midrash* in both Galilee and the Golan. This was a period of resurgence and renewal, as Jews in the Galilee began to prosper again. They have left us monuments of these developments in the many fine synagogue buildings from this period whose remains can be seen today because of the intensive program of excavations that has taken place there over the past forty years, especially through the work of Eric and Carol Meyers and James Strange in Upper Galilee.[40]

Relations with Rome had mellowed also, as the changed ethos of Sepphoris and Tiberias in the post-70 period, previously described, testifies. Nothing illustrates this change better than an early-third-century coin of Sepphoris, by then declaring itself by its new name Diocaesarea. The legend on the coin reads: "Diocaesarea the holy, city of asylum, autonomous, loyal, (a treaty of) friendship and alliance between the holy council (of the city) and the Senate and people of Rome."[41] The rabbis, in their wisdom, had learned to negotiate the issues that living in a Roman world posed for Jews everywhere, without having to continue the struggle for the political inde-

Revolt," in Collins and Harlow, eds., *Eerdmans Dictionary of Early Judaism,* 417-25. Eck, *Rom und Judea,* 59-63, discusses the offensiveness of the Roman transformation of Jewish sacred space by this action on the part of Hadrian.

39. C. Hezser, *The Social Structure of the Rabbinic Movement in Roman Palestine* (Tübingen: Mohr Siebeck, 1997); S. Millar, *Sages and Commoners in Late Antique Palestine* (TSAJ 111, Tübingen: Mohr Siebeck, 2006); D. Urman and P. Flescher, *Ancient Synagogues: Historical Analysis and Archaeological Discovery* (Leiden: Brill, 1995); L. Levine, ed., *The Synagogue in Late Antiquity* (Philadelphia: Jewish Theological Seminary of America, 1987); *The Rabbinic Class of Roman Palestine in Late Antiquity* (Jerusalem: Yad Izhak Ben-Zvi, 1989).

40. E. Meyers, J. Strange, and D. Groh, "The Meiron Excavation Project: Archaeological Survey in Galilee and the Golan," *BASOR* 230 (1978), 1-24. Since that initial survey, final reports have appeared for Khirbet Shema, Gischala, and Meiron from this team, which also includes Carol Meyers. A valuable catalog has also been published by A. Runesson, D. Binder, and B. Olsson, *The Ancient Synagogue from Its Origins to 200 C.E.* (Leiden: Brill, 2008).

41. "The holy council" mentioned on this coin may well be the Jewish Sanhedrin, which apparently continued to function in inner-Jewish affairs, according to Meshorer, *City Coins,* 37 and catalog number 95 (see above n. 30 also).

pendence that their coreligionists of previous centuries had sought. It was a matter not of betraying their inherited view of life but of finding ways to accommodate to the situations that confronted them, as various anecdotes in the rabbinic writings illustrate.[42]

The Jesus-followers are largely hidden from view in the sources that deal with this turbulent period of Jewish history in Palestine. In Roman eyes they would have been indistinguishable from other Jews, even though already in 64 C.E. Nero was able to initiate a pogrom against the Christians in Rome, making them the scapegoats for the fire that he himself had caused, as Tacitus reports (*Annals* 25.44.2-8). Those who were in Jerusalem must have left for the safety of the Greek cities like Pella in Perea or even Antioch. As discussed above, Luke deals with the destruction of the temple in ways that relate to his own projects toward the end of the first or beginning of the second century C.E. By placing the event in the past, he can recognize the centrality of the Holy City for Jesus and the early church, as the first stage on its journey to becoming the church of all the nations. Matthew on the other hand, engaged as he is in a bitter dispute with "the synagogue across the street," interprets the destruction as a judgment by God on an unfaithful Israel who has refused the invitation to come to the wedding feast of the son (Matt 22:1-10; particularly v. 7).[43] It would be some time before we find a Christian apologist addressing Rome directly, but when it happens the tone is more robust, even confrontational. Tertullian, a Christian apologist from North Africa living in Rome, suitably flatters the emperor of the day (c. 192), Septimius Severus (also from North Africa), by declaring that only "bad" emperors used laws against the Christians. For their part, Christians pray for the emperor "from the heart" to the One who alone is able to grant good things to the ruler. Having thus reassured Septimius, Tertullian boldly, and also presciently, declares his confidence in the future of the Christian movement: "We Christians are but of yesterday, and we have filled everything you have: cities, tenements, forts, towns, exchanges, yes, and camps, tribes, palaces, senate, forum. All we have left you are the temples" (*Apology* 37.4).

---

42. When Rabbi Gamaliel was queried as to why he would enter the bathhouse in Acco, thereby passing the statue of a nude Aphrodite, he replied: "I never came into her domain, she came into mine. They do not say 'Let us make a bathhouse as an ornament for Aphrodite,' but rather, 'let us make Aphrodite as an ornament for the bathhouse'" (Mishnah Abodah Zara 3.4).

43. S. Freyne, "Vilifying the Other and Defining the Self: Matthew's and John's Anti-Judaism in Context," in J. Neusner and E. Frerichs, eds., *"To See Ourselves as Others See Us": Christians, Jews, "Others" in Late Antiquity* (Chico: Scholars, 1985), 117-44.

Table Three: Roman Rulers and the Jews

31 B.C.E.	Octavian defeats Mark Antony at the battle of Actium and is declared *Imperator*. He is made sole ruler *(Princeps)* of the Roman world in 27 B.C.E. after a period of internal strife between various military factions. He is given the title *Augustus* (Greek *Sebastos*) in 22, *Pontifex Maximus* in 12, and *Pater Patriae* in 2 B.C.E. Herod pledges his support and organizes Caesarean games in Jerusalem in 27 B.C.E. to honor Augustus.
14 C.E.	Death of Augustus.
14-37	Tiberius as sole emperor, public ministry of Jesus in Palestine, 27-30 (?).
37-41	Gaius Caligula is emperor. He wants to have his statue erected in the Jerusalem temple, but dies before his orders can be implemented.
41-54	Claudius is emperor. He expels Jews and Christians from Rome in 49 C.E.
54-68	Nero is emperor. In 64 Christians are made the scapegoats for a fire in Rome, leading to the probable martyrdom of Peter and Paul.
69	The end of the Julio-Claudian line of emperors. Vespasian is the first of the Flavian line, 69-79. The Jerusalem temple is destroyed in 70 under Vespasian's son Titus, ending the first revolt of the Jews, which began in 66.
79-81	Titus is emperor. He celebrated his victory over the Jews earlier, with the Arch of Titus as a memorial of the event. Jewish historian Josephus, who was involved in the revolt in Galilee, surrendered and was brought to Rome by Titus, where he engages in his apologetic writings, *Jewish War, Jewish Antiquities, Vita,* and *Against Apion*.
81-96	Domitian, last of the Flavian emperors. Persecution of Christians in Asia, possibly reflected in the Revelation of John.
96-98	Nerva is emperor. The Jewish tax *(fiscus Judaicus)* that previously was paid to the Jerusalem temple now goes to the temple of Jupiter in Rome.
98-117	Trajan is emperor. Pliny writes to him about the Christians in the province of Bithynia. In 115 Jews in Egypt, Cyprus, and Mesopotamia revolt.
117-38	Hadrian is emperor. He invades Britain and establishes the frontier of Hadrian's Wall. Second revolt of the Jews in Palestine under Bar Kokhba, 132-35. Jerusalem becomes a Roman *colonia*, Aelia Capitolina. In 134 Hadrian visits Athens again and initiates the Panhellenion, a confederation of Greek cities.
138-61	Antoninus Pius is emperor. He is mentioned in the Talmud as having

	friendly discussions with the Jewish patriarch. The beginning of the Antonine line.
161-80	Marcus Aurelius, the philosopher emperor. He wrote his *Meditations* after 166. Wars on the frontier with Parthia and on the Danube.
180-92	Commodus, Marcus's son, is emperor. He caused trouble in Rome with the execution of senators and was murdered, thus ending the Antonine dynasty.

CHAPTER THREE

Palestinian Economy and Society

This widow has given her whole livelihood.

(MARK 12:41-44)

The Markan story of the Jerusalem widow casting the equivalent of a small Roman coin into the temple treasury even though it represented her livelihood illustrates the complicated and uneven economic systems that prevailed in Palestine by the beginning of the Common Era. Jewish, Roman, and Greek city coinage were all in circulation, each signifying the different layers of economic as well as political activity operative in the country. Little wonder that the profession of money changer was a popular one. Attempts to unravel the ways in which the different systems operated and competed with each other have been aided by the application of various sociological models for interpreting the data that has come to light. While such approaches are indeed helpful, the danger is that they may inadvertently be imposing modern economic and social theories onto ancient societies. Thus, whereas today in our global situation economic issues determine political issues to a large extent, in the ancient world it was quite the opposite. All ancient economies were politically controlled. That means that political power determined who benefited and to what extent, thus giving rise to highly stratified societies.

Where to Begin? Models and Muddles

Since economic aspects of ancient societies are embedded in other, mainly political, aspects, they have often been overlooked, not receiving the same attention as the cultural and religious dimensions, especially among biblical scholars. In more recent times, however, the increased dialogue between archaeology, the social sciences, and literary studies has drawn attention to the amount of information that ancient texts contain about economic issues. While it is true that there was no discussion of economic theory in the ancient world comparable to that of the post-industrial revolution era, "rational" economic thinking was not wholly absent. Classical scholars have highlighted the fact that the ancient world was familiar with such topics as the maximizing of resources, the manipulation of markets, and the need to keep production costs low. The huge cache of papyri from Egypt has made it possible to understand at first hand how all these factors were managed on a daily basis, information that has been helpful in understanding the Palestinian situation also, as we shall see.

As interest in these topics develops among biblical scholars, there is a notable divergence of approach between those who favor the deductive approach through the application of models and those who favor a more inductive approach of looking at the archaeological and literary data from different sites and regions. There are limitations to both approaches. A slavish use of models can lead to serious distortion in the picture that emerges, since social models are by definition generalized pictures that seek to capture certain key aspects of a society. The danger is that the results are taken as giving the whole story when, in fact, the model chosen will highlight certain aspects only. Furthermore they do not take account of changes that may be occurring over time. Thus a historical perspective that seeks to map changing values and attitudes, the shifting international as well as local power structures, key technological advances, and even the impact of natural phenomena such as earthquakes and droughts must also be included in the discussion.[1]

The inductive approach that relies on examining the data from dif-

---

1. S. Freyne, "Herodian Economics in Galilee: Searching for a Suitable Model," in P. F. Esler, ed., *Modelling Early Christianity: Social-Scientific Studies of the New Testament in Its Context* (London: Routledge, 1995), 23-46. Reprinted in Freyne, *Galilee and Gospel: Collected Essays* (WUNT 125; Tübingen: Mohr Siebeck, 2000), 86-113. K. C. Hanson and D. E. Oakman, *Palestine in the Time of Jesus: Social Structures and Social Conflicts* (Minneapolis: Fortress, 1998), 63-98 and 161-63.

ferent sites and regions is more likely to take these factors into account. Yet here, too, there are problems, especially when attempts are made to paint general pictures on the basis of partial evidence from what are often chance discoveries. Archaeologists generally talk in periods such as late Hellenistic, early Roman, and the like, periods that can often be as long as a hundred years or more, making it difficult to pinpoint developments that the material remains relate to a particular person or moment in time. In other words, a critical dialogue between spade and text is called for.[2]

Given these limitations, both approaches can assist and correct each other. The use of models can eliminate what has been described as the "intuitive" approach, that is, relying on hunches rather than hard evidence. The inductive approach on the other hand ensures that claims are not made on the basis of a chosen model without concrete evidence to support them. These introductory remarks are prompted in particular by the ways in which an understanding of Galilean economics has come to play such an important part in discussions about the aims of Jesus' ministry. Even the briefest perusal of the Gospels shows just how much of his teaching has to do with the dangers of wealth, the blessedness of the poor, and the need to follow his example in renunciation of home, property, and wealth.[3] The impact of Liberation Theology has generated a special interest in this aspect of Jesus' teaching, and inevitably varying points of view vie with each other in claiming Jesus' support for very different modern ideological positions.[4]

What kind of social and economic situation do these statements of Jesus presuppose? Do they apply especially to Galilee, or are they relevant in Judea as well? One could infer two quite opposing situations on the basis of such teaching: either they suggest that Galileans in Jesus' day were affluent and needed to be reminded of values that were embedded in their shared biblical heritage, or one could argue that there was widespread endemic poverty in the region, where the peasants were gradually being forced into a

---

2. In a paper delivered at the 2008 Society of Biblical Literature meeting, "Reappraising the Galilean Economy," J. Reed highlights the difficulty of taking a single model, such as that of M. I. Finley's *The Ancient Economy* (Berkeley: University of California Press, 1973), to cover the ancient Mediterranean economy from fifth-century B.C.E. Athens to fourth-century C.E. Rome.

3. D. Fiensy, *Jesus the Galilean: Soundings in a First Century Life* (Piscataway: Gorgias, 2007), 85-135.

4. R. Lassalle-Klein, ed., *Jesus of Galilee: Contextual Christology for the 21st Century* (Maryknoll: Orbis, 2011); cf. S. Freyne, "Jesus of Galilee: Implications and Possibilities," *Early Christianity* 1 (2010), 372-405.

situation of near penury. Variants of both answers have been given in some recent construals of Jesus' life.

Questions such as these have highlighted the Herodian period in general and that of Antipas in particular as especially significant for a proper assessment of the situation and Jesus' response to it. Is there a convergence between the changes occurring in Galilee under Antipas and the emergence of the one protest movement that occurred in Galilee (as distinct from Judea) in the first century C.E.? The answers vary, depending on how one reads the evidence from the archaeological record. Did Antipas's reign help to stimulate the Galilean economy, if we can use such a piece of modern jargon, or did it increase the burden on the small landowners, who, on the basis of both literary evidence and archaeological surveys, dwelled for the most part in villages? It may be that there were differences between micro-regions within Galilee itself, such as the lakefront area, and it could equally be true that some Galileans profited from the new regime more than others. Thus we hear of the "grandees" *(megistanes)* and the "leading men of Galilee" *(hoi prōtoi tēs Galilaias)* who were invited to the king's birthday party together with the military officers *(chiliarchoi)* according to Mark 6:21. Who are the "Herodians" that we meet in the Gospels, a new class of administrators and landowners or a small court circle? How can archaeology assist with these questions?

In order to obtain a proper perspective on these first century C.E. issues, it is important to examine the way in which the Galilean economy fared under the Hellenistic monarchies and the Hasmoneans prior to the Herodian rule. In the previous chapters, political, cultural, and religious changes that were occurring have been described. It is important in this context to highlight the economic changes that were embedded in these other aspects of society in those periods also. This "longer view" will help to put into perspective any changes that may have occurred and to assess better their likely continuing impact on the native population in the first century also.

The Hellenistic Monarchies and Economic Change

Our best information regarding the economic realities of the early Hellenistic age undoubtedly comes from the Zenon papyri from Oxyrynchus in Egypt. These deal with a tour of inspection by Zenon and others on behalf of the Ptolemaic finance minister, Apollonios, who also owned vari-

ous estates in Palestine. The main issue that emerges is that of landownership, since agriculture in its various forms was the main activity in all
pre-industrial economies. On the basis of what can be gleaned from this
correspondence, it seems that a considerable amount of the land was owned
directly by the king as royal lands and managed on his behalf by various
people, some named in Zenon's reports, such as the Judean Joseph, a member of the Tobiad family from Transjordan, who obtained the position of
tax-farmer for Coele Syria from the Egyptian king (*Ant* 12.160-85). Zenon,
accompanied by quite a large retinue, began his tour of inspection at Strato's
Tower (later Caesarea Maritima), where they had disembarked from Egypt.
They traveled through Idumea, then crossed over to Transjordan, returning
via Galilee to the port of Ptolemais. Several places are mentioned: Adora
and Marissa in Idumea and, in Galilee, Qadesh on the borders of Tyre and
Bethanath, usually identified with a site near the Netofa valley in Lower
Galilee. A number of these places have yielded strong evidence of a Hellenized ethos from slightly later times, suggesting that they may have acted
as regional market centers for the produce of the surrounding countryside.[5]

What emerges from Zenon's correspondence as well as from other
Egyptian papyri is a tightly managed leasing and accounting system, with
various levels of bureaucracy, ranging from estate stewards to regional overseers, in what was essentially a state-run enterprise, similar to that which
obtained in Egypt. The size of the various holdings varied, but in general the
tendency was for considerable increase from the small family-run holdings
of the earlier Israelite period to estates as large as 50 to 100 hectares (120-
250 acres). Each of these was dedicated to the production of single crops —
grapes, olives, or wheat. Those specializing in wine production required a
considerable amount of labor, both seasonal and permanent. According to
the Roman writer Cato winemaking demanded four times as many laborers
as olive oil production because it called for intensive activity in picking and
treading the grapes at a particular time of the year.[6]

It is unclear whether or not free small landowners existed, at least
in the Ptolemaic period, and if so, how numerous they were likely to have
been. A lengthy inscription from shortly after 200 B.C.E. describes the situation that obtained in the Jezreel plain. Ptolemy, the son of Thraseas, a high-

---

5. V. Tcherikover, *Palestine under the Ptolemies: A Contribution to the Study of the Zenon Papyri* (Mizraim 4/5; New York: Stechert, 1937), 4-5 and 9-90.

6. John S. Kloppenborg, *The Tenants in the Vineyard* (WUNT 195; Tübingen: Mohr Siebeck, 2006), 288.

ranking Ptolemaic general who had defected to the Seleucid side after the Seseucid victory at Paneion in 198 B.C.E., was duly rewarded in terms of the leasing of a number of extra villages in addition to those that he had owned previously. He also obtained tax concessions with regard to the movement of goods between those villages that he owned or leased. His property was also to be free from the billeting of soldiers, which was ordinarily extremely burdensome for property owners. However, permission had to be obtained from a higher official in order to move goods to or from villages outside his territory. In addition to underlining the restrictions on an important figure, on the basis of other ancient documents, this arrangement suggests that the majority of the inhabitants of these estates were classified as *laoi,* that is, as villagers bound to the soil with no independent status.[7]

In general, one can say that the impact of Hellenization on the economy of the whole country, north and south, was to introduce specializations in terms of production, with the emphasis on exports to Egypt, especially oil, wine, and wheat. It is probably during the period of Ptolemaic rule (300-200 B.C.E.) that the beginnings of the fishing industry around the Sea of Galilee are also to be dated. Josephus mentions that an unusual type of fish, found elsewhere only in the Nile in Egypt, the *coracin,* was also present in the Sea of Galilee (*War* 3.520). The reference to the Nile suggests that there was a special connection with Egypt and that this is related to developments introduced by the Ptolemies. It will be recalled that two centuries later, when Jesus called fishermen from Bethsaida as his first followers, James and John left their father Zebedee "with the hired servants" (Mark 1:20), suggesting a family-run business rather than mere subsistence fishing. The name of Migdal Nun (Magdala), itself meaning "fish tower," was changed to the Greek name Tarichea, a reference to the salting of fish, a process which made it possible to preserve and export fish from the region. Greek technical know-how seems to have come early to Galilee, and the Zenon papyri mention salted fish as one of the exports from Judea to Egypt.[8]

While the Ptolemies sought to introduce into Palestine an adminis-

7. Y. Landau, "A Greek Inscription Found near Hefzibah," *IEJ* 16 (1966), 56-70; P. Briant, "*Laoi* et Esclaves Ruraux," in *Actes du Colloque 1972 sur l'esclavage* (Paris: Girea, 1974), 93-133.

8. K. C. Hanson, "The Galilean Fishing Economy and the Jesus Tradition," *BTB* 27 (1997), 99-111; Mendel Nun, *The Sea of Galilee and Its Fishermen in the New Testament* (Kibbutz Ein Gev: Kinneret Sailing, 1989); two Zenon papyri, *PCZ* 59004 and 59006, mention salted fish being sent to Egypt.

Ruins of a fisherman's house at Bethsaida. Home of Jesus' first permanent
followers, the town was upgraded by Philip the Tetrarch and renamed
Bethsaida Iulias in honor of the empress.
(Todd Bolen/BiblePlaces.com)

trative arrangement similar to that which operated in Egypt, they had also
to take account of the mixed population of the country in this period: the
Judeans around Jerusalem, the Idumeans in the south, the Phoenicians in
the coastal plain that was shared by various cities from Gaza to Sidon along
the Mediterranean coast. The Greek historian of the period Polybius says
that the inhabitants of Palestine were particularly attached to the Ptolemies,
yet the Seleucid king Antiochus III met with very little resistance in Palestine when he launched his successful campaign that led to the end of the
Ptolemaic rule with the victory at Paneion in 198 B.C.E. Indeed, there is direct evidence that this change of rulers brought real benefits to the Judeans,
at that time living mainly in the south within the territory of the temple
state. Josephus reports a decree of the king to the governor of the region as
a whole, known officially as Coele Syria at that time. The preamble recounts
the ways in which the people of Jerusalem had received his army and assisted in removing the Ptolemaic garrison from the citadel. As a result, they
were to be rewarded by receiving aid to restore the city and to complete the
building of porticoes at the temple. No tax was to be charged on the timber
required for this project, which was to be imported from Lebanon. In addi-

tion they were to be provided with an allowance of sacrificial animals, wine, oil, and frankincense for the temple worship, as well as a substantial supply of wheat and salt (*Ant* 12.138-44).

Such concessions from the new rulers allowed the Judean economy to begin to develop, even prosper. The presence of Hellenistic influences among the priestly elite that emerged some thirty years later at the time of Antiochus Epiphanes' intervention was not only cultural but economic as well. Chapter 1 mentioned the incident of Judeo-Greek residents of Jerusalem being sent to Tyre with a large amount of money to assist with the celebration of the quinquennial games at Tyre in honor of Herakles (2 Macc 4:18-20). We may well ask where this money came from or how it had accumulated. How much of it was the fruit of Judean peasant labor? Indeed Antiochus Epiphanes' first sally on Jerusalem was to rob the treasury of the temple to finance his ill-fated campaign in Egypt and to pay a war indemnity to the Romans that his father had incurred. The prosperity of the temple state was in no small part due to other concessions made by Antiochus III that must have stimulated the economy further. Freedom from taxes was granted for three years to all returnees in order to encourage them to return, and thereafter their share of the tribute to be paid to the Seleucid rulers was reduced by one third.

It is difficult to measure the amount of commercial exchange that was likely to have taken place between the surrounding Greek cities and the Judeans. The Zenon papyri make it clear that commercial activities were carried out with Ptolemais, which is mentioned in the correspondence eleven times in all. Ancient Acco had been upgraded to the status of a Greek city and renamed Ptolemais by one of the early Ptolemaic kings, Ptolemy II Philadelphus, in 261 B.C.E. As we saw in Chapter 1, the Hellenization process at Tyre and Sidon had not interfered with their long-standing independence as free cities with strong mercantile connections throughout the Mediterranean.

There were also well-established commercial contacts between Tyre in particular and the Israelite kingdom dating back to Solomon's exchanges with Hiram, king of Tyre, when building the first temple (1 Kings 5-8; 2 Chronicles 2-5). The prophet Ezekiel, writing in the sixth century B.C.E., fills out the picture of the relationship further. The Tyrians are described as "merchants of the peoples on many coastlands," and Judah's role in its commercial activities is that of supplier of wheat, olives, early figs, honey, oil, and balm, most of these items being the produce of Galilee (Ezekiel 27). As late as the first century C.E., Luke signposts Tyre's continued dependence on the Judean countryside for essential foodstuff (Acts 12:20). The city's geographical position on an island at a point where the coastal plain narrows considerably meant that, unlike both Ptolemais and Sidon, the city's own territory could not supply its needs.

The discovery of Tyrian coinage at many Judean sites as well as in hidden hordes in Galilee has been interpreted by some as indicative of the strong commercial links between Galilee, especially Upper Galilee, and the city.[9] However, several factors need to be kept in mind when deciding on the relevance of this evidence. For one thing, there were far more Tyrian coins in circulation than those of any other mint. It has also been pointed out that many of the coins found at Galilean sites were bronze rather than silver and therefore do not indicate major trading relations.[10] For almost two hundred years, from 126 B.C.E. to 56 C.E., the Tyrian shekel (= Greek *tetradrachma*) and half shekel (= Greek *didrachma*) retained international confidence as a means of exchange due to the consistency of their weight and silver content. This may well explain why the Tyrian half-shekel became known in Jewish sources as "the coin of the sanctuary" despite the fact that it bore the image of Herakles as well as the symbol of an eagle with a Greek legend. Such a conclusion would indicate just how accepting of Hellenistic standards, especially in the matter of trade and commerce, the Hasmoneans had become, even when their own coins continued to display caution with regard to symbols and legends that might be deemed offensive by more observant groups such as the Pharisees and the Essenes.[11]

While Tyre, Sidon, and Ptolemais are listed repeatedly as opposing Hasmonean expansion, it is Ptolemais that seems to have had the most fractious relationship with the Judeans of Galilee, and was therefore least likely to have developed trading and commercial relationships with its Judean hinterland. As was discussed in Chapter 1, various armies, Seleucid and later Roman, embarked on campaigns against the interior from this city. In

---

9. R. Hanson, *Tyrian Influence in the Upper Galilee* (Cambridge: ASOR Publications, 1980). Cf. however, the critique of R. Horsley, *Archaeology, History and Society in Galilee: The Social Context of Jesus and the Rabbis* (Valley Forge: Trinity, 1996), especially 66-106.

10. D. Barag, "Tyrian Currency in Galilee," *INJ* 6/7 (1982/3), 7-13; U. Rappaport, "Phoenicia and Galilee: Economy, Territory and Political Relations," *Studia Phoenicia* 9 (1992), 262-68.

11. On the Hasmonean coinage, see E. Schürer, *The History of the Jewish People in the Age of Jesus Christ*, rev. and ed. G. Vermes, F. Millar, and M. Black (Edinburgh: Clark, 1973-84), vol. 1, Appendix iv: "Hebrew Coins," 602-6; M. Chancey, *Greco-Roman Culture and the Galilee of Jesus* (SNTSMS 134; Cambridge: Cambridge University Press, 2005), 166-92.

all probability it was this fact that led to continuing animosity between Ptolemais and the Maccabees. Jonathan, the second of the Maccabean brothers, was lured to his death there (1 Macc 12:46-48). Later Alexander Jannaeus was minded to lay the city waste, as he had done with Samaria and Scythopolis, but in the end he had to abandon the project because of the support the citizens of Ptolemais received from the Ptolemaic ruler of Cyprus, Ptolemy Lathyrus (*Ant* 13.324-34).

It would appear then that with the possible exception of Tyre, interregional and interethnic commercial activity that had flourished under the Ptolemies and Seleucids in the best spirit of Hellenism had to give way to cultural and religious differences once the independent Jewish state had emerged. However, the expansion of the borders of Judea meant the development of an internal economy, and the importance of Jerusalem was also greatly enhanced, not just as the religious center, but also as the hub of the Hasmonean administration and government.

Economic Realities and Society in the Hasmonean State

As discussed in a previous chapter, the successors of the Maccabees, the Hasmoneans, were able to win further concessions of land and taxes from successive contenders for the Seleucid throne as that empire began to fall apart (1 Macc 10:21-45; 11:30-37). Eventually, an independent Jewish state emerged, one that set about destroying the Greek cities such as Samaria, Scythopolis, and Marissa and taking control of their territories.[12] The Itureans who had settled in Upper Galilee and the Idumeans in the south were either forcibly converted to Judaism or compelled to leave, and Judean settlers were introduced into what were deemed to be ancestral lands (1 Macc 15:33). These operations undoubtedly brought about rapid economic as well as demographic changes within an enlarged Judean kingdom. The territory of the temple state was now greatly increased and offered new possibilities for the inhabitants.

Alexander Jannaeus, the longest serving of the Hasmonean rulers (103-76 B.C.E.), engaged in several campaigns against the coastal cities, so

---

12. For the details of this expansion under John Hyrcanus (134-104 B.C.E.), Aristobulos I (104-103 B.C.E.), and Alexander Jannaeus (103-76 B.C.E.), see M. Avi-Yonah, *The Holy Land from the Persian to the Arab Conquests (536 B.C. to A.D. 640): A Historical Geography* (Grand Rapids: Baker, 1966), 52-76.

important for external trade, as Josephus was keenly aware (*Ag. Ap.* 1.60). At the end of his life, Alexander is said to have controlled a number of such places, but at the cost of continual warfare with the rulers of Egypt and several of the larger cities, such as Gaza and Ptolemais (*Ant* 13.396). When, after the death of his wife Alexandra, the Roman general Pompey intervened in the civil war that had broken out between their two sons, part of the Roman settlement was to restore freedom to those cities that had been either destroyed or annexed (*Ant* 14.87-88).

Access to the sea meant that the Judeans could engage in international trade, opening up, however briefly, the possibility of contact with the wider Mediterranean region. This included the large Jewish Diaspora, not just in Egypt, but in Asia Minor and even Rome itself. One indication of the increased trade is the number of stamped Rhodian jar handles that have been found in Jerusalem from this period. Indeed Josephus is happy to cite the Greek historian Strabo about the size and expansion of the Jewish Diaspora and the amount of public money that the Jews had amassed. Writing for a Roman readership, he adds that there "is no public money among us except that which is God's," referring to the contribution of the Diaspora to the Jerusalem temple (*Ant* 14.110-18). A little after Pompey (53 B.C.E.), the Roman general Crassus, preparing for an unsuccessful campaign against the Parthians to the east, was able to plunder the Jerusalem temple and remove the gold ornaments, which amounted to 8000 silver talents (*Ant* 14.105-9).

However, the use and distribution of that wealth was the issue, as far as Judean society as a whole was concerned. Once the Judeans had effectively gained their independence, they did not have to pay the annual tribute to the Seleucids. Yet the development of a state structure, including a permanent army, would eventually put serious financial demands on all Judeans, including those settled in the conquered territories. Perhaps the presence of foreign mercenaries in an army that was originally assembled with the aim of defending the Judean religious heritage comes as the greatest surprise (*Ant* 13.374, 378, 427). It demonstrates how, within a period of a few generations, the Judean rulers had come to accept Hellenistic practices, including the waging of professional warfare, as quite normal.

The new rulers combined charge of the temple and priesthood with control of the affairs of the state. Crown lands that previous regimes had owned for their personal use now fell into the hands of the native elite. These were situated in the neighborhood of Jericho, the plain of Esdraelon, the district of Lydda (Lod), and in the region aptly named "The King's Mountain Country," a district that covered the western foothills of Judea and Samaria (Mishnah *Shebi'it* 9.3).[13] Thus, access to the two sources of revenue, temple and land, enabled the Hasmonean rulers to develop an affluent lifestyle, but also to ensure sufficient revenue to maintain the permanent army.[14] Inevitably there were other taxes, the extent of which is uncertain. Later rabbinic sources speak of three different taxes, or rather the division of the annual tithe of all agricultural produce into three parts, one for the priests and Levites, one for the treasury, and one for the poor and the widows in Jerusalem.

However, this information in all probability reflects later idealizations long after the temple was destroyed. The reality in the newly emerging Judean state was that the ruling elite was in a position to combine religious and state taxes for their own interests. That is why John Hyrcanus, and after him Alexander Jannaeus, refused to agree with the plea of the Pharisees that they should relinquish the High Priesthood and concentrate only on the affairs of state (*Ant* 13.291-92; 13.372-73). In the ancient world, temples were both sources of revenue and repositories of wealth, and to be in charge of the temple was to take control of its finances, which could be appropriated for whatever purposes the ruler thought fit. In a series of official documents from a little later renewing the treaty of friendship between Rome and the Jews, Julius Caesar decrees, among other things, that the people will "pay tithes to Hyrcanus and his sons, *just as they paid to their forefathers*" (*Ant* 14.203). The Hyrcanus in question here is the son of Alexander Jannaeus, but the reference to what was paid to the forefathers strongly suggests that religious and state taxes were firmly in the hands of the Hasmonean rulers from the outset, and this would explain why the literary sources present us with a rather confused picture of how the tax situation had evolved over time.

A spike in the Judean population, probably due, in part at least, to the fact that many had returned from the Diaspora, occurred during the first century B.C.E. These were the circumstances in which the conquered territories, north and south, were colonized by Judeans, as we have seen already in the case of Galilee. Even though the Hasmoneans maintained some large estates for their own and their friends' private use, the evidence of settlement patterns in other areas suggests smaller allotments, with the

13. S. Applebaum, "Economic Life in Palestine," in S. Safrai and M. Stern, eds., *The Jewish People in the First Century: Historical Geography, Political History, Social, Cultural and Religious Life and Institutions* (CRINT 1; Philadelphia: Fortress, 1976), 2:631-700, at 634-36.

14. I. Shatzman, *The Armies of the Hasmoneans and Herod* (TSAJ 25; Tübingen: Mohr Siebeck, 1991).

owners living in villages that could be easily fortified against hostile attack or banditry.[15] This pattern of land sharing was, of course, in line with the pentateuchal ideal of all Israelites owning a plot within the Promised Land. It thus suited Hasmonean propaganda quite well. At the same time it also took the pressure off the center in terms of overcrowding and ensured a strong peasantry, loyal to Judean customs and laws, scattered throughout the conquered territories, north and south.

It is safe to assume that the same style of agricultural production established under the Ptolemies and Seleucids continued under the Hasmoneans. Insofar as the Judean small landowners were free, unlike those we met under Seleucid rule, they could therefore transport their goods. Local marketing and trade would have increased. While tolls did still operate, it would seem, they were not between villages but rather between different territories, as in the case of the toll collector Levi (Matthew), whom Jesus called while he was sitting on his toll seat not far from Capernaum (Matt 9:9). The number of large estates would, in all probability, have decreased somewhat from that which obtained when the whole country was treated as royal land. While some of the produce of these estates might have been available for export, small landowners would be operating more at subsistence level.

Those who were fortunate enough to be settled in the more fertile regions of Galilee and Judea where the *terra rossa* soil (which covers almost 50% of the arable land in the country) was to be found, would have fared better, even though the deposits of this soil are shallow and the ground must be terraced to prevent erosion. Water supply was also a factor, less so in Galilee than in Judea, but there are plenty of examples of deep storage cisterns and collection pools in both regions. Josephus describes the fertility of the valley region of eastern Galilee in idyllic terms, not surprisingly, since there is a combination of mineral-rich basaltic soil and a plentiful supply of springs there (*War* 3.516-21). These differences in climatic and soil conditions no doubt explain the fact that the rabbinic sources speak of different produce for the temple coming from different sub-regions (Tosefta *Menahot* 8.3).

It was certainly a major bonus, especially for the small landowners, that they did not have to pay tribute from their produce to a foreign over-

---

15. U. Leibner, *Settlement and History in Hellenistic, Roman, and Byzantine Galilee* (TSAJ 127; Tübingen: Mohr Siebeck, 2009), 315-28 for the number and character of the settlements and their distribution.

lord. According to the decrees of Caesar mentioned earlier, this amounted to as much as a quarter of "the produce sown" every second year. However, the religious taxes for Jerusalem probably included additional elements to that of the tithe of produce "of what was sown as well as the firstlings of the flock," which ideally should be consumed in the temple, as stipulated in the Torah (Deut 14:22-23). However, this proved unworkable for people living at any distance from the temple, and so the Torah also permitted the sale of the produce, provided the money was spent in Jerusalem in purchasing the necessities for a sacred meal "before the Lord" with one's household and the Levites from one's town, who did not own any land because they served the temple (Deut 14:25-27). While this provision was a boost for Jerusalem and its traders, it was a serious burden for people living at a distance, who had the additional cost of traveling annually for at least one of the festivals, Passover, Pentecost, or Tabernacles (Deut 16:16). Ideally, of course, all the male members of the family who had made their bar mitzvah were expected to make the journey three times a year, but, in view of the fact that the festivals were held at the busiest times in the agricultural cycle, that would have been impracticable for many.[16]

An indication that the burden of taxes was found to be highly objectionable, at least in some circles, comes from two documents, one Essene and the other Pharisaic. The famous Temple Scroll found in Qumran (11QTemple) is dated to the beginning of the reign of Alexander Jannaeus, who in all probability was the first in the line to adopt the title "king." In commenting on a passage from Deuteronomy known as "the law of the king" (Deut 17:14-20), the Qumran text adds to the Deuteronomic injunction "He must not return the people to Egypt in order to acquire more horses" (v. 16) by rendering it as follows: "He must not multiply horses for himself, or cause the people to return to Egypt *for war* in order to increase

---

16. The tithing obligation arose from the recognition that the land was Yahweh's gift to Israel and this had to be recognized at his sanctuary. Over time the number of tithes increased to three, a second for the Levite in the town and a third for the poor (Tob 1:7-8). Josephus mentions that the Galileans were prepared to pay him and his companions the tithes that "were their due because they were priests," but he himself declined to accept the tithes (*Life* 63, 80). However, he also states that before the revolt the high priests sent their servants to the countryside to forcibly collect the tithes, suggesting that by the first century the system had become a means of maintaining the priestly elite in their luxurious lifestyle and was resented by the country people (*Ant* 20.181, 206-7). See S. Freyne, *Galilee, Jesus and the Gospels: Literary Approaches and Historical Investigations* (Dublin: Gill and Macmillan/Philadelphia: Fortress, 1988), 191-93 on later rabbinic concerns with the issue of agricultural gifts.

the gold or the silver" (11QTemple 56.16). The same theme is struck in a collection known as the *Psalms of Solomon,* attributed to Pharisaic circles and dated to c. 40 B.C.E., at the very end of the Hasmonean rule. Among the attributes of the ideal future king that was hoped for is that he "would not multiply gold and silver *for war*" (*Pss. Sol.* 17:33).

Both texts link the waging of war with gold and silver, implying that acquisition of wealth was an unworthy motive for a Judean king to embark on such an enterprise. They may also be intimating that the prolonged campaigns of Alexander Jannaeus had impoverished the people. As mentioned above, we do not have any detailed information as to what other taxes Jannaeus may have imposed in addition to those associated with the temple, but the probability is that the cost of maintaining a standing army and paying mercenaries over the twenty-seven years of his reign put a serious drain on the country's resources. As part of his military strategy he built several fortresses on the borders of the conquered territories, which subsequently were taken over by the Herodians and developed further. Among the most important of these was Machaerus on the border with Arabia, Masada overlooking the Dead Sea, and lesser ones in Samaria and Transjordan. He also built a palace in Jerusalem, overlooking the city and the temple.

In addition to these defensive building projects, various members of the dynasty developed three palaces in the Jericho region. This was a strategic location on the north-south axis of the Jordan valley, but it also had a benign winter climate. The remains of a royal estate have also been uncovered in this region that was renowned for its date palms and balsam trees. These were highly regarded commodities and commercially very profitable in the ancient world.[17] In this respect, the Hasmoneans were following best Hellenistic practice, as established by the Ptolemies in particular, of more specialized farming in order to maximize the natural resources of the micro-climate in the Jericho region. A four-hundred-meter-long buried channel of clay pipes brought water from the nearby Wadi Qelt, supplying both the farm and the first palace. At a later phase in the development a second aqueduct was installed to meet agricultural and recreational needs, an indicator of the increase in the number of the inhabitants of the area.

The question was posed in the earlier discussion of the Hasmoneans'

---

17. Strabo, *Geography* 16.2.41; Pliny, *Natural History* 12.113-23; Josephus, *War* 2.459-75. Dates were deemed a luxury, and the balsam tree produced a highly prized perfume. Mark Antony bequeathed the district of Jericho to Cleopatra later, according to Josephus (*War* 4.362).

cultural commitments as to whether they had "become Greek" or merely "acted Greek." The manner in which they engaged in wars of conquest with the aid of foreign mercenaries, especially during the long reign of Alexander Jannaeus, would seem to suggest that they had indeed thoroughly absorbed the Hellenistic ethos. The very names Alexander, Aristobulos, and Antigonos are further indications of their allegiances. However, a recent study of their three palaces in the region of Jericho raises some very interesting issues. Applying a method based on social archaeology, Eyal Regev seeks to uncover the ideological concerns of the dynasty through an examination of the way in which internal space was structured and the purposes that different spatial arrangements were intended to serve.[18]

By employing what is described as "access analysis," that is, the degree of ease of accessibility to the monarch that the layout of the palaces presupposes, Regev discovers that, when compared with Herod the Great and other Hellenistic monarchs, the Hasmoneans were unostentatious and somewhat removed from their clientele. The palaces were not designed to impress and were only modest in size, the largest being that of John Hyrcanus, which was subsequently covered in to allow the so-called "fortress" palace of Alexander Jannaeus to be built. There was only limited use of typical Hellenistic features such as colonnades, mosaics, and reliefs. Neither was there any display of wealth in the tableware or much evidence of imported fine ware or wine from Rhodes, which was considered a luxury. Likewise, the dining areas *(triclinia)* where entertainment of guests would have been conducted were modest in both size and ornamentation.

Using the same type of analysis, a real contrast seems to occur when the gardens and outdoor pools are examined. In total there are eleven pools of varying sizes in the complex, and eight were in use simultaneously. The pools in particular were not connected directly to the palaces, suggesting to Regev that they were not reserved for private use only. By contrast the indoor bathhouses with terra cotta bathtubs and heating furnaces, four in all, were situated in inaccessible places. They are the one clear example of Hellenistic luxury in the palaces and were meant to be available only for the immediate royal family. One highly significant aspect of the water installations in the palaces is the number of stepped pools, which served as ritual baths. They are quite separate from the bathrooms and on occasion in close proximity to the kitchens, thus ensuring that food was prepared in

18. E. Regev, "Royal Ideology in the Hasmonean Palaces of Jericho," *BASOR* 363 (2011), 45-72.

ritual purity. Twelve of these installations have been discovered, four with storage pools attached. These served the purpose of collecting water for ritual washing by natural means, in accordance with the halakhic regulations of the Pharisees.[19]

This early evidence for observance of ritual purity among the Hasmonean elite is somewhat surprising. It is true that after Jannaeus's death his wife, Salome Alexandra, acting as regent, was very influenced by the Pharisees, who had opposed her husband and had suffered under him. But this would not explain the presence of ritual baths in the earliest stages of the palace complex already under the father of the dynasty, John Hyrcanus. It should be remembered that the Hasmoneans insisted on retaining the high priesthood, and the purity laws were originally intended to ensure that the sanctity of the temple was preserved, especially by the priests. One of the aims of the Pharisaic movement was to extend the notion of purity to the everyday situation of people living in the land, something that brought them into conflict with Jesus and his movement also.

Jerusalem Rediscovers Its Former Glory

The architectural achievements of Herod the Great, to be discussed shortly, overshadow somewhat the Hasmoneans' efforts to extend and embellish the religious and political capital of the newly established independent state. Several of their buildings were sacrificed in the Herodian redevelopment of the city, especially in the area of Herod's palace on the western hill. Herod had a large podium constructed so that his palace overlooked the whole

---

19. *Miqva'oth* or stepped pools are not mentioned in the Torah's instructions regarding purity regulations (Lev 15:13), though they became an important feature for purity maintenance in both private and public places during the Second Temple period. They seem to have virtually disappeared after the temple's destruction. While they vary somewhat in size and the configuration of the steps, they can be distinguished clearly from bathing pools and storage tanks, as can be seen in both Herodian palaces, at Qumran, and also in Sepphoris where they are found in proximity to such other water installations. A tractate of the Mishnah in the division on Purities is principally concerned with how water for a *miqveh* is to be collected without human intervention. In some instances storage pools with a connecting pipe *(otzar)* have been identified in archaeological remains; it served to maintain the principle of "living water," that is, water that had not been collected by humans. Cf. S. Freyne, "Jewish Immersion and Christian Baptism: Continuity on the Margins?" in D. Helholm, et al., eds., *Ablution, Initiation and Baptism: Late Antiquity, Early Judaism and Early Christianity* (Berlin/Boston: de Gruyter, 2011), 1:221-54, especially 225-36.

city, and underneath the remains of that some ritual baths and cisterns from the Hasmonean times have been uncovered. Apparently many parts of the city from the first temple period were still not rebuilt until the Hasmoneans arrived. The population increased considerably, so that a new residential quarter was established on the western hill (the upper city) where the palace was situated, and what is known as the "first wall" was rebuilt around the southwestern hill, where it had fallen into disrepair. Further residential quarters were built to the north and were surrounded by what has come to be called "the second wall." Furthermore, in order to meet the needs of the growing population, an aqueduct was built to bring water to the city from springs in the southern hills.[20]

The physical expansion of Jerusalem was symptomatic of its growing importance as both a temple city and a state capital under the Hasmonean regime. The ever-increasing number of pilgrims that visited the city for the great festivals brought new wealth to Jerusalem, thereby boosting its revenues. More and more of the country priests came to live in the city to perform their sacred duties more easily. Other temple officials also crowded the busy streets, adding to its ever-burgeoning population. Zealous young scholars such as Paul of Tarsus moved permanently to Jerusalem to study at the feet of the great teachers. The first-century C.E. Greek inscription from a building in Jerusalem, the *Theodotus Inscription,* mentions Torah study as an activity carried on there and in attached lodgings, presumably to accommodate Diaspora Jews coming to study Torah in the holy city.

These were the circumstances in which a settlement, whose physical location was highly unfavorable, came to achieve a status that was almost equal to that of Athens or Rome. The attraction it continued to hold for the far-flung Judean Diaspora, east and west, was certainly a factor in its reputation, despite the fact that it was not on any of the major highways of the ancient world. Even the Roman historian Tacitus begins his quite unfavorable account of the Jews by alluding to the fact that their city is "famous" (*Histories* 5.2). His contemporary Pliny is more fulsome, describing Jerusalem as "by far the most outstanding of the cities of the East" (*Natural History* 5.90). At the same time, Jewish literature of the late Hellenistic and early Roman periods reflects differing opinions as to how the city should fulfill its symbolic role and who should be in charge of its ceremonial activities. This corresponds to the idealization of the holy city from an earlier

20. N. Avigad and H. Geva, "Jerusalem: The Second Temple Period," in *NAEHL* 2:717-29.

period, as can be seen in the Zion tradition, especially in Isaiah and in several psalms.

One early work, the Wisdom of Jesus ben Sira, comes from a Jerusalem scribe and is dated to c. 180 B.C.E. It was translated into Greek by his grandson for the benefit of Jews of the Egyptian Diaspora in c. 130 B.C.E. Several aspects of the work shed light on the world of a pious but affluent Jerusalemite of the period. He seems to be familiar with early Stoic philosophical ideas about the unity of the cosmos when he describes God as "the All" (Sir 43:27). He can also give practical advice as to how to behave at a banquet and manage one's money. In what is undoubtedly a self-portrait (38:24–39:11), he contrasts his own privileged position with that of other residents whose business it is to maintain the fabric of the world (38:34). Deeply rooted in his own tradition, he can draw on older notions about Mount Zion to highlight his attachment to and delight in the Temple city. According to ch. 24, Wisdom has made its home in Jerusalem, having sought a suitable resting place among every people, and is to be identified with the Book of the Covenant of the Most High God.

As an educated cosmopolitan, not only has Ben Sira the leisure to study his own tradition, he is also familiar with contemporary political and philosophical trends. Thus the role of the scribe is outlined in terms of his importance as a counselor in international affairs in contrast to that of various craftsmen, whose labors "maintain the fabric of the world" (38:34). These others do not have "the opportunity of leisure," whereas the scribe/wise man does not have to engage in such mundane affairs. As a result, he can seek out the wisdom of the ancients, penetrate the subtleties of parables and the hidden meanings of proverbs, appear before rulers, traverse foreign lands, and learn what is good and evil in the human lot. Yet this cosmopolitan figure is also deeply spiritual, rising before dawn and petitioning the Most High and asking pardon for his sins (39:1-5).

Later in the book his description of the High Priest Simon, the son of Onias, appearing in the temple, surrounded by "the sons of Aaron in their splendor," paints a glowing if nostalgic picture of the ceremonial action in the Jerusalem temple (50:1-21). Clearly, the High Priesthood and temple rather than the king and the royal palace are at the center of Ben Sira's world. The book closes with an invitation to his readers, to come and "lodge in the house of instruction" and acquire "wisdom without money" (51:23-26). In this conclusion we can catch a critique of the new affluence that Jerusalem was experiencing along with acknowledgment of its importance as the context in which the scribe can flourish. In the next chapter, when discussing the wisdom of the teacher from Nazareth in Galilee, Yeshua the craftsman (cf. Mark 6:3), we shall return to the figure of Ben Sira as a representative of a class of professional scribes in Jerusalem who obviously felt that their reputation and authority had been challenged by the country healer/teacher.

Ben Sira's grandson translated his book for the Egyptian Diaspora, suggesting that conditions had not changed dramatically in the interim. The *Letter of Aristeas* was actually written in Egypt and gives us an insight into the way in which Jerusalem and the homeland were viewed from the perspective of the Diaspora there.[21] While there are several different theories as to the real purpose of this work relating to Jewish propaganda in Egypt, there can be no denying the idyllic view of the priesthood, the temple, and the land that the work envisages. The High Priest's vestments are described in great detail: a garment decorated with precious stones, a girdle woven of the most beautiful colors, and a hallowed diadem with the name of God the ineffable inscribed in golden letters (*Letter of Aristeas* 96-98). The land is abundantly stocked with every kind of tree; the local farmers are full of zeal; they have many flocks and herds of various kinds. In addition the land is well suited for commerce; Jerusalem has many crafts and there are a number of convenient harbors through which to import goods. The district is well watered and there is an abundant water supply for the temple (112-16).

Several other Jewish writers from the same period also deal with the centrality of Jerusalem and its temple, but with somewhat different perspectives on how its role is to be understood and who should be in charge. In five fragments of the Greco-Jewish writer Eupolemus dated to the middle of the second century B.C.E., the story of Solomon's building of the first temple in 1 Kings 5–8 is retold in such a way that the author envisages Solomon demanding assistance from the kings of Tyre and Egypt in honoring "the Great God who made heaven and earth." Other neighboring regions are expected to help with provisions for the workmen, but later the same chore is imposed on the "twelve tribes of the *Judeans*" (not of "the Israelites" as we might have expected), one tribe for each month. In all probability this account reflects some of the hopes of the early Maccabeans, envisaging, as it does, a restoration of temple and land within the new Judean state, which will be in a position of supremacy over Israel's traditional enemies.

21. Although the book is set in the reign of Ptolemy Philadelphus (285-247 B.C.E.), most scholars date it to the second half of the second century B.C.E., approximately 100 years later.

The Book of the Watchers, an apocalyptic work of uncertain date that now forms part of the composite work *1 Enoch* (chs. 1–36), provides a very different view of the temple personnel. We saw in Chapter 1 (pp. 25-26) that this work deals with a group whose wicked deeds mean that the Most High has passed a sentence of condemnation against them which even the intercession of Enoch, "a scribe of righteousness," before the throne of God cannot reverse. (Having prepared himself at "the waters of Dan southwest of Hermon" [*1 Enoch* 13.7], Enoch receives his "throne vision" at that holy mountain, the account of which is echoed in the story of Jesus' transfiguration experience in the same region of Upper Galilee, as recorded in Mark 9:2-8 and the other Synoptics.) In all likelihood, those who are condemned and for whom Enoch intercedes are the temple personnel, who are deemed to be no longer worthy to act on behalf of the people before the Most High God. This stinging criticism of the priests as polluters of the temple is very similar to that found in other writings, such as the *Damascus Document:*

> . . . they also defiled the temple, for they did not keep apart in accordance with the law, but instead lay with her who sees the blood of her menstrual flow. And each man takes as a wife the daughter of his brother and the daughter of his sister. (CD 5.6-8)

and the *Psalms of Solomon:*

> They stole from the sanctuary of God as if there were no redeeming heir. They walked on the place of sacrifice of the Lord, (coming) from all kinds of uncleanness; and (coming) with menstrual blood (on them), they defiled the sacrifices as if they were common meat. There was no sin they left undone in which they did not surpass the gentiles. (8:11-13)[22]

The former text is from the Qumran Essenes, who had separated themselves from the Jerusalem temple by returning to the desert and claiming that their community constituted the true temple.[23] The latter critiques the

---

22. Florentino García Martínez and Eibert J. C. Tigchelaar, eds., *The Dead Sea Scrolls Study Edition,* vol. 1 (Leiden: Brill and Grand Rapids: Eerdmans, 1997), 557. Robert B. Wright, "Psalms of Solomon," in *The Old Testament Pseudepigrapha,* vol. 2 (Garden City: Doubleday, 1985), 659.

23. B. Gärtner, *The Temple and the Community in Qumran and the New Testament* (SNTSMS 1; Cambridge: Cambridge University Press, 1965).

Hasmonean priests for having "defiled the sacrifices," thereby provoking God's anger, which allowed Pompey to enter the temple's sacred precincts.

This account of the way in which the Judean state developed and the internal tensions that emerged is essential for our understanding of the social as well as the religious matrix of the Jesus movement in the early first century C.E. While the advent of Rome adds a further element to the economic and social mix, as we shall presently discuss, the internal fissures that occurred under the Hasmoneans continued to grow once statehood was lost and relations with new overlords had to be negotiated. The Galileans that we meet in the Gospels were for the most part descendants of those Judeans who had been planted in Galilee as elsewhere during the expansion. Indeed, the tradition that Jesus' family was from Bethlehem in Judah and had migrated to Galilee has more than an element of probability when it is situated within this larger setting of movements between the different regions in this period. The journeys of Jesus to the surrounding regions of Galilee that Mark refers to without much comment also take on a special significance against the backdrop of the Hasmonean expansion and the belief that the Judeans were merely reclaiming ancestral lands. Jesus, too, was aware of the notion of a "greater Israel" whose outer limits were described by various writers of the Second Temple period looking for the restoration of Israel. Unlike the Hasmoneans, however, Jesus taught that these lands were to be recovered not by the sword but by the power of the word that proclaimed the God of Israel as the God who welcomed all to his banquet.

Economy and Society in Herod's Judea

In the previous chapter, the importance of the reign of Herod the Great was discussed from the perspective of his espousal of the Augustan propaganda regarding the new age that was dawning for humanity. Here the focus will be on how his and his successors' rule impacted on the internal dynamics of the Judean territory, both socially and economically.

The transition from the Hasmonean to the Herodian period was not an easy one, given the fact that it coincided with a turbulent period in Roman history also, namely, the transition from republic to empire. This took place through the agency of various alliances of triumvirs, consisting of strong military men, whose influence and power virtually sidelined the senate as the sole instrument of governance in the Roman world.

The break-up of the Hasmonean state was quick and decisive. Pompey, a member of the first triumvirate, was operating in the eastern Mediterranean at the time, and as "friend and ally" intervened in order to resolve the civil war between Jannaeus's two sons. The outcome was to be typically Roman, namely "divide and rule." Judea was reduced to the status of an ethnarchy, and its territory was greatly reduced. The Greek cities of the interior and on the coastal plain were restored, and various local councils were established in the different Jewish regions as was deemed appropriate. In Galilee, Sepphoris was the chosen center, confirming the fact that the region was now seen as a Judean territory in Roman eyes.[24]

At an early stage, Herod won his spurs in the north, successfully pursuing a brigand chief along the Syrian border in Upper Galilee and being suitably rewarded by the Romans. His father, Antipater, an Idumean by birth but with a Judean wife, had been acting as viceroy to a weak and ineffectual Hasmonean, Hyrcanus II, one of the two warring brothers, whom Rome had appointed as the Judean ethnarch and High Priest. Herod continued to impress various Roman power brokers, including Mark Antony, who together with Caesar's son Octavian (the future Augustus) had formed the second triumvirate. Eventually, in the year 40 B.C.E., Herod was declared "king of the Jews" by the Roman senate. It took him three years, however, before he was able to take control of his kingdom since Antigonus, the son of the ousted Hasmonean brother Aristobulus II, having summoned help from the Parthians across the Euphrates, sought to restore the kingdom of his grandfather Alexander Jannaeus. Herod's troubles did not end with his victory over Antigonus, since now a final struggle for control of the Roman world was brewing between Antony and Octavian, with Herod constrained to support Antony, who with his paramour Cleopatra, the queen of Egypt, was operating in the eastern Mediterranean. However, Octavian was finally victorious at the battle of Actium, off Greece, in 31 B.C.E., and so ended a turbulent period in Roman history.

Herod was quick to curry favor with the victor of Actium, hurrying to pay his homage at Rhodes and explaining that it was out of a sense of duty to Rome that he had fought on the side of Antony but that he was now ready to offer his services to Octavian. Thereafter, he continued to have a close relationship with the man who was now the sole ruler *(imperator)* of

---

24. S. Freyne, *Galilee from Alexander the Great to Hadrian: A Study of Second Temple Judaism* (Wilmington: Glazier / Notre Dame: Notre Dame University Press, 1980; reprint Edinburgh: Clark, 1998), 57-63.

the Roman world and was richly rewarded for his loyalty. As discussed previously, he was one of the earliest rulers in the East to honor Octavian with imperial games in Jerusalem, and he later built three temples to Roma and Augustus in different parts of his enlarged kingdom.

This very brief summary of Herod's coming to power must suffice. However, his achievements, especially his building program, made a lasting impression on the landscape of Jerusalem and Judea in particular. We may well ask how Herod funded his buildings at home and his philanthropic work abroad and what impact his reign made on economic and social conditions within his kingdom. In seeking to answer those questions it must be recalled that though his title was "king of the Jews," he was in fact a client king *(rex socius),* which means that his primary role was to promote Roman rule within his territories, to aid in maintaining the Roman peace when it was threatened, and, in particular, to ensure that Rome's rival in the East, the Parthians, were kept in check. As an Idumean, appointment as "king of the Jews" was also highly problematic, especially for the supporters of the Hasmoneans, to whom Herod was never acceptable. This double bind helps to explain those ambiguous and seemingly contradictory aspects of Herod's personality that have often been explained in psychological rather than sociopolitical terms.[25]

Herod's annual income from his kingdom has been calculated as roughly 1000 talents.[26] This is calculated on the basis of the arrangements Augustus made for his three sons at his death (*Ant* 17.318-20). While this amount was more or less the equivalent of that which Caesar had allowed to the last of the Hasmoneans, Herod was more efficient, indeed ruthless, in ensuring its collection and overseeing its distribution. As a half-Jew he could not aspire to the priesthood, but he quickly took control of the temple by removing the Hasmonean claimants to the High Priestly office and appointing his own candidates from the Diaspora. This meant that he was able

25. In addition to the studies by Richardson and Rocca already cited (Chapter 2, n. 4), I have found the following older accounts both accessible and helpful in understanding Herod's multifaceted character and achievements: A. M. H. Jones, *The Herods of Judaea* (Oxford: Clarendon, 1938; reprint 1967); M. Stern, "The Reign of Herod and the Herodian Dynasty," in Safrai and Stern, eds., *The Jewish People in the First Century,* 1:216-304; A. Schalit, *König Herodes* (Berlin: de Gruyter, 1969).

26. S. Rocca, *Herod's Judaea* (TSAJ; Tübingen: Mohr Siebeck, 2008), 227-39 is an excellent discussion of Herod's economic resources. Cf. also E. Gabba, "The Finances of King Herod," in A. Kasher, U. Rappaport, and G. Fuks, *Greece and Rome in Eretz Israel* (Jerusalem: Yad Izhak Ben Zvi, 1990), 160-68.

to decide the amount of the tithes that went to the priests and could retain the rest for his other projects. These included a lavish building program: several palace/fortresses, the magnificent harbor at Caesarea Maritima, and the three temples to Roma and Augustus, along with promotion of the imperial games. In addition there was the upkeep of a large court and philanthropic works abroad as discussed in the previous chapter.

It is generally agreed that Herod, like other client-kings, did not have to pay tribute to Rome, but he was restricted in terms of minting his own money other than copper coinage. In addition to his annual income from his subjects, he inherited the royal estates of the Hasmoneans, including the lucrative date and balsam plantations in Jericho and Ein Gedi. Other royal estates in the non-Jewish parts of his realm, such as the Plain of Esdraelon, Samaria, and Batanea in Transjordan were used for the placing of veterans, thereby ensuring a steady income. Furthermore, it seems certain that Herod had some discretion as a tax-collector on behalf of Rome in Syria and in Cilicia in Asia Minor, a role that, according to Josephus, gave him some discretion in granting favors to certain locals while also benefiting greatly himself (*War* 2.428). His entrepreneurial spirit was manifested in his leasing the copper mines in Cyprus from Augustus for a one-time payment of 300 talents, but he received half the annual income thereafter (*Ant* 16.128).

Herod's building projects throughout his kingdom impress the modern as well as the ancient observer, but they also highlight the massive expenditure that must have taken place during his reign. The ambitious plans developed for the various buildings involved the use of Roman architects, engineers, and craftsmen as several of his buildings were based on Roman originals. While the "building boom" that Herod initiated was undoubtedly a boost to native employment, it must also have been a drain elsewhere on the economy, especially in the lives of ordinary people.

The development of an artificial deep harbor at Caesarea was the most ambitious of all his projects. Since there were no natural deep-water harbors along the coast, Herod had to build his out into the open sea, the piers on the north side measuring 250 meters and on the south and west 750. The entrance was at the northwestern corner and was 30 meters wide, with two large towers on either side.[27] This entrance led into three different basins,

---

27. Josephus mentions that one of these towers was named after Drusus, the stepson of Augustus who conducted campaigns in Germany but died as a result of a fall from a horse in 9 B.C.E. Josephus does not give a name for the second tower, but Werner Eck, *Rom und Judaea. Fünf Vorträge zur römischen Herrschaft in Palaestina* (Tübingen: Mohr Siebeck, 2007), 16-17, suggests that in all probability it was named after Tiberius, the future emperor and Drusus's

presumably for use by different-sized crafts. The technical expertise needed to construct such an edifice in the seabed was considerable and involved among other things the use of a particular type of concrete that utilized volcanic ash imported from Italy. The possibilities that this project had to offer for commercial contacts with the wider Mediterranean world were immense. It is a testimony to Herod's shrewdness in this regard that he was able finally to remedy the lack of such a facility for previous Judean rulers, who were dependent on shallow harbors along the Mediterranean coastline, often controlled by Phoenicians rather than Judeans.

Herod's plans for the rebuilding of the Jerusalem temple "at his own expense" were also ambitious, but highly strategic. Clearly, he was seeking to curry favor with the populace following the riots generated by his efforts to stage imperial games in the city to honor Augustus in 28 B.C.E. In the speech that Josephus attributes to him on the occasion of the announcement of his plans, he declares that he wants to restore the temple building *(naos)* to the dimensions of its Solomonic precursor, judiciously noting that neither the returnees from Babylon nor the Hasmoneans had been able to accomplish this. The actual temple building, which housed the holy of holies, was erected to an impressive height, and a massive wall surrounded both the temple building itself and the court of the priests, where the altar of sacrifice was located. According to Josephus, Herod had a thousand priests trained as masons and carpenters, so that the work could be accomplished without any violation of Jewish purity laws.

The archaeological excavations and remains in the vicinity of the temple mount testify today to the grandeur that Herod aspired to, most clearly evident in the size and craftsmanship of the large ashlar blocks that were used in the construction. In addition to the temple itself and the court of the priests that lay behind the protecting wall of the temple, there were two other courts, an inner and outer one, the former for Israelites including women, and the latter for Gentiles. There was a low dividing wall between the two with signs in Greek indicating that any Gentile who crossed this would be liable to the death penalty.[28]

The area of the *temenos* or sacred precinct was extended to the south

---

older brother. This identification is based on an inscription from Caesarea, first published in 1961, which refers to a *Tiberium* that Pontius Pilate, prefect of Judea, "restored." This interpretation of the inscription is based on a reconstruction by G. Alföldy, "Pontius Pilatus und das Tiberium von Caesarea Maritima," *Scripta Classica Israelica* 18 (1999), 85-94.

28. E. Netzer, *The Architecture of Herod the Great Builder* (Grand Rapids: Baker, 2008), 137-78.

with considerable difficulty because of the steep incline of the Tyropoean valley. A surrounding wall with various entrances and an impressive roofed *stoa* enclosed the whole area, measuring in all approximately 450 by 315 meters. These *stoas* consisted of colonnades separated by two rows of Corinthian columns on the west, north, and east sides and one of three rows on the southern side. This was by far the most elaborate of the *stoas*, with its central colonnade raised higher than the other two and the ceilings ornamented with various wood carvings (*Ant* 15.411-16). Since Herod, unlike his Hasmonean predecessors, could not publicly enter the holy of holies, he may have used the "royal *stoa*" for private meetings and entertaining foreign visitors. In addition he was making a statement about his own royal status and allegiance to the emperor, since the building itself has been compared to the Kaisareion built in honor of Augustus in Alexandria.

A particularly interesting feature at the southwestern corner of the complex was a staircase and passageway (known today as Robinson's arch) whereby it was possible to enter the royal *stoa* from the upper city, where the royal palace was located, without mingling with the crowds in the streets below. The main access to the temple for the worshipers was through the Hulda Gate on the south side. This was divided into two entrances in order to preserve ritual purity for those entering and exiting. In addition there were many ritual baths located nearby on the outside. The pilgrims entered the temple by a tunnel under the royal *stoa*, exiting inside into the large plaza, which may have served both as a courtyard for the Gentiles and as an agora-like gathering place where commercial activity to do with the temple took place.

There are various proposals as to the exact location of the tables of the money changers that Jesus overturned (Mark 11:15-18).[29] A decision on the most likely location would assist in interpreting the symbolic significance of his action. The least likely suggestion claims that his action took place in the street underneath Robinson's arch, where trading would have taken place. Did Jesus intend to put an end to all sacrifice by banning the sale of doves? Or was he protesting against the use of a pagan coin as the coin of the sanctuary? Or could he have been making a protest against the luxurious lifestyle of the Herodian elite, of which the temple's architecture, especially that of the royal *stoa*, was symbolic, thereby linking his protest with his praise of the poor widow in this same setting? All these suggestions

29. R. Millar, "Historical Method and the Deeds of Jesus: The Test Case of the Temple Demonstration," *Forum* 8 (1992), 5-30.

have their various supporters, depending on what particular understanding of Jesus' ministry as a whole is being proposed.[30] Nor need they be mutually exclusive. We shall have to defer judgment until the next chapter, therefore, before finally coming to an understanding of Jesus' action within the larger framework of his ministry as a whole.

It should be recalled that work on the temple, which began in 20-19 B.C.E., continued up to the outbreak of the first revolt, therefore also including the time of Jesus' public ministry (cf. John 2:20). Even allowing for Josephus's well-known propensity for exaggerating numbers, the impact of the temple construction must have been considerable. He reports that when construction ceased in 62 C.E. eighteen thousand workers were out of work and that the people suggested to Agrippa II, Herod's great grandson and the curator of the temple at that time, that building should continue in the temple area, where the eastern wall of the *stoa* was in need of refurbishment, due presumably to subsidence. Agrippa's reasons for refusing the request are interesting: "The work would take time and a great deal of money." Instead he allowed for the paving of the city with white stone (*Ant* 20.219-22). Apparently, money was not as plentiful as it had been a century earlier, but in the meantime Herod's kingdom had been subdivided and Roman provincial structures, including a tax census, had been put in place.

When one takes account of Herod's other projects outside Jerusalem, especially the palaces and fortresses, as well as his benefactions abroad, it is little wonder that several commentators have seen his reign as extremely oppressive on the ordinary people of the land.[31] This opinion needs to be critically assessed, however, in the light of all the available evidence. True, Josephus does give a highly negative judgment of Herod's treatment of his subjects while bestowing lavish honors on his Roman friends such as Marcus Agrippa and Augustus (*Ant* 16.150-58; cf. 17.191-92). Moreover, on Herod's death, the Jerusalem crowd demanded, among other things, that Archelaus, the heir apparent, should reduce the yearly payments and remove the sales taxes that had been ruthlessly exacted (*Ant* 17.205). The Jewish delegation that was sent to Rome subsequently was even more scathing in its criticism of Herod's tactics in extorting taxes and bribes in addition to the annual tribute (17.308). They even went so far as to request that Augus-

---

30. A. Yarbro Collins, "Jesus' Action in Herod's Temple," in A. Yarbro Collins and M. Mitchell, eds., *Antiquity and Humanity: Essays in Ancient Religion and Philosophy Presented to Hans Dieter Betz* (Tübingen: Mohr Siebeck, 2001), 45-61.

31. For Herod's palaces, see E. Netzer, *Die Paläste der Hasmonäer und Herodes des Großen* (Mainz: von Zabern, 1999).

tus put an end to the Herodian kingship and that Judea be joined with the Roman province of Syria (17.314).

The probability is that these complaints were partly standard practice on the death of a monarch in antiquity and partly the complaints of the elites, who had suffered most under Herod since they would have been the most likely targets of the sales tax he is said to have imposed.[32] Even the revolts that took place in the various regions of the kingdom on his death, including one in Sepphoris in Galilee, in all probability originated among the remnants of the Hasmonean aristocracy that had survived Herod's attempts to wipe them out entirely and were not the protests of a totally impoverished peasantry. It should be remembered that Josephus was from that same priestly lineage, and his negative evaluation of Herodian rule in contrast to his opinion of the Hasmoneans must be judged in that light.

In actual fact, there is counterbalancing evidence that Herod did show concern for his landowning subjects at times of particular difficulty. The occasion of the two-year drought (25-24 B.C.E.) and subsequent plague due to the failure of the wheat crop is the most frequently cited example of his magnanimity (*Ant* 15.299-315). Herod arranged for wheat to be imported from Egypt, where grain-production was dependent on very different climatic factors to those of Palestine/Syria. Because of his friendship with the Roman governor of Egypt, a large shipment of approximately 30,000 tons of wheat, comprising between 180 and 220 shiploads, was made available to those in need within Herod's realm. According to Josephus, he bore the brunt of the cost of this himself, even melting down gold and silver ornaments in order to pay the price demanded, which was almost four times the normal (cf. *Ant* 3.220-21). The wheat was carefully distributed to those in need, and the aged were supplied with bread already baked. The drought meant that domestic animals had perished also, and there was, therefore, a shortage of wool and other material for winter clothing. This too was taken care of, so that Herod's popularity increased greatly and his previous brutality was forgotten, at least temporarily. On two further occasions (20 and 14 B.C.E.) we hear of reductions of the taxes due, in the first case by a third because of a poor harvest (*Ant* 15.365), and on the second occasion he reduced the taxes of the previous year by a quarter on returning from a successful tour of Ionia with Augustus's heir-apparent Marcus Agrippa (*Ant* 15.64-65).

It seems probable, therefore, that the impact of Herod's reign on the

---

32. Jones, *The Herods of Judaea*, 86-92, gives a balanced account of Herod's revenues and his shrewd development of the resources at his disposal.

economics of his kingdom was both varied and uneven. It has been suggested that his approach was harsh and cruel in the earlier years of his reign
up to his reconciliation with Octavian in 31 B.C.E. Thereafter his position
was much more secure, financially as well as politically, leading to acts of
magnanimity to the peasants and attempts to placate the opposition to him
from the townspeople who were loyal to the Pharisees. These had remained
the party of opposition, as they had been also under Hasmonean rule, refusing to take the oath of allegiance which he was seeking to impose on the
whole population (*Ant* 15.370; cf. 17.151-64).

The final years of Herod's life were blighted by court intrigues among
his varied offspring, which probably meant that venality and corruption
were on the increase. The peasantry came under increased pressure to meet
the needs of the court. The story of the slaughter of the innocents in Matt
2:16-18 captures well Herod's paranoia towards the end of his life, even if
some aspects of the story are clearly legendary. The arrangement that Augustus came to with regard to Herod's will, refusing to appoint any one of
the three pretenders to the kingship, suggests that he was aware of the need
for a more varied approach to the rule of Judea than that which Herod's
centralized and authoritarian style of government tolerated. Of the three
claimants, Antipas in Galilee was the most successful in negotiating the balance between loyal recognition of Rome and maintaining the peace among
his Judean subjects. It is to his period of rule that we now turn: an essential
if somewhat hidden component in the public career of Jesus and his first
followers.

Galilean Economy under Antipas

In the introduction to this chapter, the issue of the use of models in preference to an inductive approach that relies on actual data was raised. I suggested that both approaches are meaningful and necessary once the limitations of each are taken seriously. Precisely because Galilee has been seen as
the main theater of Jesus' ministry but also as the home of rabbinic Judaism
after the two revolts, there has been unprecedented interest in the archaeological record of the region, covering various periods from the Iron Age
(ninth century B.C.E.) to the Byzantine Period (fourth–seventh centuries
C.E.). There is, therefore, a sizable amount of data relating to the early Roman period, that is, the first century C.E., when Jesus' ministry occurred.
However, that has not precluded different scholars from opting for different

models in order to profile the Galilean economy at the time of Jesus, as we shall presently discuss.

However, there is a prior issue, previously alluded to, that can be easily overlooked but is absolutely essential for our understanding of the region's economy, namely Galilee's natural features in comparison with other regions of the country.[33] The Mishnah (*Shebi'it* 9.2) clearly defines three different regions in Galilee for purposes of harvesting: Lower Galilee, Upper Galilee, and the valley. The differences among these subregions can be described as ecological in that different crops grew more easily in one rather than the others and the time of harvesting varied accordingly. Because the soil and water quality varied, the inhabitants were engaged in different agricultural and ancillary activities over the centuries. Josephus too is aware of this traditional division of Galilee, but he concentrates his attention particularly on the valley, that is, the region bordering on the Sea of Galilee. In particular he describes the Plain of Gennossar, situated in the northwestern corner of the area, in idyllic terms. The seasons vie with each other, he writes, in bestowing their gifts on this territory, because of its plentiful supply of spring water and the variety of plants that it can produce. Nor is he unaware of the importance of the lake because of the purity of its water, with its source in Mount Hermon, and the quality of its air (*War* 2.506-21; 3.41-44). Both air and water are recognized in ancient medical literature as highly significant for good health, raising the question whether Jesus may have focused much of his Galilean ministry in that region precisely because of the physical factors that made it attractive for those in search of healing, as already discussed in relation to the number of healing spas in the rift valley.[34]

Given this ecological diversity, we can expect that the inhabitants of Galilee were engaged in various occupations, even though, as in all ancient economies, agriculture was predominant. Land ownership, was, therefore, of primary importance. The inference that there was an increase in absentee landlords, landless serfs, and day laborers during the first century is often based on the assumption that Jesus' parables reflect the actual rather than the imagined social world of Galilee. These images may indeed have been drawn from firsthand experience, yet they need

33. S. Freyne, *Jesus, a Jewish Galilean: A New Reading of the Jesus Story* (New York and London: Clark, 2004), 24-53.

34. See the Hippocratic treatise *Airs, Waters, Places*, Greek text and translation by W. H. S. Jones (Loeb Classical Library 147; Cambridge: Harvard University Press, 1924), 1:65-137.

not have all been drawn from Galilee, since there is no evidence of royal estates in the region.

As we have seen in the previous section, Herod the Great inherited the royal lands of previous regimes, but none of these were in Galilee proper. If Jesus spent some time in the Judean desert with John the Baptist, as we will discuss in the next chapter, then he could well have been aware of the Herodian holdings at Jericho, or equally those in the Plain of Esdraelon or the King's Country as he journeyed with other pilgrims to Jerusalem. When Herod did inherit land in Batanea and Trachonitis as a gift from Augustus, he planted this with Babylonian Jews, who lived in villages and received relief of all taxes. This was in return for their support in pacifying the region, which traditionally had been the home of bandits. As mentioned previously, the number of different surveys that have been conducted in different sections of Galilee present a fairly consistent picture of small plots of land comprising on average some ten to twelve acres. This pattern is at least as old as the Hasmonean conquest of the north, when the biblical pattern of private ownership of individual plots of land became the norm (cf. 1 Macc 14:4-15, especially v. 12).[35] It corresponds with the evidence from both Josephus and the Gospels, both of which assume that "the Galileans" who flock to Josephus's aid or "the crowds" who follow Jesus are neither landless nor particularly impoverished. While one might be suspicious of Josephus's lauding of the Galileans' industrious qualities as a way of boosting his own skill as a general and ruler, the number of 204 settlements that he mentions for Galilee is by no means out of line with the numbers that modern surveys of the region suggest for the early Roman period (*Life* 235).[36]

Against this background of a shared primary resource, based on the archaeological and literary evidence, the question arises as to how this picture might relate to the various models that have been proposed for the study of the region as a whole. The debate is ongoing, it should be noted, as new and more representative archaeological evidence is forthcoming and as sociological models are being applied with greater awareness of their limitations in dealing with specific regions because of the abstract and generalized picture that they suggest.

35. For a discussion with differing points of view on land ownership, see Freyne, *Galilee from Alexander the Great to Hadrian*, 156-69; D. Fiensy, *The Social History of Palestine in the Herodian Period: The Land Is Mine* (Lewiston: Edwin Mellen, 1991), 21-74; R. A. Horsley, *Galilee: History, Politics, People* (Valley Forge: Trinity, 1995), 207-21.

36. Chaim ben David, "Were There 204 Settlements in Galilee at the Time of Josephus Flavius?" *JJS* 62 (2011), 21-36.

According to what has come to be known as "the Lynski-Kautsky model" (after the names of two sociologists), aristocratic agrarian empires concentrate all the power in a small ruling elite.[37] These are represented at the apex of a pyramid-style model of social stratification in agrarian societies. A retainer class of artisans — scribes, tax collectors, and other officials who are both sufficient and necessary for the maintenance of order in the whole system — serve this privileged group and are located beneath them on the pyramid of power and privilege. The urban poor, slaves and other expendables, are situated at the base of the pyramid, with the landed peasantry just above them in this hierarchical network of social relationships.[38] Since the reign of Antipas in Galilee saw the refurbishment of Sepphoris and the foundation of a new city, Tiberias, this model is often augmented with insights drawn from the idea of the consumer city as parasitic on the countryside as this has been developed in particular by Moses Finley.[39]

At a relatively early stage in the debates between archaeologists of early Roman Galilee and sociologically informed historians, clear differences of opinion quickly emerged. In a follow-up volume (1998) to his 1993 study of the historical Jesus, John Dominic Crossan expressed a preference for the Lynski-Kautsky model because, in his view, it highlights the plight of peasants within agrarian empires. According to Crossan, the emergence of the two urban centers in Galilee was not good news for Galilean peasants, as some had claimed. Focusing in particular on the studies of Galilean pottery production by David Adan Bayewitz, Crossan (following, it should be noted, the dictates of the chosen model rather than the data that Adan-Bayewitz had presented) rejects the notion that the emergence of pottery-making centers in various villages was indicative of increased diversification among the peasantry of Antipas's Galilee. Rather, according to a cross-cultural study of pottery-making on which Crossan relies, it indicates a deterioration in the status of some peasants who are forced to engage in ceramic production "not for entrepreneurial opportunity but out of agricultural necessity." In other words, artisans, as "dispossessed peasants," are even lower on the social scale.[40]

In a similar vein, Richard Horsley challenged the interpretation of the

---

37. R. Horsley, *Sociology and the Jesus Movement* (New York: Crossroad, 1989); J. H. Elliott, *What Is Social-Scientific Criticism?* (Minneapolis: Fortress, 1993).

38. Hanson and Oakman, *Palestine in the Time of Jesus,* 63-98 and 161-63.

39. M. Finley, *The Ancient Economy* (2nd ed.; London: Hogarth, 1981).

40. J. D. Crossan, *The Birth of Christianity: Discovering What Happened in the Years Immediately after the Execution of Jesus* (New York: HarperSanFrancisco, 1998), 226-27.

findings of Eric Meyers and his team working in Upper Galilee. They had suggested the possibility of trading relations between some Galilean villages and the region of Tyre on the basis of the coin profiles and artifacts they discovered at four different excavated sites, as well as evidence of industrial activity. For Horsley, however, such a scenario was impossible within a politically controlled economy. In various publications he consistently placed a strong emphasis on the Roman imperial presence as the dominant social structure in Galilee. Its demands on subject peoples led to "disintegration of the fundamental forms of social life that accompanied these economic burdens."[41] This disintegration, Horsley claims, manifested itself in social banditry and other forms of protest. Thus, a picture of Galilean social life emerges that is dysfunctional and oppressive, especially for the people at the bottom of the pyramid. In such a scenario of almost complete state control, the idea of peasants engaging in commercial transactions with the surrounding regions is simply not convincing, as far as Horsley is concerned. When the burden of the Herodian tax system is combined with the demands of the Judean temple state, the native Galilean peasants were caught in a double bind, he claims.

In an earlier study I, too, have attempted to model the Galilean economy under Antipas.[42] The ideas of historical sociologist Thomas Carney seemed to be tuned appropriately to address the issue of whether rapid social and economic change was occurring under Antipas. According to Carney, it is important to distinguish between profiling a stable economy and detecting the pattern of rapid changes that might be occurring, which is a more difficult task. In the latter instance, both external and internal factors need to be considered, and it is only when changes in the market, in the modes of exchange, and in the values and attitudes of the society can be charted as occurring simultaneously that rapid economic developments can be postulated. When I now reflect on the exercise, especially in the light of the ongoing archaeological investigation in the region, it seems to me that the earlier Hellenistic period as discussed earlier in this chapter might have been a better candidate for analyzing rapid economic change in the region.

However, there is one important aspect of Carney's suggestions that

41. *Galilee: History, Politics, People,* 221. See R. Horsley, "Archaeology and the Villages of Upper Galilee," *BASOR* 297 (1995), 5-15, with a response by E. Meyers, pp. 17-25.
42. Freyne, "Herodian Economics in Galilee," 86-113. See T. F. Carney, *The Shape of the Past* (Lawrence: Coronado, 1975).

certainly applies to Antipas's Galilee, namely, the need to consider the importance of changing values and the resultant loss of confidence in the institutions that were responsible for propagating and maintaining these values. On reflection two competing value systems were operating simultaneously, now that there was a direct Roman presence in the province in the person of Antipas and his court. The Judeans who had settled in Galilee and who made up the bulk of the village populations were still attached to Jerusalem. This presumably meant readiness to pay tithes and the half-shekel offering for the temple (*Life* 63, 80). The extent to which other wealth-leveling mechanisms based on the Pentateuch were operative is unclear. The decrees of Caesar explicitly reduced the tax burden in the seventh year "because in that year they neither plough nor take fruit from the trees" (*Ant* 14.202, 206), referring directly to the Sabbath year regulations. The Pentateuch also suggests other mechanisms for alleviating social and economic differences such as the poor person's tithe, interest-free loans, and the duty to leave parts of the crop for the poor when harvesting.

In contrast to the principles of egalitarianism and communal solidarity that were at the heart of Israel's social organization, Roman society was dominated by a patron-client dynamic that inevitably led to social stratification. This reached all the way up to the emperor, who was the universal patron. Rulers such as the Herodians were deemed to be his clients, even when they themselves took on a patron's role in their territories. Closely related to this structure were the notions of honor and shame, which have been described as "pivotal Mediterranean values."[43] Put simply, honor had to do with the amount of public recognition a person could generate by acquiring wealth, performing some outstanding public service, or having a significant number of dependent clients. Obviously, the higher up the social ladder one was able to climb, the more honor one was deemed to have, as in the case of those who were designated "friends" of a patron, be it the emperor, the governor or, in the case of Judea, the Herodian rulers. Wealth was a definite status indicator, and acts of philanthropy, as in the case of Herod the Great's action to alleviate hunger during the drought, was a way of increasing honor in the eyes of one's subjects. Shame on the other hand was the result of "not knowing one's place" as this was ascribed according to the accepted norms and roles within the society. Women in particular could be deemed shameful if they transgressed the strict social boundaries

43. B. Malina, *The Social World of Jesus and the Gospels* (New York: Routledge, 1996), 143-75.

set for them within a highly structured patriarchal world. In the early imperial period, however, there is some evidence of high class Roman matrons beginning to negotiate the transition from the private to the public sphere, the classic example being Livia/Julia, the wife of Augustus and mother of Tiberius discussed in the previous chapter.

Clearly, these two contrasting views of social organization, the Judean and the Roman, were operative in Antipas's Galilee. One obvious example of the latter is the Markan story of Antipas's birthday celebrations, already mentioned (Mark 6:17-29). This event was attended by *megistanes, chiliarchoi,* and *hoi prōtoi tōn Galilaiōn.* Each of these terms designates people of relatively high status in the Galilean hierarchy. The *megistanes,* usually translated as "great ones" or "grandees," were people who had achieved notable wealth and belonged, therefore, to the official circle of Antipas's friends. *Chiliarchoi* on the other hand were military personnel, literally "rulers of a thousand." Their presence in the account is somewhat surprising since Antipas would not have been allowed to have a large permanent army. However, Mark may have included them in his list of guests as typical for such an event and as those whose status would normally have been acquired by prowess in defending the realm. The *hoi prōtoi tōn Galilaiōn,* literally "the first (or leaders) of the Galileans," is a term that occurs frequently in the account of Josephus's dealings in the region in 66 C.E. They were local leaders, possibly synagogue elders, from the different toparchies or districts into which Galilee was divided for administrative purposes, and would have been of Judean stock.[44] Their presence in such a gathering is an indication of their acceptance of, or at least their acquiescence in, the Roman value system, especially when this brought them public honor, presumably among some at least of the village population.

The profile of this last group in particular is indicative of the kind of erosion of older values that could occur when the Judean heritage was confronted with an alternative lifestyle, one that offered honor and status to those natives who were prepared to embrace it. As we shall see in the next chapter, the "values revolution" that Jesus inaugurated was a direct challenge to such accommodation. His message drew its inspiration from the

44. One should also note the presence of Herodias at this event, even if her role as described by Mark was not as one of the guests but rather as the organizer of matters political behind the scenes. See S. Freyne, "Zwischen Römischem Imperium und Synagoge. Die Rolle von Frauen im römischem Palästina durch die Brille des Markusevangelium," in M. Navarro Puerto and M. Perroni, eds., *Die Bibel und die Frauen. Eine exegetische-kulturgeschichtliche Enzyklopädie.* 2.1: *Evangelien* (Stuttgart: Kohlhammer, 2012), 39-59, especially 54-58.

ideals of Israel's communal charter as this was laid out in the Pentateuch. In Mark's gospel we encounter an alliance between a group described as "the Herodians" and the Pharisees who conspired together against Jesus, both in Galilee and Jerusalem (Mark 3:6; 12:13). At first glance this appears to be a strange association, yet a number of considerations suggest that it is not at all as unlikely as appears at first sight. The Pharisees were no strangers to political engagement, as their involvement in the affairs of the Hasmonean state makes clear. Josephus tells us that they were particularly popular with the townspeople, and the Evangelist Luke goes further still, declaring that they were "lovers of money" (Luke 16:14). Similarly, the most likely profile of the Herodians is that suggested by Josephus, who mentions a number of the leading men in Tiberias who bear the name Herod, one of whose associates was absent from the city on his estates across the Jordan in Perea (*Life* 32-33). They might easily be identified with the grandees who attended Antipas's birthday celebrations. Neither group would have been enamored of a movement that espoused the radical lifestyle of Jesus and his followers in Galilee, with its critique of affluence, status, and luxury.

These textual indicators point us firmly in the direction of the changes occurring in Antipas's reign, if we are to properly understand the matrix of the Jesus movement. A second generation of students of early Roman Galilee are beginning to question the over-reliance on the use of models in earlier studies and point to the dangers of distortion that are inherent in the too rigid application of these models to some of the data that archaeology has uncovered. Thus the excitement generated by the discovery of Sepphoris, so close to Nazareth, has given way to a more sober assessment of its status in the early first century C.E. Now that some recent excavations have taken place in Tiberias, it emerges that it, rather than Sepphoris, was the more Roman of the two cities in terms of layout and typical architectural features in the first century.[45] Josephus's description of Antipas making Sepphoris "the ornament of all Galilee" undoubtedly led to over-interpretation of the discoveries at the site, many of them belonging to the second century when the city came to be known as Diocaesarea, as was discussed in the previous chapter.

This downgrading of Sepphoris's role in the first century C.E. poses a question with regard to its fitting the typology of the "consumer city" as described by Moses Finley with reference to the parasitic role of cities as

---

45. Z. Weiss, "Josephus and Archaeology on the Cities of Galilee," in Z. Rodgers, ed., *Making History: Josephus and Historical Method* (Leiden: Brill, 2007), 385-414.

residences for the elite in aristocratic empires.[46] Nevertheless, as a toparchic or main regional center, one of five such in Galilee, Sepphoris clearly had an important role to play within the Galilean social and economic systems. Justus of Tiberias bemoans the fact that the archives and the royal bank had been moved from his own city to Sepphoris after Nero's partitioning of Galilee in 56 c.e., with the transfer of Tiberias and Tarichea "together with their toparchies" to the control of Agrippa II.

This arrangement certainly meant that Sepphoris had an important administrative position within the truncated province. The *archeia* refer to records generally, which probably included tax and debt records, especially if there was a land and poll or head tax, as was probably the case, if not under Antipas, then later when Galilee came under direct Roman rule in 44 c.e. The royal bank also suggests commercial activity, probably referring to the minting of coins and their storage. This new role would also explain why the city did not take part in the first revolt, asking for protection from the Galilean zealots and receiving assistance from the Roman governor of Syria, Cestius Gallus (*Life* 31). This suggests that the Sepphoreans had indeed opted for Roman rather than Judean values and lifestyle, a fact that Josephus confirms by his stinging criticism of their lack of loyalty in refusing to join in support of "the temple which is common to us all," though the city was situated in the center of Galilee and in a position to help the revolt, "surrounded, as it was, by many villages" (*Life* 346).

This observation raises the issue of the possible commercial and other links those villages might have had with the urban center. Adan-Bayewitz and others have shown that one of those villages, Shikin, just 2 km away, was the supplier of large amphorae and storage jars to the city. No doubt other villages were suppliers of other services and produce to the market there also. A lead weight with the names of two market managers (*agoranomoi*) inscribed in Greek between two rows of columns has been found in the excavations. The columns suggest a colonnaded building, probably the marketplace of the city.

This pattern of clusters of smaller settlements associated with larger centers and engaged in some local trading is likely to have been replicated elsewhere in Galilee also. The fact that various subregions were associated with different produce, such as wine and oil in Upper Galilee, grains in the

---

46. M. Finley, *The Ancient City* (Berkeley: University of California Press, 1973); "The Ancient City from Fustel de Coulange to Max Weber," *Comparative Studies in Society and History* 19 (1981), 305-27.

Colonnaded street at Sepphoris, "the ornament of Galilee,"
refurbished and expanded by Antipas as one of the
main toparchic centers of Roman Galilee.
(Todd Bolen/BiblePlaces.com)

Bet Netofa plain, and fish as well as other produce in the lake district indicates a degree of industrial specialization. The movement of these products gave rise to ancillary trades such as ceramic production, boat making, and related activities, which would have gone beyond the demands of mere subsistence living among "the peasants." It is true that Galileans did not engage in long-range trading, other than with Tyre, and the road system necessary for large-scale movement of goods would only be fully developed in the second century. Yet the spike in the population numbers in the early Roman period, indicated by the number and size of the settlements, gave rise to increased internal demand, something that both Josephus and the Gospels presuppose. Recent discoveries are refining further our ideas about the size and scale of operation in the villages in Galilee, whereas theoretical discussions are leading to the recognition that our notions of the peasantry need to be much more nuanced than heretofore. The emerging image of Galilee is, therefore, much more differentiated both socially and economically than that which the models being employed previously suggested.

Thus the proposal that "the urbanization of Galilee" as reflected in Sepphoris and Tiberias led to a major impoverishment of the country people is not corroborated by the archaeological discoveries. In his important study of Antipas's reign, Morten Jensen has examined the evidence from four recently excavated sites in Lower Galilee/Golan, namely, Jotapata, Gamla, Capernaum, and Khirbet Qana and claims that there is no evidence of any decline at these sites in the first century.[47] Douglas Edwards, who participated in the excavations at Capernaum and was, up to the time of his untimely death, the director of the dig at Khirbet Qana, has been a consistent supporter of the view that in the early Roman period Galilean villages participated in the economic opportunities and dangers inherent in the Mediterranean system. In his opinion "it would be a mistake to assume that the Jesus movement operated in a cultural, political or economic isolation from major urban centres."[48] This conclusion may well be true for the later Jesus movement in Galilee of the post-Easter period. However, I still want to stand with the conclusion of my earlier study, namely that the absence of any mention of either Sepphoris or Tiberias in the Gospels represents a principled avoidance by Jesus himself of these places and the urban ethos that they represented.[49]

The evidence for the claims of Jensen and Edwards comes from a better understanding of the Galilean economy. Edwards points to the beginnings of the Roman road system in the environs of Sepphoris, a development that he dates already to the first century. In addition, he points to the striking of coins by Antipas, three in total during his long reign, as mentioned previously. In terms of tracing these movements and their significance, pottery has become the most important aspect of the material remains. Several villages are known as important centers of local production, Kefar Hananya on the borders of Upper and Lower Galilee and Shikin, close to Sepphoris, being the best known, because of the support for their products in the Jewish literary sources.[50] The wares from Kefar Hananya are

47. M. Jensen, *Herod Antipas in Galilee* (WUNT 215; Tübingen: Mohr Siebeck, 2006), 162-86.

48. D. Edwards, "The Socio-Economic and Cultural Ethos of the Lower Galilee in the First Century: Implications for the Nascent Jesus Movement," in L. Levine, ed., *The Galilee in Late Antiquity* (New York: Jewish Theological Seminary of America, 1992), 53-74, at p. 72. See also Edwards, "Identity and Social Location in Roman Villages," in J. Zangenberg, et al., eds., *Religion, Ethnicity and Identity in Ancient Galilee* (WUNT 210, Tübingen: Mohr Siebeck, 2007), 357-74; "Walking the Roman Landscape in Lower Galilee: Sepphoris, Jotapata and Khirbet Qana," in Z. Rodgers, et al., eds., *A Wandering Galilean: Essays in Honour of Sean Freyne* (Leiden: Brill, 2009), 219-36.

49. S. Freyne, "Jesus and the Urban Culture of Galilee," in *Galilee and Gospel*, 183-207.

50. D. Adan-Bayewitz, *Common Pottery in Roman Galilee: A Study of Local Trade*

to be found at both Jewish and non-Jewish sites such as Tel Anafa and Acco/
Ptolemais, suggesting a wide distribution area that was determined more by
commercial interests than by religious or cultural differences. As an example of the competition that these Galilean wares faced, Edwards instances
Meiron, a thoroughly Jewish foundation in Upper Galilee: Kefar Hananyia
ware and eastern Sigillata wares, that is, imported wares, are almost equally
represented in the ceramic remains at the site. This evidence, allied to the
discovery of dovecotes, oil presses, flax grown for weaving, and quarries for
stone masonry all convince Edwards of the existence of varied and complex production and market conditions that cannot be subsumed under the
general rubric of a "politically controlled economy."[51] In this regard, the
fish industry in the lake region is particularly significant as an industry that
emerged already in the early Hellenistic period, as was suggested earlier.
The technique of salting fish, developed already in Hellenistic times, made
it possible to export them as far as Rome. The number of harbors, fish-
ponds, and breakwaters discovered around the lake dating from Roman
times is testimony to this industry in the Roman period also.

Yet not everybody is so convinced by the inference of a "vibrant economic environment" based on this evidence alone. With regard to the pottery, Andrea Berlin, for example, has shown that a special type that she
describes as Phoenician semi-fine ware, probably produced in the environs
of Tyre, is found at a range of sites in the circumference of Galilee, but
never in the interior of Galilee proper.[52] She further claims that imported
household wares from the first century B.C.E. found at Gamla and other
Jewish sites disappear in the first century C.E., coinciding with what she describes as a native resistance to Romanization, associated with the reign of
the Herods.[53] In a similar vein, the change in patterns of coinage from Tyrian to native Hasmonean found at Jotapata in the same timeframe points to

(Ramat-Gan: Bar Ilan University Press, 1993); D. Adan Bayewitz and I. Perlman, "The Local
Trade of Sepphoris in the Roman Period," *IEJ* 40 (1990), 153-72; J. Strange, D. Groh, and
T. Longstaff, "Excavation at Sepphoris: The Location and Identification of Shikin," *IEJ* 44
(1994), 216-27, and 45 (1995), 171-87.

51. Edwards, "Identity and Social Location," 366.

52. A. Berlin, "From Monarchy to Markets: The Phoenicians in Hellenistic Palestine,"
BASOR 306 (1997), 75-88.

53. A. Berlin, "Romanization and Anti-Romanization in Pre-Revolt Galilee," in Berlin
and A. Overman, eds., *The First Jewish Revolt: Archaeology, History and Ideology* (London:
Routledge, 2002), 57-73; "Jewish Life before the Revolt: The Archaeological Evidence," *JSJ* 36
(2005), 417-69; *Gamla I: The Pottery of the Second Temple Period* (IAA Reports 29; Jerusalem:
IAA Publications, 2006), especially 133-55.

a similar disengagement from the larger region.[54] Thus, it would seem, the use of archaeological evidence alone to determine the economic realities cannot be decisive. Circumstances vary from place to place and period to period. Generalized ideas about a "Mediterranean economy" in which Galilee participated need to be tempered by local circumstances, where factors other than commercial do, in fact, seem to have impacted on trade and commerce, at least to some extent.

Faced with this division of opinion with regard to the economy of Galilee in the first century, it might appear unwise to draw any inference with regard to the nature of Jesus' ministry there. However, it does seem possible to find some middle ground that could prove helpful to the quest. It would be highly unlikely that the immediacy of the Herodian presence, signified by Antipas's building projects, modest though they are in comparison with those of his father elsewhere, did not cause some problems for Galileans. Mark, as we have seen, paints a variegated picture of those who attended Antipas's birthday party. In addition to this list we must add the ubiquitous tax collectors as a reminder of the demands made on the natives in terms of both a land tax and a head tax. Josephus's mention of "imperial grain" stored in Upper Galilee reminds us of the perennial shortage of grain in Rome and the expectation that the eastern provinces, especially Syria and Egypt, would provide for this on an ongoing basis. Clearly, Rome was happy to accept payment of tribute in kind rather than cash. An incident that took place in the reign of Gaius when the Judean peasants (including the Galileans) engaged in an agricultural strike that would have threatened the payment of the annual tribute is a stark reminder of the narrow margins that were operative in terms of supply and demand (*War* 2.192-203). Drought, as occurred in the reign of Herod the Great, caused great hardship for the population, as we have seen earlier.

The benefits of "the peace under Tiberius" of which Tacitus speaks may not have touched everybody in Galilee equally, as elsewhere. There are definite signs of social stratification in some of the larger villages such as Jotapata, with its Second Pompeian style frescoes and wall paintings in one of the residences, and Gamla, with milling and olive press installations in a large villa-style complex.[55] But this is only half the story of the 204 set-

---

54. D. Adan-Bayewitz and M. Aviam, "Iotapata, Josephus and the Siege of 67: Preliminary Report of the 1992-94 Seasons," *JRA* 10 (1997), 131-65.

55. Z. Yavor, "The Architecture and Stratigraphy of the Eastern and Western Quarters," in D. Syon and Z. Yavor, eds., *Gamla I: The Architecture of the Shamarya Gutmann*

tlements in Galilee of which Josephus speaks. At the time of the revolt, we hear of the residents of the smaller hamlets retreating to fortified sites such as Jotapata and Gamla to escape the Roman onslaught. Placing these people on the social scale in Galilee is not so easy. If we were to take Mark's picture of Galilee, written about the same time as Josephus's account of his own sojourn in the province, we find reference to villages with market places (Mark 6:56), people with money who could be expected to purchase their own provisions (v. 36), those engaged in the fish industry having hired servants (1:20), synagogues, at least in the sense of local communities, even if we cannot be sure that all had buildings pre-70 (v. 39), and medical practitioners who expected payment for their services (5:26; cf. *Life* 403). Clearly, Galilee's social organization was mixed, as was its economy, and we cannot assume that all shared equally in the prosperity, if that is what we should call it, associated with Antipas's rule.

In the opening three chapters of this study we have focused on aspects of Galilean life that are, as we shall see, highly relevant in terms of understanding Jesus and his movement in Galilee and Jerusalem, namely, the continuing impact of Hellenization on the region, the nature of Galilean Jewish identity, and the economic and social situation in Galilee in the reign of Antipas. Archaeology has greatly assisted us in filling out or correcting the impression one gets from our chief literary sources. We have learned (1) that the epithet "Galilee of the Gentiles" is not an appropriate description of the region's ethos from the second century B.C.E. onward, (2) that there are unmistakable signs of continued Jewish practice and observance throughout the region, despite the "intrusion" of the Herodians, and (3) that, while there is no trace of economic or social decline in some of the larger villages, nevertheless the likelihood is that social differentiation increased among the peasantry during the reign of Antipas. The effort to situate Jesus and his movement in this context will be both a challenge and a testing of these conclusions in the following chapter.

Excavations, 1976-1988 (IAA Reports 44; Jerusalem: Israel Antiquities Authority, 2010), 13-113, especially 98-109.

CHAPTER FOUR

Situating Jesus

The author of the Fourth Gospel presents the Jerusalem authorities passing a negative judgment on Jesus at the Feast of Tabernacles. Their dismissal of the claims circulating among the crowds that he could possibly be the Messiah were based partly at least on the fact that he came from Galilee (John 7:52). Some of the people of Jerusalem believed that since Jesus' origins were known, he was already disqualified from the role: ". . . when the Messiah comes no one will know where he is from" (v. 27). Others claimed that according to the Scriptures the Messiah would be descended from David and would come from Bethlehem in Judah and that, being a Galilean, Jesus could not possibly be the chosen one (vv. 41-42).

An underlying current to these discussions that comes to the surface later in this episode is a Jerusalem/Judean disdain for Galileans as unlettered and ignorant of the Torah (v. 49). In other words, the Galileans belong to the *am ha-aretz* or "people of the land" as defined in later rabbinic discussions.[1] Indeed there is a strong suspicion that John 7 was written with

---

1. The term *am ha-aretz* (literally "people of the land") does not appear in the New Testament but is used in the Hebrew Bible to refer to different groups among the people. It appears in rabbinic writings to designate those who do not take seriously the teaching of the sages on tithing and other purity matters. A. Büchler, *Galiläische Am ha-Aretz des Zweiten Jahrhunderts* (reprint, Hildesheim: Olms, 1968), distinguished between two types, *am ha-aretz le-mitzwoth* and *am ha-aretz le-torah,* claiming that the former term only emerged in the second century C.E. with reference to the descendants of the priests who migrated to Galilee after the destruction of the temple and rejected the authority of the rabbis. The *am ha-aretz le-torah* applied to all who rejected the Torah at any time. However, A. Oppenheimer, in his detailed study *The Am ha-Aretz: A Study of the Social History of the Jewish People in the*

a view to the developing dispute between the Johannine community and the Jewish synagogue authorities that runs through the gospel as a whole and reflects a later situation than the actual career of Jesus. The earliest date would probably be the post-70 period, when the remnants of various Jerusalem groups, including the Pharisees, were forced to abandon Judea and migrate to other parts of the land including Galilee and competing claims to Jewish identity were being formulated. Nevertheless, the attitude toward Galileans that the episode indicates did not arise for the first time then but in all probability was prevalent at the time of Jesus also.[2]

Birth and Infancy: The Connection with the Baptist

The stories of Jesus' birth and infancy that Matthew and Luke use to preface their accounts of his public ministry (Matthew 1–2 and Luke 1–2) suggest that the issue of Jesus' place of origin, as distinct from the theater of his public ministry, had surfaced in other contexts also. Perhaps the fact that Mark, the earliest of the four canonical gospels, does not deal with the topic at all and that Paul, likewise, is unconcerned about the matter, had caused objections to be raised against early Christian claims regarding Jesus' messiahship that needed to be addressed. While sharing a number of facts about his origins, both Matthew and Luke feel free to develop their accounts in quite different directions, often echoing aspects of the public ministry that surface later in their differing accounts of Jesus' adult career. Thus, Matthew merely mentions in passing Jesus' birth in Bethlehem (Matt 2:1) and alludes to it again in respect of the slaughter of the children in Bethlehem and the surrounding area by Herod (v. 16). Luke relates the fact that Jesus' birth in Bethlehem was due to the census that Caesar Augustus had ordered for the whole world (Luke 2:1-6). Luke, it would seem, assumes that Jesus' family

---

Hellenistic-Roman Period (Leiden: Brill, 1977), takes the opposite view, suggesting that *am ha-aretz le torah* surfaced as a term of abuse among the rabbis only in the second century C.E. because of the neglect of study of Torah among certain elements of the population in the period after 135 C.E., when Torah study had replaced temple worship as the central act of Jewish piety.

2. S. Freyne, "Jesus and the Galilean *Am ha-Aretz*: A Reconsideration of an Old Problem," in Z. Weiss, O. Irshai, J. Magness, and S. Schwartz, eds., *"Follow the Wise": Studies in Jewish History and Culture in Honor of Lee I. Levine* (Winona Lake: Eisenbrauns, 2010), 37-52; "Jesus and the Galilean *Am ha-Aretz*: Fact, Johannine Irony or Both," in P. Anderson, F. Just, and T. Thatcher, eds., *John, Jesus and History: Aspects of Historicity in the Fourth Gospel* (Atlanta: SBL, 2009), 139-54.

was living in Galilee but was of Judean extraction, whereas Matthew accepts the Bethlehem birth without any explanation. Matthew links Jesus' later Galilean residence with opposition from the Herodian house, first from Herod the Great and subsequently from his son Archelaus (Matt 2:16-23).

Deciding between the two claimants to Jesus' actual birthplace is not easy. Both Evangelists are more interested in presenting Jesus' birth as a messianic event in which the hand of God is present, directing the movements of the child and his family by angelic messengers (Luke) or heavenly dreams (Matthew). Clearly, place of origin was an important factor in the authenticity of the claims about Jesus being made by his later followers. While Martin Hengel believes that the family of Jesus was actually aware of its descent from David and that, therefore, Jesus was conscious of his Davidic origins from the outset, others have resorted to the unlikely suggestion that Jesus was born in a village of Galilee also called Bethlehem, which was changed to Bethlehem in Judea when he appeared as a messianic claimant. In my opinion, neither suggestion is likely. As explained previously, many Judeans migrated to Galilee in the wake of the Hasmonean expansion, and this would explain how a Galilean-born Jesus could equally have had Judean family associations. The likelihood of such a memory being maintained over a century at most is far more probable than the suggestion that details of Davidic descent were passed on over many centuries in his family, as Hengel's position implies.[3]

Irrespective of what solution one opts for, what is significant for understanding Jesus' life and ministry, as well as that of his first followers, is the fact that he too was committed to Judean claims about the divine presence in Jerusalem. This was so even when his interpretation of how that presence should function for all Israel varied considerably from that of the Judean religious establishment. Not everybody interested in the career of the historical Jesus thinks that this was so, however. Thus, for example, John Dominic Crossan writes that Jesus probably only visited Jerusalem once and that he was so incensed by what he encountered there that he launched the protest against the temple and the holy city that would eventually lead to his death.[4] As mentioned in the Introduction, the emphasis in recent scholarship on Jesus' Galilean ministry has given rise to a serious danger

3. M. Hengel and A. M. Schwemer, *Jesus und das Judentum* (Tübingen: Mohr Siebeck, 2007), 292-94; J. P. Meier, *A Marginal Jew: Rethinking the Historical Jesus* (New York: Doubleday, 1991), 1:214-19.

4. John Dominic Crossan, *The Historical Jesus: The Life of a Mediterranean Jewish Peasant* (Edinburgh: Clark, 1993), 360.

of the specter of a non-Jewish Jesus emerging in another guise. However appealing such a universalist understanding of Jesus' ministry might appear to be, New Testament scholarship should never again fall into the trap of the "Aryan Jesus," the product of nineteenth-century anti-Semitism, which had such pernicious consequences in the anti-Judaism of the twentieth century.[5]

It is here that the relationship between John the Baptizer and Jesus is a crucial but often neglected facet of the adult Jesus' own formation. The contrast that Jesus makes between himself and John — the one a bon vivant and the other a prophet of judgment — should not in any way detract from his declaration of deep admiration for John: "No one born of women is greater than he" (Q Luke 7:28/Matt 11:11).[6] In his account of the infancy of Jesus, Luke seeks to make that link very real: their mothers were kinswomen and the child in Elizabeth's womb danced for joy when Mary approached, thereby underlining John's subordination to Jesus, which would surface later in the tradition. This contrast is particularly pronounced in the Fourth Gospel, where, on the one hand, Jesus is presented as engaging in a baptismal rite that is similar to John's but leads to a dispute between their respective disciples, and, on the other, John declares that "he [Jesus] must increase and I [John] must decrease" (John 3:22-30).

In his infancy account, Luke also links John with the temple since his father Zechariah is a country priest engaged in the offering of the daily sacrifice when he is informed about Elizabeth's miraculous conception in her old age.[7] The family's association with the temple worship makes John's appearance in the desert, promoting a baptism of repentance for sins, all the more curious. According to Torah regulations there was an annual rite of repentance for all Israel, *Yom Kippur,* so John's activity must be seen as a protest or at least as dissatisfaction with the Temple and its rituals. This would put him in the same category as other protest movements, most no-

5. S. Heschel, *The Aryan Jesus: Christian Theologians and the Bible in Nazi Germany* (Princeton: Princeton University Press, 2008).

6. Meier, *A Marginal Jew,* 2:142-44, argues that Luke 7:28b/Matt 11:11b — "The least in the kingdom (of heaven) is greater than he" — is part of the authentic logion, while others are less certain, seeing it as a later "Christian gloss." What is significant is that the clause does not in any way detract from the encomium for John, since the remark refers to the change of the aeons: John is the greatest and last prophet of the first dispensation, whereas "the least in the kingdom" belongs to the new dispensation inaugurated by Jesus.

7. Meier, *A Marginal Jew,* 2:19-27, especially 24 and note 25, p. 69, regards this one element of Luke's infancy account as having historical probability.

tably the Essenes as known from the Qumran Scrolls. They had seen a return to the desert as a way of renewing a commitment to Israel's original calling and of preparing themselves for God's coming salvation, as foretold in various prophecies having to do with "the day of Yahweh."[8]

Several of the scrolls give expression to a deep-seated dissatisfaction with the existing temple and its worship. For example, 4QMMT, a letter from the desert group to those who were in charge of the cult, claimed that this was not being performed in the manner that was laid down in the Torah. It was for this reason that they had separated themselves from the Jerusalem worship, asserting instead that it was they who performed the correct rituals in the desert. This dissatisfaction is further underlined by the self-description of the *yahad* (i.e., "the unity," as the group described itself), who declared that they constituted "the temple" (1QS 5.5-8; 9.3-5). This self-understanding is underlined also by the obvious concern with ritual purity that is expressed in several other documents from the group, as well as in the archaeological remains from Qumran itself.[9] Perhaps most telling of all is the Temple Scroll, which envisages three temples, the present one occupied by the sons of Belial, the one that the group hopes to build where Yahweh will allow his name to dwell, and the end-time temple that he himself will build (11QTemple 29). This scenario combines a serious critique of the present situation in Jerusalem, a statement about the group's own claim to authenticity in the interim, and an expression of apocalyptic hope for the future definitive intervention with regard to the temple built by God himself.

The *Book of the Watchers* in *1 Enoch,* previously discussed in relation to Banias (pp. 25-26), also provides another window on inner-Judean critique of the Jerusalem temple and its personnel. Indeed, there were, we saw, linguistic connections with the Essene critique in terms of the corruption of the Watchers, that is, the Jerusalem temple personnel, and the imminent judgment against them, which Enoch was commissioned to pronounce.[10]

For our present purposes of locating dissatisfaction with the existing

8. In the postexilic period, the idea of "the Day of Yahweh" as a day of judgment against the nations came to be applied to the unrepentant in Israel, whereas originally it referred to Israel's enemies: Amos 5:18-20; Mal 3:19-23 (4:1-6); Isa 33:10-16.

9. J. Magness, *The Archaeology of Qumran and the Dead Sea Scrolls* (Grand Rapids: Eerdmans, 2002); S. Freyne, "Jewish Immersion and Christian Baptism: Continuity on the Margins?" in D. Hellholm, et al., eds., *Ablution, Initiation and Baptism: Late Antiquity, Early Judaism and Early Christianity* (Berlin: de Gruyter, 2010), 1:221-54, especially 230-37.

10. Chapter 3 above, p. 110.

temple as a context for understanding John's ministry in the desert, these parallels are quite sufficient. John too shares the expectation of an imminent judgment and, in the manner of other prophets before him, issues a call for repentance of heart on the part of Israel as a whole, introducing a rite of washing as a public statement of such repentance that has echoes of Israel's "passage" to the Promised Land. Isaiah's injunction to "prepare the way of the Lord in the desert" (Isa 40:3) is one of John's rallying calls also (Matt 3:1-2; Mark 1:3; Luke 3:4-6), one that, incidentally, was shared by the Teacher of Righteousness, the putative founder of the Qumran Essenes, according to the Damascus Document.[11]

The apocalyptic atmosphere behind this thinking, one that expresses hope for a new age in which evil in all its forms will be banished, points to the social location of these prophetic voices within first-century Judean society. They are operating on the margins, literally and metaphorically. It is this social aspect of John's ministry that Josephus highlights, possibly ignoring his implied criticism of the temple because of his own priestly connections (*Life* 1-2, 80). Unlike Mark's account of John's death as the result of Antipas's drunken oath and Herodias's desire for revenge, Josephus tells us that John, imprisoned at Machaerus, was put to death because of his popularity with the crowds who responded enthusiastically to his call for "justice toward all." Antipas feared an insurrection and thought it better to preempt any disturbance by having John dispatched (*Ant* 18.118). Clearly, Judean society, or at least a sizable proportion of it, was divided between allegiance to the central symbol system and its guardians and concern about the social deprivation and distance from the power structures that the populace at large was experiencing. As we shall presently see, both aspects — the apocalyptic worldview *and* the passion for social justice — are hallmarks of Jesus' public ministry also, despite the change of location from the desert to the fertile region of Galilee.

By aligning himself so emphatically with John in the Q passage cited earlier, Jesus was inevitably placing himself in the public eye also. Yet curiously, as we have already noted, Antipas does not impinge at all on Jesus' Galilean ministry in the earliest accounts. Only Luke reports that some

11. CD 1.10-12. This figure thus appears in the Damascus Document, an early Jewish work that was found in two medieval manuscripts, fragments of which have also been found in Qumran. The Teacher is usually regarded as the founder of the Qumran group, an inspired teacher who is also mentioned in the *pesharim* or biblical interpretations from Qumran. Some scholars have identified him with the High Priest ousted when the Maccabees took control of that office in the late second century B.C.E.

Pharisees warned Jesus about Antipas's threat, but in characteristic fashion Jesus restates his purpose and intention to continue with his message and ministry (Luke 13:31-32). It is interesting that the three Synoptic Evangelists mention that Jesus' coming into Galilee took place only after John's arrest (Mark 1:14; Matt 4:12; Luke 3:19-20). Was his return a flight from Antipas, who may have made Machaerus in Perea his residence, or a homecoming to Nazareth, or a mission to his native province with an urgent message?

The fact that his opening declaration was couched in a highly political statement about the imminent arrival of God's *basileia* or kingly rule leaves the matter in no doubt, as far as the Evangelists were concerned. However, now the strategy has changed from one of association with John's desert ministry toward those who came out to him to one of engaging with the people of Galilee. By traveling among them, healing their sick, and instructing them in the values of God's *basileia* through his own actions and lifestyle, Jesus was directly but subtly challenging the values that Rome and its collaborators were espousing. If the Evangelists decided to tell this story without including Antipas directly in the plot, that is indeed understandable given their audiences and their purpose. Yet it should not lure us into ignoring the real presence of mediated Roman power that Jesus would have encountered at every turn, in Galilee and in Jerusalem, as was discussed in the previous chapters.

"Beginning in Galilee"

We may well ask: Why Galilee? One might have expected that Jesus, like other country prophets before and after him, would have gone directly to Jerusalem, there to announce his message about the imminent arrival of God's kingly rule. Indeed, in one recent account of his life, the author, Joseph Ratzinger (Pope Benedict XVI), suggests just that, prioritizing the Johannine gospel rather than the Synoptics.[12] Whereas the latter suggest at most one year of public ministry culminating in the Passover at which Jesus was arrested and crucified, the Fourth Gospel mentions three and possibly four Passovers, the Passover, of course, being an annual festival.[13]

12. Joseph Ratzinger (Pope Benedict XVI), *Jesus of Nazareth* (New York: Doubleday, 2007), especially 218-37.

13. The date for the beginning of Jesus' public ministry is computed on the basis of Luke's statement that Jesus was thirty years old when he began his public ministry (Luke 3:23), taken in conjunction with the assumption that he was born toward the end of Herod

Most commentators do opt for the Johannine timeframe or some variant of it on the basis that one year is too brief a period for the activity and movement attributed to Jesus even in the Synoptics. Ratzinger's suggestion that, had Jesus gone to Galilee, he could have avoided any confrontation with the Judean authorities would appear to be wide of the mark, however, in view of what we have seen about Judean influences and concerns among the Galileans in previous chapters. Nor can it be claimed, as some have, that Jesus wished to confront the Hellenistic/pagan culture of Galilee directly. As previously discussed, such suggestions are based on the misunderstanding that Isaiah's description "Galilee of the Gentiles" implied that the region continued to be largely pagan even in the first century B.C.E. In fact, the likelihood was that there was just as much if not more interest in and contact with the Greek world in urban Jerusalem, especially among the elite upper classes, than was the case in rural Galilee.

A better approach to this question is to examine those aspects of the Galilean situation with which Jesus' ministry there can be shown to have been particularly concerned. In the previous chapter we have seen that there has been considerable recent discussion of the economic and social world that Jesus encountered in Galilee, and we shall return to this issue later in this chapter also. However, there are two other aspects of the Galilean situation that seem to be important for Jesus based on his actions, namely, the tribal and the geographical associations of the region. While I no longer follow Alt's or Horsley's idea that there was an old Israelite population still living in Galilee in the first century C.E., I do concur that these aspects of Galilee's past were important and significant for the Judean immigrants and their progeny, as well as for any would-be messianic prophet figure who might appear among them.

Some scholars have suggested that the establishment of the Twelve as a group should not be attributed to the life of the earthly Jesus but was rather a creation of the early church as it sought to establish claims to being the new Israel. However, such a suggestion is highly improbable on critical grounds. Our two earliest written sources, Mark and Q, are aware of

---

the Great's reign, that is, 6 B.C.E., on the basis of Matthew's account of the slaughter of the innocents. Luke also says that John the Baptist began his mission in the fifteenth year of the reign of Tiberius, which would be 26 or 28 C.E., depending on whether the two years of his coregency with Augustus are taken into account. 28 C.E. is the more likely date, indicating that Jesus began his public ministry sometime shortly thereafter and died at the Passover of 31 C.E., on the supposition of a three-year public ministry, following the Johannine scheme. For a detailed discussion, see Meier, A Marginal Jew, 1:372-433.

the group's existence and identity, and the notion of the restoration of the twelve tribes was a regular motif in Second Temple restoration literature. Jesus' promise that his disciples would sit on thrones "judging the twelve tribes of Israel" in the future reign of the Son of Man (Matt 19:28; Luke 22:28-30) fits into such a scenario of a restoration to come in which all Israel will at last attain its allotted role as one people, north and south.[14]

Of the four northern tribes, Naphtali and Zebulun retained their Israelite identity until the conquest of 732 B.C.E., since both are mentioned in the account of the Assyrian conquest of the north and in Isaiah's promise of restoration to come (2 Kgs 15:29; Isa 8:23[9:1]). The other two, Asher and Dan, appear to have been less successful in maintaining a separate identity since they are not mentioned by Isaiah and instead we hear of "Galilee of the Gentiles" and "the way of the Sea" as other regions that can hope for future redemption. Both tribes were vulnerable to non-Yahwistic influences, since both were chided in the ancient Song of Deborah for their failure to answer a call to arms against Jabin. the Canaanite king of Hazor, as the northern tribes struggled to obtain control of the allotted land (Judg 5:17). Both tribes are said to have found the benefits of maritime activity too alluring, a charge that suggests that they may have over time been absorbed into the culture of the seafaring Phoenicians.[15]

If we interpret Jesus' going first to Galilee rather than to Jerusalem against this background of tribal claims and failures, the association of his mission with the hopes for the restoration of the tribes would seem to be quite deliberate. The schism that had separated north from south after the death of Solomon had driven a wedge between David's royal city and the land of Israel. A certain sense of superiority was associated with Judah in the literature emanating from Jerusalem, as in the blessings of Jacob, where Judah's prowess is praised by the other tribes and Judah is designated as the future holder of the royal scepter for the messianic king who is to come (Gen 49:8-10).

This preeminent role for Judah among the tribes is based on the promise to David that his house would rule forever, a promise that became the basis for the expectation of a Son of David as the messianic figure in later literature, and explains the views attributed to the Jerusalem populace

14. S. Freyne, *The Twelve: Disciples and Apostles: An Introduction to the Theology of the First Three Gospels* (London: Sheed and Ward, 1980); Meier, *Jesus: A Marginal Jew*, 3:125-97.

15. For a more detailed discussion of the conquest and tribal structure of early Israel, see S. Freyne, *Jesus, a Jewish Galilean: A New Reading of the Jesus Story* (New York: Continuum, 2005), 60-91.

in John 7, discussed above (2 Sam 7:4-17; cf. Mark 12:35-37). As David's city, Jerusalem continued to take on an increasingly sacral character through the centralization of the worship in the temple there following the cultic reform of Josiah in the seventh century B.C.E. (Deut 16:2). Prophets such as Isaiah developed further the myth of Yahweh's presence on Mount Zion, to which the nations will also stream on pilgrimage (Isa 2:2-3). This picture was reinforced in various festal psalms sung by pilgrims, including presumably Jesus and his family, as they approached Mount Zion, "an unshakable fortress" because "God is within" (Psalms 46-48).

Despite this special focus on Jerusalem because of the presence of Yahweh, the promises associated with the coming of the Messiah from Judah included all Israel within their compass. Thus, the oracle of salvation for the north that mentions the Galilean tribes (Isa 8:23 [9:1]) functions as an introduction to a joyful poem with strong messianic coloring. It celebrates the arrival of the Messiah king in the form of a child whose birth signals an end to war, whose names include the titles of Wonderful Counselor and Prince of Peace, and who will rule with justice and integrity (9:2-6). A later oracle in a similar vein celebrates "a shoot from the stock of Jesse" (David's father) who is endowed with the spirit of wisdom and understanding and whose integrity will ensure justice for the poor of the land (Isa 11:1-9). While this second poem does not refer explicitly to the tribes, its immediate sequel continues the motif of national harmony by announcing that Ephraim will no longer be jealous of Judah, nor Judah of Ephraim. Together they will take charge of the land, and Yahweh will make a pathway for the remnant of his people left from the exile in Assyria (vv. 10-16).

The election of the Twelve as a symbolic statement about the meaning and purpose of Jesus' ministry had a strong messianic subtext, therefore, even though he never made a direct claim to be the Messiah during his public ministry, as we shall presently discuss. Closely related to the tribal issue is that of the boundaries of the Promised Land and the possible significance of Jesus' journeys outside the political Galilee of his day. In the account of the conquest of the Promised Land by the northern tribes, a section described as "the land remaining" is mentioned as not having been captured. Its boundaries are described in relation to certain named places in southern Lebanon, reaching as far north as the pass of Hamath, through which the Litani River flows (Josh 13:2-6). While neither ancient Israel nor the Hasmoneans actually controlled this whole region, it continued to be included within the borders of the ideal Israel in various accounts of the boundaries of the allotted land, which are quite separate from the tribal boundaries (Ezek 47:15; Num 34:7-9). This idea of a "greater Israel" continued to have some currency in later Judean literature also, not least in the Genesis Apocryphon from Qumran, in which Abraham's journeys through the land, as described in Gen 13:14-18, are greatly expanded. According to this Qumran text Abraham, in a night vision, saw himself traveling from the Great Sea (the Mediterranean) to the Euphrates and from the Taurus mountains in the north to the Red Sea in the south. He then returned and built an altar "to the God most high," having been joined by three Amorite brothers who "were his friends."[16]

According to Mark, Jesus' reputation traveled throughout the whole "outer circle" *(perichōron)* of Galilee (Mark 1:28). Later in the narrative Mark presents Jesus himself traveling in the borders of Tyre and Sidon, in the Dekapolis region, and in the district of Caesarea Philippi under Mount Hermon (Mark 5:1, 20; 7:24, 31; 8:27). While all these places were, as we saw in the first chapter, thoroughly Hellenized and not part of the Judean territory, the question arises as to why Mark and, following him, Matthew feel free to present such a picture of border crossing.[17] Some scholars have dismissed this information as part of the narrative framework of Mark's story that has very little historical value, and others attribute it to a desire of the later community to predate the opening of the Gentile mission to Jesus' own day. However, while these notices do indeed shed light on the situation in Mark's day (post-70 C.E.), as we shall argue in a later chapter, the idea of the "greater Israel" does suggest a plausible scenario for understanding Jesus' actual journeys as well.

This sense of surrounding territories and their relationship to the land of Israel was well understood by the later rabbis also. Thus, for example, the Mishnah declares that as far as the obligation of bringing gifts to the temple was concerned, "one who owns a plot of land in Syria is like one who owns one in the outskirts of Jerusalem" (*Hallah* 4.11). There is also evidence of rabbinic preoccupation with defining the borders of the land, especially in western Galilee, bordering on the territory of Tyre. When these are compared with Josephus's account of the same border in 66 C.E., it is clear that the territory of Jewish Galilee had shrunk somewhat and that in traveling to

16. 1QapGen 21. On the notion of a "greater Israel" in the restoration literature of the Second Temple period, see S. Freyne, "The Geography of Restoration: Galilee-Jerusalem Relations in Early Jewish and Christian Experience," *NTS* 47 (2001), 289-311, especially 292-97.

17. Luke omits these forays into the Gentile territory, presumably because he sees the mission as expanding from Jerusalem, as he recounts the movement out from Jerusalem in his second volume, the Acts of the Apostles.

the "borders of Tyre" Jesus was in fact operating within what had once been claimed as the land of Israel and therefore of interest to a Judean prophet/preacher intent on proclaiming the imminent arrival of God's kingly rule to all Israel.[18]

The story of Jesus' encounter with the Syro-Phoenician woman on the borders of Tyre (Mark 7:24-30) does raise the more general question of Jesus' attitude toward and concern for non-Jews. His initial response to her request was typical of ethnocentric Judean views of Gentiles, even if his qualifier of the need for the children to be fed *first* does suggest that others are not thereby excluded. Yet her response, her *logos* or reasoned reply as Mark describes it, suggests that both she and he belong in the same household and eat at the same time, albeit in different positions, and it brought about a change of outlook on his part. Without Jesus actually visiting the woman's house, the demon departed from the child, not because of the woman's faith (as Matthew supplies in his version of the story, Matt 15:21-28) but because of her word, a creative declaration that opens Jesus up to the reality of a messianic banquet where Jew and non-Jew share equally at the same table.[19]

Nevertheless, Jesus' reply to the woman was based on the principle of Jew first and then Gentile, arising from the notion of the special election of Israel according to the divine plan, a view shared by Paul also (Rom 1:16). From a more general Judean perspective, the ways in which the Gentiles might share in the future salvation varied, from the notion of the nations streaming toward Zion to partake of its wisdom to the idea of their inclusion by God in the great eschatological drama that would unfold eventually. In the interim, individual Gentiles could fully convert to Judaism by undergoing circumcision (becoming proselytes), or worship the God of Israel (as God-fearers), or even be acknowledged as righteous Gentiles, as some rabbis declared.[20]

---

18. In a text known as "the Baraita of the Borders," two detailed lists of villages in western Galilee are given. One deals with the "forbidden villages in the territory of Tyre" and the other describes the borders of "the land held by those who came up from Babylon." These lists may well have originated during the Hasmonean conquest of the north, or they may reflect later rabbinic idealizations of the land. Either way they indicate a concern with defining the land for purposes of observance of such demands of the Torah as payment of tithes and the obligation to bring other offerings.

19. P. Alonso, "The Woman Who Changed Jesus: Texts and Contexts," in R. A. Lassale-Klein, ed., *Jesus of Galilee: Contextual Christology for the 21st Century* (Maryknoll: Orbis, 2011), 121-34.

20. J. Jeremias, *Jesus' Promise to the Nations* (London: SCM, 1958).

Jesus favored the idea of the eschatological banquet, especially when confronted with rejection by some of the more zealous of his coreligionists such as the Pharisees. A Q saying that draws on a frequently used image of the scattered Israelites in exile returning from east and west, north and south, is reinterpreted to apply to the banquet for "all peoples being prepared on this holy mountain" (Isa 25:6-8).[21] Those who are now refusing to listen to Jesus' urgent invitation will be envious on being excluded from the celebration, which includes the patriarchs Abraham, Isaac, and Jacob (Q Matt 8:11-12; Luke 13:28-29). Mention of these three figures, especially Abraham, to whom the promise was made that "all the nations of the earth would be blessed in him," indicates that Jesus had in mind not just the Israelite exiles but Gentiles as well. Indeed his parable of "the banquet," in which outsiders are included as replacement for those who were invited but refused to come, makes the same point in a provocative and pointed manner (Matt 22:1-14; Luke 14:16-24; cf. *Gospel of Thomas* 64).

It is not that, like Paul, Jesus was forced to change the focus of his mission from Israel to the nations. His familiarity with the biblical stories and characters ensures that he could never have entertained a purely ethnocentric view of God's care, which was directed to the whole of the creation. Indeed his declaration that he "had not seen such faith in Israel" when he encountered the plea of a centurion to heal his son balances somewhat his rather abrupt response to the Syro-Phoenician woman (Matt 8:10). As a skilled wisdom teacher, part of his strategy was to draw on older images such as the symbol of the Twelve or that of the returning exiles and reinterpret these in the light of his own understanding and vision. Thus, while the Twelve recalls the structure of early Israel, Jesus was unconcerned about tribal boundaries and territories, issues that had given rise to internecine struggles and violence over the centuries. Nor did he think of reconquering "ancestral lands" by force as the Hasmoneans had done in their efforts to re-create the "greater Israel" (1 Macc 15:33). Perhaps the single most remarkable saying in his teaching is the injunction to "love your enemies" (Matt 5:44-45), where "enemy" should not be construed merely in terms of individuals but rather to include neighboring nations as well, who were traditionally viewed as hostile and enemies of Israel.[22]

These considerations concerning Jesus' decision to begin his ministry

---

21. Isa 43:5-7; 49:12; Zech 8:7-8; Bar 5:5; *Psalms of Solomon* 11:2; *1 Enoch* 57.1.

22. R. Horsley, "Ethics and Exegesis: 'Love Your Enemies' and the Doctrine of Non-Violence," *JAAR* 54 (1985), 3-31.

in Galilee can assist in addressing the question posed at the outset of this section. A prophetic figure who felt charged to proclaim God's kingly rule to all Israel may well have decided to begin in Galilee, since it was there that the breakdown of the old tribal league first occurred with the disappearance of Asher and Dan. Memories of the subsequent schism and breakup of David's kingdom were still alive in the region, as two inscriptions from different periods from Tel Dan suggest.[23] The institution of the Twelve points to a desire to return to pre-monarchic realities, even though some people were prepared to greet Jesus as the son of David, the ideal earthly king who would restore Israel's fortunes to their former glory. However, Jesus rejected such a temptation, since his call was pointing in another direction that would challenge all human notions of kingship, Israelite, Judean, Greek, and Roman. His would be a different way with different values.

Discerning Jesus' Role

In seeking a better understanding of Jesus' ministry in Galilee and Jerusalem, it is important to distinguish between the roles ascribed to him by various segments of the population and the role that he himself regarded as the true expression of his own self-understanding, which was confirmed for him at his baptism according to all the accounts.[24] When he put the

23. Fragments of a ninth-century B.C.E. Aramaic stele referring to an Israelite king and "the house of David" have been discovered outside the ancient gate at Tel Dan. See A. Biran and J. Naveh, "An Aramaic Stele Fragment from Tel Dan," *IEJ* 43 (1993), 81-98. A second bilingual (Greek and Aramaic) inscription from the Hellenistic period dedicated to "the God who is in Dan" has also been discovered. See A. Biran, "To the God Who Is in Dan," in Biran, ed., *Temples and High Places in Biblical Times* (Jerusalem: Hebrew Union College, 1981), 142-51. Biran discovered this inscription in a cultic setting at Tel Dan and leaves open the possibility that, because the God in question is not named but is associated with the Danites *(en Danois)*, Zoilos, who made the vow, may have intended the Israelite God. However, V. Tzaferis, "The 'God Who Is in Dan' and the cult of Pan at Banias in the Hellenistic and Roman Periods," *Eretz Israel* 23 (1992), 128-35, has suggested that the inscription refers to the god Pan, whose shrine is located just a few km to the east of Tel Dan.

24. Jesus' baptism in the context of John's ministry is mentioned in all the canonical gospels. Because the event clearly caused problems for later Christian claims about Jesus' sinlessness, as can be seen, e.g., in the discussion between John and Jesus as reported by Matthew (Matt 3:13-15), it is highly unlikely that the *fact* of the baptism was invented by later Christians. While the Fourth Gospel does not say directly that Jesus was baptized by John, nevertheless John connects the purpose of his ministry with revealing Jesus to Israel (John 1:31). Mythological features such as the voice from heaven and the descent of the dove do

question to his disciples as to who people thought he was, the answer he received was revealing: "Some say John the Baptist, others Elijah, and others still one of the prophets." Jesus insisted, "But you, who do you say that I am?" Peter answered him, "You are the Messiah (Christ)." "And he sternly charged them not to tell anyone about him" (Mark 8:27-30).

In this exchange a distinction emerges between what people generally thought of Jesus and what the inner circle of his followers were expected to think about the matter. Popular opinion varied, but, interestingly, there is no mention of a royal Messiah but rather an emphasis on a prophetic figure, whether it be John *redivivus* (cf. Mark 6:14), Elijah, who was expected to return before the end and make such preparations as restoring the scattered tribes of Jacob (Sir 48:10), or still another promised prophet like Moses (Deut 18:18). As spokesperson for the group, Peter's answer indicates that they were thinking of a royal figure, "the anointed one." Mark, in fact, confirms this later in his narrative when he reports that James and John asked for special places in Jesus' kingdom, which they were apparently anticipating would come about in Jerusalem (cf. Mark 10:35-37). That request was quickly dismissed, just as Peter's confession was sidestepped with the order not to tell anyone about the royal claim. Rather than building on Peter's confession, Jesus immediately begins to refer to his own fate under a highly enigmatic designation, namely, "the son of man," however we are to understand his usage of this image based on the book of Daniel.[25]

Jesus' command to Peter to keep silent fits into a recurring pattern in Mark's gospel, one that has given rise to the theory that Mark has generated the notion of the "messianic secret" as part of his presentation of Jesus'

---

reflect later theologizing about the event, but there is no good reason to doubt that this experience was highly significant in the career of Jesus. For a full discussion of all the issues, see Meier, *A Marginal Jew* 2:100-130.

25. On the basis of some usage in rabbinic writings, G. Vermes, *Jesus the Jew: A Historian's Reading of the Gospels* (London: Collins, 1973), 162-68, has proposed that the Hebrew expression *bar 'enash* (son of man) is a synonym for the Aramaic *hahu gabra* meaning "that man." It thus serves as a circumlocution for "I" or "this one here," sometimes meaning the speaker himself, and it is in this sense that it is used in many gospel instances. Vermes claims that the appeal by most New Testament scholars to "one like a Son of Man" of Dan 7:13 as determining Jesus' usage is misplaced because it fails to take account of regular Palestinian linguistic usage or recognize the phrase's non-titular signification in Jewish literature. For a counter-position, cf. A. Yarbro Collins, "The Influence of Daniel in the New Testament," in J. J. Collins, *Daniel: A Commentary on the Book of Daniel* (Hermeneia; Minneapolis: Augsburg-Fortress, 1993), 90-112.

career.[26] While such a claim has indeed considerable merit, which will be discussed in a later chapter, a good case can also be made for ascribing this trait in the tradition to Jesus' own reticence about his role during his earthly ministry. In an early Q passage that is quite independent of Mark, Jesus refuses to give a direct answer to the disciples of John who were sent to enquire whether he was "the one who is to come." Instead of answering the question, Jesus tells them to report to John what they have heard and seen, alluding to several passages in Isaiah that could reasonably be associated with the Messiah's activity (Q Luke 7:18-23 / Matt 11:2-6). Both versions of the incident end with the enigmatic comment of Jesus: "Blessed is the one who finds in me nothing that will make him stumble." While the answer to John's question is unmistakably "Yes," Jesus recognizes that aspects of his ministry may indeed be shocking for some of his contemporaries. Yet the manner of his communication is deliberately indirect, avoiding as far as possible any title, while subtly indicating that he is not following any ascribed role, even one that could be legitimated by appeal to Scripture. It was for God, not humans, to decide under what conditions the true meaning of the messianic role would be revealed and to whom it should apply.[27]

As already mentioned, the precise role of the Messiah varied among different circles of Judean society of the period. However, by far the most widely expected figure was that of an ideal king, who would not only rid Israel of injustice and foreign domination, but would usher in an era of peace and prosperity. This was in accordance with the various expressions of messianic hope in the literature, reaching as far back as Isaiah. Because of the militarism of the later Hasmoneans, some depictions of the future ideal king were indeed warlike and hostile to outsiders (*Pss. Sol.* 17:22-25). As we shall presently discuss, Jesus' career of "preaching good news to the poor" and "the liberation of captives" did not fit such an image, and yet his death by crucifixion is indicative of the public threat he posed to Roman and some Judean interests alike.

26. The theory that the messianic secret was a creation by the early church dates back to W. Wrede, *The Messianic Secret in the Gospels* (Reprint, London: Clarke, 1971; first published in 1901). For Wrede, Jesus' concealment of his messianic status was a theological idea of the Evangelist rather than a historical fact. He based this view on, among other features, the gospel's frequent commands to silence: Mark 1:34, 43-45; 3:12; 5:43; 7:36; 8:26, 30; 9:9. Cf. C. Tuckett, ed., *The Messianic Secret* (London: SPCK, 1983), for more recent discussions of the issue.

27. For a stimulating discussion of this aspect of Jesus' self-communication, see B. Meyer, "Jesus' Ministry and Self-Understanding," in B. Chilton and C. Evans, eds., *Studying the Historical Jesus: Evaluations of the Current State of Research* (Leiden: Brill, 1994), 337-52.

It is surely significant that the only "outside" opinion of Jesus other than that reported by Peter, that of the Judean Josephus, corroborates the gospels' account of a ministry of word and work. It is generally accepted that Christian scribes have embellished the so-called *Testimonium Flavianum* in the course of its transmission. However, these later additions are readily discernible, and when they are expunged there is still an important statement about Jesus:

> At this time there appeared Jesus, a wise man, *if indeed one ought to call him a man.* For he was a doer of amazing deeds, a teacher of people who receive the truth gladly. He won over many of the Jews and many of the Greeks. *He was the Messiah.* When Pilate, upon hearing him accused by men of the highest standing among us, had condemned him to be crucified, those who had in the first place come to love him did not give up their affection for him. *For he appeared to them the third day alive again, the divine prophecies having spoken these things and a myriad of other marvels because of him. And the tribe of the Christians, so-called after him, has still to this day not disappeared.* (*Ant* 18.63-64)[28]

That Josephus himself did not rely on Christian witnesses about Jesus' activity emerges from the vocabulary he employs. Jesus is said to be a "doer of amazing/startling deeds" *(poiētēs paradoxōn ergōn)*. *Paradoxa* does not appear in the NT in relation to the works of Jesus, which are typically called *erga* (deeds), *sēmeia* (signs), or *dynameis* (deeds of power). These terms relate to LXX usage in regard to God's acts of creation and redemption, whereas *paradoxa* in connection with *erga* has more the nuance of strange or unusual deeds. Indeed while Josephus uses the word quite frequently in other contexts, it only appears twice in relation to deeds, here as descriptive of Jesus' actions and in *Ant* 9.182 in regard to Elisha, another Galilean prophet and wonder-worker.

---

28. Meier, *A Marginal Jew,* 2:56-88, has a detailed discussion of the passage and the issue of interpolations. Even in the edited version of the text without the phrases italicized here, he notes some differences from the Evangelists: the idea that Jesus evangelized both Jews and Greeks, the fact that no reason is given for Pilate's condemnation, and the modified role of the Jews. However, all three issues can be resolved given that Josephus was himself a Jewish priestly aristocrat and unlikely to paint his fellow aristocrats in a bad light on this issue. When he was writing *Antiquities* in the last decades of the first century, the Christian community did indeed have many Greeks among its members. In the context of *Ant* 18, Pilate's action against Jesus is part of a sequence of stories in which Pilate shows little respect for Judean religious sensitivities. The action against Jesus serves as another example of his hostility.

In a similar vein, the description of Jesus as a teacher differs somewhat from NT usage. Josephus describes Jesus as a wise *(sophos)* man, and qualifies this by adding "a teacher *(didaskalos)* of those who receive the truth gladly." This latter phrase refers to the eagerness of Jesus' audiences rather than the claims of Jesus' teaching per se. Nevertheless, the designations "wise man" and "teacher" accurately reflect both the genre and content of Jesus' instruction and the recognition he received, even on occasion from enemies, as a mode of address: *rabbi/didaskale.*

In attempting to evaluate the likely impact of Jesus' deeds and words it will be important to recall the results of the discussion in previous chapters. It was suggested that the amalgam of Greek culture, Roman presence, and changing economic and social structures brought about a conflict of values in all of Judean society. Because much of Jesus' public ministry was conducted in Galilee, according to our earliest sources, it was there that one can best capture the impact of his ministry while keeping the symbiotic relationship that many Galileans had with the Jerusalem center in mind also. This relationship existed, even when those in power there often showed little concern for the mere provincials who were deemed suspect in terms of their knowledge of and commitment to some of the teaching emanating from one or another of the competing groups. The Jerusalem center had gradually become dysfunctional in terms of its primary responsibility as the seat of the divine presence for all Israel because of the power alliances that had been entered into with the officers of Roman rule. The popularity of Jesus as a teacher and the unquestioning acceptance of his healings must be attributed, in part at least, to the fact that his own ascetic lifestyle and demeanor differed from that of official teachers, thereby clothing his actions with an aura of the divine in the popular mind and his teachings with a sense of authenticity.

The Messianic Deeds of Jesus

The terminology used by the Evangelists for the deeds of Jesus removes them from the realm of thaumaturgic activity, locating them rather in the sphere of God's continual care for his people. It is worth noting that the scribes who came down from Jerusalem in Mark's account, did not question the *fact* of Jesus' exorcisms, but rather the *source* of his power: "This one casts out demons by Beelzebul, the prince of demons" (Mark 3:22; cf. Q Luke 11:15/Matt 12:24). Such a charge is a classic example of those in power seeking to vilify others whose popularity and success with the crowds threaten their own authority. Mark stresses the fact that they had come from Jerusalem, thereby signaling the ways in which the center sought to control the periphery and giving the episode a formal tone.

However, Jesus' response is to underline the source of his power, namely, the Spirit of God.[29] At the same time, he signals the real threat that his actions pose for those in power, Roman and Judean alike. By introducing the notion of the demonic, the Jerusalem authorities were already placing the issue within the larger cosmic framework of current apocalyptic thinking, in which it was believed that heavenly forces of good and evil were engaged in an ongoing struggle that replicates those of humans on earth. Jesus, as we shall see, shared that worldview also, and his reply highlights his confidence that God's kingdom, not that of Beelzebul, will eventually prevail (see Luke 10:18).[30] There were political implications to the charge and the response, however, since the apocalyptic worldview had strong resonances in the context of oppression and social exclusion. The book of Daniel is the earliest example in the Jewish world of a response to the threat of Antiochus Epiphanes. Thereafter this genre became highly influential among dissident groups, such as the Essenes, who felt socially and politically excluded. It is no surprise therefore, that Jesus and his followers should also avail themselves of the strategy afforded by the genre, since it allowed those who otherwise felt excluded to imagine a very different world order to that which was now causing so much distress.

29. In Mark's account, the source of Jesus' power, namely, the Spirit, is implied in the final declaration that the scribes are guilty of an eternal sin of blasphemy against the Holy Spirit (Mark 3:29). The Q version shared by Matthew and Luke differs slightly from Mark in that the charge is made by the Pharisees (Matthew) or "some of the crowd" (Luke). In this version, Jesus speaks directly to the opponents, alluding to the fact that some of their children were also involved in exorcisms of which he approved: "If I by the finger [Matthew 'Spirit'] of God cast out demons, by whom do your children cast them out?" (Luke 11:19-20; Matt 12:27-28). It is generally accepted that Luke's reference to "finger of God" is the more original, recalling as it does the reaction of the Egyptian sorcerers to the plague which Moses and Aaron had brought on the people (Exod 8:19). See also Hengel and Schwemer, *Jesus und das Judentum*, 429.

30. C. Grappe, "Jésus Exorciste à la Lumière des Pratiques et des Attentes de son Temps," *RB* 110 (2003), 178-96, draws attention to the fact that several Jewish texts from the Second Temple period, including some from Qumran, point to the simultaneous arrival of the kingdom of God and the defeat of Satan. The fact that after several of his acts of healing and exorcism Jesus is hailed by his audience as "the son of David," especially in Matthew, also recalls the power that is attributed to Solomon, a son of David, as healer because of his knowledge of all wisdom (see 1 Kgs 4:29-34; Wis 7:17-20; Josephus, *Ant* 8.42-49).

Against this background, the political implications of Jesus' reply to the Jerusalem scribes become more apparent. His choice of the images of divided houses and kingdoms that will inevitably collapse must have had an immediate impact on his hearers (Mark 3:24-25). These are not generalized images but rather ones that would immediately resonate with audiences in first-century Galilee and Jerusalem. Within living memory Augustus had divided Herod the Great's kingdom into three segments, and one of these, Judea, had quickly devolved into a Roman procuratorship due to Archelaus's treatment of his subjects. It would be the end of the first century before the last of the Herodians, Agrippa II, would depart from the stage, but it must have been obvious to many already in the time of Antipas that neither he nor any of his clan would ever attain his ambition of becoming king of the Jews. Divided "houses" are houses that are doomed.[31]

Equally the "house of Israel" was a dangerously divided house in the first century, something that emerged in the clear light of day during the first revolt in 66 C.E. According to Josephus, different philosophies emerged for the first time in the reign of John Hyrcanus, and thereafter the Pharisees and the Sadducees vied for power within the theocracy that was Judea, with the Essenes engaged in developing an alternative commonwealth in the desert. Indeed Jesus' own renewal movement, addressing itself to "all Israel," as we have seen, was already seeking to heal the divisions, political and religious, that had emerged within Judean society in his day. The movement continued to address itself to this vision of the Master even after his death, but with no lasting success, as far as the ideal of "all Israel" was concerned. It would be several centuries before rabbinic Judaism and catholic Christianity would emerge as two opposing "houses" arising from the same original source. But that story too is for a later chapter.

The Beelzebul controversy opens up a much larger window, therefore, on the activity of Jesus and its possible ramifications. Mark, more than the other Evangelists, sees Jesus' healing ministry as one of exorcisms. In this he aligns Jesus with folk medicine as this was practiced throughout the Mediterranean world rather than with the more scientific approach to illness that was beginning to be current, especially in the Greek world. However, there was a fine line between the two approaches and they could easily overlap. Even Luke, who traditionally is believed to have been a physician, often combines a medical description of a condition with the more traditional

31. S. Freyne, "Jesus and the Urban Culture of Galilee," in *Galilee and Gospel: Collected Essays* (WUNT 125; Tübingen: Mohr Siebeck, 2000), 183-207, especially 199-203.

understanding of the bodily invasion of a person by an evil spirit that needs to be expelled.[32]

By retaining, for the most part, the folkloric approach in his description of Jesus' healings, Mark assists in our understanding of the social and political aspects of Jesus' work as this was perceived by his contemporaries. Some modern discussions of healthcare systems in the ancient world place the focus on illness as a social construct as distinct from disease as a biological condition. Whereas diseases were beginning to be understood scientifically in the first century, illness involved community decisions as to who can and cannot be included within a particular social arrangement. In this scenario, illness is seen as deviance from accepted cultural and social norms, thereby warranting stigmatization or even exclusion from the group and its activities.[33] An example of such stigmatization is the strictness of the regulations with regard to the participation of lepers in the temple worship (Leviticus 14–15). The blind and the lame were also excluded from the temple, according to 2 Sam 5:8, a regulation that the Essenes also practiced, according to the Annex to the Community Rule (1QSa 2.4, 9).

Several of the Markan exorcism stories illustrate Jesus' rejection of such taboos. At Mark 1:40-44 Jesus does not hesitate to touch a leper who has asked for healing, something that would be deemed to violate the purity laws, according to Leviticus. At this point, however, Jesus does follow the Levitical instruction, namely, that the leper must have himself examined by the priest before rejoining the cultic community, thereby respecting its cultural norms. In the case of the Gadarene demoniac (Mark 5:1-20), no such regulation applies, since Jesus is dealing with a Gentile. Once again, however, the effect of Jesus' dismissal of the legion of demons is to restore the man "to his right mind," and he is ordered to return home. His new condition differs markedly from the previous situation in which nobody was able to restrain him. The Syro-Phoenician woman's daughter is found without the invading demon after the mother has persuaded Jesus that she and he both belong to the same household (Mark 7:24-30). Finally, in the

32. A. Weisenrieder, *Images of Illness in the Gospel of Luke* (WUNT 164; Tübingen: Mohr Siebeck, 2003), 304-5, discusses this aspect of Luke's stories of healing.

33. Weisenrieder, *Images of Illness*, 43-64; J. Pilch, "Healing in Mark: A Social Science Analysis," *BTB* 15 (1985), 142-50; *Healing in the New Testament: Insights from Medical and Mediterranean Anthropology* (Minneapolis: Fortress, 2000); H. Avalos, *Health Care and the Rise of Christianity* (Peabody: Hendrickson, 1999); Y. Eliav, "Medicine and Hygiene," in J. J. Collins and D. Harlow, eds., *The Eerdmans Dictionary of Early Judaism* (Grand Rapids: Eerdmans, 2010), 929-31.

case of the possessed deaf and dumb boy whose father beseeches Jesus to assist, the demon is expelled in a highly dramatic scene in which the father's faith plays a part, and again the boy is restored to his parent, so that normal relationships can be reestablished (Mark 9:14-28).

Some other exorcism stories in Mark have a more mythological dimension. The demons recognize Jesus and engage in a contest with him by claiming to know his name as Son of God or Son of the Holy One, thereby claiming control over him (Mark 1:24, 34; 3:11-12; 5:7). In each case Jesus silences them, thereby displaying his greater power as a sign that God's kingly rule will prevail in God's time, as the Beelzebul episode proclaimed. Other stories refer to healing without any overt demonic presence. Thus in the case of Peter's mother-in-law we hear that Jesus took her by the hand and raised her up and that the fever left her, reflecting a view of the illness as an invasive force (1:29-31). Two cures, one of a deaf and dumb man and the other of a blind man (7:31-35 and 8:22-26) are structured in a similar way: in both instances Jesus functions more as a traditional folk healer, performing the cure separately, away from the crowd and applying spittle to the malfunctioning body parts. In contrast to this very active healing ministry in Galilee, Jesus performed only one healing in Judea according to Mark, when he responded to the pleas of the blind man of Jericho by restoring his sight so that he followed Jesus on the pilgrim way that led to Jerusalem (10:46-52).[34]

Mark describes Jesus as a healer only once, and then obliquely. In answer to a complaint from "the scribes of the Pharisees" that Jesus was associating with classes of people whom they regarded as sinners, Jesus replied: "Those who are well have no need of a physician *(iatros),* but those who are ill" (Mark 2:17). Clearly, healing, in the sense of restoring to wholeness those who were marginalized socially or physically, was a hugely significant aspect of Jesus' career for both the Evangelist and his audience. In presenting Jesus as challenging the accepted norms with regard to various taboos, Jewish and pagan, the Evangelist is filling out the picture that Jesus had drawn already when responding to John the Baptist's query. There Jesus

---

34. As well as retaining the folkloric dimension, probably stemming from the oral tradition, these stories also serve the Evangelist well in his narrative presentation. Thus the cures of the deaf and dumb man and the blind man encase a passage which is highly critical of the Twelve's understanding of Jesus, in which Jesus queries them regarding their failure to *see* or *hear* what they have experienced (Mark 8:11-21). Likewise the blind man of Jericho who follows Jesus eagerly on the way is a real contrast to the disciples' timid and fearful following at 10:32.

appealed to passages in Isaiah that regarded healing as part of the messianic brief: "Go and relate to John what you have seen and heard: the blind receive their sight, the lame walk, lepers are cleansed, the deaf hear, the dead are raised, and the poor have good news preached to them" (Q Luke 7:18-23; Matt 11:2-6). A virtually identical selection of passages from Isaiah has been published from Qumran (4Q521). It is prefaced there with a direct reference to the Messiah: "Heaven and earth will listen to his Messiah."[35] Jesus' exorcisms/healings were an important aspect of his messianic claims, as far as his contemporaries were concerned, it would seem, and Mark also was quite aware of this in his presentation of Jesus' career as healer/exorcist.

In the opening chapter of this study attention was drawn to the healing centers that were found in the Jordan valley, and the issue of Jesus' healing activity as rivaling that of professional healers was touched on. It will be recalled that Josephus's description of the quality of the air and the water in the lake region recalled the instruction of the Hippocratic work *Airs, Places, and Waters,* which advises physicians *(iatroi),* on arriving in a new location, to examine these aspects of the environment thoroughly because of their importance for good health.[36] Could this aspect of the local environment have played a role in Jesus' choice of this region for much of his ministry, as described by all the Evangelists? At least it provides a context for understanding the social aspect of his healing ministry, especially since we hear that Josephus was brought to physicians at Capernaum when he was injured in a fall from his horse *(Life* 403-4). On the basis of the archaeological remains from places such as Hamath Gader and Hamath Tiberias, the health spas were frequented by the elites, and the physicians who were attached to such places were professionals to whom fees had to be paid.

One of Jesus' healings reported by Mark addresses this very topic in dramatic fashion (Mark 5:25-34).[37] A woman with an issue of blood for twelve years had attended many physicians and was not cured, but in fact had deteriorated. In the process she had spent all her money, suggesting that she must have been a wealthy widow. It is usual to interpret the wom-

---

35. This reply combines several discrete references from Isaiah: Isa 26:19; 29:18-19; 35:5-6. See J. J. Collins, *The Scepter and the Star: The Messiahs of the Dead Sea Scrolls and Other Ancient Literature* (Anchor Bible Reference Library; New York: Doubleday, 1995), 117-22, for a discussion of the Qumran text.

36. See Chapter 3 above, p. 120. Cf. W. H. S. Jones, trans. and ed., *Hippocrates* (Loeb Classical Library; New York: Putnam, 1923), 1:65-137.

37. R. von Bendeman, "Christus der Artz. Krankheitskonzepte in der Therapieerzählungen des Markus Evangeliums," *BZ* 54 (2010), 36-53, 162-70, here especially 46-51.

an's flow of blood in relation to the Jewish purity regulations concerning women's menstruation. Thus, the fact that she touched the hem of Jesus' garment would have meant that he incurred uncleanness according to the purity regulations of Leviticus. However, that is not the inference that Mark draws from the story. Rather the stress is on the failure of the physicians and the devastating cost to the woman. In this instance, Jesus does not perform any action but is merely aware of his healing power being accessed by the woman's touch of his garment. This detail merely highlights further the healing power of Jesus as a recognized *hasid,* or holy man, similar to other Jewish healers that we hear about in rabbinic sources. The impression of Jesus' healing ministry that Mark's story is intended to illustrate is the fact that, unlike the professionals who minister to the elites, Jesus' gift is freely open to all, rich and poor alike, as a sign of God's reign now occurring among the Galilean populace.[38]

"He Was a Wise Man, a Teacher of Those Who Receive the Truth Gladly"

By describing Jesus as a "wise man" Josephus locates him within the scribal tradition even though the Jerusalem authorities are said to have dismissed him as "not having studied" and therefore a member of the *am ha-aretz,* the unlettered people of the land (John 7:15). In the previous chapter we encountered a Jerusalemite of the same name from an earlier period, Jesus ben Sira, whose description of the privileged role of the scribe contrasts starkly with that of Jesus of Nazareth. Indeed ben Sira contrasts the role of the *tektōn* or craftsman (Sir 38:27), whose task it is to maintain "the fabric of the world," with his own superior position in society, engaged in foreign travel and acting as counselor to rulers and kings. The people of Jesus' own village, Nazareth, use the very same term to describe Jesus, as they wonder about the possible source of his wisdom: "Is not this the *tektōn,* the son of Mary and brother of James and Joses and Judas and Simon, and are not his sisters here with us?" (Mark 6:3). In all probability there were village scribes in Galilee also, men who had mastered the art of writing and whose task it

38. Vermes, *Jesus the Jew,* discusses Jesus within the setting of Hasidic Judaism. See especially the chapter entitled "Jesus and Charismatic Judaism," 58-85, which deals with miracle stories of several figures such as Hanina ben Dosa and Honi "the Circle Drawer" and the possible parallels with the gospel accounts of Jesus' actions.

was to keep official records, but Jesus and his family clearly did not belong to that class.[39]

In fact, wisdom as a way of viewing the world and as a profession was a broad category, ranging from the proverbial wisdom of the peasant at one end of the scale to that of the court advisor and diplomat at the other. Clearly, Jesus was much closer to the former than the latter, but that is merely indicative of the respective social standings of the practitioners rather than a barometer of the insights that each might possess. In addition to these two types a third should also be included, namely, the visionary with his revealed wisdom. In the Jewish context, the court scribe would have been formally schooled and is a teacher of wisdom with his own *beth midrash* or house of study focused on the Torah as the source of universal wisdom (Sir 51:23; see 24:1-29). The peasant, on the other hand, was the repository of ancient lore arising from human experience that was often cross-cultural and passed on orally from one generation to the next. It was based on observation of the rhythms of nature, the movements of the heavenly bodies, and the changes of the seasons. The visionary stands outside these two streams, is the recipient of revealed knowledge, usually communicated through visions, dreams, and oracles, and normally operates on the margins of society, avoiding cities but often attracting crowds, especially if he is deemed to have supernatural powers as well.[40]

The lines between these different types are by no means rigidly drawn, yet the "map" is helpful in clarifying Jesus' role as teacher within appropriate settings of Judean society. Clearly he does not fit into the first category, the members of which are among his bitterest opponents according to all the gospels. On the other hand, a perusal of his attributed sayings shows a combination of peasant wisdom and visionary insights, containing tropes such as the proverb based on observation and the apocalyptic revelation of coming events. There has been a tendency in some recent treatments of Jesus to expunge the apocalyptic elements from his sayings entirely on the assumption that wisdom and apocalyptic are two completely discrete genres

---

39. C. Keith, *Jesus' Literacy: Scribal Culture and the Teacher from Galilee* (Library of New Testament Studies, Edinburgh: Clark, 2011).

40. J. Z. Smith, "The Temple and the Magician," in W. Meeks and J. Jervell, eds., *God's Christ and His People: Studies in Honor of Nils Altsrup Dahl* (Bergen: Universtetsvorlaget, 1977), 233-47; G. Nickelsburg, "Revealed Wisdom as a Criterion for Inclusion and Exclusion: From Jewish Sectarianism to Early Christianity," in J. Neusner and E. Frerichs, eds., *"To See Ourselves as Others See Us": Jews, Christians and Others in Antiquity* (Brown Studies in the Humanities; Chico: Scholars, 1985), 73-92.

representing two very different worldviews. However, an examination of much of Second Temple literature, including the Qumran scrolls, makes it clear that this is by no means the case, and that wisdom and apocalyptic elements intermingle freely, belonging to the same worldview.[41] Indeed, two of the most prominent of Jesus' personal utterances, the "Our Father" prayer (Q Luke 11:2-4/Matt 6:9-13) and his so-called *Jubelruf* or joyful exclamation of thanksgiving to God (Q Luke 10:21/Matt 11:25-27), demonstrate the way in which these two dimensions of Jesus' consciousness fit very comfortably together as he addresses God with the intimate familial term "Abba."

The earliest version of the "Our Father," that found in Luke rather than Matthew, consists of a balanced structure of four petitions/wishes addressed directly to God after the opening praise of his name Abba/Father. The first and last petitions refer to God's coming kingdom and the judgment that will ensue, while the middle two deal with the everyday needs of humans — bread and debt-relief:

Abba, May your name be blessed;
A1 May your kingdom come;
B1 Give us each day our daily bread,
B2 And forgive us our debts as we forgive our debtors;
A2 And do not bring us to the time of trial.

The opening address to God as Abba and reference to the *shem* or name, in characteristic Jewish fashion, recalls a frequent image of the heavenly court in which God's majesty or blessedness is constantly celebrated by the choirs of angels (cf. Rev 4:6-11). This is followed by a petition for the immediate completion of the project that Jesus has inaugurated, namely, the full realization of God's rule or *basileia* now. This wish is matched in the closing petition of the prayer that the suppliant be spared in the final judgment of separation between good and evil, which was also an important element of the standard apocalyptic expectation for the end.

The two middle petitions ask for the daily sufficiency of bread and forgiveness of debt on the basis that the suppliants also forgive their debtors. Both reflect a social situation of mere subsistence and indebtedness,

41. S. Freyne, "Apocalypticism as the Rejected 'Other': Wisdom and Apocalypticism in Early Judaism and Early Christianity," in D. Harlow, K. Martin Hogan, M. Goff, and J. Kaminsky, eds., *The "Other" in Second Temple Judaism: Essays in Honor of John J. Collins* (Grand Rapids: Eerdmans, 2011), 247-61; D. Harrington, *Wisdom Texts from Qumran* (London and New York: Routledge, 1996).

indicative of the daily struggle for survival in peasant societies generally, one that would have been quite familiar to some, at least, of the Galilean crowds that followed Jesus. The petitions also recall two separate biblical images that may well have played an important role in Jesus' own program for an alternative social arrangement in which all Israel would share equally in the land. The notion of daily bread recalls the gift of the manna in the desert, which was given on a daily basis. This demanded total trust in Yahweh's constant care for his people (Exod 16:1-30), a topic which Jesus also addresses in his instruction about freedom from care in matters of food, drink, and clothing (Q Luke 12:22-29/Matt 6:25-33). The forgiveness of debts was part of the Jubilee legislation as this is developed in Leviticus 25, especially in vv. 8-17. These detailed regulations were intended to maintain equitable landownership within the clan and the family, since the land really belonged to Yahweh and Israelites shared in it is as leaseholders only (Lev 25:23).[42]

The "Our Father" thus reflects the ways in which Jesus can combine wisdom and apocalyptic dimensions in one worldview. Apocalyptic enabled him to envisage the present very differently to the social realities that he encountered, whereas wisdom's focus on the daily plight of people ensured that he did not remain locked into a utopian world that dreamed only about the future.

Each of the Evangelists present Jesus as praying with somewhat different nuances, even though a lonely or desert place seems to be his preferred location. It is remarkable that none of the recent wave of studies of the historical Jesus has dealt with this aspect of his personality and practice. We must assume that his sense of mission to Israel was confirmed and clarified in these encounters, after the pattern of the prophet Elijah, who is said to have visited Horeb, there to beg that he be released from his task of challenging the pagan impulses of the royal house, only to have his mission renewed in a theophany (1 Kgs 19:1-18). There too, Jesus' familiarity with the psalms, especially those dealing with the national identity and God's care in the midst of personal suffering, would undoubtedly have nourished his determination to continue with his ministry despite the fact that he was receiving differing reactions, ranging from over-enthusiastic acceptance by

42. S. Freyne, "Jesus, Prayer and Politics: 'Contemplative Action for Justice,'" in D. Luckensmeyer and P. Allen, eds., *Studies of Religion and Politics in the Early Christian Centuries* (Early Christian Studies 13; Brisbane: St Paul's, 2010), 3-28; J. Jeremias, *The Prayers of Jesus* (London: SCM, 1967), 82-107.

the crowds, lack of true understanding of his mission from his chosen inner circle, and vilification and rejection by the teachers of Israel.

Jesus' *Jubelruf* reflects such a background of prophetic vision also in which reassurance for the tasks ahead is imparted through confirmation of the source of the Master's teaching (Q Luke 10:21-22/Matt 11:25-27). In Jesus' case, this reassurance came from the fact that the Father, "Lord of heaven and earth," had revealed *(apekalypsas)* "these things" to "little ones" *(nēpioi)* and hidden them from the "wise and the learned" *(sophōn kai synetōn)*. His outpouring of gratitude arises from his own visionary reassurance that the revealed wisdom of his *basileia* teaching could be described as good news for the poor and afflicted, whereas his learned opponents had excluded themselves from God's revelatory message.[43] The saying reflects the situation brought about by the charge from the Jerusalem scribes that he was in league with the prince of demons. In making this charge they had sinned against the Spirit as the real source of Jesus' power and thereby cut themselves off from future redemption, as long as they persisted in their blindness (Mark 3:28-30). The impression of an insider-outsider dichotomy that emerges here is in line with other aspects of Jesus' ministry, especially his view of the parables as revelatory expressions for his chosen ones of the *mystery* of the kingdom, which he had been proclaiming openly from the beginning, but which functioned as mere riddles for "those outside" (Mark 4:10-12).

Taken in isolation, the apocalyptic worldview does indeed draw hard lines between the chosen and the excluded. This is an aspect of the Jesus story that was further accentuated subsequently by his followers, who would have felt particularly vulnerable in the wake of their leader's violent death. Nevertheless, such attitudes must surely have emerged in his own lifetime also, given the fate of his mentor John the Baptist and the opposition that his teaching aroused with its political implications for those in power. At the same time, the impact of the revelatory wisdom to which Jesus' permanent followers laid claim has to be balanced against his use of ordinary peasant wisdom, with its universal appeal and significance. Indeed both modes of thought and expression, the apocalyptic and the wisdom, play off each other to reveal the hidden mysterious nature of God's involvement in the everyday, a hiddenness that spoke to Jesus' Jewish piety of a God who is mysterious and nameless and cannot be represented in images. Yet this is

43. J. Jeremias, *New Testament Theology: The Proclamation of Jesus* (London: SCM, 1971), 56-61.

a God who can still be affectionately named Abba/Father, who "makes the rain to fall on the just and the unjust alike" (Matt 5:45) and "is kind to the ungrateful and the wicked" (Luke 6:35). The God of Jesus is in love with the whole creation.

In drawing on the everyday images of peasant wisdom Jesus is not seeking to reaffirm the stability of the status quo, however, nor is he merely offering a way of coping with the inevitable. Instead, in his use of images drawn from nature and everyday human experience he refashions and sublimates the observations and the language of ordinary people.[44] He can speak pithily and courageously about God's care, unencumbered by the learned exegesis of the law teachers or by the pretentiousness of elite scribes like ben Sira. There are qualities of the enigmatic, the unexpected, and the subversive in his utterances that challenge the hearers/readers to reappraise their own assessments of the way things really are and reorder their lives accordingly. It is little wonder, therefore, that following Jesus, not learning from him, became the hallmark of the true disciple in his "school."

In this, respect Jesus' parables are perhaps the most characteristic feature of his style. These short stories have been mined for information about the social world of Galilee, because at one level they ring so true to life. Yet, legitimate though such an investigation might be, it can easily miss the element of exaggeration and surprise that is part of the parables' plots. This aspect of the parables has been correctly interpreted by philosopher Paul Ricoeur and others as an example of "the application of the metaphorical mode to the narrative form" in Jesus' stories.[45] Good metaphors, according to Aristotle, are based on perceived likenesses, yet likeness implies not identity but comparison. Jesus' parables are often introduced by "The kingdom of God is like . . . ," suggesting comparisons with human experiences such as sowing, reaping, banqueting, searching for lost objects, and the like, familiar, everyday events that are readily recognizable. However, just at a point in the story line when the reader is lured into its internal logic, it takes an unexpected and unforeseen twist, and one is left wondering what the point really was. As a pedagogic device, this unusual twist in the story line engages the hearers' imagination to rethink their own presuppositions and

44. B. Brandon Scott, "Jesus as Sage: An Innovating Voice in Common Wisdom," in J. G. Gammie and L. Perdue, eds., *The Sage in Israel and the Ancient Near East* (Winona Lake: Eisenbrauns, 1990), 399-416.

45. P. Ricoeur, "Biblical Hermeneutics: The Metaphorical Process," *Semeia* 4 (1975), 29-148; M. A. Tolbert, *Perspectives on the Parables* (Philadelphia: Fortress, 1979); G. Shillington, ed., *Jesus and His Parables: Interpreting the Parables of Jesus Today* (Edinburgh: Clark, 1998).

revaluate their notions of what "the kingdom of God" might really be like. Often, as in the case of the parable of the wicked tenants (Mark 12:1-12), the story can operate on two levels. While it does reflect recognizable social situations in the experience of the hearers such as that of absentee landlords, it also builds on images derived from the Hebrew Scriptures, such as Isa 5:1-10, which refers to Israel as the Lord's vineyard, thereby giving a theological depth to the parable's meaning for those who have ears to hear.

The German New Testament scholar Gerd Theissen has aptly described Jesus' teaching and lifestyle as inaugurating a "values revolution" in that Jesus challenged the prevailing attitudes toward wealth, power, and knowledge.[46] These attitudes were endemic to both Roman and Judean society, especially since the reign of Herod the Great, as was discussed in previous chapters. We have already seen here how Jesus' drawing on the wisdom of everyday experiences was a far cry from the learned discussions of court scribes and the superior social status that accrued to them on the basis of their learning. By adopting and adapting the language of the simple people to speak about the kingdom of God, Jesus was privileging their lives and their world as the locus of revelation in terms of God's care for the whole creation. For Jesus, wealth and power were not indicators of high status, as many of his contemporaries believed, nor were their opposites, poverty and weakness, badges of shame. The beatitudes in their earliest Q form as preserved by Luke are the summation of Jesus' teaching and living in these matters, which subvert the prevailing cultural norms (Q Luke 6:20-21; Matt 5:3-11).

Instead of advocating a philanthropic use of wealth, as even Herod the Great had done on occasion, Jesus, in contravention of standard Jewish belief as prescribed in Deuteronomy, declared the poor blessed. Freedom from the anxiety that possessions brought meant that the poor could trust in a provident deity who would look after them, just as he had cared for Israel in the desert. To be practicable, that ideal was, of course, dependent on the regulations associated with the gift of the land being implemented. The reality was, as we have seen, that especially from the Hellenistic period onward, alternative value systems had replaced such a kin-based ideal, something that was accentuated further during the Herodian period as the possibility of international trade increased. Small groups such as the Qumran Essenes and perhaps also the early Jesus movement in Jerusalem attempted to put such ideas about having everything in common into prac-

46. G. Theissen, "Jesus Bewegung als charismatische Werterevolution," *NTS* 35 (1989), 343-60.

tice. However, there was never any likelihood that the vast majority of the people could replicate Jesus' program, given the more complex society that had evolved. Thus, already in Luke's gospel we can see how Jesus' teaching on the blessedness of the poor finds expression in a call to the rich to share their possessions with "the poor, the blind, the maimed, and the lame" (Luke 14:21). These were the very people who had been excluded from full participation in both the temple community and the larger Greco-Roman society because of the stigma of poverty or physical impairments.

As regards the exercise of power, Jesus deliberately contrasts the ways in which authority would function in his community in contrast to the norm in the Greco-Roman world. In response to two disciples' request for special places in his kingdom, Jesus refers directly to the prevailing power structure: "You know that among the Gentiles those whom they recognize as rulers lord it over them, and their great ones are tyrants over them. But it is not so among you; but whoever wishes to become great among you must be your servant; and whoever wishes to be first among you must be the slave of all" (Mark 10:42-45). Slaves and servants as "great ones" and "grandees" would be unimaginable without the impetus of an apocalyptic imagination to see the new age of God's *basileia* as the mirror opposite of the present situation of oppression and tyranny.

One of the great boasts of Augustus in his *Res Gestae* was that his reign had brought peace to the Roman world, the *Pax Romana*. Yet by the end of the first century, Tacitus could write as follows about his rulers: "They make a desolation and call it peace" (*Agricola* 3.30-31). Despite the propaganda, Rome's peace was imposed, never more forcibly than in the manner in which the Jewish revolt was so systematically put down and the Roman victory celebrated in triumph. The image on the *Judea Capta* coins of a female figure kneeling with a Roman soldier brandishing a spear over her head speaks louder than words about the Roman attitude toward subject peoples who might dare to challenge its self-proclaimed right to rule the world. In contrast, Jesus' ideas of peace were drawn from the great prophetic images in Isaiah, in which harmony between humans and with the animal and natural worlds were envisaged. The beatitudes do not suggest different types of people who might enter the kingdom but rather different qualities that the true disciple is expected to cultivate and practice. Thus the peacemaker is both "poor in spirit" and "meek," that is, not seeking to exploit or dominate others but gentle and empathetic, especially in acknowledging the dignity of the needy and the excluded.

A trawl through the sayings of Jesus shows just how consistent he was in challenging the prevailing assumptions of both the Roman world and the Judean priestly establishment, reflecting his own style and practice:

- By adopting the lifestyle of a wandering charismatic healer Jesus has no share in the land of Israel: "The Son of Man has nowhere to lay his head" (Matt 8:20).
- Traditional family patterns are disrupted in favor of a new "fictive kinship" arrangement that includes "sisters" as well as "brothers": "Who is my mother? And who are my brothers?" (Mark 3:33).
- Traditional piety is to be ignored if the radical demands of the kingdom are to be followed: "Let the dead bury their dead" (Matt 8:22).
- Jesus' behavior is deemed a rejection of the ascribed roles for sons in the village economy: "Where did this one get all this? . . . Is not this the carpenter, the son of Mary?" (Mark 6:2-3; cf. Matt 13:55: "the carpenter's son").
- Love of enemy, rather than violence and retaliation, is the way to peace: "Love your enemies and do good and lend, not expecting anything in return" (Luke 6:35).
- The religious regulations around food are unimportant: "Why do the disciples of John and the disciples of the Pharisees fast and your disciples do not fast?" (Mark 2:18). "Why do your disciples ignore the tradition of the elders and eat their bread with unwashed (common) hands?" (Mark 7:5).
- The Sabbath regulations are subservient to human need: "The Sabbath was made for humans, not humans for the Sabbath" (Mark 2:27).
- Money and possessions can take over one's life: "Take heed, beware of all greed. A person's life does not consist in possessions" (Luke 12:15). "Do not lay up for yourselves treasures on earth, where moth and rust corrode and thieves break through and steal" (Matt 6:19). "You cannot serve God and mammon" (Matt 6:24; Luke 16:13).
- The Jerusalem temple is meant for worship of God, not business deals: "My house shall be called a house of prayer for all peoples, but you have made it a den of thieves" (Mark 11:17).
- Authority consists in service, not domination: "Persons who would save their lives must lose them" (Mark 8:35). "Whoever would be greatest among you should become least of all and servant of all" (Mark 9:35). "Whoever wishes to be great among you, let that person be your servant, and whoever wishes to be first among you, let them be the slaves of all" (Mark 10:44).

Jesus and the Future

If the wisdom tradition provided Jesus with the raw material for his teaching about life as it is to be lived in the present, the apocalyptic strand of thought described the consummation that was imminent. The apparent tension between these two aspects of Jesus' sayings has given rise to a lively debate over the past century and a half as to how they can best be reconciled. As mentioned previously, these discussions have often been conducted on the false assumption that only one of the alternatives can be attributed to Jesus and that the other was the creation of his followers after his death. However, a more careful assessment of the evidence both from contemporary Jewish literature and the Jesus tradition suggests that this is a "false alternative," in some instances, at least, based on a modern discomfort with the apocalyptic worldview.

The apparent ambiguity is created already by Mark's initial report that Jesus came into Galilee declaring that "the kingdom of God has drawn near" *(ēngiken)* and that this was "good news" *(euangelion)*, indicating the fact that "the time *(kairos)* was fulfilled *(peplērōtai)*" (Mark 1:14-15). This is indeed a dense proclamation employing a number of highly technical terms that already had currency in the Hebrew Scriptures for God's coming to the aid of Israel. The announcement implied that a period of expectation had come to an end and that this was the long-awaited good news for Israel. Yet the Greek term for "draw near" or "is close at hand" suggests a hint of "not yet" or "not fully, yet." That such a nuance is present in this opening summary by Mark of Jesus' preaching is confirmed by a number of subsequent statements attributed to Jesus himself. Thus in the "Our Father" Jesus prays for the coming of the kingdom, and at the same time in the beatitudes he can assure the poor that they are already blessed, while promising the hungry and the mourners that they *will* (future) be filled and consoled (Q Luke 6:20-21/Matt 5:1-4, 6). Perhaps the parables, especially the so-called growth parables, capture the idea best: the kingdom is hidden, yet present and active, like the seed in the ground, and the final realization can be likened to the joy of harvest time (Mark 4:26-32). At the same time images such as the future banquet with the patriarchs (Q Luke 13:28-29/Matt 8:11-12) and Jesus' own expectation as he approaches his death (Mark 14:25) have a definite future orientation.

Jesus' association with and admiration for John the Baptist has already been discussed. There is general recognition that the urgency of John's preaching about the need for immediate repentance makes clear that he did expect an imminent arrival of God's kingly rule. This would bring both blessing and bane in accordance with prophetic warnings, especially after the exile, about "the day of Yahweh" as a day of judgment on the unrepentant in Israel (Amos 5:18-20; Mal 3:19-23[4:1-6]; Isa 33:10-16). Hence the emphasis on repentance in John's preaching. Some recent discussions of Jesus' relationship with John, such as those of John Dominic Crossan and Marcus Borg, argue that once Jesus broke with his mentor he adopted a very different outlook and strategy, in effect adopting the role of wisdom teacher or Cynic-like preacher rather than that of eschatological prophet.[47] Jesus, it is alleged, no longer stressed repentance or imminent judgment. However, such a conclusion scarcely stands up to scrutiny when one examines the number of sayings in the Q version of the Sermon on the Plain, for example, that stress the need for higher standards of ethical behavior from disciples and the warning about the judgment that will accrue if these are not maintained (Q Luke 6:37-45). Galilean towns Chorazin, Bethsaida, and Capernaum are condemned for their obstinacy (Q Luke 10:13-15/Matt 11:21-24), and Jesus' disciples are told to shake from their feet the dust of those places that refuse to receive them as his messengers (Q Luke 10:10-12/Matt 10:14-15). This threat of judgment applies also to Jerusalem and its temple (Q Luke 13:35/Matt 23:37-39).

Once Jesus came into Galilee, there was undoubtedly a shift of emphasis and strategy in his approach. The contrasts that he drew between himself and John did not diminish his continued endorsement of his mentor. At the same time, he claimed that his own ministry represented another dimension of their shared end-time expectation, a further step along the eschatological timeline beyond that of John.[48] However, Jesus' teaching was, as we saw in the previous section, not an affirmation of the status quo but a call for a radically different view of the world and of humans' role within it. Such a proclamation calls for a very different view of both the present and the future. This corresponds to the Jewish apocalyptic understanding of the temporal sequence of two contrasting ages, namely the present evil age and the future good age. Insofar as Jesus was calling for a radical renewal of Israel now, he was effectively declaring that the future good age had already broken into the present. The kingly rule of God was no longer future but already here and realizing itself in and through his ministry.

47. Crossan, *The Historical Jesus*, 265-302; M. Borg, *Jesus in Contemporary Scholarship* (Valley Forge: Trinity, 1994), 47-68.

48. Dale C. Allison, *Jesus of Nazareth: Millenarian Prophet* (Minneapolis: Augsburg, 1998), 105.

Such a claim inevitably raises again the issue of Jesus' own self-awareness. In his most recent study, *Jesus and das Judentum* (2007), Martin Hengel has argued that the baptismal experience of the "voice from heaven" provided a major confirmation for his approach to his ministry, even though Hengel also attributes a full messianic consciousness to Jesus from his family background. Without dismissing the significance of the Jordan experience, many scholars would question such an explicit awareness, preferring rather to allow Jesus' self-understanding and sense of mission to develop in the maelstrom of his life experiences.[49] However, Hengel correctly insists that John's understanding of his own ministry should not be seen as just that of another prophet, but rather as Elijah, the last of the prophets, whose task it was to prepare for the arrival of the Messiah. Such a self-understanding on the part of John would have suggested to Jesus that his own role was that of the expected one. As we saw, he was reluctant to make any such public claims, while insisting that his healing and teaching activity were to be understood as manifestations of God's kingly rule finally breaking into the present evil age. The final determination of his messianic status was for the Father to affirm in the future.

Once it is accepted that Jesus did share the apocalyptic worldview, which for him was also transformative of the present for his followers, we may well ask how he saw his own and Israel's future in the end-time scenario that he expected. One issue that has arisen on the basis of some texts is the claim that Jesus expected the end during his own lifetime, or at least during that of his disciples. Three very formal declarations (Mark 9:1; Matt 10:23; Mark 13:30), all following a definite pattern, claim that the definitive consummation of the present will have occurred within the current generation. The consummation in question is variously described: the arrival of the kingdom, the return of the Son of Man, or simply "all these things," referring to the end-time scenario as depicted in Mark 13. While the trend in recent scholarship has been to attribute these sayings to the early church, Allison's suggestion that they all stem from a single saying of Jesus himself arising from the disappointment of the disciples during his ministry is quite persuasive, given the common structure that they share.[50]

49. Hengel and Schwemer, *Jesus und das Judentum*, 291-94 and 320-22. See S. Freyne, "Reflections on the Galilean Jesus in the Light of Martin Hengel's *Jesus und das Judentum*," in C. Breytenbach and J. Frey, eds., *Reflections on Early Christian History and Religion* (Erwägungen zur Frühchristlichen Religionsgeschichte 1; Leiden: Brill, 2012), 101-14.

50. The common pattern is as follows: (1) "Amen, Amen," (2) "I say to you," (3) something will not have occurred: disciples will not have tasted death, this generation will not have

What could have given rise to such a disappointment, and might Jesus also have shared it? Of the three locations where the saying occurs, that of Matthew would appear to be the most historically plausible, since the mission charge which the disciples are to deliver is associated with the imminent arrival of the kingdom in both Q and Mark. The Twelve, in their symbolic role as representatives of all Israel, had been sent on an urgent mission to announce the coming event and to perform healings that would replicate Jesus' own ministry. However, in both the Q and Markan versions of the mission charge, they were warned that rejection might well be their lot (Mark 6:10-12; Q Luke 10:10-12/Matt 10:14-15). The urgency of the message and the symbolism of the actions they are to perform when rejected, taken in conjunction with the mention of the fate of Sodom in the Q version, all point to a situation of extreme urgency in Jesus' own estimation as far as Israel's fate is concerned.[51] This warning is similar to that about the possibility of sharing in or being excluded from the banquet with the patriarchs in the hope that all Israel too could join in the universal celebrations (Q Luke 13:28-29/Matt 8:11-12). The fact that Paul, faced with the apparent failure of his mission to "his own people," could still envisage a final act of God whereby Israel would be grafted together with the Gentiles onto the one root (Rom 11:13-24), shows that the Jesus movement, both in the homeland and in the Diaspora, never abandoned the hope that "all Israel" would share in the messianic festivities.

Such a suggestion immediately raises again the question of Jesus' use of the Son of Man image with regard to his own identity and mission, one of the most hotly debated issues in gospel studies. The fact that in the New Testament the expression is found only on the lips of Jesus highlights its

---

passed, or the mission of the disciples to the towns of Israel will not be over, (4) before a final consummation will have taken place. Allison, *Jesus of Nazareth,* 149-50, makes a good case for seeing all three as versions of a single saying of Jesus, which suggests a sense of crisis with regard to the expectations that his ministry had generated.

51. Matthew, in line with his *heilsgeschichtlich* understanding of the mission to Israel (ch. 10) and the nations (28:18-20), emphasizes that the mission of the Twelve, as well as that of Jesus himself, went only to Israel (Matt 10:5-6, 23; 15:24), but this was already implicit in his reply to the Syro-Phoenician woman. Allison, *Jesus of Nazareth,* 148-50, believes that the reference to the Son of Man coming in Matt 10:23 could have been uttered at a moment of disillusionment among the disciples "as their apocalyptic enthusiasm was on the wane." This is a variant of A. Schweitzer's suggestion that Jesus himself became disillusioned at a certain point in the ministry, causing him to change his strategy and opt to go to his death in Jerusalem, a decision that would appear to be indicated at Mark 8:31. See Schweitzer, *The Quest of the Historical Jesus,* trans. J. M. Robinson (New York: Macmillan, 1968), especially 387-97.

importance, raising the possibility that this is a veiled reference to his messianic status. Two alternative suggestions as to its background and meaning have been put forward. One of these, already mentioned, associated with Geza Vermes but with a much older provenance among specialists in the Aramaic language, claims that Jesus could have been using a Palestinian Aramaic idiom that simply means "man" in general or "someone," or was even a circumlocution for the personal pronoun "I." Vermes's proposal went even further, however, suggesting that there was evidence for an additional nuance associated with the idiom, whereby one could refer to oneself in this manner when a direct statement would have been seen as immodest or inappropriate, as for example the saying about the Son of Man (= "I") having power to forgive sins (Mark 2:10). While such a suggestion would seem to fit well with Jesus' indirect mode of communication, already discussed, serious objections have been raised to the proposal, not least the late and unclear examples that Vermes adduces for his claim.[52]

The second alternative, namely, that the Son of Man sayings originate in apocalyptic literature, beginning with Dan 7:13, has raised other questions among New Testament scholars. Rudolf Bultmann distinguished three different categories of "Son of Man" sayings within the Synoptic tradition: those that speak of a future role as judge/savior, those that refer to Jesus' present activity, and those that describe his sufferings in Jerusalem.[53] Of these, the sayings related to his suffering are usually seen as examples of "prophecies after the event" put on the lips of Jesus after the resurrection and based on various details from the Passion narratives. This does not imply that Jesus was unaware of the possibility of his death in Jerusalem, but merely that the details of the sufferings and the irony of a glorious figure suffering at the hands of men would seem to belong to the post-resurrection setting.

This narrows the question of the authenticity of the "Son of Man" sayings to those referring to the future and the present. While Bultmann was prepared to see some of the future "Son of Man" sayings as authentic, other scholars believe that they must all be attributed to the post-Easter setting.[54]

---

52. Vermes, *Jesus the Jew*, 162-91. See A. Yarbro Collins, "Jesus as Son of Man," in A. Yarbro Collins and J. J. Collins, *King and Messiah as Son of God: Divine, Human and Angelic Messianic Figures in Biblical and Related Literature* (Grand Rapids: Eerdmans, 2008), 149-74, especially 156-66, for a discussion of the proposals regarding the Aramaic idiom.

53. Rudolf Bultmann, *Theology of the New Testament* (London: SCM, 1951), 1:30.

54. G. Theissen and A. Merz, *The Historical Jesus: A Comprehensive Guide* (London: SCM, 1998), 541-53, especially 549-51.

However, such skepticism is both unwarranted and unlikely. If these say-ings were all the product of the post-Easter enthusiasm of Jesus' followers, how is it that they occur only on the lips of Jesus himself? The expression "Son of Man" appears once in Acts (7:56) and not at all in the New Testa-ment epistles, an omission that would be surprising indeed if it was a later creation.[55]

Must we then choose between the present and future sayings, and if so on what basis? Or could both be plausibly seen as originating with Jesus himself? There seems to be no good reason to rule out this second position. As mentioned previously, Jesus' use of "Son of Man" in the ev-eryday sense would fit well with his contrasting of himself with John the Baptist (Matt 11:19) or his question to the disciples (Matt 16:13). The fact that the expression was used in everyday parlance in Palestinian Aramaic, even if the nuance suggested by Vermes is uncertain, would seem to offer sufficient contextual probability that Jesus did in fact employ it on occa-sion, meaning "this one" or "I," possibly to avert immediate attention from himself.

This conclusion does not rule out the "visionary" statements about the future Son of Man stemming from Jesus also. There is evidence that the "one like a Son of Man" in the original vision in Dan 7:13 was reworked in later Jewish tradition to refer to an individual figure, either the Messiah (1 Enoch 48:10; 52:4) or an end-time warrior (4 Ezra 13:1-13). If, as we have been suggesting, Jesus too shared aspects of the visionary strand of Jewish thinking, he could well have been familiar with the reworking of images that promised future salvation for the oppressed, as well as the messianic overtones of the designation in the present, as in 1 Enoch.[56]

Jesus' statements about the future role of the Son of Man in our two earliest sources (Mark and Q) are to do with his roles as savior and judge, both described with reference to Dan 7:13. The disciples are promised that they "will see" the Son of Man "coming on the clouds in glory with his angels to gather the elect" (Mark 13:26-27), whereas his accusers at his trial are told that they "will see" the Son of Man "seated at God's right hand" and "coming in glory" (Mark 14:62). It is only in this second instance that Jesus clearly identifies himself with the figure who is to come, whereas in an ear-lier saying (Mark 8:38) there is a certain ambiguity as to whether Jesus sees

55. Allison, *Jesus of Nazareth*, 115-20.

56. Theissen and Merz, *The Historical Jesus: A Comprehensive Guide*, 543-45; Yarbro Collins, "Jesus as Son of Man," 166-68.

himself in that role or is referring to a heavenly being other than himself: "Whoever is ashamed of me and my words in this wicked and sinful generation, of him will the Son of Man be ashamed when he comes in the glory of his Father with his holy angels." The relationship between Jesus and the heavenly figure is quite clear: the latter will pass judgment on the basis of fidelity to Jesus' teaching, but Jesus' own identity as the future Son of Man is left open. In that case, it may be that this formulation goes back to Jesus himself. It reflects the apocalyptic worldview of the two ages and reassures the disciples that his teaching is indeed the true way, while at the same time pointing to the separation that will occur in the future on the basis of acceptance or rejection of his words.

The other early source, Q, also has sayings about the Son of Man's role in the future, reflecting the Markan coloring but also striking a definite note of warning. Thus Q Luke 12:8-9/Matt 10:32-33 resembles closely Mark 8:38, while stating the point more positively: "Whoever acknowledges me before others (literally 'men') the Son of Man also will acknowledge before the angels of God; but whoever denies me before others (literally 'men') will be denied before the angels." Other sayings stress the sudden nature of the appearance of the Son of Man (Q Luke 12:39-40/ Matt 24:43-44). This visionary aspect of his coming is reflected in its being compared to a flash of lightning (Q Luke 17:23-24/Matt 24:27), and the example of the flood story is used to illustrate humans' lack of preparedness for the sudden arrival of the day of reckoning (Q Luke 17:26-27/Matt 24:38-39).

This brief survey suggests the continuing influence of the Son of Man figure within the Jesus traditions. The trend discovered in the earliest sources was further accentuated in the later gospels, including the Fourth Gospel. Yet, important as this identification is, it points to a larger issue of the role of the book of Daniel in Jesus' and his early followers' understanding of their mission and destiny. It should be remembered that, in its original setting within the book, the figure to whom power and authority has been given is a human figure ("one like a human being/Son of Man"), in contrast to "the beast" that is about to launch his attack, namely, Antiochus Epiphanes. The vision suggests that, just as there is a battle between good and evil on earth, this is being replicated in the heavenly realm, with the victory over the "beast" confirmed in advance. This emerges clearly in the explanation of the vision that Daniel receives, where the Son of Man now represents the collective of "the people of the saints of the Most High" who are to receive the kingly rule of God, not as individuals but as a group:

He [the beast] will speak words against the Most High, will wear out the holy ones of the Most High, and will attempt to change the sacred seasons and the law, and they shall be given into his power for a time, two times, and a half a time. Then the court will sit in judgment, and his dominion will be taken away to be consumed and totally destroyed. The *kingship* and dominion and the greatness of the kingdoms under the whole heaven will be given to the people of the holy ones of the Most High; their *kingdom* shall be an *everlasting kingdom,* and all dominions will serve and obey them. (Dan 7:25-27)

This interpretation of the vision focuses, not on the Son of Man, but rather on the notion of kingship/kingly rule that is being transferred from the earthly tyrant to "the holy ones of the Most High." The emphasis here on kingly rule/kingship is all the more remarkable given the relative paucity of usage of such terms in the Hebrew Bible as a whole.[57] It thereby directs our attention to Jesus' original proclamation about the arrival of God's *basileia* now (Mark 1:14-15). As Norman Perrin, following in the footsteps of his mentor Joachim Jeremias, declares, "The central aspect of the teaching of Jesus was that concerning the Kingdom of God. On this there can be no doubt. . . . Jesus appeared as one who proclaimed the Kingdom; all else in his message and ministry serves a function in relation to that proclamation and derives its meaning from it."[58] If, as we have been repeatedly insisting, Jesus was constantly diverting attention from himself to his message, then we should attend to the ways in which he understood the nature of the community he was gathering around him in the name of God's *basileia.*

To fully appreciate the significance of this line of argument it is important to recall the setting of the book of Daniel, namely, the crisis for Jewish faith generated by Antiochus Epiphanes, as discussed in Chapter 1 (pp. 13-14). Daniel's vision of the Son of Man, to whom universal "dominion and glory and kingship" was given by the Most High, Ancient of Days (Dan 7:13-14), occurs in the context of another vision of the overthrow of Antiochus, by far the most threatening of the beasts that have come out of the sea to attack the saints of the Most High (vv. 1-12). Daniel and his companions are presented at the outset as *maskilim* or "learned in all wisdom" (1:4, 17), a gift that goes well beyond Daniel's powers to interpret dreams, as his prayer

---

57. See Meier, *A Marginal Jew,* 2:243-53, for a detailed survey of the evidence.
58. N. Perrin, *Rediscovering the Teaching of Jesus* (London: SCM, 1963), 54, cited in Meier, *A Marginal Jew,* 2:237.

to the Most High God acknowledges (2:20-23). Toward the end of the book, a group described as the *maskilim* or wise ones again emerges, this time referring to those who have "instructed many" but have suffered at the hands of "the beast," and some had perished (11:33-35).

In the context of the book as a whole, Daniel and his companions are prototypes for this group who suffered most at the hands of the Syrian oppressor. They are said to have received only "a little help" from others, a veiled reference to the different factions within the Judean resistance. Unlike the Maccabean freedom fighters, the *maskilim* had adopted a pacific role, trusting in God's protection rather than human resistance.[59] In the end they are the ones who will triumph, since once "the time of anguish" is over, "many of those who sleep in the dust of the earth shall awake, some to everlasting life and some to shame and everlasting contempt. Those who are wise *(maskilim)* shall shine like the brightness of the sky, and those who lead many to righteousness like the stars forever and ever" (Dan 12:2-3). This is the first clear statement of the possibility of an afterlife for individuals in the Hebrew Bible, a belief that would play such an important role in the understanding of the early Jesus-followers after the trauma of his violent death.

By promising that the coming Son of Man would soon vindicate his permanent group of followers who had been loyal to his teaching, Jesus was aligning his community and its future fate with that of the *maskilim* as this emerges in the book of Daniel. The Jesus-followers too were expected to lead people to righteousness, and they too could expect persecution, and even death, at the hands of imperial powers and others who did not agree with their ideas of peace, justice, and the righting of wrongs, following the example of Jesus. However, they could also look forward to future glory, shining like the stars forever.

As a teacher of revealed wisdom, Jesus would have thought of his own future in such terms also. Yet it is noteworthy that when the Sadducees, who, unlike the Pharisees, did not believe in resurrection from the dead, once challenged him on the matter, he did not refer to Daniel and the *maskilim*. Instead he built an argument from Scripture that his interrogators would have accepted, namely the book of Exodus. When Moses sought reassurance regarding the name of the God who was directing him to lead

---

59. Efforts to identify the group in terms of those known to us from this period have not been wholly successful. See P. Davies, "The Scribal School of Daniel," in J. J. Collins and P. Flint, eds., *The Book of Daniel: Composition and Reception* (Leiden: Brill, 2002), 1:247-65.

Israel out of Egypt, Yahweh identified himself only as being "the God of Abraham, Isaac, and Jacob." Since the Patriarchs were long dead and God's reply was in the present tense ("I *am* the God of . . ."), Jesus infers that God is the God of the living, not of the dead (Mark 12:18-27; Exod 3:6), thereby also alluding to a frequent epithet for God in the Hebrew Bible, "the *living* God."

In identifying Jesus' followers with the *maskilim* of Daniel, I have argued elsewhere that this profile also connects them to the figure of the Suffering Servant and his "offspring" as this is developed in the last section of the book of Isaiah.[60] The paean to the servant begins with Yahweh declaring that "his servant shall prosper ('be wise'); he shall be exalted and lifted up and shall be very high" (Isa 52:13). Thereafter, however, there is a long description of the suffering and rejection that the servant has experienced. The servant's own demeanor was one of silent acceptance of his treatment at the hands of those who are now the narrators within the poem and who have come to realize what the purpose of the servant's sufferings was: "He was wounded for our transgressions, crushed for our iniquities. . . . His life was an offering for sin. . . . The righteous one shall make many whole." Though the servant has suffered an ignominious death, the poem ends with his receiving his due reward: "He shall see his offspring and prolong his days; through him the will of the Lord shall prosper. Out of his anguish he shall see light and he shall find satisfaction through his knowledge." This promise of future reward would seem to be fulfilled in the final chapters of Isaiah, where a group described as "the servants [plural] of the Lord" (Isa 54:17) emerges whose lifestyle seems to be modeled on that of the servant of Isaiah 52–53. Likewise, their treatment at the hands of others within the triumphant Zion community constituted by the returnees from Babylon is similar to that of the servant figure. However, a number of oracles speak of their subsequent vindication because of their fidelity to the ideal of humility and trust as displayed by their prototype, the Suffering Servant.[61]

It is not possible to find many verbal links between the story of Isaiah's Suffering Servant and the early Christian accounts of Jesus' death and subsequent vindication by God. Yet the pattern of the two narratives is unmistakably similar. Not merely was Isaiah's servant figure a model for Jesus in terms of understanding his inevitable death as redemptive for others in God's plan, the servant's wisdom in trusting in God's care for the just must

60. *Jesus, a Jewish Galilean*, 116-21.
61. *Jesus, a Jewish Galilean*, 105-8.

have been an inspiration for Jesus also. In particular the idea that the servant's "offspring" would continue to bear witness to his values and vision must have brought reassurance to Jesus as the inevitable clash of values with the political and religious leaders began to surface in the full light of day. Three sayings of Jesus seem to encapsulate this view of his own and his disciples' future. As Allison has shown, they follow a common pattern of honor now / shame later as against shame now / honor later:[62]

1. For all who exalt themselves shall be humbled,
   And those who humble themselves will be exalted.
   (Q Luke 14:11; cf. Matt 23:12)
2. Those who try to save their life will lose it,
   But those who lose their lives will keep them.
   (Mark 8:35; Q Luke 17:33; Matt 10:39)
3. Many who are first will be last,
   And the last will be first.
   (Mark 10:31)

There is no indication as to when the reversal of fortune that these sayings envisage will take place. Indeed they appear as detached and strange utterances unless one keeps in mind the apocalyptic worldview of the one who uttered them. Two of his closest followers, James and John, the sons of Zebedee, were still thinking in terms of an earthly kingdom as they approached Jerusalem (Mark 10:35-37). Their failure to appreciate the radically different understanding of how human life should be lived under the reign of God as proclaimed by Jesus underlines just how domesticated even they, Galilean fishermen, had become with the reign of Caesar. Jesus was not about to replace one kingdom with another, as they expected. It would take the "failure" that was about to be accomplished in Jerusalem to open their eyes to appreciate just how radically different his vision was, and the consequent urgency of the present moment.

This realization resulted in a vibrant missionary drive by all branches of the Jesus movement at an early stage after his death. While he may not himself have formally commissioned a mission to the Gentiles, this was the inevitable outcome of his life and ministry, especially in his use of such images as the eschatological banquet shared with the patriarchs and the abundant and unexpected harvest that will follow the seemingly insignif-

---

62. Allison, *Jesus of Nazareth*, 131-36.

icant dimension of the present sowing. Even his abrupt reply to the Syro-Phoenician woman did not preclude such an outcome. However, the final confrontation in the Holy City that was about to unfold was the necessary trigger in bringing about the change of consciousness that was required for the disciples to begin to understand Jesus' real purpose and mission and their own role as his true followers.

"Jerusalem, Jerusalem"

Luke tells us that when Jesus was twelve years old he accompanied his parents to celebrate the festival of Passover in Jerusalem, a journey they made each year (Luke 2:41). The story is precious in that it is our one insight into the adolescent Jesus' private life in the canonical gospels. Yet the account is so thoroughly Lukan in language, style, and theme that in the absence of any independent corroborating evidence it clearly does not meet the usual criteria for historicity. Yet, Luke the artist paints a lifelike picture of a situation that must have confronted Galilean Jews every year, possibly even three times a year. It prompts the questions as to the frequency of Jesus' visits to the holy city and how, as a country prophet, he might have been received there.

In Chapter 4 (pp. 133-34) we encountered the Fourth Gospel's treatment of Jesus' visit to the Feast of Tabernacles and caught a glimpse of the attitude of the Judean religious authorities toward their country cousins (John 7:10-43). Again we can well suppose that this account is based on experience of the attitudes that Galilean pilgrims were likely to have encountered in an urban setting that was dominated by a class who considered themselves to be superior, not just as urbanites, but as people charged with responsibility for the sanctuary and the holy city. In this instance, we have a corroboration of sorts from Josephus, who tells of the difficulties encountered by Galilean pilgrims at the hands of the hostile Samaritans as they passed through on the way to Jerusalem for a festival.

The event took place in the reign of the emperor Claudius (c. 50 C.E.) and was sufficiently serious to warrant an intervention by the Roman procurator, resulting in the subsequent punishment of some of the perpetrators. Of interest here is the way in which the Judean authorities reacted. We are told that when news of the incident reached the city they hastened out to meet the Galileans, pleading with them not to retaliate as follows: "In their desire for reprisals against the Samaritans they would bring down the wrath of Rome on Jerusalem. . . . The country and the sanctuary, as well as their own wives and children, were threatened with destruction merely for the object of avenging the blood of a *single Galilean*" (*War* 2.237; cf. *Ant* 20.118-36).[63] Josephus was of Jerusalemite priestly stock, and the sentiment he describes here echoes that expressed by the high priest Caiaphas in the Fourth Gospel when the Jerusalem authorities were concerned about Jesus' popularity with the crowds on the eve of Passover. He feared that the Romans would come and destroy their sanctuary *(topos)* and the city: "You know nothing at all!" Caiaphas said, "You do not understand that it is expedient for you that *one man* should die for the people, and that the whole nation should not perish" (John 11:49-50).

While this deliberation is loaded with Johannine irony and in all probability reflects a post-70 situation, it nevertheless corroborates the earlier views about Galileans, as judged by Jerusalem priestly standards. Yet Jesus was no ordinary pilgrim, but a country prophet whose movement had come to the attention of the Jerusalem scribal establishment, which had tried to discredit him, as already discussed. One saying preserved in Q, Luke 13:34-35/Matt 23:37-39, Jesus' lament for Jerusalem, suggests that his final visit to the city was by no means the only one: "Jerusalem, Jerusalem, who kills the prophets and stones those sent to her. How often I wanted to gather your children together as a hen gathers her nestlings under her wing, and you would not. Look, your house is forsaken. I tell you: You will not see me again until (the time comes when) you say, 'Blessed is the one coming in the name of the Lord.'" While this saying may well have served the community behind the Q source later, in terms of their own dealing with the calamity that was about to befall Jerusalem in 70 C.E., there is no good reason for not seeing it as expressive of Jesus' own sentiment also.[64]

---

63. S. Freyne, *Galilee from Alexander the Great to Hadrian: A Study of Second Temple Judaism* (Wilmington: Glazier / Notre Dame: Notre Dame University Press, 1980; reprint Edinburgh: Clark, 1998), 74-76.

64. "Q" stands for the German word *Quelle* meaning "source," a term that came to be used in the nineteenth century for the putative collection of sayings of Jesus that scholars postulated to explain the literary relationships in respect to the sayings of Jesus between the gospels of Matthew and Luke. The issue of the relationships between the Synoptic Gospels came to the fore in the context of nineteenth-century discussions of the historicity of the Gospels, and Q and Mark were deemed to be the earliest pillars of what has come to be called the "two-source hypothesis." C. Tuckett, *Q and the History of Early Christianity: Studies on Q* (Edinburgh: Clark, 1996); J. Kloppenborg, *Q Parallels: Synopsis, Critical Notes and Concordance* (Sonoma: Polebridge, 1988); J. Kloppenborg Verbin, *Excavating Q: The History and Setting of the Sayings Gospel* (Edinburgh: Clark, 2000); J. M. Robinson, P. Hoffman, and J. Kloppenborg, *The Critical Edition of Q* (Leuven: Peeters, 2000).

Seam separating Herod the Great's extension to the south and the earlier eastern retaining wall of the temple. (J. H. Charlesworth)

Jesus' lament is directed at the city (Jerusalem) and the temple ("your house"). Both were intimately connected economically, socially, and religiously: the city was the "holy" city because the holiness of the temple extended to the city and the temple relied on the city and its inhabitants for the resources and personnel to sustain its daily routine of worship. It should not be forgotten that the rebuilding program of Herod the Great was still underway during Jesus' public ministry and any suggestion that the temple was doomed or abandoned would touch the nerve center of the city's economy also. The expression "how often" surely implies that Jesus had engaged in public appeals to the Jerusalem religious authorities on several occasions and that these had fallen on deaf ears. Yet the final statement of v. 35b, "Blessed is the one coming in the name of the Lord," strikes a note of hope, taken as it is from Psalm 118 (v. 26), one of the *hallel* psalms sung by pilgrims as they approached Jerusalem on the great feasts. The reference to a "coming one" suggests a general expectation that occurs more than once in the Q source, including the query of John the Baptist's messengers to Jesus (Q Luke 7:19-20/Matt 11:2-3).[65] Its use here on the lips of Jesus once more leaves open his own identity, an identity that, according to Mark, the crowds had come to recognize as he entered Jerusalem for

65. Kloppenborg, *Q Parallels*, 52-53.

the last time, when they greeted him chanting this same verse from Psalm 118 (Mark 11:9).

Gerd Theissen helpfully suggests that Jesus' lament and subsequent prophecy about the destruction of the temple should be seen in the context of a long-standing tension between the temple and the land, one that had become exacerbated throughout the first century c.e.[66] Theissen notes that all the prophets before Jesus who challenged Jerusalem were also from the country: Micah was from Moresheth (Mic 1:1), Uriah from Kiriath Jearim (Jer 26:20), and Jeremiah from Anathoth (Jer 1:1), and Jesus was from Nazareth in Galilee.

Of these early prophets, the case of Jeremiah is the closest analogue to that of Jesus. They both engaged in a combination of prophetic words and actions to challenge the temple hierarchy in terms of their respective understandings of what was amiss in Judean religious attitudes and practice. Jeremiah broke an earthenware jug as a symbol of what Yahweh Sabaoth would do to "this people and this city" because of the syncretistic religious practices that the people of Jerusalem and their religious leaders had engaged in (Jer 19:1-11). A sentence of death had been passed against Jeremiah (18:18), but he reiterated his earlier condemnations, declaring that Yahweh would make Jerusalem and its temple a ruin like the old Israelite shrine of Shiloh (7:1-15; 26:4-6). In the end, Jeremiah was saved from the wrath of the people and the priests by some friends and thus avoided execution.

Jesus' symbolic action with regard to the temple was his overturning of the tables of the moneychangers, driving out those who bought and sold within the temple court or traded in doves, and he would not allow anyone to carry anything through the temple court (Mark 11:15-18). These actions have been variously interpreted, ranging from what has been called "the tantrum in the temple" to declaring an outright end to sacrificial worship with his prohibition against carrying anything through the temple courts.[67] The comment on his action that Mark places on his lips combines elements from both Isaiah and Jeremiah: "My house shall be called a house of prayer for all nations (Isa 56:7), but you have made it a den of thieves (Jer 7:11)."

---

66. G. Theissen, "Die Tempelweissagung Jesu. Prophetie im Spannungsfeld zwischen Tempel und Land," *Theologische Zeitung* 32 (1976), 144-58.

67. For an evaluation of the recent proposals, see A. Yarbro Collins, "Jesus' Action in Herod's Temple," in A. Yarbro Collins and M. M. Mitchell, eds., *Antiquity and Humanity: Essays in Ancient Religion and Philosophy Presented to Hans Dieter Betz* (Tübingen: Mohr Siebeck, 2001), 45-61. Yarbro Collins concludes that Jesus' protest was prompted by the transformation of the temple area into a Roman-style agora by Herod's renovations.

The Isaiah citation is from a passage in which Yahweh declares that both eunuchs and foreigners who "observe my Sabbaths and cling to my covenant" will be welcome to offer sacrifices on his altar (Isa 56:1-8). Jeremiah's "den of thieves" comes from his temple speech which berates the Jerusalem audience for declaring their attachment to Yahweh's temple in fine words but proceeding to break all the commandments of the Decalogue, including those forbidding the worship of false gods (Jer 7:1-15).

Perhaps this combination of scriptural interpretations of Jesus' action is our best clue to why his whole career and ministry was seen as such a threat to the Jerusalem temple aristocracy. After all, the Essenes continued to be critical of the temple, its personnel, and its rituals. They declared that only they represented the temple's role correctly in their community life and maintained that there would be a new temple that would replace the existing one inhabited by the sons of Belial. Jesus and his movement were not alone, therefore. John the Baptist, too, could be seen as a threat to the centrality of the temple's role in the life of the people. However, Antipas had taken care of that threat by having John removed. Jesus, we saw, had adopted a different strategy to John's while still publicly affirming his admiration for him. The Jesus movement involved instigating a people's movement throughout the villages of Galilee, one that could potentially undermine the authority and prosperity of Jerusalem as the temple city. The nature of the threat that it posed was all the more serious because it sought to appropriate the central symbols of the people, namely, the temple and the land, the cornerstone on which the temple based its claims and depended for its maintenance. In the process, it offered a different interpretation of those symbols in terms of God's original design for all Israel.

From that perspective, the Jesus movement is a classic example of one in which the periphery poses a serious threat to the center by undermining its claims to be acknowledged as *the* center. The views of a contemporary anthropologist ring true for the Jesus movement in its Galilean setting: "The people of the periphery encounter the meanings and symbolic forms of the centre with perspectives that are both formed and capable of being formed, and the very fact that they are shaped by the experience of periphery will contribute to making them different from the centre."[68] In other words, being peripheral can mean being creative with regard to the established symbol system, of which the center is both guardian and propagator.

68. U. Hannertz, "Culture between Centre and Periphery: Towards a Macroanthropology," *Ethnos* 54 (1989), 200-216.

Peripherality can create the freedom to adapt to the real situations being encountered at the boundaries, where coexistence with other cultural systems rather than blind loyalty to one's own center's norms may be the more pressing challenge. The story of Jesus' encounter with the Syro-Phoenician woman on the border of Tyre, to which reference has been made more than once in this study, perfectly encapsulates the point.

We need only recall briefly the supporting evidence for these claims already touched on in this chapter. The Isaiah passage that, as Mark's citation suggests, best explains Jesus' views on the current temple practice, is highly informative. Reference to "a den of thieves" envisages a situation in which those who were excluded from full participation in the temple worship according to the priestly code of Leviticus would be free to participate fully, "offering gifts on my altar" (Isa 56:7). All that was required of them was observing the Sabbath and clinging to the covenant. The conditions mentioned here pointedly avoid any mention of the purity regulations, so important to the priestly class and their offshoot the Pharisees. Presumably Jesus, like every other pilgrim, would have immersed in one of the many ritual baths that were provided in proximity to the temple.[69] There is fairly general agreement, however, that he did not take any formal position on the question of purity regulations with regard to food, hand-washing, sexual taboos, or corpse uncleanness. Some of these matters continued to be an issue later in the community's life (Gal 2:11-14; Acts 10:44-46; 15:28-30), apparently without any appeal to Jesus' own practice or teaching to resolve the matter, unlike the case of his teaching on divorce, for example (1 Cor 7:10-11).[70] Instead, his own behavior was one of seeming indifference to the regulations surrounding such issues: he touched corpses, allowed menstruating women to touch him, moved among demoniacs and others who were

69. A papyrus fragment (P Oxy 840), to be dated probably to the second century C.E., assumes that suspected violations of the purity regulations for entering the temple were carefully monitored. According to the papyrus fragment the High Priest challenges Jesus as to whether he and his disciples had actually bathed before entering the temple precinct. Jesus' answer is to distinguish between inner and outer cleanliness. See F. Bovon, "Fragment of Oxyrhynchus 840," *JBL* 119 (2000), 705-28.

70. Meier, *A Marginal Jew*, vol. 4 (2009), pp. 343-477, "Jesus and the Purity Laws," has a thorough and careful study of all the evidence regarding Jesus and the Purity Laws and concludes that, apart from the saying about *qorban* (Mark 7:10-12), nothing in Mark 7 goes back to the historical Jesus. This does not mean that Jesus rejected the whole Mosaic dispensation, however, but rather that, as a charismatic prophet, he focused on certain aspects of the tradition that he believed were more important, "the weightier matters such as justice, mercy and faith" (Matt 23:23), and exercised freedom in other areas.

deemed impure, and declared that Sabbath observance had to cede to human need. His encounter with the Syro-Phoenician woman had changed his views as to when and where Gentiles should be admitted to the great banquet, at which he believed all peoples would eventually participate and to which all were invited (Q Luke 14:16-24/Matt 22:1-10). In short, as I have argued in *Jesus, a Jewish Galilean,* his vision was more Abrahamic than Mosaic, following the promptings of Isaiah, which envisages a universal rather than purely ethnic role for Israel's restoration.[71]

Much has been made of the fact that Jesus predicted the imminent destruction of the temple (Mark 13:1-2), and in some versions he is associated directly with this event: "I will destroy . . ." (*Gospel of Thomas* 71; see John 2:19). Such a charge against him was made at his trial also, but there it is said to be false (Mark 14:58; 15:29). As to whether he would also have spoken of his building a new temple is not as certain, since this element is missing in the *Thomas* version of the saying. Jesus himself was not of priestly background and therefore less likely to have seen the future in terms of temple imagery. Hopes of a new temple do indeed feature in some strands of Second Temple period literature, where God is most frequently seen as the builder (Tob 13:10; *1 Enoch* 90:28-29; *Jubilees* 1:17; 11Q29 8-9). E. P. Sanders suggests that Jesus may have been merely a prophet of doom, similar to his namesake Jesus the son of Ananias, "a rude peasant" who for several years prior to the first revolt continuously uttered prophecies of doom against "the temple, the people, and the city," until he was killed by a ballista during the final siege (*War* 6.300-309).[72]

While the parallels with the accounts of the trial and punishment of both characters are interesting, Jesus of Nazareth had a definite view of restoration in describing how he viewed the future of his community. Images such as gathering the flock, inviting guests, celebrating marriage festivals, and managing households are typical in terms of his references to the community that was forming around him. The household is a particularly interesting image given the close kinship ties that were characteristic of Judean society and the patriarchal structures that prevailed. But even then Jesus' subversive redefinition of what constituted a family was quite striking. When informed that his mother and his brothers were outside calling for him, he replied: "Who are my mother and my brothers?" And looking at those who sat around him he then said: "Behold my mother and

---

71. *Jesus, a Jewish Galilean,* 67-70 and 97-105.

72. E. P. Sanders, *Jesus and Judaism* (London: SCM, 1985), 61-76, especially 66.

my brothers. Whoever does the will of my Father is mother *and sister* and brother" (Mark 3:31-35). When this story is read in conjunction with the account of his visit to Nazareth (Mark 6:1-6), some interesting insights into his purpose emerge. The latter story assumes that he had brothers, who are named, and sisters who are unnamed. The sisters are not mentioned among the family members who had sought to bring him home in the earlier episode in ch. 3. Presumably this was in deference to village custom of women being restricted in public. However, in his response Jesus includes sisters as part of the new family that he is in the process of gathering.[73]

These considerations suggest that while Jesus may indeed have spoken about the destruction of the temple, its imagery or associated piety did not play a major role in his version of the restored Israel. Yet when the action in the temple is viewed in the context of the larger picture of his ministry, it becomes clear that the whole career of Jesus can be seen as a major challenge to the religious center of the nation, a challenge that could not be allowed to continue, as indeed the author of the Fourth Gospel states explicitly (John 11:47-53). Interestingly, at an early point in his narrative of the Galilean ministry, Mark mentions that the Pharisees and Herodians had made a pact that Jesus should be done away with (Mark 3:6). Presumably, Herod Antipas could have implemented such a decision, as he had done in the case of John the Baptist. Indeed, it may well be that the popular reaction to John's death prevented Antipas from moving against Jesus, since Josephus relates that the people had judged that his defeat at the hands of Aretas, the Nabatean king whose daughter he had divorced, was divine punishment for his execution of John (*Ant* 18.116; cf. Mark 6:14-16).

The Roman procurator in Judea, Pontius Pilate, had no such constraints, once he was convinced that this was a case of *stasis,* that is, possible disruption of the Roman order. Alone of the Evangelists, Luke makes this explicit in his account of the charge brought against Jesus, namely, encouraging people not to pay taxes to Caesar, calling himself king and stirring up the people by teaching throughout all Judea, beginning in Galilee (Luke 23:2-5). The first of these charges is untrue on the basis of the discussion about the image on the denarius and Jesus' reply: "Render to Caesar what is Caesar's" (Mark 12:16). As regards the second item on the list, we have seen how reticent Jesus was to claim the messianic title with its implied notion of kingship, at least in the popular mind (cf. John 6:14-15). However, the third

73. R. F. Talbot, "Jesus as Rebellious Son: Deviance and Downward Mobility in the Galilean Jesus Movement," *BTB* 38 (2008), 99-112.

item, "teaching the people in all Judea, beginning in Galilee," points unmistakably to Jesus' values revolution as we have described it, with its rejection of Roman ideals of peace, power, and possessions.

Once again, the citation at Jer 7:11 about the temple being made a "den of thieves" *(lēstai)* points to the social upheaval that was occurring in Judea ever since the death of Herod the Great in 4 B.C.E. and the subsequent deposition of Archelaus in 6 C.E. Pretenders in various parts of the kingdom sought to move into the vacuum created by Herod's death, giving rise to serious disturbances in Galilee, Perea, and Judea (*War* 2.55-65; *Ant* 17.269-85), and the Roman legate from Syria, Varus, was under severe pressure to quell the troubles. A census of property initiated by Quirinius, the new legate of Syria, as Judea became a procuratorship in 6.C.E. was the signal for the emergence of the Fourth Philosophy under Judas the Gaulanite (Galilean in *War*) and Saddoq, a Pharisee. They had a passion for freedom, saw the census as the first act of enslavement by Rome, and urged noncompliance (*War* 2.118; *Ant* 18.23). Josephus repeatedly uses the term *lēstēs* for the members of this movement, often as a term of vilification, implying that they were little better than highway robbers (cf. *Ant* 18.3-10).[74] Hengel's claim that the movement started by Judas the Galilean was identical with the Zealot party and that it continued to operate throughout the whole period from 6 to 66 C.E. has not been universally accepted.[75] Yet there can be little doubt that there was an undercurrent of opposition to Rome, often merging into open brigandage toward various officials and personages throughout the land, right up to the beginning of the first revolt in 66 C.E.

The Jesus movement was one of several protest movements that emerged throughout this period, but, unlike some of the others, its leader eschewed violence and preached love of enemies, seeking to engage through a symbolic rather than a military campaign with the Romans and the native elites, both in Galilee and Jerusalem. For those who might be opposed to Jesus and his teaching for other reasons, representing him and

74. D. M. Rhoads, *Israel in Revolution, 6-74 C.E.* (Philadelphia: Fortress, 1976), 159-62, notes that Josephus uses the term in various forms eighty-four times when covering the period from 6 to 66 C.E.

75. M. Hengel, *Die Zeloten: Untersuchungen zur jüdischen Freiheitsbewegung in der Zeit von Herodes I. bis 70 n. Chr.* (3d ed., WUNT 283; Tübingen: Mohr Siebeck, 2011). See, in particular, his treatment of the Zealot movement and the career of Jesus, 336-40. M. Smith, "Zealots and Sicarii: Their Origin and Relation," *HTR* 64 (1971), 1-19, is critical of Hengel's view, claiming that the Zealots appear for the first time only during the revolt. See Freyne, *Galilee from Alexander the Great to Hadrian*, 216-29.

his movement to the procurator as seditious was not difficult. His Galilean origins and ministry could easily be used to link him with Judas the Galilean and his militaristic anti-Roman philosophy. Provincial governors were not concerned with symbols but with power. Even though the gospels present Pilate as somewhat detached and not unsympathetic to Jesus, we get a very different picture of him from Josephus, especially in his attitude to the Judeans and their temple. As a procurator, ultimately responsible to the legate of Syria for maintaining the Roman peace, Pilate was not likely to take any chances with Jesus. A public death by crucifixion, after first having him flogged, was standard Roman practice in order to deter any would-be followers.[76] The wonder is that some at least of the "ringleaders" did not suffer the same fate as Jesus, as happened in the case of some of the other protest movements later. The likelihood must be that they were able to merge with the crowd of Galilean pilgrims in the city for Passover and then return to their homes and their erstwhile occupations. Only time would tell how they would deal with their disappointment of the failed experiment that was meant to embrace all Israel. Fortunately, some faithful women disciples remained to the end and were able to make the connection when they were surprised by the good news that God had indeed vindicated his servant. Jesus' promise that he would "go before them to Galilee" (Mark 14:28), even though they would be scattered like sheep whose shepherd was taken from them, provided a ray of hope for the future, one that would encompass both Jerusalem and Galilee, as we shall see in the following chapters.

Table Four: Rome and the Christians

6 (?) B.C.E.	The birth of Jesus.
4 B.C.E.	The death of Herod the Great.
4 B.C.E.–39 C.E.	Antipas is tetrarch of Galilee.
10 C.E.	Archelaus is deposed as ethnarch in Judea, and Roman procuratorship established there in his place.
19	Tiberias is founded in Galilee.
29-39	Pontius Pilate is procurator of Judea.
30 (?)	Jesus is crucified.

76. M. Hengel, *Crucifixion in the Ancient World and the Folly of the Cross* (London: SCM Press, 1977), 33-45; idem, *Jesus und das Judentum*, 601-24.

33 (?)	Stephen is killed and the Christian Hellenists are dispersed from Jerusalem.
41-44	Reign of Herod Agrippa, grandson of Herod the Great and friend of the emperor Gaius Caligula. James the son of Zebedee is killed in Jerusalem.
60-62	Porcius Festus is governor of Judea. Agrippa II sends Paul to Rome for trial.
62	James the brother of the Lord is tried and executed by the Jewish Sanhedrin during an interregnum of the Roman procuratorship. The Jewish Christian community in Jerusalem leaves for Pella in Transjordan.
64	Peter and Paul are martyred in Rome.
94	Christians in Asia are persecuted, as reflected in the Revelation of John.
110	Ignatius, Christian bishop of Antioch, is martyred in Rome.
115	Pliny's letter to Trajan regarding the Christians in Bithynia.
132-35	The Bar Kokhba revolt in Judea. Jewish Christians are persecuted in Palestine for refusing to join the revolt.
144	Marcion in Rome as well as other "heretics" such as Valentinus the Gnostic.
156	The martyrdom of Polycarp of Smyrna.
165	Justin Martyr in Rome writes his *Dialogue with Trypho*.
180	Irenaeus writes his *Adversus Haereses*.

CHAPTER FIVE

The Jesus Movement in Jerusalem and Its Later History

In the previous chapter it was argued that the shape and intention of Jesus' ministry was based on an older, prophetic view of Israel's destiny, one that retained the *symbolism* of temple and land as pledges of Yahweh's presence and protection, while being highly critical of the existing situation that obtained among the dominant elite of the Jerusalem temple state. The Jesus movement was not the only reformist group within Second Temple Judaism that shared this view of the Jerusalem priestly leaders and their collaboration with Rome. Both the Essenes and the Pharisees, as well as other apocalyptically minded groups, had different visions of how the new Israel should be construed and how the temple symbolism should be represented. The Essenes envisaged an alternative "temple" in the desert while the Pharisees sought to extend the notion of purity as this pertained to the actual temple itself to the home and the village also. Nor should the various sign prophets and zealot-style movements that we hear about from Josephus be excluded from any account of the religious ferment that was occurring throughout the first century, as this was discussed in the first part of this study.[1]

Jesus had gathered a small group of permanent followers during his healing and teaching ministry that accompanied him to Jerusalem on the last fateful journey. This group was given a symbolic role relating to one of the hopes of restoration, namely, the return of the twelve tribes who would partake in messianic blessings. However, the later tradition dealing with the trial and arrest of Jesus is very clear about the fact that the group, including

1. R. Horsley and J. Hanson, *Bandits, Prophets and Messiahs: Popular Movements at the Time of Jesus* (Minneapolis and Chicago: Seabury, 1985).

its leader, Peter, had deserted their master and were dispersed, once Jesus was arrested. As the account of the trial and crucifixion evolved it reflected many aspects of later Christian responses to the challenges facing the new movement. Yet the failures of the chosen ones continued to be told as an important signal, of warning, but also of hope, for future followers faced with similar situations within a hostile environment.

In light of the tragic event of Jesus' crucifixion and the hostility that he and his followers experienced in Jerusalem, it is quite surprising to discover that shortly after his death a community of his followers was established in Jerusalem and that an outsider to the original group, James the brother of the Lord, had become its leader and spokesperson. Why and how did this situation come about? We do have Luke's account of the early days of the Jerusalem community in his companion volume to his Gospel, the Acts of the Apostles. There we read that the risen Jesus spoke with his followers gathered in the holy city for forty days prior to his definitive departure, described in terms of an ascension into the clouds. They were promised the gift of the Holy Spirit in order to be his witnesses to Jerusalem, Judea, Samaria, and the ends of the earth.

Gathered in the Upper Room where they had celebrated the final Passover meal with Jesus and accompanied by Mary his mother, they elected one of their number who had been with them from Jesus' baptism to his ascension to fill the place of the traitor Judas, who had committed suicide on realizing the heinousness of his deed of betrayal (Acts 1:15-26). The promised Spirit duly arrived on Pentecost day as they all came together for prayer, and they immediately began to preach boldly to an audience of "devout Jews from every nation under heaven, living in Jerusalem" (Acts 2:5). Each heard what was being spoken in their own native tongue, a veritable reversal of the tower of Babel story when God had confused the language of the different peoples because of their sin of hubris in seeking to build a tower that would reach to heaven (Gen 11:1-9).

After this dramatic and idealized introduction to the origins of the universal mission of the church, which Luke has crafted in a manner similar to his introduction to the story of Jesus in the infancy narratives in his gospel, the mission as delineated by Jesus at Acts 1:8 can begin. Inspired by the Isaian vision of the servant of Yahweh's universal mission (Isa 49:6; cf. Acts 13:47), the Christian missionaries are to follow a path that will lead eventually from Jerusalem to Rome, where Luke's story ends with Paul, still proclaiming the good news to those who came to him there, though under house arrest. Well crafted though this narrative structure is, from a historical perspective it brushes lightly over many aspects of a complex process about which we are not so well informed.

It is generally agreed today that Acts is an apologetic history written in a context in which varied accounts were circulating about the origins of the movement and the conflicting lines of authority based on the roles of different individuals. In particular Paul's role has to be acknowledged and clarified in the post-Pauline world. Yet in subtle ways, such as the absence of his own favorite self-designation "apostle," which Luke reserves for the Twelve, he is made subservient to them and to the Jerusalem church. This depiction was surely intended to counteract alternative versions that were circulating later, as Luke seeks to reassure his readers of "the safety of the things in which they have been catechized" (Luke 1:1-4; Acts 1:1-2). His theological agenda in this two-volume work must be recognized, namely, the need to establish continuity between Jesus and Luke's readership despite the distance and difference in time and place between their situation and the originating experience of Jesus' own time in Galilee and Jerusalem. To this end "beginning from Jerusalem" was a linchpin of the Lukan construct. Yet the historical process whereby all this actually came about needs to be critically established.

At the end of Luke's gospel the departing Jesus instructs the disciples to remain in Jerusalem until they receive the gift of the Spirit, the point where Acts takes up the story (Luke 24:49). However, this information does not tally with the endings of both Mark's and Matthew's gospels. A well-attested early ending of Mark's gospel at Mark 16:8 reports an instruction given by a "young man, dressed in a white robe" to the women who had gone to the tomb to go and tell the disciples and Peter that Jesus had risen and would "go ahead of them to Galilee" (Mark 16:7). However, Mark tells us, they told no one, because they were afraid.

Matthew elaborates on this rather enigmatic ending of Mark by repeating the instruction to the women about a return to Galilee and reports an actual encounter of the women with Jesus, who tells them not to be afraid and suggests that they should go to Peter and the others. Next we are informed that Peter and the rest of the Twelve (minus Judas) go to a mountain in Galilee to which Jesus has directed them and are there given a universal mission to "make disciples of all the nations" (Matt 28:16-20). The concluding chapter of the Fourth Gospel (John 21), a chapter that is usually deemed to be a later ending to the work, also knows of a meeting between the disciples and Jesus in Galilee, not on a high mountain as in Matthew, but rather by the seashore where the disciples had returned to their erstwhile fishing career. In the next chapter we shall seek to follow these leads on a return to Galilee in tracing the origin(s) and course(s) of the early Christian mission there. In this chapter, however, the likelihood and significance of the continued centrality of Jerusalem will be explored. But first the question of Jesus' resurrection needs to be discussed since it is the cornerstone on which the continuation of the movement in all its varied forms was based.

"He Is Risen, He Is Not Here"

Perhaps the best place to begin this discussion of what was implied for the early Christians in claiming that Jesus was raised from the dead is with Paul of Tarsus. A self-confessed zealous Jew of Pharisaic persuasion, he had come to Jerusalem to study at the feet of the famous Jewish teacher Gamaliel shortly after the death of Jesus in the early thirties C.E. Since Paul was closely associated with the Pharisees, he would have been quite familiar with their notion of resurrection from the dead, as described by Josephus (*Ant* 18.14; *War* 3.373-75; see 2 Macc 7:9). Paul, on the basis of an appearance of the risen Christ to him personally, a story that Luke later tells in terms of Paul's Damascus Road experience (Acts 9:1-9), claimed the right to be an apostle of Jesus Christ on a par with other authoritative figures such as Peter and the Twelve and James and all the apostles, who also had had similar experiences (1 Cor 9:1-2; 15:8-11; cf. 15:3-7). In writing to the Corinthian church that he had previously established, Paul dealt with the question of Jesus' resurrection since apparently some of the new converts either queried the notion altogether or had a different understanding of Jesus' fate, such as, for example, an exaltation to heaven similar to that of Elijah or Enoch.

In dealing with the issue, Paul begins by reaffirming his belief that Jesus was indeed raised from the dead, based on his appearance to him (1 Cor 15:8, 12).[2] He then mounts a different argument inspired by his own Pharisaic upbringing, which, on the basis of an apocalyptic understanding of history, had taught him that the just would indeed be raised and "shine like

2. The Greek term used here in v. 8 is *ōphthē*, which is the perfect passive of the verb "to see," *horaō*. The perfect tense suggests a past event with continuous effect in the present, and the passive mode, meaning that the effect is not brought about by the person who experiences it, is to be translated as "was seen" rather than "saw." This careful use of language suggests that the experience was outside the normal human capacity of the people experiencing the appearances of the Risen One.

the stars forever" (Dan 12:2-3; cf. *Ant* 13.172; 18.14).[3] As he develops his case Paul twice declares, "If there is no resurrection from the dead, then Christ is not raised" (vv. 13 and 16). Ultimately, resurrection is an act of God's justice in vindicating those faithful ones whose lives manifest their commitment to God's law (*1 Enoch* 104:2-6). For Paul, Jesus' vindication is the firstfruits of a great harvest (1 Cor 15:20-24), one that he expects to be completed in the near future (vv. 51-54). In a later letter to the Corinthians he again affirms his belief in the resurrection of Jesus, this time seeing it as a new act of creation on the part of God in which the believer already participates. "It is the One who said 'Let light shine out of darkness' [cf. Gen 1:3] who has shone in our hearts to give the light of the knowledge of the glory of God in the face of Jesus Christ" (2 Cor 4:6). This knowledge assures both Paul and his converts that "the One who raised the Lord Jesus will raise us also with Jesus, and bring us with you into his presence" (v. 14).

When we turn from Paul's theological reflections on the resurrection and its implications for Christian living to the narrative accounts of the Evangelists, we appear to be operating in a very different landscape. Unlike the narrative realism of the Passion stories, the post-resurrection stories are somewhat disjointed, individual characters are disconcerted and frightened, mysterious happenings such as earthquakes occur, and the appearance of figures of a distinctly otherworldly hue give a somewhat eerie quality to the whole. Two different types of stories occur: descriptions of the discovery of an empty tomb and accounts of appearances of the Risen One. Each serves a different purpose within the overall proclamation of the different Evangelists, and this makes it impossible to construct a plausible historical sequence of events on the first Easter days from these accounts.[4]

The stories of *the empty tomb* highlight the fact that Jesus had actually died and was buried, a fate that was not necessarily granted to all convicted criminals. Furthermore, the desire of two of his female followers to ensure that his body was duly anointed (Matt 28:1) was in accordance with Jewish burial customs. That they found that the body was missing was not in itself a proof of resurrection, since it could simply have indicated that it had been stolen and disposed of in some other way. Matthew seems to be aware of this possibility when he reports that the Jewish authorities had asked Pilate

---

3. G. Nickelsburg, *Resurrection, Immortality and Eternal Life in Intertestamental Judaism and Early Christianity* (Cambridge: Harvard University Press, 2006).

4. C. H. Dodd, "The Appearances of the Risen Christ: An Essay in Form-Criticism of the Gospels," in D. Nineham, ed., *Studies in the Gospel: Essays in Memory of R. H. Lightfoot* (Oxford: Blackwell, 1957), 9-35.

to place a guard on the tomb in order to preclude any deceit by Jesus' followers (27:62-66). In this regard, it is interesting to note that while Paul is aware of Jesus' burial, he does not mention the empty tomb stories in his very early report, presumably emanating from the Jerusalem community (1 Cor 15:4). This suggests that these particular stories may have been intended to counteract rumors that the disciples had indeed disposed of the body of Jesus surreptitiously, rumors that were still circulating when the gospel of Matthew was written some sixty years later (Matt 28:11-15).

The *appearance stories* serve several different purposes. Paul declares that he himself has received and handed on the account in 1 Cor 15:3-6, suggesting a very early pre-Pauline formulation of the Easter faith. Its primary function is an endorsement of the roles of certain key figures and the groups attached to them: Peter and the Twelve, James and all the apostles, and the five hundred brethren, "some of whom are alive and some have died," all have had appearances of the Risen One. There is no mention here of any of the women witnesses, particularly Mary Magdalene, who in the gospel narratives is the first to encounter and recognize the Risen One (Matt 28:8-10; John 20:11-18). The manner in which Paul seeks to attach his own experience of the Risen Christ to those of others (1 Cor 15:6-11; cf. 9:1) confirms the view that the chief function of the appearance stories had to do with sanctioning the authority of different key figures within the early church.[5]

A second function of the appearance stories is to emphasize that the crucifixion did not end Jesus' teaching role for his disciples by relating the various instructions he gives to different characters. This tendency would later be further developed in several of the gnostic gospels, where the Risen Christ appears to different key figures, James, Peter, Judas, and Mary, for example, and engages in lengthy dialogues and discourses with them. Indeed, Luke may well have sought to challenge this open-ended approach of appeal to the continued teaching role of the Risen One when he writes that Jesus "appeared to his disciples *for forty days,* speaking about the kingdom of God" (Acts 1:3). Having promised the gift of the Spirit, Jesus departed from his disciples definitively, with an assurance uttered by "men dressed in white" that "this Jesus who has been taken up from you into heaven will come in the same manner as you have seen him go" (v. 11). However, no specific time frame is given for such a return, in conformity with Luke's extended view of the present age.

5. J. Jeremias, *New Testament Theology: The Proclamation of Jesus* (London: SCM, 1971), 300-312: "Easter: The Earliest Tradition and the Earliest Interpretation."

A third function of the stories is to highlight Jesus' corporeality, while at the same time emphasizing the fact of his bodily, that is, his personal, transformation. The need for these apparently contradictory indicators arose from outsiders' ridicule of the notion of an individual's resurrection, typical of the attitude that Paul encountered when he addressed the Areopagus in Athens, as Luke indicates (Acts 17:18). It was important to demonstrate continuity between the Risen One and the earthly Jesus, since fear and non-recognition on the part of those who encountered the Risen One are highlighted:

> Jesus himself stood among them and said to them: "Peace be with you." They were startled and terrified and thought they were seeing a ghost *(pneuma)*. He said to them: "Why are you frightened, and why do doubts arise in your hearts? Look at my hands and feet; see that it is I myself. Touch and see, for a ghost *(pneuma)* does not have flesh and bones as you see that I have." And when he had said this, he showed them his hands and his feet. While in their joy they were disbelieving and still wondering, he said to them: "Have you anything here to eat?" They gave him a piece of broiled fish, and he took it and ate it in their presence. (Luke 24:36-43)

The Thomas story in John 20:19-29 is a Johannine version of the same theme, except that the Lukan language of fear, disbelief, and wonder is absent. Instead the Johannine disciples rejoice, and the Holy Spirit is bestowed on them there and then. Thomas's doubt is removed a week later and he too is declared "blessed," even if, from a Johannine perspective, belief in the witness of others rather than physical contact with the Risen One should be the basis for faith.

This emphasis on the corporeality of the Risen One would appear to have come about because of some later tendencies that are best exemplified within the Johannine community, where some were denying the fact that the pre-resurrection Jesus had come in the flesh (1 John 1:1-4; 4:2). Docetism, as this heresy was labeled, ran counter to the almost universal early Christian claims of Jesus' real humanity in that it claimed that he merely seemed to be human but in fact was a divine being appearing in human garb. The early appearance stories in which the Risen One defies the laws of physics by appearing among the disciples even though the doors are shut (John 20:26) or is not immediately recognizable until he has performed some characteristic action such as breaking bread (Luke 24:30-32) or giving instructions to the disciples to go fishing (John 21:4-8) may well have contributed to the perception that he had always been a ghost, not a real flesh and blood person.[6] No doubt, Paul's discussion of the nature of the risen body in which he starkly contrasts the physical *(sarkikos)* with the spiritual *(pneumatikos)* body, the perishable with the imperishable (1 Cor 15:35-49), also contributed to this distortion, which passages such as that cited from Luke's later description of Jesus' corporeality sought to correct.

The Resurrection Event and History

Since the resurrection of Jesus is properly understood not as an event in time and space but as a vindication by God of Jesus' life, we can only discuss historical traces of the event in terms of its effects on the lives of those who were privileged to encounter the Risen One. In this regard all the canonical gospels are quite circumspect. None of them describes the resurrection as it happened, but they all recount different facets of its impact among Jesus' followers. It is only in this sense that one should speak of the resurrection of Jesus as a historical event. There are several areas in which its effects can be captured and its historic meaning for life deciphered. These have to do with the ways in which the disciples came to an understanding of Jesus' identity and purpose, the manner in which that realization clarified their own role, and the possibility of drawing on their earlier experiences and memories in dealing with the challenges that confronted them as they embarked on their mission.

Understanding Jesus' Mission

During the period of Jesus' public ministry the inner circle of his followers centered on the Twelve clearly experienced something remarkable about this man who had summoned them to follow him in his ministry of preaching and healing. The Synoptic Gospels' portrayal of their being peremptorily summoned to abandon home, occupation, and family to follow Jesus is probably more likely than the Johannine account, which portrays some at least of the group as being already disciples of John the Baptist and asking to

6. R. E. Brown, *The Community of the Beloved Disciple* (New York: Paulist, 1979), 110-23.

join Jesus (John 1:35-51).[7] As Galilean village people they would have been well aware of the political and social ferment that was taking place in their region during the reign of Antipas, especially the forcible moving of people from the surrounding villages to inhabit his new foundation Tiberias, a city that was intended to honor the new Roman emperor, Tiberius, as discussed in Chapter 2 (pp. 64-66). Some of them were fishermen who could make a reasonably good living from the Lake of Kinnereth, especially because of the facilities at nearby Tarichea/Magdala for salting the produce of the sea, thereby making it possible to export the fruits of their labor farther afield. By comparison with their coreligionists in the other subregions of Galilee, who had to labor long and hard to eke out a living from their plots of land, these natives of the lake region were relatively affluent and mobile.

We can only speculate as to what prompted Jesus to summon these particular people to join his movement, or what inspired them to answer his call so promptly. The Evangelists have deliberately crafted their narrative accounts of the call of the two pairs of brothers (John and James, Simon and Andrew) in such a stark and sparing manner in order to highlight the personal demand that following Jesus would make on the lives of those who would join his permanent retinue (Mark 1:16-20). Somewhat later Jesus himself articulated that demand for a would-be disciple: "Leave the dead to bury their dead" (Q Luke 9:59-60; Matt 8:21-22). This goes against the grain of all that Jewish law and piety demanded of a son or daughter.[8] But then Jesus himself seemed to have broken the ties of kinship and family responsibility for a different vision of human community. The summons of his mother and brothers for him to return home, as prescribed by long-standing custom of village society (Mark 3:31-35), went unheeded, and when eventually he did return to Nazareth it is clear that the locals had very little understanding or sympathy for his activity (6:1-6). In the previous chapter

---

7. The Fourth Gospel is aware of annoyance among the disciples of John over Jesus' popularity with the crowds, presumably because of the latter's more liberal views about the need for Jewish purification (John 3:25-26). In all probability this reflects later rivalries, possibly in Ephesus, between followers of the Baptist and Christians, since according to Acts 19:1-7 Paul encountered followers of John there, who had undergone his baptism but knew nothing of Jesus. The notice in the Fourth Gospel may well reflect such an ongoing rivalry between the two groups, which the Evangelist seeks to resolve by highlighting the close connections between John and Jesus. The story of disciples of John wishing to join Jesus' followers would serve the interests of such a reconciliation.

8. M. Hengel, *The Charismatic Leader and His Followers* (Edinburgh: Clark, 1981), especially 1-3.

it was suggested that Jesus himself, as distinct from his Galilean followers, had been a disciple of John the Baptist before his return to Galilee, on the basis of his fulsome encomium of John. If this is a plausible suggestion, then Jesus' itinerant lifestyle had deeply religious implications based on an older view of Israel's vocation and ethos as an "exodus" people. Jesus sought to enact such a vision in the land rather than in the desert as John and other dissident groups such as the Essenes had chosen to do.

Clarifying the Disciples' Role

However, his Galilean disciples were far from clear about the true implications of Jesus' mission or their own role in regard to it. The incident that Mark locates in the journey to Jerusalem section is surely indicative of their misunderstanding. James and John, the sons of Zebedee, asked for special favors "when you come into your glory" — a clear indication that they expected a triumphant outcome to his ministry. However, Jesus curtly dismissed the request, declaring that they "do not know what [they] are asking," and went on to speak to the whole group of his chalice and his baptism, veiled references to the suffering and death that he suspected lay ahead (Mark 10:35-40).

In the instruction that followed Jesus proposed a model of leadership that contrasts starkly with that of Gentile (i.e., Roman) rulers who lord it over their subjects and press down on them. A model that is based on royal power is not what he had in mind, but rather one of service and meekness (Mark 10:42-45). In disabusing the disciples of any ideas of a glorious outcome, Jesus was rejecting the most popular current understanding of Israel's future ruler, namely that of a powerful earthly king, a new David, who will restore Israel's fortunes to their former greatness among the nations. The disciples' subsequent abandonment of their teacher and his betrayal by one of them are clear indications that, right to the end, this intimate group did not fully grasp the true purpose of Jesus' life as this was unfolding in their presence, despite their experience of rejection while participating in the mission in Galilee and Jesus' avoidance of the enthusiasm of the crowds desirous to take him by force and make him king (John 6:14-15; see also Acts 1:6).

However, as Luke tells the story, the Pentecost experience following Jesus' meeting with them changed the disciples from fearful and timid followers into bold proclaimers of the good news that God had vindicated

Jesus' claims by raising him from the dead. However, recent rhetorical analysis of Luke's writings tends to dismiss this account of new beginnings as an idealized and symbolic narrative with little or no historical information, whereas in the past, the emphasis was more on Luke's reliability as a historian of earliest Christianity. However, the search for putative sources in these early chapters of Acts could never be very successful in view of Luke's rewriting of whatever traditions he may have drawn on.[9] Furthermore, the recent tendency to date the work to the second century has changed the understanding of Luke's main concerns when writing his second volume, and these, it is alleged, have to do with issues facing the Jesus movement at that time, rather than giving reliable information about the earliest days.[10]

However, while taking account of these discussions, we should not dismiss Luke's opus as mere fiction, in the sense of a purely fabricated history. Ancient historiography had varied purposes, and Luke does show himself to be interested in dealing with the past independently of his own present. We should recognize that he is capable of recapturing in his narrative the texture and tone of original incidents and speeches, as he considered "suitable to the occasion" — in best Thucydidean fashion.[11] One has only to think of his account of Paul's address to the Areopagus at Athens (Acts 17:16-34) to appreciate his ability to project himself into different situations and audiences. Indeed some older scholars deemed the speeches that Luke puts on the lips of Peter so "fitting" in terms of syntax and style as well

---

9. See J. Dupont, *The Sources of Acts* (London: Darton, Longman and Todd, 1964). By way of conclusion to this study Dupont writes: "There are so many indications that set us on the track of pre-existing sources. We seize a link which is very clear; we try to follow the source from which it comes and, almost immediately it becomes lost and disappears.... This can be explained by the literary work of the author; he is not satisfied with transcribing his sources, he rewrites the text by putting the imprint of his style and vocabulary everywhere" (p. 166). For a more recent discussion, building on Dupont's study, see R. Pervo, *Dating Acts: Between Evangelists and Apologists* (Santa Rosa: Polebridge, 2006), Appendix 1, 347-58.

10. Cf. the remarks of J. Tyson, "Source Criticism of Acts," in A. McGowan and K. Richards, eds., *Method and Meaning: Essays in Honor of Harold W. Attridge* (Atlanta: SBL, 2011), 41-57, who concludes that "decisions about the sources are closely related to decisions about the date, authorship and purpose of Acts" (p. 56). In his earlier study *Marcion and Luke-Acts: A Defining Struggle* (Columbia: South Carolina University Press, 2006), Tyson argues that the crisis generated by Marcion's schism and its widespread popularity created a serious problem for proto-orthodox Christianity, especially because of his foregrounding of Paul as the only apostle. See further p. 342 n. 53.

11. For a different perspective, cf. S. Mason, "Speech-Making in Ancient Rhetoric, Josephus and Acts: Message and Playfulness," *Early Christianity* 3 (2012), 147-71.

as content that they concluded he must be drawing on Aramaic traditions originating in Jerusalem.[12]

Addressing Challenges

Irrespective of such claims about sources, the highly respected British New Testament scholar C. H. Dodd long ago suggested a deliberately "primitive" quality to the early speeches in Acts (Acts 2:14-36, 37-38; 3:12-26; 4:8-12; 10:34-43). He suggested that they all follow a definite pattern, thus underlining their authorial unity. The suggested structure is as follows: (1) the age of fulfilment has dawned; (2) this has taken place through the ministry, death, and resurrection of Jesus, events of which Peter and his companions are witnesses; (3) the resurrection means Jesus' exaltation to the heavenly realm, meriting him various titles associated with Israel's future redemption; (4) the presence of the Holy Spirit means that messianic times have arrived and will shortly reach their consummation; and (5) the hearers are appealed to to repent, offered forgiveness for their part in Jesus' crucifixion, and invited to join the messianic community. At each point of the development various scriptural passages are appealed to, many of them from the Psalms and Isaiah.[13]

The crucifixion and subsequent resurrection are central to all these accounts, but unlike Paul's and later theology, where Jesus' death is understood as an "atoning sacrifice for sin" (Rom 3:24-25; Heb 10:12; Acts 13:38-39), the emphasis of the early speeches is on the fact of the Judean leaders' complicity in the unjust handing over of Jesus to Pilate and his subsequent vindication by God. It is this latter experience, not Jesus' death, that was crucial to these first preachers. As Luke presents it, God's plan, foretold in the prophets, has been wonderfully realized. Thus we hear of Jesus' "mighty works and wonders," which are described as "signs which God has done through him" in the Pentecost speech (2:22). Peter's speech in the house of the Roman centurion Cornelius is the most detailed in terms of a description of Jesus' ministry, but the pattern and message are the same as the earlier ones:

12. C. C. Torrey, *The Composition and Date of Acts* (Harvard Theological Studies; Cambridge: Harvard University Press, 1916). However, as Pervo notes, the work of J. Fitzmyer and others on Palestinian Aramaic as this is found in, e.g., the Qumran Scrolls makes Torrey's hypothesis altogether unlikely.

13. C. H. Dodd, *The Apostolic Preaching and Its Developments* (London: Hodder and Stoughton, 1936), 7-35.

As for the word which he, the Lord of all, sent to the children of Israel, preaching the gospel of peace through Jesus, the Messiah, you know the thing [literally "the word"] that happened through all Judea, beginning from Galilee after the baptism which John preached: that God anointed Jesus of Nazareth with Holy Spirit and power, and he went about doing good and healing all who were oppressed by the devil, because God was with him. And we are witnesses of all that he did in the country of the Jews and in Jerusalem. Him they killed by hanging him on a tree. God raised him up on the third day and permitted him to be manifest, not to all the people, but to witnesses chosen beforehand by God, namely to us, who ate and drank with him after he rose from the dead. (Acts 10:36-41)

The significance of this speech is the manner in which the life and ministry of Jesus are now construed, suggesting an early biographical outline similar to that used by Mark subsequently for his gospel, even to the highlighting of casting out of demons as part of Jesus' healing ministry. Peter speaks with confidence now about the meaning of the things that he has previously experienced but either misunderstood or did not fully grasp earlier. His new role and that of his companions is one of boldly witnessing to the truth about Jesus for Jews and Gentiles alike. Far from being a criminal deserving of death by crucifixion, Jesus was in fact God's anointed one, fulfilling his destiny as this had been foretold in the Scriptures.

Those very Scriptures could now be mined for suitable epithets for Jesus and his role: he is *mare'* (Lord) and *Mashiaḥ* (Christ); he is the Holy and Righteous one; he is the rejected stone that has become the Cornerstone, as announced in Ps 118:22 with regard to the new temple; or, finally, he is the savior of all. Of all the declarations about Jesus' role and identity in these speeches, one in particular stands out as being very early indeed, thereby confirming Luke's historical sensitivity about the events he is reporting: Jesus is described as the Messiah who is "waiting in heaven" until "the time of universal restoration that God announced long ago through his holy prophets" comes about (Acts 3:21). This formulation shows an awareness of how fluid the earliest proclamations could be in terms of Jesus' identity as Messiah, or merely Messiah designate, as in this formulation.

Unlike other instances in the speeches where his exaltation to God's right hand has constituted him as God's Messiah (Acts 2:36), or when his healing ministry is already seen as the activity of God's anointed one (10:38), the statement in Acts 3:21 has a different, one can say primitive, ring to it. In this case the revelation of Jesus' messianic status is associated with the final consummation of all things, soon to be realized according to Jewish apocalyptic expectations, while there also appears the terminology of the Stoics in regard to the cosmic cycle in which a renewal of all things was expected to follow a great conflagration, but the apocalyptic framework remains Jewish.[14] Because the early Jewish-Christian mind was so steeped in apocalyptic thinking, there was no contradiction between these different moments with regard to Jesus' messianic identity, however. Though not necessarily himself sharing the perspective, Luke was aware that in this worldview past, present, and future could all blend easily into a complex picture of a single process or be separated out into different moments from a human perception.

It is somewhat puzzling that there is no mention of Jesus as teacher in these early speeches, especially since the followers are constantly described as his disciples in the gospel accounts. This suggests a master-pupil relationship, but the designation is reserved solely for the account of his pre-Easter association with them and does not occur elsewhere in the New Testament.[15] While various collections, both oral and written, of Jesus' sayings and teaching must have circulated from an early stage, possibly already during his lifetime and certainly after his death, these do not seem to have played an important part in the early Jerusalem proclamation as construed by Luke. Perhaps this is because the focus of these early speeches was convincing the Jerusalem crowds of the messianic status of Jesus, while his teachings were reserved for those who would join the movement that quickly arose in his name and imitated his lifestyle, the topic of the next chapter. Here it is sufficient to point out that the resurrection experience leading to the gift of the Spirit was to contribute greatly to the understanding of Jesus' teachings also.

The author of the Fourth Gospel is most explicit on this matter. Twice he declares that it was only after the resurrection that the disciples remembered *and understood* things that Jesus had said to them while he was with them (John 2:21-22; 12:16). It is in this gospel also that the promise of the Spirit/Paraclete that they would receive after Jesus' departure is couched in terms of teaching and bringing everything to their minds (14:25-26; 16:12-15). However, this understanding of the transmission and interpretation of

14. Luke uses two technical terms in Acts 3:20-21, *anapsyxis*/refreshment and *apokatastasis*/restoration, both of which are rare in the NT but found in various Greco-Roman philosophical writings.

15. P. Trebilco, *Self-Designation and Group Identity in the New Testament* (Cambridge: Cambridge University Press, 2012), 208-46.

Jesus' teachings is not confined to the gospel of John. It is found in Matthew's gospel also, where Jesus' presence is understood to continue with the community in its organizational and teaching activities "to the end of time" (Matt 18:15-20; 28:20).[16] Thus, while recent discussion of the sayings tradition emphasizes the stability of oral memory, thereby countering the skepticism of some scholars with regard to the possibility of ever hearing the "very words" of Jesus, we should not ignore the freedom with which various teachers and preachers adapted and applied Jesus' sayings to meet new situations in their communities, precisely because the resurrection of Jesus and the gift of the Spirit gave them the freedom to do so.

Jerusalem as Center for the Jesus Movement

The claim of the previous section has been that, thanks to Luke's historical sensitivity, in the opening chapters of Acts we can catch echoes of the very early preaching of Jesus' followers gathered in Jerusalem. Because their leader had been executed there as a criminal, it is quite surprising to find any traces of Jesus' followers in the holy city. Indeed, some modern scholars who think that we cannot retrieve any reliable historical information about the early Jerusalem Jesus-followers from Luke's account, go so far as to question whether any such group in Jerusalem ever existed. However, such a hypercritical position is in my view unwarranted.[17] Allowing for the fact that Luke's rhetoric is directed toward his own (later) readership, it would have been counterintuitive for him to have fabricated the whole account of the early Jerusalem community, and, in addition, Paul is aware of the importance of Jerusalem as a center for the new movement, even though he also wants to assert his own independence from an early stage (Gal 1:16-20). In other words, there is independent evidence for the centrality of Jerusalem, even when, as we shall see, many of the details are uncertain.

The underlying reason for Jesus-followers' presence there is quite clear, however, when one considers the transformative effect of the resurrection experiences on their understanding of Jesus and his mission. Once

16. Matt 18:20 has an interesting rabbinic parallel: "Wherever two or three are gathered studying the Torah, the Shekinah (presence) of Yahweh is there" (*m. Aboth* 3.2).

17. See the articles of C. R. Matthews, M. P. Miller, D. E. Smith, and L. H. Martin, all in their different ways challenging the "Lukan myth" of the Jerusalem church and its role in the development of early Christianity, in R. Cameron and M. P. Miller, eds., *Redescribing Christian Origins* (Atlanta: SBL, 2004).

they were assured that Jesus was indeed the Messiah of Israel, but a very different Messiah from what they had previously anticipated, and that his life could be presented as the inauguration of the messianic age, a presence in Jerusalem was both expected and demanded. The promises associated with Zion in the Hebrew Scriptures would be fulfilled, and the speeches to the various Jerusalem audiences, as well as early hymns that Paul would draw on later, as in Phil 2:6-11, could integrate the fact of Jesus' humiliation and death with his now triumphant reign and his reception of a new name, *mare'/kyrios/Lord.*[18]

This triumph over apparent failure redounded to the glory of God the Father and encouraged them to announce the good news of their witness about Jesus in Jerusalem, irrespective of whatever hostile reception they could expect from the Jerusalem political and religious leaders. Noteworthy in these speeches is the irenic tone that they adopt, avoiding any prophetic condemnation of the Jewish leaders and their actions, or of the temple itself for that matter. The condemnation to death of an innocent man is described as having been "done in ignorance," thereby providing an excuse of sorts by highlighting the wonderful outcome for all Israel that the resurrection of Jesus has now inaugurated.[19] There is then "contextual plausibility" as well as positive evidence for maintaining the notion of a community of Jesus-followers in Jerusalem from a very early date after the crucifixion.

The centrality of Jerusalem in Israelite and Judean history went back to David's choice of this Jebusite fortress on Mount Zion as the capital of his new kingdom that would supersede the old tribal federation (2 Sam 5:6-12). Solomon's building there of the temple for Yahweh, who now became the patron god of the city (1 Kings 5:4-5), further enhanced its reputation. Expectations regarding a future anointed one, a Son of David, as the ideal king, continued into the first century, even prompting Jesus to challenge the scribal interpretation of Ps 110:1 as reference to the promise (Mark 12:35-37). It is no surprise, therefore, that Peter's speech on Pentecost day to his Jerusalem audience should draw on this expectation by alluding to the link with David, not, however, by recalling his exploits as king but rather underlining his prophetic powers as author of the Psalms in declaring that God "would not allow his holy one to see corruption" (Ps 16:10; Acts 2:25-28, especially

18. For a discussion of the Semitic (Aramaic) background to the use of the title *kyrios,* see J. Fitzmyer, *A Wandering Aramean: Collected Aramaic Essays* (SBL Monograph Series 25; Missoula: Scholars, 1979), 115-42, especially 130-32.

19. B. F. Meyer, *The Early Christians: Their World Mission and Self-Discovery* (Wilmington: Glazier, 1986), 77-78.

v. 27). David could not have been referring to himself, Peter argues, since he had indeed died and his tomb was still in Jerusalem, and so was in fact "speaking of the resurrection of the Messiah" (v. 31).[20] This is quite a remarkable adaptation of the psalm, since the expectation surrounding the Davidic Messiah was of an earthly king, not a crucified "criminal" whom God would subsequently vindicate.

The Zion tradition as a symbol of God's election and protection had also developed independently of the royal associations, especially in the exilic and post-exilic periods (the sixth to fourth centuries B.C.E.), when Judea was without a king. German Old Testament scholar Martin Noth neatly characterizes the change of emphasis by declaring that Jerusalem was gradually transformed from a royal capital to a cult city. Zion and its people could replace the discredited monarchy as bearers of the promise to David.[21] The book of Isaiah, which reached its completed form only in the Persian period (the fifth century B.C.E.), develops this motif further in an opening oracle where Zion is the source of the wisdom that the nations are searching for (Isa 2:2-3). Ben Sira in the second century B.C.E. had, as we saw in Chapter 3, developed the theme further, stressing Zion's importance to the scribal tradition and identifying Wisdom and Torah (Sir 24:1-29). Thus Jerusalem became the focal point for pious Diaspora Jews such as Paul to come and study at the feet of one of the renowned Torah teachers.[22]

---

20. David's tomb must have been a well-recognized monument in first-century Jerusalem. Josephus describes David's burial by Solomon with "the splendor customary for royal burials," but relates how the tomb was twice robbed because of the vast amount of money that it was reputed to contain. The first occasion was when the Hasmonean Hyrcanus II took 3000 talents in order to get the Syrian king Antiochus Sidetes to end a siege of Jerusalem and remove his army (*Ant* 7.392-94; 13.249). Herod the Great entered the tomb also hoping to find "a large sum of money" to defray the cost of his lavish gifts. However, one of his guards was struck by lightning, and Herod retreated quickly. In order to make reparation he adorned the entrance with a memorial of white marble (*Ant* 7.394; 16.179-82). Later tradition locates it on Mount Zion beside the Cenacle or Upper Room where the Last Supper is traditionally located. Cf. J. Murphy-O'Connor, *The Holy Land* (3rd ed.; Oxford: Oxford University Press, 1992), 111.

21. S. Freyne, *Jesus, a Jewish Galilean: A New Reading of the Jesus Story* (New York: Continuum, 2005), 96, with reference to the mythicization of Zion in the psalms of Zion. Psalms 46–48 form a mini-cluster of thematically linked poems, with the shortest at the center (Psalm 47) celebrating the universal kingship of Yahweh, bracketed by Psalm 46, which speaks of the Holy City in cosmic terms, and Psalm 48, hailing the wonders of Zion, impregnable because "God is in the temple."

22. The famous *Theodotos Inscription* found in Jerusalem and dated to the pre-70 period, speaks of a synagogue for "the reading of the Law" and "the teaching of the command-

There is a further development of the myth of Zion in the book of *Jubilees,* a rewriting of a section of Genesis dating from the mid–second century B.C.E. that was prompted by the attempted Hellenization of the Jerusalem cult by Antiochus Epiphanes. The city could now be described as "the center of the navel of the earth," one of three holy places facing each other, namely, the Garden of Eden, Mount Sinai, and Zion (*Jub* 8:12-21, especially v. 19). The image occurs in the listing of the nations following the division of the earth after the flood among Noah's three sons Shem, Ham, and Japheth (Gen 9:18-19). In the rewriting of this episode in *Jubilees,* Zion's position is at the center of the territory of Shem, the most favored of the sons, and hence its special location between Eden and Sinai, mediating between the universality of Adam and the particularity of Moses.[23] This very issue of mediating between these two poles would confront the Jesus-followers quite early with the success of the Pauline mission to the Gentiles, as we shall presently discuss.

This long history of the significance of Zion provides the rationale for the emergence at an early date of a community of Jesus-followers in Jerusalem. In two brief summaries, Luke describes the group as "having all things in common" and gathering in their homes "for the breaking of bread" while continuing to visit the temple (Acts 2:43-47; 4:32-37). This description, especially the sharing of goods, is reminiscent of the Essene community, a radical expression of the intended egalitarianism within an ideal Israel. Since there is some circumstantial evidence of an Essene group in Jerusalem located close to Mount Zion (the so-called Essene Gate), it could well be that some Jesus-followers adopted a similar lifestyle in Luke's estimation. However, the continued attendance at the temple would certainly not be consonant with an Essene influence, nor does it echo Jesus' declaration that the temple was doomed. Luke may well be painting an idealized picture of harmony in the early days of the nascent community, a harmony that was broken internally by the story of Ananias and Sapphira falsifying their income (5:1-11) and externally by the opposition from the Jewish temple ar-

---

ments" that was built by one Vettenos, a priest and synagogue leader, who was the son and grandson of two synagogue leaders. In addition it had lodgings for visitors from the Diaspora as well as water installations, presumably *mikvaoth* for ritual washings. Vettenos's father and the elders were responsible for the commemorative stone. See J. Kloppenborg, "The Theodotos Synagogue Inscription and the Problem of First-Century Buildings," in J. Charlesworth, ed., *Jesus and Archaeology* (Grand Rapids: Eerdmans, 2006), 236-82.

23. P. Alexander, "Early Jewish Geography," in D. N. Freedman, et al., eds., *The Anchor Bible Dictionary* (New York: Doubleday, 1992), 2:977-88, especially 980-93.

istocracy. Thus, for Luke, the primitive unity of the group was under threat, and a further episode of internal discord arose when the Greek-speaking widows complained that they were not receiving their fair share in the daily distribution of food in the community (6:1-2). This complaint was all the more ironic in view of the fact that in the earlier accounts of the groups meeting to break bread together in their homes, Luke explicitly mentions that they did so with "glad and generous hearts" (2:46).

Hebrews, Hellenists, and Stephen

The dispute allowed Luke to introduce the "Hebrews" and "Hellenists" as separate groupings within the community, even though they had not been mentioned previously in the narrative. In order to resolve the seemingly trivial problem of philanthropy that had arisen, the Twelve resorted to what would appear to be a much bigger community decision, namely, the election of seven deacons, all of whom had Greek names. These would take charge of such matters, leaving the apostles to devote themselves to the ministry of the word (Acts 6:3-6). Luke thereby describes a form of church order that probably reflects the situation of his own day. We hear nothing further of the dispute, but rather of one of the seven deacons, Stephen, "full of grace and power" (v. 8), emerging as an inspired evangelist for the new movement. His ministry eventually gave rise to a serious dispute between him and members of different "synagogues" belonging to various Diaspora Jews living in Jerusalem, Saul of Tarsus being among them (7:58). Stephen was eventually arraigned and condemned for speaking against Moses and God, or alternatively against the holy place and the Law (6:11, 13).

Clearly, Luke sees this whole episode as a critical stage in his account of the development of the early Christian mission. His narrative goes on to tell of the "dispersion" that followed the death of Stephen and of the success of these new evangelists in proclaiming the word wherever they went. He instances the success of Philip in Samaria (Acts 8:4-8) and later mentions "the dispersed" again as having great success in Phoenicia, Cyprus, and Antioch, all places where a Hellenistic ethos prevailed (11:19-21).[24] It is Luke's

24. It was in Antioch that the Jesus-believers were called Christians for the first time, a Latinism, probably developed first by outsiders, that signifies supporter or adherent of a person, in this case *Christos/Messiah*. Clearly, the Jesus-followers were distinctive enough as messianic Jews to be recognizable as different from other Jews in the city. See Trebilco, *Self-Designation*, 272-97.

intention to show the beginnings of the mission to the Gentiles as being the work of Greek-speaking Jews who were Jesus-followers from Jerusalem, even though he did not profile them in the early chapters of Acts, where the attention is all on Peter and the Twelve addressing the Judean authorities. Nevertheless, the list of places represented by Diaspora Jews in the Pentecost day experience, each hearing Peter's words in their own language (2:5-13), prepares the reader in advance for the role played by Diaspora Jews in breaking new and fertile ground where Paul and others would subsequently reap a rich harvest.[25]

There has been much discussion about the identity and significance of the Hebrews and Hellenists, in terms of both the role they play in Luke's narrative and their possible contribution to the original development of the new movement in its earliest phase. As Luke tells the story the distinction between them must have been considerable, since it was only the Hellenists that had to leave the city in the wake of the disturbances caused by Stephen's death, whereas the Hebrews were not involved, it would seem. However, Luke does not develop this point or suggest that there was a theological rift between the two groups. That could wait for later in the narrative when Paul was accused by Jews from Asia of disloyalty to his Mosaic birthright, eventually leading to his arrest and trial, also in Jerusalem (Acts 21:27–22:29).

As previously mentioned, critical New Testament scholarship going back to the early nineteenth century has on the whole taken the Lukan account at face value, even when highlighting Luke's own theological agenda. In a recent study that focuses on Luke the writer and his rhetorical skills, Todd Penner seeks to break new ground that seriously challenges the reliance on Acts for historical information. Penner argues that Luke's narrative is an example of epideictic rhetoric, that is rhetoric that seeks to establish a favorable contrast between the new *politeia* of the Jesus-followers and that of the unbelieving Jews. In this view, Stephen's speech, drawing as it does on examples from Israelite history to demonstrate that their ancestors had always been unfaithful in following the leaders that God had appointed, performs its rhetorical function perfectly.[26] In Penner's view the whole epi-

---

25. M. Hengel, "Die Ursprünge der christliche Mission," *NTS* 18 (1971), 15-38.

26. T. Penner, *In Praise of Christian Origins: Stephen and the Hellenists in Lukan Apologetic Historiography* (Emory Studies in Early Christianity; New York and London: Clark, 2004), 303-27. This view of Stephen's speech contrasts with the traditional view that Luke is drawing on different sources here and that the speech does not respond to the charges brought against Stephen. Cf. M. Simon, *Stephen and the Hellenists in the Primitive Church* (London: Longmans, 1958), 39-77.

sode of the Hellenists and Stephen fits into Luke's scheme of the gradual expansion outward of the new movement, a scheme that maintains continuity with the origins and prepares for the eventual extension further to Rome through the journeys of Paul. There is no suggestion that the Hellenists were more "liberal" than their Hebrew coreligionists and therefore more suited to a missionary approach to the Gentiles. Penner writes: "Regardless of their actual importance *or even existence* in the real nascent Christian community in Jerusalem, it is evident that for Luke the Hellenists form the bridge between the apostles in Jerusalem and the Pauline mission among the Gentiles."[27]

In order to prepare his argument for this paradigm shift in the study of Acts, Penner has critically surveyed previous scholarship that has, as was noted, been dominated by source and historical criticism. One of his main targets is the work of Martin Hengel, who has brought his encyclopedic knowledge of ancient Judaism to bear on the issue of "filling in the gaps" in Luke's account of Stephen and the Hellenists. At first sight, the conclusion that emerges could not be more different from that of Penner.[28] Luke, for Hengel, was a companion of Paul, familiar with the situation in Jerusalem and therefore reliable in his information about the earliest days of the new movement. He is an Evangelist rather than a trained rhetorician. His Greek is colloquial rather than classical, and his main concern is to ensure his readers' sense of security in their faith in Jesus.

In reconstructing the situation that pertained in Jerusalem, Hengel relies heavily on the claims, based on archaeological as well as literary evidence, that there was a sizable Greek-speaking population of Diaspora Jews living in the city.[29] Luke seeks to capture this vibrant situation in his description of the presence of Diaspora Jews who were present from all parts of the ancient world on the feast of Pentecost (Acts 2:8-12), some of whom must have joined the new movement following Peter's speech. The Hellenists and Hebrews within the Jesus movement were soon separated on linguistic grounds, according to Hengel, something that showed up particularly in their religious gatherings. The Greek speakers would have used the Septuagint (LXX) or Greek translation of the Hebrew Scriptures, and,

27. Penner, *In Praise of Christian Origins,* 329.

28. Penner, *In Praise of Christian Origins,* 23-39.

29. M. Hengel, "Zwischen Jesus und Paulus. Die 'Hellenisten,' die 'Sieben' und Stephanus," reprinted in M. Hengel, *Paulus und Jakobus. Kleine Schriften III* (WUNT 141; Tübingen: Mohr Siebeck, 2002), 1-58, with updating of the original 1975, 58-67. English translation in Hengel, *Between Jesus and Paul* (London: SCM, 1983), especially 1-29.

depending on geographic as well as other background factors, they organized themselves in various "synagogues" or worship communities within the city.

Not all returnees to the holy city, Saul of Tarsus included, were convinced by the claims about Jesus, however. And it was from those belonging to the Synagogue of the Freedmen — Cyrenians, Alexandrians, Cilicians, and Asians — that opposition to Stephen's charismatic, Spirit-filled preaching and ministry arose (Acts 6:7-11). He was accused of speaking against the Jewish religious institutions of temple and Torah, in a fashion not dissimilar to the charges brought against Jesus, and he suffered a similar fate. However, even though Luke signals the parallels between the two men's demise, Jesus was tried before the Jewish Sanhedrin, including the High Priest, as well as by the Roman provincial governor, whereas Stephen was the victim of lynch law, being stoned by the mob, with no sign of an official Jewish or Roman presence. Thus the Stephen affair was an inter-synagogal dispute that went horribly wrong.

Even though Luke merely mentions in passing that there was a persecution against the church in Jerusalem following Stephen's death, and that "those who were scattered went from place to place, proclaiming the word" (Acts 8:1-4), Hengel has no difficulty in filling out the picture for us, combining detailed knowledge of the sources and operating with a lively imagination ranging over the whole body of tradition about Jesus and the early Christians. Thus he attributes to those dispersed to Phoenicia, Cyprus, and Antioch the beginnings of the Christian mission among Greek-speaking Jews and so-called God-fearers. It is they who must be credited with the beginnings of christological reflection about Jesus as Son of man and Lord, fueled by their knowledge of Greek and the Greek Scriptures. They would have been responsible also for the translation into Greek of Jesus' sayings and parables. Aramaic-speaking followers (the "Hebrews") would not have been able to join them in their "eschatological, Spirit-filled" freedom in carrying further the Torah and temple criticism of Jesus. In a word, for Hengel, Stephen and the Hellenists fashioned Greek-speaking Christianity. It was not contacts with the pagan Greek *Geist*, as other German scholars have maintained, but the Greek-speaking *Jewish* believers and their sympathizers who laid the foundations for the Christian religion to become eventually a "world religion."

When one compares these two accounts of Stephen and the Hellenists based on very different methodologies and presuppositions, they are not as far apart as both scholars might want to claim. While Penner could rightly be accused of adopting a minimalist position in terms of the historicity of the episode, Hengel's approach is maximalist in his desire and ability to "fill in the gaps" in our received narratives and give a plausible account of what might have happened. At least they both agree that the episode of Stephen and the Hellenists played a pivotal role in the spread and development of the Jesus movement as it gradually cut loose from its Jerusalem moorings. Penner's study is confined to that single episode and his desire is to develop an alternative methodology in approaching early Christian texts. As a result he does not deal with the Hebrews and what, if any, role they play in Luke's rhetorical composition. Hengel does indeed discuss the name *Hebraioi,* but only in passing. Several times they seem to embody for him the conservative peasant ethos of the Galilean Jesus movement and so were less well equipped, both linguistically and culturally, to expand their horizons to the Spirit-filled heights that Pentecost opened up for their Greek-speaking coreligionists.[30]

New Horizons and Identity Formation

Later in this chapter we shall deal with the topic of the role that James and his Jewish Christian followers played within nascent Christianity, but before doing so it is worth pondering the suggestions of Ben F. Meyer regarding the Hebrews and the Hellenists and their roles within the early Jesus movement. Instead of seeing them merely as literary creations to serve rhetorical purposes, or envisaging them as being somehow in cultural opposition, the one closed and withdrawn, the other open to the prevailing *Zeitgeist,* he sees the question of their identities through the lens of their understanding of what was involved in a world mission. How did the decision to embark on such an enterprise change self-understandings within both groups? What *horizon* did each have? How did that move introduce the issue of *self-identity* as a conscious issue for both groups within early Christianity? Both italicized words are important for the analysis, the former referring to a field of vision which opens up possibilities for meaning-making and the latter to the reorienting of life in order to become one's true self, an idea

30. Hengel, "Zwischen Jesus und Paulus," 49, writes: "Within Palestinian Judaism there was no freedom for an open criticism of the temple and the Law that might even touch Moses the Lawgiver himself. However, the Aramaic-speaking community, in agreement with the preaching of Jesus may not have had the rigorous approach to the Law that it later displayed under the leadership of the Lord's brother James after Peter had departed c. 44 C.E."

brilliantly encapsulated by the Greek poet Pindar in his aphorism, "Become what thou art."[31]

Applying such a model to group identity formation has its inherent risks, yet it enables Meyer to profile the way in which the ultimate horizon of "world mission" played itself out among these two manifestations of early Christian identity formation in a brilliantly insightful way. It does not pit the one against the other or allow the insights or initiatives of the one to cast the other in a negative light. Meyer poses the issue at stake succinctly as follows: "How is it that, alone of the parties, movements and sects of Second Temple Judaism, Christianity discovered the impetus within itself to found Gentile religious communities and to include them under the name of the 'Israel of God'?" (Gal 6:16). He answers his own question by suggesting that despite the influence on the new movement of the diverse worlds in which it operated, early Christianity had its own "deep structure" derived from the memory of Jesus and the Easter faith in his triumph over death. It was that belief that allowed them to conceive of Jesus, not only as the Christ/Messiah, the fulfiller of the promises to Israel, but also as "the first born of many brothers," the first human of a new humankind (1 Cor 15:40-49; Rom 8:29). Early Christian history was, he claims, self-orienting, in that its proclamation and the selfhood of the proclaimers reflected a phenomenon that was unique in the history of religions: "eschatological reversal realized in historical time."[32]

How do these insights translate into a better understanding of the roles of the Hebrews and the Hellenists within the shared horizon of Jesus' reversal of fortune from executed criminal to victorious Lord and the focus on his life as the culmination of all history? Finding the evidence for a world mission at an early stage of the community's life is not easy. Neither Judaism, even in the Diaspora, nor Jesus himself during his lifetime for that matter envisaged such an enterprise.[33] We argued in the last chapter that Jesus did indeed expect Gentiles to share in the great banquet of all nations that Isaiah, in particular, had in mind, something he expected would come about soon as the consummation of God's kingly rule. But as far as mission was concerned, his own focus and that of his immediate followers was on

---

31. In these formulations, Meyer is drawing on the reflections of philosopher/theologian Bernard Lonergan on human cognitive intentionality and its application to groups rather than individuals. See *The Early Christians*, 23-35.

32. Meyer, *The Early Christians*, 17-20.

33. See the discussion of this topic by M. Goodman in *Mission and Conversion: Proselytising in the Religious History of the Roman Empire* (Oxford: Clarendon, 1994).

the restoration of Israel, even when this led him and them to breach the political borders of Galilee of his own day in search of the lost sheep of the house of Israel. We have already emphasized the centrality of Zion for Jesus' followers, once they realized the full meaning of the resurrection experience and had begun to articulate that meaning in symbols and images drawn from the rich repertoire that their own tradition had to offer in the Hebrew Scriptures and other Second Temple literature.

This was the seedbed in which the *Hebraioi* began to grow into the realization of who they were and what their role was within the greater scheme of things. The name by which the group was known was indicative of their linguistic and cultural background as part of Jesus' permanent retinue in Galilee. At their core was the Twelve, whose symbolic importance continued to be highly significant in the early days, even to the point where they could envisage a judging (i.e., ruling) role for themselves in regard to the twelve tribes of Israel, when the Son of Man would return in glory (Matt 19:28; cf. Luke 22:28-30). Old ways die hard, it would seem: if there was to be no place at his side in an earthly kingdom, then better still an authoritative role in the heavenly kingdom. Other Galilean followers such as Jesus' mother, Mary Magdalene, and the other women who stayed true to him to the end, as well as James, one of his blood brothers, who according to 1 Cor 15:7 had been singled out for a resurrection experience, were also among those who had, however belatedly, come to recognize the true significance of Jesus' life. Presumably there were also sympathizers from Jerusalem, people like Nicodemus and Joseph of Arimathea, and nameless others who filled the Upper Room in those early days and broke bread in memory of Jesus as he had requested they should do.

These meals became one of the principal sites in which the group's identity came to be articulated, since as well as providing an occasion for remembering and understanding Jesus, they also pointed to the great banquet to come. Meyer speaks of the group drawing on the image of the new temple as one of the ways in which they articulated their identity, and naturally this image had association with sacred meals also. In the prophetic literature Zion and the temple had become synonymous, and the community was gathered on Mount Zion, which made the connection both obvious and illuminating. Meyer writes:

> As God's dwelling place, the community was the first-fruits of messianic salvation; and as the first-fruits sanctify the whole harvest to come, this community on Zion sanctifies all Israel on the point of entering its her-

itage. Not the community *in place* of Zion, but *on* Zion. Between Zion and the community there was a bond of reciprocal dependence. If it was the community that made Zion the Zion of fulfilment, it was Zion that established the accord between the Scriptures and the community, between the terms of prophecy and fulfilment.[34]

It is against this horizon of being the new temple with all that that implied for the restoration of Israel and the coming of the nations that the *Hebraioi* came to understand and "know" themselves for what they truly were — no longer Galilean pilgrims coming annually to celebrate one of the festivals but the pillars and foundation of the temple "not made with hands" of which Jesus spoke (Mark 14:58).[35]

Meyer concludes that the *Hebraioi*, consisting of a nucleus of Jesus' Galilean followers, saw themselves as not only the heirs but the living fulfillment of the biblical prophecies on Zion. Based on these prophecies they had indeed a horizon of universal salvation, but they lacked the enabling conditions for a universal mission. For them the salvation of the nations would occur in mythic time, and therefore their task was to create the conditions for the myth to be realized in God's own time. In the next section we will trace their subsequent history both in Jerusalem and "in exile" after the destruction of the temple in 70 c.e.[36]

Meyer's model helps to profile the *Hellenistai* also, especially in regard to the ways in which they differed from the *Hebraioi*. To begin with, their Greek background gave them an advantage when it came to engaging with the larger Mediterranean world, and language provided an entrée to a different horizon of understanding about life's meaning. As Diaspora Jews or their descendants, their attachment to Jerusalem was unquestioned, yet as people "zealous for the law" after the manner of Paul of Tarsus, there may well have been a sense of disappointment or at least frustration with what they actually encountered in the holy city.

Meyer takes his cue from the charge against Stephen as reported by Luke, in which Stephen was linked with a statement that claimed that "Jesus of Nazareth will destroy this place [i.e., the temple] and will change the customs of Moses" (Acts 6:14). Such a charge suggests that Stephen was propa-

34. Meyer, *The Early Christians*, 37.

35. In describing the Jerusalem-based apostles James, Peter, and John, Paul uses the unusual description *styloi apostoloi*, "pillar apostles" (Gal 2:9), an image that evokes the notion of a building, namely, the new temple, made up of people rather than columns.

36. Meyer, *The Early Christians*, 52-66.

gating a rather different aspect of Jesus' ministry to that which the *Hebraioi* were articulating. Of course there were sayings in the Jesus tradition that could be understood as radical attacks on the central symbols of Judaism, but that would be to misinterpret Jesus' real intention of renewal and fulfillment, not destruction. The violent attack on Stephen and his group therefore depended on how he understood Jesus' ministry and how this might have changed his own horizon as a Diaspora Jew in Jerusalem.

Unlike the *Hebraioi*, for whom the resurrection experience was a vindication of the past of Jesus, providing them with a lens through which to re-envisage that past, the *Hellenistai* viewed it within a different horizon, namely, the judgment on unrepentant Israel and the destruction of the temple. Thus for them the resurrection meant the transcendence of the old order rather than its renewal and fulfillment. Jesus' resurrection signified that the new age had already dawned and the symbols of temple and Torah were superseded, mere types of the true reality, which the risen Jesus represented. As Meyer concludes, "If the *Hebraioi* were the link of the earliest community with the past of Jesus, the *Hellenistai* by their self-understanding made themselves the link with the future: not as the vanguard of Israel but as the vanguard of a purified humanity."[37]

Jesus-Followers in Samaria?

In view of the historical hostility between Judea (including Galilee) and Samaria outlined in Chapter 1 (pp. 44-47), it comes as a major surprise to discover that the early Jerusalem church sent Philip to Samaria and that he was quite successful there (Acts 8:4-25). The account of Samaria's successful evangelization by one of the Twelve fits into Luke's overall scheme in Acts for the advance of the Christian mission outward from Jerusalem, a journey that was to extend from "all Judea and Samaria" to "the ends of the earth" (1:8). The name Philip suggests a Greek background, and this is confirmed by the fact that as a native of Bethsaida he was approached by "some Greeks" who wanted to meet Jesus (John 12:20-22). It was appropriate, therefore, that it was he who should go to a Hellenized "city of Samaria" (Acts 8:5), where he encountered competition from one Simon Magus, who had the reputation among the citizens of being "the Power of the Great God" but who latched onto Philip's successful mission. However, when Peter and John visited Sa-

37. Meyer, *The Early Christians*, 83.

maria to confirm those who had accepted Philip's teaching, they denounced Simon for attempting to purchase their powers with regard to the gift of the Spirit. Luke's account of the success of this first outreach of the new movement ends with an explicit mention that Peter and John preached to many of the Samaritan villages as they returned to Jerusalem (v. 25).[38] If this was truly the case, it was a very different reception to what they would have encountered as Galilean pilgrims previously, and indeed John, together with his brother James (nicknamed Boanerges/"sons of thunder" according to Mark 3:17), had wanted to call fire down on a Samaritan village for refusing to admit Jesus and the disciples, as they passed through on their way to Jerusalem (Luke 9:51-56). Perhaps the realization that the new movement was based on the memory of a dissident Jewish prophet from Galilee who had been betrayed to the Romans by the Jerusalem temple aristocracy made Samaritans more open to hearing the good news about him.

It is not easy to evaluate the further import of this account beyond the role it plays within the narrative structure of Acts, especially in view of Luke's interest in Samaria and Samaritans in his gospel also. The "good Samaritan" (Luke 10:25-37) and the cured Samaritan leper who alone returned to give thanks (17:11-19) are positive characters for the Evangelist. Their role as "outsiders" can be used as "shaming" figures in contrast to the Judean characters in both stories in terms of the values of unconditional love and gratitude that the Lukan Jesus proposed. This positive role is all the more surprising for the reader of Luke's two-volume work in view of the fact that, as just alluded to, a Samaritan village had refused to receive Jesus and his disciples because "his face was set toward Jerusalem" (9:53). There seems to be little connection between this profile of the Samaritans in the gospel and the account in Acts other than the fact that John appears in both stories, albeit with very different roles.

The city of Samaria/Sebaste, home to Herodian veterans, would not appear at first sight to be a likely place for a successful mission to do with a Judean prophet. The city had a checkered history, especially its destruction during the Hasmonean expansion, as described by Josephus (*Ant* 13.275-81).

---

38. Josephus uses "Samarian" *(Samareis)* to refer to the inhabitants of the region in general (*Ant* 9.125) and "Samaritan" *(Samareitai)* for the religious connotation of worshipers of Yahweh on Mount Gerizim as opposed to Jerusalem (*Ant* 9.290). Because he has a pronounced anti-Samaritan bias, he dates the origin of the schism back to the fall of the northern kingdom and the planting of the region with Persian (Cuthean) settlers, according to 2 Kgs 17:24-28. The New Testament writers do not make this distinction, and *Samareitai* is the constant usage in both Luke and John.

Steps of the temple to Roma and Augustus at Samaria/Sebaste,
built by Herod the Great in 26 B.C.E.
(Todd Bolen/BiblePlaces.com)

However, despite the destruction and scattering of the population, Samaria had recovered sufficiently to be listed among cities freed from Hasmonean rule in 63 B.C.E. by Pompey. It was resettled by Gabinius, the Roman governor of Syria in 57 B.C.E., who had taken over from Pompey the reorganization of the former Hasmonean kingdom (*Ant* 14.88). The ethos of the city thereafter must have been that of a thoroughly Hellenized and Romanized place, prompting Herod the Great to rename the city Sebaste, plant five thousand veterans in the neighborhood and adorn the place with a magnificent temple to Roma and Augustus, as well as other architectural features of a typical Roman city, in 27 B.C.E.[39]

The religious Samaritans had at some stage previously moved their center from Samaria to Shechem (Tel Balata), close to their sacred mountain, Gerizim, as reported by Josephus (*Ant* 11.322-24; 13.256), leaving Sa-

39. E. Netzer, *The Architecture of Herod the Great Builder* (Grand Rapids: Baker, 2008), 81-93; J. Zangenberg, *Frühes Christentum in Samarien. Topographische und traditionsgeschichtliche Studien zu den Samarientexten im Johannesevangelium* (Tübingen: Francke, 1998), 47-55; *Samareia. Antike Quellen zur Geschichte und Kultur der Samaritaner in deutscher Übersetzung* (Tübingen: Franke, 1994), 68-91, presenting all the texts dealing with Samaria/Sebaste in the Herodian period.

maria to the Macedonian colony located there.[40] Both the temple and the city were destroyed by John Hyrcanus in the first wave of Judean expansion to the north, possibly as early as 128 B.C.E., though 107 B.C.E. is the more likely date on the basis of the coin finds. The temple was not rebuilt, but Gerizim continued to be regarded as a sacred mountain in the first century C.E., as indicated by the Samaritan woman in her conversation with Jesus (John 4:20).[41]

The presence of Simon Magus in Samaria/Sebaste indicates a mixed religious environment, typical of a Greco-Roman city, even before Herod's building of the temple to Roma and Augustus. Remains of a temple to the Egyptian goddess Isis, attested by a Greek inscription dating from the Hellenistic period, were discovered underneath a Roman period temple with an altar dedicated to Kore/Persephone, the goddess of the underworld. Another inscription found with the remains of a statue reads: "One God, the ruler of all things, Great Maiden (megalē Korē) the Invincible." While the excavators date the inscription to the late second or early third century, the likelihood is that the cult of Persephone had reached Samaria from Greece earlier. Two aspects of the inscription are interesting in this context. First, "one god" (heis theos), an epithet so characteristic of Israelite monotheism (Deut 6:4), is given here to a female Greek goddess, reflecting the syncretistic tendencies of Hellenistic paganism. Furthermore, the description of the goddess as megalē Korē, "great maiden," corresponds to the claim that Simon Magus was presenting himself as "the power of the God called Great (megalē)" (Acts 8:10).[42] Against such a background of Hellenistic rather than Jewish inspiration, it is at least plausible to suppose that an account of the "mighty deeds" of Jesus, as in Mark's gospel or in his putative source of a "catena" of miracle stories, might easily have made an impression on some of the city's population.[43]

The Fourth Gospel also gives considerable prominence to Samaria and Samaritans in its account of Jesus' ministry. Apart from the meeting with the Samaritan woman at Jacob's well near Sychar (John 4:4-42), the Jerusalem authorities call Jesus a Samaritan, by way of insult, because he

40. E. Campbell, "Shechem," NEAEHL 4:1345-54.

41. Zangenberg, Frühes Christentum in Samarien, 27-30.

42. D. Flusser, "The Great Goddess of Samaria," IEJ 25 (1975), 13-20; G. R. Horsley, "The Great Goddess of Samaria," in Horsley, ed., New Documents Illustrating Early Christianity 1 (Sydney: Ancient History Documentary Research Centre, Macquarie University, 1981), 105-7.

43. H. Clark Kee, Community of the New Age: Studies in Mark's Gospel (Philadelphia: Westminster, 1977), 32-38.

dares to challenge their claim that Abraham was their father, and he makes no effort to rebut the charge (8:48-49). Other geographic indicators associated with the region of Samaria are the reference to "Aenon near Salim" in the Jordan valley, where both Jesus and John the Baptist conducted their baptizing ministries (3:22-30), and a place called Ephraim where Jesus repaired to after the raising of Lazarus in order to avoid hostile Jews (11:54). Even though the location of this place is uncertain, because of its presumed links with one of the Israelite tribes, Ephraim, it is usually identified with Aphairema, a town located on the border of that tribal territory with Judah (1 Macc 11:34).

Jesus' stopover in the region of Samaria and his subsequent evangelization of the inhabitants of Sychar are in stark contrast to both Luke's notice of the hostility of the Samaritans toward Galilean pilgrims and the Matthean Jesus' instruction to the twelve disciples: "Go nowhere among the Gentiles and do not enter a town of the Samaritans, but go rather to the lost sheep of the house of Israel" (Matt 10:5-6). The symbolic Twelve are sent to Israel, and yet the Samaritans are not included! This rebuff is almost as harsh as that to the Syro-Phoenician woman in Mark, and yet the Samaritans are singled out as being different from Gentiles. Clearly, the Judean bias, one that Josephus shared, namely that these people were Cutheans even when they pretended to be friendly with the Judeans, was shared by the Judeo-Christian Evangelist Matthew or his source.

Despite this negative view of Samaria and the Samaritans in some early Christian circles, the subtly crafted story of the Samaritan woman has been interpreted by some as pointing to a strong Samaritan influence on the so-called Johannine community. Raymond Brown in particular has constructed an elaborate developmental profile of how this alleged community originated as a small Jewish Christian sect, probably located in Jerusalem but separate from the James group and centered instead on an unnamed figure called in the gospel "the beloved disciple."[44]

---

44. R. Brown, *The Community of the Beloved Disciple: The Life, Loves and Hates of an Individual Church in New Testament Times* (New York: Paulist, 1979). The "Beloved Disciple," who is mentioned but not named in the gospel (John 13:23-26; 18:15-16; 19:25-27; 20:2-10; 21:7, 20-23), has given rise to different views on the role of this figure, both with regard to the gospel itself and also within the pre-literary (i.e., pre-gospel) history of the community. Brown suggests that he was not a member of the Twelve but originally a disciple of John the Baptist and that he had an influential leadership role in the early stages of the community's history, but not in the writing of the gospel (*Community*, 31-34). By the late second century the author was identified as John the son of Zebedee, but this

Over time this group evolved into an independent Hellenistic Christian community situated outside Palestine, probably in Asia Minor. A strong Samaritan input is postulated as the catalyst for the second stage of the process described by Brown, and this is symbolically reflected in the story of the woman at the well and her interaction with Jesus. The story moves from a discussion about the significance of "living water" (John 4:7-15) to a debate about the identity of Jesus as the prophet/Messiah (vv. 16-26). The male disciples are somewhat indignant at the Master talking with a Samaritan and a woman, but she becomes the messenger to her townspeople, who flock to Jesus and end up declaring that Jesus is not just the Messiah, as the woman had suspected, but "the Savior of the world" (vv. 39-42).[45]

Brown suggests that a distinctive Samaritan expectation of a prophet like Moses (Deut 18:15, 18), combined with strong opposition, even possible persecution from "the Jews," contributed to the group's development of a "high christology" that insisted on Jesus' heavenly origins, thereby compensating for the group's alienation from both their Jewish roots and other Jewish Christians. This meant that in order to express their new understanding of Jesus' true mission among humans, some of the traditional titles such as Son of Man, Son of God, and Messiah had to be reconfigured and a new role, that of *Logos*/Word, developed, based on the notion of heavenly wisdom coming to dwell in their midst.[46]

Jesus had told the Samaritan woman that "the time was coming and *now is*" when the true worshipers would no longer worship on Gerizim or Jerusalem, but "in spirit and in truth" (John 4:23-24). This solemn declaration may reflect that moment in the late sixties when the Jerusalem temple was under serious threat from both Judean zealots and the Roman legions. It could well be that it was then that, like other groups of Jesus-followers,

---

identification is open to question. Clearly, if the work went through several editions over a considerable period of time, as seems probable, it is unlikely to have been the work of one individual. However, because of the consistency of style, vocabulary, and ideas in the completed work, the notion of a "Johannine school" has been canvassed. See M. Hengel, *The Johannine Question* (London: SCM, 1989). Some have suggested that "the beloved disciple" is a literary fiction rather than a historical figure. For a recent discussion, see H. Attridge, "The Restless Quest for the Beloved Disciple," in D. H. Warren, A. G. Brock, and D. W. Pao, eds., *Early Christian Voices in Texts, Traditions and Symbols: Essays in Honor of François Bovon* (Leiden: Brill, 2003), 71-80.

45. For a very different reading of the episode from that of Brown, cf. D. Lee, *Symbolism, Gender and Theology in the Gospel of John* (New York: Herder and Herder, 2002).

46. Brown, *Community*, 36-55. He includes in stage one opposition from the Jews, leading to expulsion from the synagogue as a result of the "high christology."

the Johannine group had to emigrate, eventually ending up in Ephesus, if the early tradition is to be believed. They had to move not just geographically but also spiritually, however, since together with the temple, all the rituals and sacred festivals had come to an end also. However, rather than abandoning their spiritual heritage they could draw on the symbolical significance of the various feasts and the ceremonies associated with them — Passover (ch. 6), Tabernacles (chs. 7–8) and Dedication (ch. 10) — to give expression to their belief in the fact that God was Spirit (4:24) and that Jesus was his divine emissary, in fact "the Way, the Truth and the Life" (14:6).

Not all Johannine scholars would agree with Brown's approach, claiming that it too readily engages in reading external events and situations into a text that calls for a more holistic reading strategy, one that interprets the irony and intricate symbolism of the work as a whole on its own terms.[47] However, the fact is that any critical interpretation of the Fourth Gospel is faced with various difficulties that the text presents, difficulties to do with order, repetition, and later additions, all suggesting that, though appearing to be like the seamless robe of Jesus for which the soldiers cast lots (John 19:23), the text is in fact the product of several hands and a number of editions. While some of Brown's reconstruction of the situation may be based on conjecture rather than clear evidence, it is nonetheless the end product of a lifetime of study of the gospel, including his magisterial two-volume commentary on the gospel and his volume on the Johannine epistles in the Anchor Bible series.[48] Its great benefit is to open up the text as a window on the world in which it was generated, enabling us to catch sight of a very special strand of early Christian life. What is revealed is the manner in which a community of Jesus-followers of a particular disposition and background

---

47. Cf. J. Ashton, *Studying John: Approaches to the Fourth Gospel* (Oxford: Clarendon, 1994), for perceptive discussions on some of the more recent trends in Johannine studies, in particular his discussion of literary approaches, especially narrative criticism, 141-65. B. Hall, "Some Thoughts about Samaritanism and the Johannine Community," in A. Crown and L. Davey, eds., *New Samaritan Studies: Essays in Honour of G. D. Sixdenier* (Sydney: Mandelbaum, 1995), 207-15.

48. Raymond E. Brown, *The Gospel according to John, I–XII; The Gospel According to John, XIII–XXI; The Epistles of John* (Anchor Bible 29, 29a, and 30; New York: Doubleday, 1966, 1970, and 1982). Brown repeated his views on the history of the community in his *Introduction to the New Testament* (New York: Doubleday, 1997), 333-82, especially 373-76. However, cf. the discussion by F. Moloney, who edited Brown's later study of the Fourth Gospel, written shortly before his death in 1998, *An Introduction to the Gospel of John* (New York: Doubleday, 2003), especially Moloney's excursus on theories of Johannine community history, 69-85, and his editorial conclusion, 317-25.

engaged in their own unique mythmaking process and the social configuration that this gave rise to.[49]

Others, such as Brown's colleague at Union Theological Seminary in New York, J. Louis Martyn, while also seeking to reconstruct the community's history, emphasize more the expulsion from the synagogue as the catalyst for the development of the Johannine group identity. This event, Martyn claims, resulted from a putative ban on *minim* or heretics by the rabbis who gathered in Jamnia in the post-destruction period.[50] Evidence for this is based on the fact that the parents of the man born blind are reluctant to acknowledge that it is Jesus who healed their son, for fear of being "excluded from the synagogue" (John 9:22). The same Greek expression, *aposynagōgos ginesthai,* occurs again in 12:42 and 16:2, in both instances referring to a punishment for any person who might recognize Jesus as the Messiah (cf. also Luke 6:22). Martyn was aware that the idea of a universal ban was problematic, since in the Jewish sources it only referred to teachers of *halakah,* as decided by the sages. Such was the case of a certain Aqabia, who had given four rulings that the sages rejected, and he was expelled. Aqabia died while the ban was in vogue and they stoned his coffin (Mishnah *Eduyot* 5.6). However, there is other evidence that synagogue communities did in fact exercise some form of supervision on their members, as in the case of the pre-Christian Paul, who had gone as far as Damascus in order to root out followers of Jesus, a fate that ironically befell himself later (Acts 9:1-2; 2 Cor 11:24).

These instances do not, however, amount to a ban imposed by a supposed synod held at Jamnia after the revolt, as Martyn and others have claimed. Indeed as we shall discuss in Chapter 8, the "parting of the ways," as the separation between Jesus-followers and observant Jews is usually described, was a lengthy process that did not occur overnight. There is evidence from as late as the fourth century that Christians in Antioch continued to frequent the synagogue, much to the displeasure of their bishop, John Chrysostom. Nevertheless there can be no doubt that a close-knit group, such as the Johannine community appears to have been, would have found it difficult, if not impossible, to remain close to the post-70 emerging

49. W. Meeks, "The Man from Heaven in Johannine Sectarianism," *JBL* 91 (1974), 44-72.

50. J. L. Martyn, *History and Theology in the Fourth Gospel* (revised and enlarged edition; Nashville: Abingdon, 1979); "Clementine Recognitions 1, 31-71: Jewish Christianity and the Fourth Gospel," in J. Jervell and W. Meeks, eds., *God's Christ and His People: Studies in Honour of Nils Alstrup Dahl* (Oslo and Bergen: Universitetsforlaget, 1977), 265-95.

Jewish orthodoxy as defined by the rabbinic schools, especially in Galilee. Geographical shifts would have inevitably meant contact with other strands of Greco-Roman philosophical and mystical thinking, as well as a more universalistic outlook. One gets the impression that, as American scholar George McRae wrote, the Fourth Gospel in its final form is a missionary document, was forged at the crossroads of Greco-Roman religious, philosophical, and mystical writing, and by implication claims to address the concerns of all the different strands.[51]

One example of similar cultural adaptation is that of the first-century C.E. Jewish philosopher, Philo of Alexandria, who had already interpreted the Hebrew Bible in the light of Plato's philosophy, giving rise to an allegorical reading, an approach that went beyond the letter to the spirit of biblical texts. His *On the Life of Moses* could be seen almost as a companion volume to the Fourth Gospel's Life of Jesus. Thus, for example, in extolling Moses as king, lawgiver, and priest, Philo describes Moses as God's partner and friend. As a citizen of the world Moses does not belong to any one city but shares the whole creation "as property prepared for the heir." Yet even more than being partner with God the Father and Maker of all, it was a greater joy still to be considered worthy of God's own name, "for Moses was called God and king of the whole nation." Having thus described Moses' intimacy with God, Philo concludes: "It is said that Moses entered into the very same darkness within which God was; that is, into the formless, invisible, non-corporeal, original pattern of being of existing things, where he perceived what is forever invisible to natural, mortal sight" (*Life of Moses* 1.156-58). In Philo's thought, Moses did not see God directly but rather God's *Logos* or Word, which was the pattern and exemplar of God's self-expression in creation. The opening hymn to the *Logos* in the Fourth Gospel (John 1:1-14) is cut from the very same cloth as this and serves as a perfect introduction to the Johannine Jesus' claim that he and the Father are "one thing" since he "knows the Father" and knowledge creates union with the object known in this Platonic thought world (John 10:30-38).[52]

---

51. G. McRae, "The Fourth Gospel and *Religionsgeschichte*," CBQ 32 (1970), 13-24.

52. C. H. Dodd, *The Interpretation of the Fourth Gospel* (Cambridge: Cambridge University Press, 1965), is the classic treatment of the various possible cultural influences on the Fourth Gospel, especially 54-73 on Philo's writing as a background for the Fourth Gospel.

James the Just and the Afterlife of the *Hebraioi*

Most histories of early Christianity focus on Jesus and Paul, often high-lighting the differences between them to the point where the question as to which of them is to be deemed the real founder of Christianity can be seriously raised.[53] The consideration of the roles of the *Hebraioi* and the *Hellenistai* in the previous section shows the importance of seeing the connections between the two principal figures and the manner in which the past of Jesus was received and interpreted by different groups in the post-resurrection period. Paul was, of course, a Hellenist, not initially a Jesus-follower, but rather, as Saul, a violent persecutor of his fellow Hellenists who were Jesus-followers. He must have seen their espousal of Jesus as a betrayal of their birthright. He claims to have been officially charged to track down the followers of Jesus, even as far as Damascus (Acts 9:1-2; cf. Gal 1:13, 23; Phil 3:6). We do not know when and how the word about Jesus had reached that important city, but the likelihood must be that it was the *Hellenistai* who had been dispersed after Stephen's death who had proclaimed Jesus there also.

Even after his Damascus Road experience it is noteworthy how Paul, whose letters can give us an insight into the thinking of the *Hellenistai,* shows little interest in memories of the historical Jesus for developing his own theological synthesis.[54] He builds it, rather, on the cross-resurrection axis, which challenges new believers to pattern their lives on these events, thereby participating now in the new cosmic age that Jesus' resurrection has inaugurated. Indeed some formulations in his letters that are deemed to be pre-Pauline show us how the thought patterns of the *Hellenistai* fit in easily with Paul's developing synthesis. In Phil 2:6-11, for example, Paul draws on an early hymn about Jesus' self-humiliation in order to exhort his converts to have the same mind as Jesus had, "even to death on the cross." It was be-

---

53. S. Freyne, "The Jesus-Paul Debate Revisited and Re-Imaging Christian Origins," in K. O'Mahony, ed., *Christian Origins: Worship, Belief and Society* (JSNTSS 241; Sheffield: Sheffield Academic, 2003), 143-62.

54. With regard to the Synoptic sayings tradition, only four actual sayings of Jesus have been identified: 1 Cor 6:15-16 on the role of sexual intercourse in marriage; 7:10-11 on divorce and remarriage; 9:14 on support for missionaries; 11:23-26 on the Lord's Supper. Cf., however, D. Dungan, *The Sayings of Jesus in the Churches of Paul* (Oxford: Blackwell, 1971), who claims that since even in these cases Paul is using the sayings tradition allusively rather than directly, "he is intimately related with that complex of traditions now preserved in the Synoptic Gospels" (p. 146).

cause of this emptying of himself that God had exalted him and given him the name *Kyrios* or Lord, which *every tongue* should acknowledge and *every knee* bow to, in recognition of his universal dominion.

Under the influence of the *Hellenistai* in the Antioch church, Paul's horizons quickly broadened to preaching his gospel to Greeks of non-Jewish background also (Acts 13-14). The difficulties this decision gave rise to in terms of what, if any, aspects of Jewish religious practice these new converts should adopt necessitated consultation with the mother church in Jerusalem. After his Damascus Road experience Paul himself claims that he did not go immediately to Jerusalem but went instead to Arabia, returning first to Damascus, before going up to Jerusalem three years later to visit (or discuss) with Kephas (Peter), remaining with him fifteen days.[55] The only other of the apostles he encountered on this visit was James "the brother of the Lord" (Gal 1:17-19). The usual date for this first visit of Paul is computed on his claim to have made a second visit fourteen years later, a visit in which he came to an agreement with the "pillar" apostles about the admission of Gentiles without circumcision, the so-called Council of Jerusalem also described in Acts 15. Most scholars date this second visit to 49 C.E., and in that case the first visit was probably 37 C.E.[56] We shall discuss the significance of these meetings presently because of what they can tell us about the different perspectives on the developing mission to the Gentiles, but for now the significant datum is that in less than a decade after Jesus' death, James the brother of the Lord was clearly in a leadership role in Jerusalem, side by side with Peter, the leader of the Twelve.[57]

How did this come about, especially since the gospels suggest that the

---

55. On Paul's visit to Arabia, see J. Murphy-O'Connor, "Paul in Arabia," *CBQ* 55 (1993), 732-37, who sees this as an indication of Paul's awareness of his role as "Apostle of the Gentiles" from his conversion. Alternatively, M. Hengel, "Paulus in Arabien," in *Paulus und Jacobus. Kleine Schriften III* (WUNT 141; Tübingen: Mohr Siebeck, 2002), 193-214, suggests that Arabia here means the Nabatean kingdom, which had constituted part of Israel's "ancestral lands" and so would form part of the messianic kingdom to come.

56. Brown, *Introduction to the New Testament*, 428-30, summarizes the different scholarly opinions in terms of the dating of Paul's career.

57. James is mentioned first in the list of the "brothers" of Jesus in Mark 6:3/Matt 13:55. The view that these brothers and sisters of Jesus were the children of Mary and Joseph was held in antiquity by Tertullian and is accepted by most scholars from the Reformation background, where the perpetual virginity of Mary is not as important as in the Roman Catholic Church. A second-century work entitled the *Protevangelium of James* claims that these brothers and sisters of Jesus were Joseph's children from an earlier marriage. See J. P. Meier, *A Marginal Jew: Rethinking the Historical Jesus* (New York: Doubleday, 1991), 1:316-32.

family of Jesus, including his brothers, were less than impressed with him during the public ministry, as noted in the previous chapter (pp. 182-83)? James is named in the official list of witnesses on the basis that he was the recipient of an appearance from the Risen One (1 Cor 15:7), information that Paul had received, possibly on the occasion of his first visit to Jerusalem. Though James had a preeminent and privileged position from an early stage, we hear remarkably little about him in the New Testament, especially in Acts. In this case, statistics are telling. James is mentioned just eleven times in the whole New Testament, whereas Peter's name occurs on 190 occasions. To put the matter bluntly, James was not wholly written out of the official version of Christian origins, but only because those who were responsible for that version, including Luke, could not have omitted him and remained credible. It is only when we see the importance of James for *all* the different branches of later generations of Christians — "orthodox," "heretical," and "gnosticizing" alike — that we can see that the legend of James "the Just" (as he came to be known later) makes it imperative to explore his historical role in the new movement, up to the time of his execution in 62 C.E.[58]

Paul's letter to the Galatians, written probably in 57 C.E., is the earliest source that touches on his relationship with James and the Jerusalem church, as was just mentioned. It can yield considerably more information about the situation than just the dating of Paul's visits. In regard to both, he wants to declare his independence by claiming that he acted on the basis of a revelation he had received (Gal 1:12; 2:2), yet he does feel the need to connect with the Jerusalem center. He is clearly on the defensive in regard to the second visit also, with his rather dismissive remark about "those who were *supposed* to be leaders; what they are makes no difference to me" (2:6). Furthermore he declares that the second visit was held in private (v. 2), whereas in Luke's account a formal meeting of the Jerusalem church is held, in which Peter and James both speak (Acts 15:13-21), with the latter apparently making the final decision (v. 19). That James was the key figure in what Meyer calls "the partial fusion of horizons" is clear from the fact that Paul tells us that "certain men who came from James" arrived in Antioch, presumably to ascertain whether the compromise arrived at in Jerusalem was being implemented there.[59] James was clearly now in control in Jeru-

---

58. S. Freyne, *Retrieving James/Yakov, the Brother of Jesus: From Legend to History* (Annadale on Hudson: Bard College Institute of Advanced Theology, 2008).

59. Meyer, *The Early Christians*, 97-102.

salem, and Peter had embarked on a mission to "the circumcised" as had been agreed to at the Jerusalem meeting, visiting Antioch on his journeys, which took him to Corinth also (1 Cor 1:12), it would seem, and eventually to Rome.

What does "partial fusions of horizons' imply for Paul, James and Peter? Reading between the lines in Galatians, but also in Philippians and 2 Corinthians, it seems clear that there was other missionary activity in progress that Paul believed was challenging his own approach in accepting Gentile converts without insisting on circumcision, a rite of initiation for males which had become the symbol of full participation in the covenant community of Israel in the Hellenistic period.[60] Paul is less than polite to those conducting this alternative mission, claiming that they are perverting the gospel of Christ by proclaiming a gospel different from what he had preached and later calling them "false brothers, who had slipped in to spy" on Paul's circumcision-free teaching (Gal 1:6-8; 2:4; 2 Cor 11:1-6; Phil 3:2-3). These "intruders" should not be confused with "those from James" mentioned a little later in Galatians 2, who were presumably checking the observance of the agreement that had been reached in Jerusalem, not preaching "another gospel."

It is interesting that when Paul seeks to discredit these other missionaries, he becomes autobiographical in terms of his own pedigree as an authentic Jew: he was "circumcised on the eighth day, a member of the people of Israel of the tribe of Benjamin, a Hebrew born of Hebrews, as to the law a Pharisee" (Phil 3:4-6). Or again: "Are they Hebrews? So am I. Are they Israelites? So am I. Are they descendants of Abraham? So am I" (2 Cor 11:22). The use of the term Hebrew *(Hebraios)* in these two defensive statements would appear to be significant. While Paul may be using it in a more general sense of "the Hebrew people" rather than Luke's technical usage in Acts for a separate group within the Jesus movement, it nonetheless points clearly to

---

60. In the Hebrew Bible circumcision (literally "cutting around" of the male foreskin) was deemed to be the mark of the covenant membership of the Israelites (Gen 17:9-14). In later times, especially in the Hellenistic period, it also became an ethnic marker separating Jew from non-Jew. Those Jews who sought to undo their circumcision following the banning by Antiochus Epiphanes were deemed apostates (1 Macc 1:13-15). Pagan writers abhorred the practice and pilloried the Jewish custom (e.g., Juvenal, *Satires* 14.99; Tacitus, *Histories* 5.2, etc.). Luke reports the circumcision of both John and Jesus (Luke 1:59; 2:21). While Paul does not condemn the practice for Jewish Christians, he regards it as superfluous, even misleading, for Gentiles, who gain access to the saving reality of the new covenant through baptism and circumcision of the heart not the flesh (1 Cor 7:17-20; Gal 5:1-15; Rom 2:25-29).

the fact that the opponents were claiming that Paul had abandoned his Israelite roots. Thus the burden of their alternative teaching had to do with presenting a much more "Jewish" version of the gospel than Paul's insistence on freedom from Jewish practice as far as Gentile converts were concerned. Between these two extremes — circumcision for all or no circumcision for Gentile converts — James's (and Peter's) approval of Paul was indeed a compromise. In other words, the *Hebraioi* of Jersualem, with James as their head, had more than one point of view with regard to a world mission, and James himself can be seen as relatively moderate in his demands.

The issue of whether circumcision was necessary or not may appear somewhat trivial. Yet, as mentioned, the removal of the male's foreskin had become at once an ethnic marker and a religious symbol of Jewishness in the Mediterranean world. However, the deeper issue was theological, namely, on what conditions could the Gentiles share in the messianic blessings? Initially, as we have seen, the *Hebraioi* believed that a restored Israel would bring about the Gentile conversion, and the prophetic images of the nations coming to Jerusalem to share in its wisdom fitted the accepted order expressed in the slogan "Jew first, then the Gentile" — a slogan used by Jesus in his dealing with the Syro-Phoenician woman (Mark 7:27).

Paul too shared this notion as he explains his gospel to a Roman readership (Rom 1:16). However, in his case the circumcision-free mission had seen the Gentiles joining in the new movement, whereas most Jews continued their obstinate refusal to accept Jesus as the fulfillment of Israel's hopes. In Romans 9–11 we see Paul struggling to explain the logic of this "cognitive dissonance," explaining that Gentile conversion was actually intended by God to make Israel jealous, but that eventually God, the master horticulturalist, would ensure that the chosen people would take their rightful place, grafted on to the same root as the wild olive, which represented the Gentile converts (11:13-24). Within a decade or so, the expectations of the *Hellenistai* with regard to the world mission were beginning to be realized, but the hopes of the *Hebraioi* were being frustrated. Even Peter, who in the early days seems to have shared the hope of the nations coming to Zion, eventually took on the missionary model, sharing the field with Paul and his associates, he going to the circumcised and Paul to the uncircumcised (Gal 2:7).[61] James held his ground in Jerusalem, never relinquishing his hope for

61. That Peter visited Antioch and Corinth is known from the Pauline letters, and his presence later in Rome, leading to his death during the Neronian persecution of the Roman Christians in 64 C.E., is also well attested. See M. Hengel, *Der Unterschätzte Petrus* (Tübingen:

Zion, it would seem, yet siding with Paul on the issue of the freedom of the Gentiles, despite the fact that some among the *Hebraioi* were engaged in a mission that was insisting on circumcision for all.

These alternative missionaries have often been described simply as Paul's "opponents" or as "Judaizers," a term that can carry pejorative overtones as far as Jews are concerned. However, these labels do them less than full justice. As J. L. Martyn suggests, they are better thought of as Christian Jews who wanted to share the blessings of the Law with Gentiles, following a Hellenistic Jewish tradition that recognizes the universal significance of the Torah, reflected in such works as the Jewish romance *Joseph and Aseneth* and the Alexandrian Wisdom of Solomon. Just as Luke describes Paul drawing on Isa 49:6 ("I will give you as a light for the nations, so that my salvation may reach the end of the earth") to justify his move from a Jewish to a Gentile audience (Acts 13:47), so too the Christian Jewish missionaries could equally point to such texts as a warrant for their own mission. For them the Torah continued to be absolute, and Jesus' role was to bring it to completion, not to destroy it (Matt 5:17-20). Paul on the other hand argues that the Torah was provisional and preparatory (Gal 5:17-22), since for him Christ was "the end of the Law" (Rom 10:4).[62]

What more can be gleaned from our sources about James's position in Jerusalem and his legacy to early Christianity as a whole? As mentioned previously, Luke's main purpose was to present a unified picture of the movement as it progressed on its mission of witnessing about Jesus from Jerusalem to Rome. In doing so, he smoothed over various divergences and conflicts that occurred, especially with regard to Paul, as mentioned already. While Paul himself seeks to emphasize his independence in his letters, Luke

---

Mohr Siebeck, 2005), 78-128. A second-century novel entitled the *Circuits of Peter* purports to fill in the period after Peter left Jerusalem until he arrived in Rome. This work, emanating probably in Syria, is now lost, but its Jewish Christian and anti-Pauline bias can be reconstructed from the pseudo-Clementine writings. This work is prefaced by two letters, one from Peter to James and the other from Clement (Peter's companion on his journeys, later his successor as bishop of Rome), also to James, relating Peter's last wishes. See F. S. Jones, "The Pseudo-Clementines" in M. Jackson-McCabe, ed., *Jewish Christianity Reconsidered: Rethinking Ancient Groups and Texts* (Minneapolis: Fortress, 2007), 285-304; "Jewish Christianity of the Pseudo-Clementines," in A. Marjanen and P. Luomanen, eds., *A Companion to Second-Century Christian "Heretics"* (Leiden: Brill, 2008), 315-34.

62. J. Louis Martyn, "A Law Observant Mission to Gentiles," in *Theological Issues in the Letters of Paul* (Edinburgh: Clark, 1997), 7-24; Joel Markus, "Jewish Christianity," in M. Mitchell and F. Young, eds., *The Cambridge History of Christianity 1: Origins to Constantine* (Cambridge: Cambridge University Press, 2006), 87-102, especially 92-93.

makes him subservient to the Twelve, while at the same time crediting him with his contribution to the universal mission of being "a light to the nations" (Acts 13:47). In the early days of the community, Peter and John are the spokespersons, and there is no mention of James the brother of the Lord. It was only after his namesake in the circle of the Twelve, James the son of Zebedee, was murdered and Peter imprisoned in the persecution launched by Herod Agrippa I in the early forties c.e. (12:1-5), that James the brother of Jesus enters Luke's narrative almost incidentally. We are suddenly informed that Peter, about to leave the city "for another place" after his miraculous escape from prison, gave orders that "James and the believers should be told" of his departure (v. 17). Clearly, this implies that James was already an influential person in the Jerusalem church, something that Paul's mention of meeting with him in Gal 1:19, on the occasion of his first visit to Jerusalem after his Damascus road experience, confirms.

Luke never calls James "the brother of the Lord," nor does he mention him in his gospel, even omitting Mark's list of Jesus' brothers in Nazareth (Mark 6:3; Luke 4:21). It is only at the so-called Council of Jerusalem that James emerges from the shadows, and it is he who announces his decision in a highly formal fashion to "the apostles, the elders, and the whole church" to write to the church in Antioch, asking them to respect Jewish sensibilities concerning false worship and food and marriage regulations, but not insisting on circumcision (Acts 15:13-21, 29).[63] Subsequently, he plays a similar role when Paul returns to Jerusalem with the collection for the local church (21:17-40). It is noteworthy that Paul does not stay with James on arrival in the city but makes a formal visit to him the next day, and this time only "the elders" are present. Again the decision is one of compromise, namely, that Paul should seek to ease the suspicions that had arisen with regard to his corrupting Jews in the Diaspora by persuading them to abandon Moses and not have their children circumcised (v. 21). To this end, the suggestion was made that he should perform a public act of joining some young men

63. In his account of the Jerusalem meeting, Paul does not mention the so-called "Apostolic Decree," in which these extra stipulations for Gentile converts were suggested (Gal 2:1-10). Their background is in the Levitical requirements for "the stranger within the gate" (Lev 17:12; 18:26), which is here being suggested as a model for relations between Jewish and Gentile Christians. It is widely accepted that these particular stipulations are later than Paul since, despite the seeming omission in Galatians, he himself adopts a similar approach to the issue of meat sacrificed to idols in 1 Cor 8:7-13. Idolatry and sexual misdemeanors (porneia) are often seen as connected in the sources. The existence of these provisos would suggest a situation in which some successors of the Hebraioi and Hellenistai still shared a common fellowship.

in the temple who were under a vow, defraying their costs and presumably also ensuring his own ritual cleanness after being in contact with Gentiles (vv. 24-26).

The Martyrdom of James

Luke must have known of the murder of James, but he does not mention it, and James does not appear again in his narrative. It is Josephus who recounts the circumstances of James's death, and in doing so he introduces the difficult political background in which, as leader of a small dissident sect, James had had to operate, as the province of Judea hurtled toward anarchy in the period leading up to the first revolt. As mentioned earlier, his namesake James the son of Zebedee had been killed during the reign of Herod Agrippa, the grandson of Herod the Great who had been given the title "king of the Jews" by his friend, the emperor Gaius, in 41 c.e. As discussed in Chapter 2 (pp. 66-67), Herod Agrippa I was an ambivalent character. He is highly praised in Jewish sources for his piety, on one occasion refusing to do a reading from Scripture at a festival, declaring himself unworthy. Yet he had all the political ambition of his grandfather and was well connected in Rome, having been educated within the imperial household. It is unclear why his ire fell on the Jesus-followers, who, if Luke is to be believed, had continued to visit the temple. Perhaps it was the memory of Jesus who had been executed by Rome as a criminal that led to this belated attack on his followers.

However, in the case of James the brother of the Lord, it was the Judean religious establishment that was responsible for his death. Josephus's account suggests an anti-Saducean bias with regard to the priestly aristocracy at the time of the revolt, whereas the Pharisees are presented in a more favorable light, complaining to the incoming procurator that an unlawful act had been perpetrated:

> Caesar sent Albinus to Judaea as procurator on hearing of the death of Felix. The younger Ananus, who was headstrong in character and extremely audacious, received the high priesthood. Being a man of this kind, Ananus thought that he had an opportunity, as Festus was dead and Albinus was on his way. So he assembled a council of judges and brought before it James the brother of Jesus, known as the Christ, and several others on a charge of breaking the law and handed them over to

be stoned. But those who were considered the most fair-minded people in the city, and strict in their observance of the law, were most indignant at this. Some of them waylaid Albinus on the road from Alexandria and explained that it was illegal for him to act in this way. . . . In consequence King Agrippa deprived him of the high priesthood. (*Ant* 20.200)

Again there is no obvious reason for the execution of James, other than that of inner-Jewish rivalry, similar to that reported by Luke in the case of Stephen's death. That also was by stoning rather than crucifixion, the Roman mode of dealing with dissidents and notorious criminals.

However, Josephus's account became the basis on which a martyrology of James was developed, one that later played into Christian anti-Jewish polemic but also enhanced the persona of James the Just in all different branches of the developing Christian movement in the second century and beyond. Thus the fourth-century Christian historian Eusebius of Caesarea reports Josephus's account in full, but prefaces it with the following statement: "Josephus did not shrink from giving written testimony to this as follows: 'And these things happened to the Jews to avenge James the Just, who was the brother of the so-called Christ, for the Jews killed him in spite of his great righteousness'" (*H.E.* 2.23.19). This statement is not in any extant manuscript of Josephus's *Antiquities,* but it reflects what the second-century c.e. Christian apologist Hegesippus reported in his account of the incident, one that Eusebius also includes in his work, deeming it to be "the most accurate rendition" (2.23.19-22). Hegesippus states that after James's death, "Immediately Vespasian began to besiege them." Eusebius endorses this statement, declaring that "even the wise among the Jews thought that this was the cause of the siege of Jerusalem, immediately after [James's] martyrdom." The claim overlooks the gap in time between the two events — 62 c.e. (James's death) and 70 c.e. (destruction of the temple). Religious polemics do not always have to be historically accurate in terms of details.

Hegesippus was a native of Palestine and of Hebrew origin, according to Eusebius, in all probability a *Hebraios,* because of his admiration for James as well as his knowledge of unwritten Jewish traditions. His dates are 120-180 c.e. and he was the author of five treatises, which Eusebius drew on heavily for his information about the church in Jerusalem (*H.E.* 4.22.1-8). His account of James's martyrdom, as preserved by Eusebius (2.23.4-18), develops the event in a very different direction to that of Josephus. There is no mention of Ananus or Albinus. Instead, James's accusers are the scribes and Pharisees, and the occasion is the Feast of Passover, when they challenge James to get the people to refrain from declaring that Jesus was the Messiah. There is a deep irony to the account, in that James is transformed into a Nazirite, that is, somebody who in Jewish tradition has vowed his life wholly to God, embarking on an ascetic lifestyle, usually for a fixed period (Num 6:1-8). In James's case this was intended as a lifelong commitment, it would seem. Furthermore, he is depicted as though he were the High Priest, wearing a linen garment and entering the temple *naos* or inner sanctuary on his own, in order to make intercession for the sins of the people, just as the High Priest did on the Day of Atonement.

There is one difference however. The Jewish High Priest had to offer a sacrifice of atonement to God and sprinkle both the sanctuary and the people with the blood of the offering according to the ordinances of Leviticus 16. However, the Jewish Christians had outlawed sacrifice, to the point that Jesus is recorded as having said: "I have come to abolish sacrifice; and if you do not cease from sacrifice, the wrath of God shall not cease from you" (*Gospel of the Ebionites*, as reported by Epiphanius, *Pan.* 30.16.5-7). In compliance with this anti-sacrificial understanding of the cult, already signaled by the prophet Isaiah and confirmed by the Markan Jesus (Isa 56:6-7; Mark 11:17), James does not offer sacrifice but prays ceaselessly to God for forgiveness of the sins of the people. As the scene unfolds, James, standing on the ramparts of the temple, refuses to comply with the wishes of his adversaries in addressing the people. Instead, he makes a profession concerning the Son of Man seated in heaven at the right hand of the Great Power, who will come again on the clouds of heaven. While many of the crowd shouts "Hosanna to the Son of David," the opponents throw James down from the ramparts and begin to stone him. James, however, prays for pardon for his accusers, but while he is doing so, he is clubbed to death by an onlooker, despite the pleas of one of the priests. "And thus he bore his witness." According to Hegesippus, he was buried close by and his tombstone was still visible in his day.

This development of the James the Just legend took place less than a century after his death in 62 C.E. According to Eusebius "the men of old" gave him this name because of his virtue (*H.E.* 2.1.1). Hegesippus is also aware that this is one of his epithets, another being Oblias, which he says means in Greek "rampart of the people and righteousness."[64] Even James's

---

64. H. Koester, *Paul and His World: Interpreting the New Testament in Its Context* (Minneapolis: Fortress, 2007), 266, thinks the word *oblias* is unintelligible. Noting that Hegesippus says that the designation was revealed by the prophets, he proposes that it is a corrup-

accusers and opponents are made to address him directly as "the just one" — implying that this was the way in which he was known and revered.[65] The designation *ṣaddiq/dikaios* had acquired quasi-messianic status already in the Hebrew Bible (Isa 9:7; 11:4; Jer 23:5; 33:15), and it continued to be used of the end-time ideal ruler in later Jewish writings, where it is often associated with the gift of divine wisdom. In Hegesippus's portrayal, James is also said to be "holy" *(hagios)* from his mother's womb in addition to being described as "the just one" (*H.E.* 2.23.3). This same combination of "just one" and "holy one" is found in the early proclamation about Jesus. In a reference to the Barabbas incident in the trial of Jesus, Peter charges the Jerusalem crowd with rejecting "the Holy and Righteous One," asking instead for a murderer (Acts 3:14-15; 7:52). Thus, the association of James's status with that of Jesus, as this was articulated in the early Jerusalem *kerygma,* is a significant step in the developing legend of his martyrdom and its theological significance.

James the Just in Three Different Guises

It is a testimony to James's status from the very beginning of the Jesus movement that all branches of developing Christianity acknowledged his importance in the succeeding centuries. After his murder, the Jerusalem community fled to Pella, a city of the Dekapolis east of the Jordan, because of an oracle that warned them of the impending doom. We are dependent on Eusebius for this information (*H.E.* 3.5.3), but its authenticity has been questioned on the basis that it was a "foundation legend" for a later Jewish Christian group in Pella.[66] However, there is nothing improbable about some *Hebraioi* leaving Jerusalem after James's murder, especially in view of the fact that both Matthew's and Mark's gospels report an advance warning

---

tion of Obadiah, a name that means "servant of God." In Obadiah 1 (LXX) the Greek *periochē eis ethnous* renders the Hebrew "messenger to the nations." As applied to James, *periochē tou laou* could mean a messenger or herald to the people, especially if the connection with the name Obadiah is accepted.

65. The description "the Just" appears six times in Hegesippus's short account. It is repeated in the *Gospel of Thomas,* the *Pseudo-Clementines* (also known as the *Clementine Recognitions*), the two *Apocalypses of James,* and the *Apocryphon of James.*

66. G. Lüdemann, "The Successors of the Pre-70 Jerusalem Christianity: A Critical Evaluation of the Pella-Tradition," in E. P. Sanders, ed., *Jewish and Christian Self-Definition* (London: SCM, 1980), 1:161-83.

from Jesus for those in the city to leave before the expected impending disaster (Matt 24:16-18; Mark 13:15-16). The likelihood of their returning after the destruction is more problematic, as they too would have mourned the loss of the temple and would have been subject to the same Roman prohibition against approaching the temple as other Jews. Tracing the reception of James among the different strands of the Jesus movement in the second and third centuries C.E. opens windows on the quite different ways in which the Jesus movement developed in that period, a topic to which we shall return in Chapter 8.

James and the Ebionites

It is usual to link various Jewish Christian sects of later centuries, especially the Nazarenes and the Ebionites, with the Jerusalem refugees to Pella and therefore to see them as the heirs of James's theological and spiritual legacy. The fourth-century C.E. theologian Epiphanius describes these sects in his *Panarion*, a work that covers all the early Christian heresies. There are serious problems about his description of the Nazarenes, however,[67] yet his mention of various villages in the general area of southern Syria, the Hauran, and the Dekapolis, where other Jewish Christian groups such as the Ebionites were known to have existed, is likely to have some substance (*Pan.* 30.2.7-8).[68] While none of the second-century orthodox Christian writers knows anything of the Nazarenes as a Christian heresy, the Ebionites are well attested in two different lines of tradition, one stemming from Irenaeus already in the middle of the second century and the other from Origen of Alexandria in the early third century.[69]

The name Ebionites was suggestive since it means "poor" in Hebrew,

---

67. P. Luomanen, "Ebionites and Nazarenes," in Jackson-McCabe, ed., *Jewish Christianity Reconsidered,* 81-118; *Recovering Jewish-Christian Sects and Gospels* (Leiden: Brill, 2012), 79-81.

68. Luomanen, *Recovering,* 59-60; H. Häikanen, "Ebionites," in Marjanen and Luomanen, *Companion,* 272-75. Eusebius refers to: "Choba, to the south of Damascus, in the same region having Hebrew inhabitants, who, believing in Christ, *observe all the precepts of the Law* and are called Ebionites. *Paul wrote the Epistle to the Galatians against this teaching.*" The italicized words refer to Eusebius's Latin additions to Jerome's Greek text referring to the Choba of Gen 14:15. See E. Klosterman, ed., *Eusebius. Das Onomasticon* (Hildesheim: Olms, 1966), 173.

69. Häikkinen, "Ebionites," 248-58.

and Ebion as founder may have espoused poverty as an ideal, thus also linking him and his followers with Paul's repeated references to "the poor among the saints in Jerusalem," for whom his collections among the Gentiles were destined (2 Corinthians 8–9; Gal 2:10; Rom 15:25-27; Acts 15; cf. Acts 4:32-37 as a possible foundation story). As regards Ebion's other links with Jerusalem and therefore with the Christianity emanating from James and his circle, Irenaeus writes:

> Those who are called Ebionites, then, agree that the world was made by God; but their opinions about the Lord are similar to those of Cerinthus and Carpocrates. They use the gospel according to Matthew only and repudiate the apostle Paul, saying that he was an apostate from the Law. As to the prophetical writings, they do their best to expound them diligently; they practice circumcision, persevere in the customs which are according to the Law, and practice a Jewish way of life, even adoring Jerusalem as if it were the house of God. (*Adv. Haer.* 1.26.2)

The christology of Cerinthus, to which Irenaeus refers, has been described as a "possession by the Spirit" christology, that is, an understanding that Jesus, an ordinary human born of human parents, was seized by the Spirit of Christ at his baptism, a conclusion that was derived from the citation of Ps 2:7 in the canonical gospels: "*Today* I have begotten you." This suggests that it was only at the baptism, not from his birth, that Jesus was endowed with the messianic spirit, which departed from him again at the crucifixion.[70] The origins of this understanding of Jesus are obscure, but one can detect behind it a strong Jewish influence which stressed the unity of God alone, in accordance with the Jewish Shemaʿ prayer (Deut 6:4), and the consequent "low christology" that could be applied to Jesus. As we have seen, the christology of the early *Hebraioi* was based on Jesus' role as fulfiller of the Law, rather than as glorified Lord, and in other sources he was the prophet promised by Moses. It is noteworthy that the canonical epistle of James mentions Jesus twice only: as "the Lord" and as "the Lord of glory" (Jas 1:1; 2:1). Neither reference reflects Jesus' pivotal role as Savior for other branches of the movement. In this regard, the Law, described as "the implanted word that is able to save your souls" (1:21) and "the perfect law of liberty" (v. 25), has a much more significant role to play in the economy

---

70. M. Myllykoski, "Cerinthus" in Marjanen and Luomanen, eds., *Companion*, 213-46, especially 224-36.

of salvation, it would seem.[71] Perhaps it was this apparent diminishing of the unique role of Jesus as Savior that made this epistle one of the doubtful early Christian books, of which Eusebius speaks as late as the early fourth century (*H.E.* 2.23).

In every other respect, the Ebionites were orthodox Jewish Christians of the *Hebraioi* variety in Irenaeus's view. Their preference for Matthew's gospel (albeit, according to Epiphanius, *Panarion* 30.13.2, an abridged version that lacked the infancy stories and which they called the Gospel of the Hebrews) can be explained by the strong Jewish character of the work. It is the link with later Jewish Christianity and especially the role attributed to James in the process of that development that needs to be highlighted in this context. Of late, the pseudo-Clementine collection *(Homilies* and *Recognitions)* has come in for renewed attention among scholars, since, though dated to the fourth century in their present form, they contain older, possibly second-century, material regarding James and the Jewish Christians.[72] This is particularly true of one section of *Recognitions (pseudo-Clementina* 1.27-71), which quite possibly has as background two other Ebionite works mentioned by Epiphanius, namely, the *Anabathmoi Iakobou (Ascents of James)* and "another Acts of the Apostles" that in his view was full of impiety *(Pan.* 30.16.6).[73]

According to *Recognitions* (1.43.3), James was made bishop by the Lord, and the church in Jerusalem greatly increased under him as he governed it "with most righteous justice." Later, the narrator (Peter) calls him "our James" on several occasions, and once he is given the title *episcoporum princeps/*"chief of the bishops" (1.68.2), as he prepares to engage in debate with the Jewish High Priest Caiaphas. The debate comes at the end of sev-

---

71. Markus, "Jewish Christianity," 91.

72. For a detailed discussion of the issues see F. Stanley Jones, *An Ancient Jewish Christian Source on the History of Early Christianity, Pseudo-Clementine Recognitions 1, 27-71* (SBL Texts and Translations 37; Atlanta: Scholars, 1995), 1-38; "The Pseudo-Clementines" in Jackson-McCabe, ed., *Jewish Christianity Reconsidered,* 285-304; R. Van Voorst, *The Ascent of James: History and Theology of a Jewish-Christian Community* (SBL Dissertation Series 112; Atlanta: Scholars, 1989). For introductions and texts of various documents within the pseudo-Clementine corpus, see G. Strecker, "The Kerygmata Petrou," and J. Irmscher, "The Pseudo-Clementines," in E. Henneke and W. Schneemelcher, eds., *New Testament Apocrypha,* trans. R. McL. Wilson (Philadelphia: Westminster, 1965), 2:102-27, 532-70.

73. The extent of Epiphanius's dislike of Ebion emerges in an anecdote that he reports of the apostle John going to the bathhouse, but on hearing that Ebion was already there, John called on his disciples to leave immediately, lest the bathhouse fall on them and they would be buried with Ebion, who was there "because of his godlessness" *(Pan.* 24.1-7).

eral days in which Peter and the rest of the Twelve have engaged with the Jewish authorities in the temple precinct, discussing the identity of Jesus. The Twelve reported their experience to James, and then they spent the night in prayer before the final confrontation with the Jewish authorities. The issue concerned the proof of Jesus' identity as the Messiah, based on Scripture. Over seven days (!) James argued convincingly from the Law and the Prophets, to the point that the High Priest and the people were prepared to be baptized. However, "a certain hostile man" intervened and stirred up a riot, actually throwing James down from the parapet of the temple and leaving him for dead. However, the disciples rescued James and took him out of the city to Jericho. Word reached them there that "the hostile man" had received permission from Caiaphas to persecute believers in Jesus who had traveled as far as Damascus. This reference to Damascus reveals the identity of "the wicked man" to be that of Paul, based on the record in Acts of his desire to persecute Christians.

Clearly we are dealing here with a legendary account, but one that exalts James over all the other disciples, including Peter. The hostility toward Paul is palpable, insofar as he is not even mentioned by name yet identified on the basis of Luke's account of his journey to Damascus. There is no mention of either his subsequent conversion or his success with the Gentile mission. It is James, not Paul or Peter, who increases the number of believers, and, while the attempt to murder James was unsuccessful, the account clearly seeks to paint Paul in a bad light, actually blaming him for impeding the conversion of the Jewish people and their leaders. One suspects that this part of the story, though possibly drawing on Hegesippus's account of the martyrdom of James, was heavily dependent on the anti-Pauline "Acts of the Ebionites" mentioned by Epiphanius.

James among the "Gnostics"

The *Gospel of Thomas* is a collection of sayings of Jesus that circulated, probably in Syria, at the end of the first or the beginning of the second century C.E. It was originally written in Greek, but in 1945 a Coptic version of this work, together with a number of other treatises, was discovered at Nag Hammadi in Egypt. While the existence of such a document was known from some patristic references, the Nag Hammadi find was the first full version of the work that was known. Subsequent to the find, it was discovered that several sayings of Jesus on Greek papyri from Egypt, found at the turn of the twentieth century, corresponded with sayings from *Thomas,* possibly therefore representing the Greek version of that gospel before it was translated into Coptic. Some scholars see this collection of sayings as being very early, even predating another similar collection, namely the Q source, used independently by both Matthew and Luke. Others, however, regard it as later and derivative. In this case, it is claimed that *Thomas* shows signs of esoteric tendencies similar to those found in writings of a more full-blown gnostic or gnosticizing bent.[74]

Saying 12 in the collection is a response to the disciples' question as to whom they should approach after Jesus has departed from them. To which Jesus replies: "In the place to which you come you shall go to James the Just, for whose sake heaven and earth came into being." While the saying once again affirms James's special role as the leader and the source of wisdom, his preeminence is all the more surprising because saying 1 specifically identifies the collection as "The words which the living Jesus spoke, and Didymus Judas Thomas wrote them down." Furthermore, saying 13 speaks of Thomas as "the one who has become drunk from the bubbling spring which Jesus has measured out," thereby favorably contrasting him with Peter and Matthew, who are also mentioned in this saying.

The somewhat surprising promotion of James in this work is interesting for a number of reasons. The epistle of James, as we shall presently see, was only accepted into the canon of New Testament Scriptures quite late. This was partly due to doubts about its attribution to James the Just, even though it certainly reflects the ethos of the *Hebraioi,* particularly with regard to its treatment of the poor.[75] Of all the letters in the New Testament it shows a much greater familiarity with and interest in the sayings of Jesus, with references and allusions to more than fifty known sayings in all.[76] A further link of James with the sayings of the Jesus tradition is found in an-

---

74. For a full discussion of the discovery of the *Gospel of Thomas* and its relation to New Testament writings, see H. Koester, *Ancient Christian Gospels: Their History and Development* (London: SCM / Philadelphia: Trinity, 1990), 75-127.

75. David Hutchinson-Edgar, *Has God Not Chosen the Poor? The Social Setting of the Epistle of James* (JSNTSS 206; Sheffield: Sheffield Academic, 2001).

76. For details of the sayings of Jesus in the epistle, see Hutchinson-Edgar, *Has God Not Chosen,* Appendix, "The Epistle of James and the Synoptic Gospels," 76-95. See also J. Kloppenborg, "The Reception of the Sayings of Jesus in James," in J. Schlosser, ed., *The Catholic Epistles and the Tradition* (Leuven: Peeters/Leuven University Press, 2004), 93-140, for a discussion of how the author of James appropriates the sayings for a different milieu to that of the sayings gospel Q.

other of the Nag Hammadi documents, the *Apocryphon* or "Secret Book" *of James.* This work also lacks any narrative structure other than the opening setting, in which the apostles are gathered together recalling the sayings of Jesus after his departure and setting them down in writing. The Savior appears to them and summons James and Peter aside and begins to instruct them "so that they may become full." The opening section consists of a dialogue between James and the Savior containing proverbs, parables, and rules. Later, the dialogue form virtually disappears and Jesus delivers a monologue in which he reassures them and encourages them to follow his path, which will lead to where he is. Again some of the sayings in this work resemble sayings known in the canonical tradition, but others are quite novel. The framework of the whole is in the form of a letter written in Hebrew in which James is sending the account of this private meeting with the Lord to a group who are asked not to share it widely, since the Savior did not wish to communicate it to all the Twelve, but only to himself and Peter.[77]

Two other works from Nag Hammadi, the First and Second *Apocalypses of James,* retain a similar format of secret revelation from the Savior, and of highlighting James's privileged role. Perhaps the information from the *Gospel of the Hebrews,* which Jerome, the fourth-century biblical scholar, reports, explains the origin of this tradition. It begins with the appearance of the Risen One to James in 1 Cor 15:7, and this was embellished later. According to Jerome's report James was present at the Last Supper, and after drinking from the cup of the Lord he took an oath not to eat or drink until he had seen Jesus risen from the dead. Soon afterward Jesus appeared to James and freed him from his oath, declaring that the Son of Man was indeed risen (Jerome, *De Vir.* 3.2).

The two James apocalypses from Nag Hammadi build further on this tradition. The now familiar themes of his martyrdom, the epithet "the Just," and James's principal role among the apostles as a teacher in Jerusalem because of his closeness to Christ are all alluded to in various ways in these writings. The recently published *Tchacos Codex* contains a well-preserved Coptic translation from the Greek of the *First Apocalypse of James,* filling in many lacunae in the text of the earlier version from Nag Hammadi, particularly with regard to James's martyrdom.[78] The Savior meets with James

77. R. Cameron, *Sayings Traditions in the Apocryphon of James* (Cambridge: Harvard University Press, 2004).

78. R. Kasser and G. Wurst, *The Gospel of Judas, Together with the Letter of Peter to Philip, James and a Book of Allogenes: Critical Edition with Introduction, Translations and Notes* (Washington: National Geographic Society, 2007).

privately before his own death and prepares him for what is about to happen. Afterward he meets James again "as he was performing his duties on the mountain," praying and instructing his disciples. James embraces him and kisses him and tells of his distress on hearing of the Savior's Passion. But he is now instructed about his own martyrdom that is to come, which is necessary for the soul to ascend to "the one who is." Thus James's spiritual union with the Savior is assured.

James in the Emerging Catholic Church

Perhaps the most intriguing aspect of the reception of James is the way in which the developing Great Church accommodated him within its structures also. The fact that Eusebius, the official historian of the Constantinian reconciliation of church and empire, included Hegesippus's version of James' martyrdom, deeming it to be the most reliable despite its strong Jewish Christian coloring, shows that there was no ideological reason to write James out of the history of the church. Yet it is clear that Eusebius wanted to domesticate him into the monarchical episcopacy of his own time, not forgetting that he himself was bishop of Caesarea and that his church had taken over from that of Jerusalem as the most important bishopric in the homeland of the gospel. Already in the second century these tensions had emerged, and Clement of Alexandria had sought to smooth things over with his statement that "Peter and James and John after the ascension of the Savior did not struggle for glory, because they had previously been honored by the Savior, but chose James the Just as bishop of Jerusalem" (*H.E.* 2.1-6). There is a hint here of the finger being pointed at James, as one of the brothers of the Lord, who had not followed the earthly Jesus but had opposed him (John 7:5), unlike Peter and the sons of Zebedee, who had promptly answered the call to follow and become "fishers of men."

Eusebius introduced this citation from Clement with his own summary of the matter: "James is narrated to have been the first elected to the throne of the bishopric of the church in Jerusalem," thus anachronistically imposing the trappings of episcopacy from his own time onto the earliest period of the church. Indeed "the apostolic throne of James" becomes an important symbol of continuity from the beginning, and Eusebius notes that it was greatly reverenced in Jerusalem "to this day" (*H.E.* 7.19; 7.32.29). At the same time, Eusebius can be ambivalent, declaring once, for example, that James received the episcopate of Jerusalem from "the Savior *and* the

Apostles," thereby combining the source of James's independence and superiority as propagated by the Jewish Christians with his own version of James
taking his place within the apostolic chain of episcopal succession.[79] What
does emerge clearly in the *Ecclesiastical History* is that Eusebius wishes to
restrict James's sphere of influence to one place only, namely Jerusalem.
James is the first in a line of bishops within that church, all of them Hebrews up to the time of Hadrian's siege (*H.E.* 4.5), just as Peter was the first
in Antioch and later in Rome, Mark in Alexandria, Dionysus in Athens, and
Timothy in Ephesus.[80]

This "domestication" of James is completed by the late acceptance of
the epistle of James into the canon, even though it was addressed to "the
twelve tribes of the dispersion."[81] This at least implies that James, or whoever wrote in his name, had claimed a wider authority than just that of
the Jerusalem church, whether all Christian believers or only Jewish Christian addressees are intended.[82] This restriction of James within the framework of the apostolic succession and the monarchic episcopate of the Great
Church contrasts sharply with his profile in the Jewish Christian writings.
Already Hegesippus had suggested that James had become a true witness to
Jews and Greeks. This profile was further enhanced in the *Ascents of James*
as represented in the *Pseudo-Clementines,* where he is said to have interro-
gated each of the Twelve separately as to what they had done in each place
in front of the whole assembly of the Jerusalem church in formal session
(1.44.1). His own missionary role with regard to the Jews is also emphasized
in this work in sharp contrast to Paul's failure, as we have seen.

79. M. Hengel, "Jakobus der Herrenbruder — der erste Papst?" in Hengel, *Paulus und Jakobus,* 549-82, here 562, n. 51. In his commentary on the Psalms (on Ps 68:8-9) Eusebius even allows himself to speculate that James did not become hostile to Jesus after he had been expelled from Nazareth or alienated from his faith in him, but was one of his most faithful disciples and was the first to receive the episcopal throne in Jerusalem.

80. W. Pratscher, *Der Herrenbruder Jakobus und die Jakobustradition* (FRLANT 139; Göttingen: Vandenhoeck und Ruprecht, 1987), 178-207.

81. For a detailed discussion of the belated canonical status of this letter and its use in the early church, see John Painter, *Just James: The Brother of Jesus in History and Tradition* (Columbia: University of South Carolina Press, 1997), 234-48.

82. M. Hengel, "Der Jakobusbrief als antipaulinische Polemik," in Hengel, *Paulus und Jakobus,* 510-48, makes a vigorous and detailed defense of James the brother of the Lord as the actual author of this letter. Others are less sure on the basis of Eusebius's information (*H.E.* 3.24-25), though there is general acceptance that it originated within a Jewish-Christian milieu. Cf. Pratscher, *Herrenbruder,* 209-21.

Conclusion

This chapter began with a discussion of Luke's desire to present the ordered progression of the early Christian expansion from Jerusalem to Rome as having proceeded according to the express will and purpose of God. To this end, Luke highlighted the initiating role of Peter with regard to the Gentile mission (Acts 10), giving him and John the main roles in addressing the Jewish audience in the opening chapters. As yet, James the brother of the Lord does not intrude. The emergence of the Hellenists is a pivotal moment in Luke's narrative since it set in train the Gentile mission that Peter had already opened up in Luke's account. Paul and his associates were to play important roles, but in ways that did not challenge the centrality of Jerusalem. The ending in Rome is deliberately left open, indeed ambivalent, as Paul, though under house arrest, is still free to explain the good news about Jesus. Thus the path is clear for the future of the mission: the gospel will be preached boldly, but it will not be without challenges from the Roman administration, despite Paul's ability to negotiate that obstacle.

Yet there is another story in Acts, running just below the surface and then springing to life occasionally and at key moments. This is the story of James and the *Hebraioi*. It was important to seek to bring that story to the surface insofar as the sources, most of them even later than Luke, would allow. Clearly, the Jewish Christian issue was a difficult and demanding one for centuries, and the significance of James for all the different branches of the emerging Jesus movement proves to be more important than even that of Peter in keeping alive the issue of Jewish participation in the universal plan of God as this was developed by the early Christians over several centuries. It is part of the irony of the story that a person with blood ties to Jesus, but who played no part in his public ministry, even opposed it or at least misunderstood it should emerge as such a central figure subsequently. Part of the "success" of Luke's account is that it so emphasized the Jerusalem-Rome axis that the other axis that one might describe as the Jerusalem-Babylon axis was largely forgotten or ignored. Once the empire and the Great Church had made their peace with one another, we are dependent on scraps of biased information or fragments preserved in the sands of Egypt to obtain glimpses into the other ways that were taken by Jesus-followers. Yet tracking the figure of James the Just has enabled us to retrieve some aspects of those others and to recognize the plurality and variety that once was present within the variegated Christian family. We shall return to this topic also in Chapter 8.

CHAPTER SIX

Remembering Jesus and Broadening Horizons in Galilee

I: THE SAYINGS SOURCES

In the previous chapter, the focus was on Jerusalem and the beginnings of the post-Easter Jesus movement there, following Luke's outline. However, as was noted then, both Mark's and Matthew's gospels suggested a return to Galilee, there to see Jesus, as he had told them to. How are we to understand this direction and how can it be reconciled with Luke's picture of the Twelve staying on in Jerusalem? Perhaps those contemporary scholars who regard the Jerusalem community as a figment of Luke's rhetorical imagination were, after all, correct! However, it was argued that the presence of a group of Jesus-followers in Jerusalem was both natural and plausible, once account is taken of the central role of the holy city in all branches of Jewish restoration hopes. Since a Galilean, James the brother of the Lord, emerged as leader in Jerusalem at an early stage, there is no need to posit an opposition between the two locations, as some have argued. The differences that emerged within the new movement were not based on putative Jerusalem-Galilee opposition but rather on the cultural and religious horizons of different groups leading to different construals of the purpose of Jesus' life and ministry.[1]

Why Galilee then? There were several reasons, most obviously the fact that some of those unnamed Galileans who had come up with Jesus for the festival and who would have benefited from his healing and teaching ministry did not abandon his memory on returning home, despite their disappointment and confusion at the manner in which his life had ended. No doubt, word of subsequent events in the holy city would have reached

---

1. E. Lohmeyer, *Galiläa und Jerusalem* (FRLANT 34; Göttingen: Vandenhoeck und Ruprecht, 1936), 110-11. Cf. R. H. Lightfoot, *Locality and Doctrine* (London: Macmillan, 1938).

this tightly knit group of relatives and followers. Perhaps some of them may even have belonged to the five hundred who are mentioned in the list of early witnesses to the resurrection, "some of whom have died, but some are still alive" (1 Cor 15:6). James the brother cannot have been the only one of Jesus' immediate family to have come to understand the significance of his life. Indeed, Eusebius, drawing on Hegesippus's account, tells us that Domitian (emperor 81-96 C.E.) had sought out members of the family of David as part of his persecution of Christians. Two grandsons of Judas, the brother of the Lord, were still alive and brought before the emperor. Having ascertained that they were poor rural peasants he dismissed them, even though they proclaimed that Jesus' kingdom was heavenly and "would come in glory at the end of the world to judge the living and the dead" (*H.E.* 3.19). This anecdote suggests that the memory of Jesus was alive in various strands of Palestinian life at the end of the first century. Some of the believers, following James, would have espoused the point of view of the *Hebraioi*, but others would have been of the *Hellenistai* persuasion, and would have made their way through Galilee as they journeyed north and east to Phoenicia and Syria after their dispersal from Jerusalem in the early forties.

As we saw in the first part of this study, Galilee had been home to Judeans for well over a century, and Jesus' family roots, we suggested, may be imbedded in that internal immigration in the wake of the Hasmonean conquests of the ancestral lands. Galilean Jews, including Galilean Jesus-followers, were faced with the challenges to their ethnic and religious identities that the Herodian presence posed, in terms of both Greek influences infiltrating from the surrounding cities and Roman political control creating a new class of people, the Herodians, whose ambitions and values ran counter to those of the older peasant residents of the region. Within the areas of Lower Galilee and the lower Golan there was sufficient solidarity, it would seem, among the rural peasantry to resist actively this new phenomenon, drawing on the older Hasmonean values of their right to the ancestral land while supporting the temple in Jerusalem as the central symbol of their belief system. This combination led to confrontation, mainly with the surrounding cities, where minorities of Judeans were being persecuted, as xenophobic anti-Judaism, especially among the Syrian inhabitants of these cities, raised its ugly head in the years leading up to the first revolt of 66 C.E. (*War* 2.457-60, 477-80).

The issue we have to address in this and the next chapter is: How did the early Jesus-followers fare within this maelstrom of competing religious, social, and political interests? What, if any, niche was there for the supporters of a convicted criminal who had challenged not merely the Roman value system but also the prevailing Judean/Hasmonean one? How did they fare in the aftermath of the first revolt? Posing such questions is much easier than attempting fully convincing answers, since our sources are few and do not allow for easy identification. Josephus, our main source of general information for this period of Judean history, only mentions in passing such events as the murder of James the Just in 62 c.e., and the picture of Galilean life that he provides on the basis of his own sojourn there in 66-67 gives no hint of a Jesus movement in the region. As yet, nothing in the material culture of Galilee that archaeology provides has anything distinctly Christian about it at this early period, with the exception of the "House of Peter" at Capernaum, to be discussed later.

A Galilean Christianity?

Various attempts have been made to rediscover "Galilean Christianity" from later literary sources, but the efforts at tracing the links between the post-Constantinian situation and the first century are at best problematic.[2] Epiphanius has a lengthy account of the conversion to Christianity of a Jewish citizen of Scythopolis, Joseph, who was deputed by the emperor Constantine (ruled 306-37 c.e.) "to build churches of Christ in the cities and villages of the Jews where no one had ever been able to place churches, since there were no pagans, Christians, or Samaritans in them. Especially in Tiberias, Diocaesarea, also called Sepphoris, Nazareth, and Capernaum, they take care to have no foreigners living among them" (*Pan.* 30.11.9-10). One detects a note of Christian triumphalism here on the part of Epiphanius, as Jews began to be legally compromised within a Christian empire under Constantine and his successors.[3] Even if the report is based on some

---

2. S. Freyne, "Christianity in Sepphoris and in Galilee," in R. M. Nagy, et al., eds., *Sepphoris in Galilee: Crosscurrents of Culture* (Raleigh: North Carolina Museum of Art, 1997), 67-74, reprinted in Freyne, *Galilee and Gospel: Collected Essays* (WUNT 125; Tübingen: Mohr Siebeck, 2000), 299-308; L. E. Elliott-Binns, *Galilean Christianity* (London: SCM, 1956); W. Marxsen, *Der Evangelist Markus. Studien zur Redaktionsgeschichte des Evangeliums* (FRLANT 67; Göttingen: Vandenhoeck und Ruprecht, 1956); W. Kelber, *The Kingdom in Mark: A New Time and a New Place* (Philadelphia: Fortress, 1974).

3. S. Goranson, "Joseph of Tiberias Revisited: Orthodoxies and Heresies in Fourth Century Galilee," in E. Meyers, ed., *Galilee through the Centuries: Confluence of Cultures* (Winona Lake: Eisenbrauns, 1999), 335-44.

factual information, it raises questions about the links between this later Christian presence and that of earlier centuries. Epiphanius's accounts of the Ebionites and Nazarenes located in Choba and Beroea, discussed in the last chapter (p. 233), might provide the missing link, however tenuous, with the Jerusalem refugees in Pella. Yet, as was discussed previously, his description of some at least of these groups is biased and at best unreliable.

Rabbinic sources too mention that there were *minim* or heretics in Sepphoris and Tiberias, and these are usually identified with Jewish Christians. One incident in particular relates to this supposition. A certain Yacob of Kefar Sekhanyah (tentatively identified with Shikin, a village two km from Sepphoris) is described as a disciple *(thalmid)* of Yeshua ben Pentera (or Yeshua ha-Nozri, "the Nazarean," in a parallel account). Jacob was described as a healer in Yeshua's name and by rabbinic standards was a teacher of unorthodox views. The rabbinic authorities reject his teaching, but one of them, Rabbi Eliezer, the teacher of Rabbi Akiba (an important second-century figure in Galilee), was reported to the Roman authorities for agreeing with Yakob on a point of legal interpretation when they met in the upper market at Sepphoris. While rabbinic texts are extremely difficult to date, these anecdotes do, nevertheless, point to the fact that some followers of Jesus were operating within the orbit of the rabbis in the second century, pointing to a Jewish Christian presence in Galilee at that time.[4]

Methodological Considerations

More recently, one detects the beginning of a reevaluation of the evidence with regard to followers of Jesus in Galilee in the first century. In particular, a number of scholars who have specialized in the study of the source known simply as Q have assigned it to Galilee. Associated with Q are other collections of sayings of Jesus, particularly the *Gospel of Thomas* but also an anonymous, possibly composite, document known as "The Teaching of the Twelve Apostles," popularly called the *Didache*. Both of these works reflect forms of Jewish Christianity that may well have originated in Palestine at an early stage of the tradition. However, whereas *Thomas* in its present form has some "gnosticising" elements, the *Didache*, at least in the section dealing with church order (6.3-15) and the brief apocalyptic finale (16.1-8),

4. R. Kimelman, "Identifying Jews and Christians in Roman Syria-Palestine," in Meyers, ed., *Galilee through the Centuries,* 301-34.

indicates an affinity with the Synoptic Gospels, especially that of Matthew. In addition the opening section of this work (1.1–6.2) offers teaching about "the two ways" — a common wisdom motif in many Jewish and Jewish Christian works. However, in the absence of any indication of date and place of origin, it is difficult to situate the work in any particular geographical setting.[5]

Two of the Synoptic Gospels, Mark and Matthew, are also now being associated with greater Galilee and Syria in discussions of their likely provenance. This represents a methodological shift from a purely literary approach to these writings to a more contextual, social-world perspective. It involves a move from the world of the text to the world behind the text, thus linking up with historical and archaeological explorations in these regions, in order to suggest plausible reading sites for the gospels based on their "local coloring."[6]

Not everybody is convinced that the genre of either the sayings sources or the narrative gospels allows such a move, however. The very fact of textualization of what must have originally been oral traditions introduces a distancing of the narrative world from the actual world in which the author(s) may have been operating. In this regard, it has been suggested that different communicative strategies are at work to those in Paul's letters, for example. By and large, Paul is addressing local communities that he knows, at least indirectly, so the readers/hearers are, to some extent, visible in the issues that he deals with. By contrast, the writers of the gospels and the other sources are largely anonymous within their texts, and we can only identify the authors on the basis of titles ascribed to them in the manuscripts of later tradition. What has been described as "mirror reading," that is, using a text as a source for the circumstances in which the author operated, leads to a vicious circle, it is claimed. It does not take account of the fact that the world of the text may have been deliberately constructed in an idealized fashion to differ from that of the actual world of lived experience.[7]

---

5. R. Kraft, "The Didache," in D. N. Freedman, et al., eds., *The Anchor Bible Dictionary* (New York: Doubleday, 1992), 2:197-98, gives a brief but informed introduction to the issues involved in the study of this work. For a recent more popular treatment with a concern for showing its continued relevance in church history, see T. O'Loughlin, *The Didache: A Window on the Earliest Christians* (London: SCM, 2010).

6. G. Theissen, *The Gospels in Context: Social and Political History in the Synoptic Tradition,* trans. L. M. Maloney (Edinburgh: Clark, 1992).

7. O. Wischmeyer, "Forming Identity through Literature: The Impact of Mark for

However, this objection, though serious, is not fatal for the project of searching for traces of the social and religious worlds in the written documents. Many of the problems just mentioned with regard to contextual readings arise from literary criticism, as this has developed in relation to the modern novel, being applied to gospel studies in particular.[8] In dealing with ancient texts, we need to recognize that there can be multiple perspectives present, perspectives that can only be uncovered when we adopt multiple reading strategies that include both literary and historical considerations.[9] This is especially true of early Christian writings, since they are engaged in recording the significant past of Jesus as well as informing communities in the present and the future that are seeking to model themselves on some version of that past. To be sure, there may well be a priority in the layering of interests that the author has woven together to create a multifaceted text — rhetorical, historical, ethical, and the like.

The purpose of such a reading exercise is to identify different strands of thought and practice within the earliest Jesus movement. It would seem to be a legitimate, indeed necessary, task, therefore, to enquire from the texts we have inherited how they or the traditions they employ might reflect particular settings and contexts as suggested by both internal and external considerations. The proposal is to proceed in *two* stages. The *first* stage, in this chapter, will be to focus on the sayings sources. This will be done because the sayings of Jesus, though probably transmitted orally in Aramaic at first, were soon translated into Greek and given written form. While there are, as we shall see, many issues of tradition history involved, nevertheless they are chronologically prior to the narrative gospels and give us therefore a first insight, partial though it may be, into the way in which Jesus was remembered and represented in a Palestinian milieu in the period leading up to the first revolt. In a *second* step, the narrative gospels, especially Mark

---

Christ-Believing Communities in the Second Half of the First Century C.E." in Eve-Marie Becker and A. Runesson, eds., *Mark and Matthew I* (WUNT 271; Tübingen: Mohr Siebeck, 2011), 355-78; R. Bauckham, "For Whom Were the Gospels Written?" in Bauckham, ed., *The Gospels for All Christians: Rethinking the Gospel Audiences* (Grand Rapids: Eerdmans, 1998), 9-48.

8. J. Donahue, "Windows and Mirrors: The Setting of Mark's Gospel," *CBQ* 57 (1995), 1-26; "The Quest for the Community of Mark's Gospel," in F. van Segbroeck, et al., eds., *The Four Gospels, 1992: Festschrift Franz Neirynck* (Leuven: Leuven University Press, 1992), 2:817-38.

9. W. Jeanrond, *Texts and Interpretation as Categories of Theological Thinking* (Dublin: Gill and McMillan, 1988), 97-118.

and Matthew, will be discussed in the next chapter, thereby covering the period up to the end of the first century c.e.[10]

The *Gospel of Thomas* and Q

The discovery in 1945 at Nag Hammadi in Egypt of a codex containing a document written in Coptic named in a colophon, or endnote, as "The Gospel of Thomas" was a major impetus in the study of early Christian origins for several reasons.[11] The work in question was a collection of sayings of Jesus, a good proportion of them parallels to sayings found in the Synoptic sayings source Q. The fact that the Nag Hammadi text was formally described as a gospel on its final page, even though the work makes no mention of the passion or resurrection of Jesus, opened up the issue of the variety of genres that merited the soubriquet "gospel" for the early Christians. It would appear that for some branches of the new movement the designation "gospel" could be applied to a collection of the sayings of Jesus, based on the belief that the kingdom was uniquely present in his eschatological teaching.[12] While the Nag Hammadi *Gospel of Thomas* is written in Coptic and dates from the fourth century, the assumption is that it is a translation of a work of the same name that was mentioned by the early third-century writers Hippolytus of Rome and Origen and was presumably written in Greek. This assumption was subsequently confirmed when a number of sayings of Jesus in Greek, written on papyrus and discovered also in Egypt toward the end of the nineteenth century, were compared

10. S. Freyne, "The New Testament in Its Palestinian Background: Essaying Mark's Gospel," in A. B. McGowan and K. H. Richards, eds., *Method and Meaning: Essays in New Testament Interpretation in Honor of Harold W. Attridge* (Atlanta: SBL, 2012) 417-40, especially 417-24.

11. The *incipit* of the gospel reads: "These are the secret sayings that the living Jesus spoke and Didymus Judas Thomas recorded." Of the three names of the disciple, only Judas is a real name. Thomas is the Aramaic word for "twin" and Didymus is its Greek translation. However, in the bilingual situation of the eastern Roman Empire the double mention of "twin" was not noticed, and this figure, mentioned in the list of the Twelve, came to be known as Judas Thomas the twin. On the basis of a later work, the *Acts of Thomas*, it has been suggested that Judas was the twin brother of Jesus.

12. Mark's was the earliest of the *narrative* genre of gospel writing, incorporating the Passion and post-resurrection stories with an account of Jesus' public ministry in the form of an ancient *bios* or life. S. Freyne, "Mark's Gospel and Ancient Biography," in J. Mossman and B. McGing, eds., *The Limits of Biography* (Swansea: University of Wales Press, 2007), 63-76.

with some of the *Gospel of Thomas* sayings and could be shown to be the originals of the Coptic versions.[13]

These discoveries give rise to a number of critical questions, not least the dating of the various versions of the sayings and whether they might, in their earliest forms, go back to the historical Jesus. Harvard New Testament Professor Helmut Koester has conducted a detailed comparison between the parallel sayings of Jesus in *Gospel of Thomas* and those in Q and other early Christian writings (including the gospel of John), and has concluded that in almost every case the *Thomas* version of the saying appears to be earlier. What is of particular interest is the fact that many of the parallels between Q and the *Gospel of Thomas* occur in what forms the basis for Luke's Sermon on the Plain and Matthew's Sermon on the Mount (Luke 6:20-49; Matthew 5-7). In both works, these early sayings reflect a mainly wisdom perspective, consisting of advice, instruction, and proverbial aphorisms. However, this does not mean that the *Gospel of Thomas* as it has come to us now is itself an early document. Rather it contains some very early versions of some of Jesus' sayings. Indeed, Koester points out that there are traces of a number of early collections of sayings of Jesus also to be found in various Pauline epistles and other writings, including the epistle of James, suggesting that the emphasis on Jesus as teacher was widely accepted in different strands of the new movement.[14]

As mentioned, the modern interest in searching for early sources dates back to the nineteenth century, when the original quest for the historical Jesus was high on the scholarly agenda. This project had become a pressing theological as well as historical issue in the wake of the European Enlightenment's critique of the gospels as being mythological and unhistorical. In response to this challenge, Q and Mark's gospel were deemed to be the earliest and most authentic with regard to Jesus' life, on the widely accepted view of historians of the period that the closer a source could be dated to the events it narrated, the more likely it was to have been accurate in terms of "what really happened." In regard to Q, for example, the celebrated historian of early Christianity Adolf von Harnack wrote as follows in 1908: "Q is a compilation of sayings and discourses of our Lord, the arrangement of which has no reference to the Passion, with an horizon which is as good as

13. H. Koester, *Ancient Christian Gospels: Their History and Development* (London: SCM, 1990) 128-72, especially 75-84; J. D. Crossan, *The Birth of Christianity* (New York: HarperCollins, 1998), 239-56.

14. H. Koester, *From Jesus to the Gospels: Interpreting the New Testament in Its Context* (Minneapolis: Fortress, 2007), 277-84.

absolutely bounded by Galilee, without any clear discernible bias, whether apologetic, didactic, ecclesiastical, national or anti-national."[15] This view that Q was a simple collection of sayings of Jesus in Galilee, unsullied by any later theological adaptations, reflected a romantic view of Jesus and his life there and was typical of the original quest for the historical Jesus.

Discussion of that topic was to take a backseat for over half a century, however, with the advent of what was known as kerygmatic theology, associated in particular with the approach of Rudolf Bultmann and the *Formgeschichte* school in Germany. In this approach the Christ of faith as proclaimed by the early church replaced the issue of the historical Jesus as the focus of both historical and theological investigations for many New Testament scholars. Yet, when the question of Jesus and his movement returned to the agenda, both Q and Galilee featured prominently in the discussion, as was discussed in Chapter 4. The fact that Q mentions three Galilean towns — Bethsaida, Chorazin, and Capernaum — has led to the supposition that the document and the community to which it was addressed were situated in Galilee.[16] There are no similar geographic indicators in the *Gospel of Thomas*, yet Koester is of the opinion that it too belonged in the milieu of northern Galilee and southern Syria, since in later tradition Thomas was revered in Syria, particularly in Edessa.[17]

Canadian scholar John S. Kloppenborg in particular has made several highly influential contributions to the study of Q and its connection with both Jesus and the earliest movement of his followers in Galilee after his death.[18] For him Q is not an amorphous collection of sayings from the original Aramaic but a literary production in Greek with clear emphases discernible in the finished work, namely a polemic against the present "generation" and a particular schema of history which involves persecution of the emissaries sent to Israel, later to be vindicated, followed by the threat

---

15. Cited by J. Kloppenborg Verbin, *Excavating Q: The History and Setting of the Sayings Gospel* (Edinburgh: Clark, 2000), 330.

16. J. Reed, *Archaeology and the Galilean Jesus: A Reexamination of the Evidence* (Harrisburg: Trinity, 2000), especially "The Sayings Source Q in Galilee," 170-96.

17. On the supposition that the *Gospel of Thomas* should be located close to the gospel of John, a work that shows particular familiarity with a number of Palestinian places, see H. Koester, "The Synoptic Sayings Gospel Q in the Early Communities of Jesus Followers," in D. H. Warren, A. G. Brock, and D. W. Pao, eds., *Early Christian Voices in Texts, Traditions and Symbols: Essays in Honor of François Bovon* (Leiden: Brill, 2003), 45-58, here 48-49.

18. *Excavating Q* provides a detailed and learned discussion of Kloppenborg's studies in Q. See in particular chapter 5, "Reading Q in Galilee," 214-70.

of the coming judgment on "this generation." These features give a unity to the whole, yet Kloppenborg believes that it is possible to identify three successive stages in Q's composition, based on identifying repetitive literary patterns, recurring motifs, and clusters of sayings with a similar import at each stage.[19]

It is important to emphasize that Kloppenborg's reconstruction is based on literary features only and does not imply that material that occurs at the second or third stage is, therefore, historically "late" and less trustworthy. Others, particularly Richard Horsley, challenge the very notion of Q as a literary work, claiming rather that its origins were in an oral culture. Traditions from and about Jesus were passed on through performance by missionaries who continued to imitate his lifestyle and praxis as they set about the renewal of village life in accordance with older Israelite customs in a Galilee that was ravaged by Herodian urbanization and Judean priestly impositions.[20] In earlier chapters we have already dissented from Horsley's views about the continuity of an Israelite tradition in Galilee over the centuries (pp. 45-46) and his description of the disastrous social and economic conditions prevailing there (pp. 122-23). Here it is his views on Q as a purely oral collection of sayings that call for comment. The literary and verbal similarities in both Matthew's and Luke's use of the source, as well as the underlying order, which can be discerned by Luke's use of the document in particular, would seem to confirm that Q must have existed as a literary work at some point, even if the earlier collections of sayings were most likely passed on orally.[21]

---

19. In this analysis, Q1 is an instructional layer based on general crosscultural common wisdom, the product of village scribes; in Q2 the rhetoric is heavily dependent on woes, warnings, and prophetic oracles directed against "this generation." The group to whom the work is addressed feels the need to defend itself and to legitimate its position over against its hostile opponents. As part of its strategy, it appeals to Israel's epic traditions (Abraham, Noah, Lot, Isaac, and Jacob), but there is no reference to Moses or David, betraying, in Kloppenborg's view, a "northern bias" that is hostile to the Jerusalem scribes and the temple. Q2 was the work of scribes with a more advanced educational level than those of Q1. Finally Q3 adopts a more conciliatory approach to the temple and the Pharisees, especially in the temptation stories (Q Luke 4:1-12) and in the insistence on the abiding validity of the Torah (Q Luke 16:17). J. S. Kloppenborg, "Literary Convention, Self-Evidence and the Social History of the Q People," in J. S. Kloppenborg and L. Vaage, eds., *Early Christianity and Jesus, Semeia* 55 (1991), 77-102.

20. R. Horsley and J. Draper, *Whoever Hears You Hears Me: Prophets, Performance and Tradition in Q* (Valley Forge: Trinity, 1999), 123-49.

21. C. Tuckett, *Q and the History of Early Christianity: Studies on Q* (Edinburgh: Clark,

Missionaries, Householders, and Village Scribes

In our efforts to identify various possible strands of the Jesus movement's early activity, both Q and *Thomas* are particularly interesting witnesses, therefore, focusing as they do on Jesus' sayings. The mission instructions preserved in Q can provide an insight into the circumstances and point of view of the outreach behind these documents.[22] Q preserves both Jesus' instructions for those being sent to announce the kingdom of God (described as agricultural workers, incidentally), and the perspective of those who were to receive them in local communities (Q Luke 10:1-12). On the one hand, the missionaries are told not to carry purse, shoes, or knapsack, thereby imitating Jesus' homelessness (Q Luke 9:57-60; 10:4/Matt 8:19-22; 10:10), yet these instructions are prefaced by a general exhortation to pray that the Lord of the harvest would send other workers also. Furthermore, the households that those sent would visit should receive them and support their efforts "for the laborer is worthy of his hire," just as Paul also claimed in writing to the Corinthians (Q Luke 10:2, 5-7; cf. 1 Cor 9:14). It is this double perspective of itinerant preachers and householders that enables us to catch a glimpse of the Jesus-followers as both settled communities and radical followers who sought to continue his memory, values revolution, and lifestyle in the post-Easter setting of first-century Galilee.[23]

1996), opts for Q as a literary work, but without the detailed layering of Kloppenborg's account of the work's development. Tuckett points to the lack of continuity between the different stages in Kloppenborg's analysis and therefore defends a basic theological and literary unity of perspective in the work from the outset, even when it is possible to differentiate between tradition and redaction at various points.

22. Mark also has an instruction by Jesus for the Twelve as he is about to send them out two by two (6:7-13, 30). These instructions are similar to but not identical with the Q instructions, and therefore both Matthew and Luke had two versions to work with in writing their gospels. Matthew combines both accounts to form a single mission discourse, emphasizing the mission to Israel only during the public ministry of Jesus (Matt 10:5-6, 23). Luke has retained the two separate accounts, the mission of the Twelve (Luke 9:1-6) and that of the seventy(-two) (10:1-12), suggesting a mission to Israel and a mission to the nations as this is developed in his second volume, Acts. The number seventy or seventy-two (variant reading) is undoubtedly symbolic, the former recalling the number of elders who shared Moses' work (Num 11:16-17) or the latter the number of nations in the world according to Gen 10:1-32 (LXX). For a discussion of the complex tradition history of the instructions, see Kloppenborg, *Q Parallels*, 66-73.

23. G. Theissen, in several studies, has used the Q missionaries as ciphers for the early Jesus movement. See his *Sociology of Early Palestinian Christianity* (Philadelphia: Fortress, 1978); *The Gospels in Context*, 203-34.

In this regard it is significant that both the *Gospel of Thomas* and the *Didache* also refer to missionary activity by Jesus-followers. Whereas *Thomas* practically repeats the Q injunction of exchanging healing for hospitality (*Gos. Thom.* 14.4-5), the *Didache* presupposes a situation in which abuse of the hospitality rule is occurring and seeks to eradicate it. With regard to the itinerant missionaries, the *Didache* gives the following instructions:

> Now concerning the apostles and prophets, deal with them as follows in accordance with the rule of the gospel. Let every apostle who comes to you be welcomed as if he were the Lord. But he is not to stay for more than one day, unless there is need, in which case he may stay another. But if he stays three days he is a false prophet. And when the apostle leaves, he is to take nothing except bread until he finds his next night's lodgings. But if he asks for money he is a false prophet. (11.3-6)

These instructions are formulated from the perspective of the householders, who are in danger of being deceived by apostles and false prophets. Q and *Thomas,* on the other hand, address the missionaries, who are instructed to stay in one house once the greeting of peace that they utter has been received. Nor should they move around from house to house, no doubt to avoid any suspicion of preying on householders. Yet both documents reflect a similar social situation within the Jesus movement — a settled community and itinerant preachers, prophets, and healers. The situation envisaged in the *Didache* would appear to be later and involves abuse of the privileges that missionaries could claim in the name of Christ. The instruction goes on to condemn in particular those who were appealing to the Spirit in making their demands. Presumably, appeal to supernatural powers and visions were ways of manipulating the unwary among the settled community. "By his conduct the true and false prophet can be distinguished" (*Didache* 11.8).[24]

In contrast to both Q and the *Didache,* the *Gospel of Thomas* presents a more radical vision for the followers of Jesus, and hence the notion of mission as an outreach to those outside appears to be missing. While it does share with Q some proverbial wisdom sayings, based on human observation, a much more dominant strand of the document's teaching could be described

---

24. Contra Koester, *From Jesus to the Gospels,* 286-87, who sees these instructions as reflecting "an archaic collection of community rules" reflecting a situation in which appeal to the Spirit rather than to institutional legitimation was very much alive. *Did.* 15:1-2 envisages another form of church leadership, namely the appointment of permanent *episcopoi* and *diakonoi.* Does this represent a later stage of development from that presupposed in *Didache* 11?

as countercultural. This arises from the fact that the fully committed follower of Jesus has come to realize the worthlessness of the world. Saying 111.3 declares: "Does not Jesus say: Whoever has found oneself, of that person the world is not worthy?" This sentiment is expressed in an alternative way in saying 110: "Jesus said: Let one who has found the world, and has become wealthy, renounce the world." This "enlightenment" comes from a deeper awareness of who one really is: "Jesus said: If they say to you, 'Where have you come from?' say to them, 'We have come from the light, from the place where the light came into being by itself. . . .' If they say to you, 'Is it you?' say, 'We are its children, and we are the chosen of the living Father'" (*Gos. Thom.* 49).

This self-understanding of the believer in the *Gospel of Thomas* echoes the Johannine perspective, suggesting that the two works may have originated in similar milieus, both groups tending to see themselves over against the world. Unlike Q's and the Synoptics' understanding of the kingdom of God as an external event that will be brought to completion in an apocalyptic occurrence, *Thomas* shares with the Johannine disciples the idea of the future kingdom as internal to the self and being realized now in the true disciple. Thus, the radical itinerancy of the disciples, rejecting family, popular piety such as fasting, and shrewd business sense in regard to money (*Gos. Thom.* 55:14) are not just imitation of Jesus' practice as in Q, but originate in a deeper recognition of the self as oriented toward regaining the primordial state of perfection that has been lost and therefore as ignoring the world. "Jesus said: Be a passerby" (*Gos. Thom.* 42), that is, do not become engaged with the world.

Returning to the question of the location of the Q group/community, the woes against the Galilean towns Chorazin, Bethsaida, and Capernaum (Q Luke 10:13-15/Matt 11:21-24) are placed in Luke's version immediately after the mission charge, implying that the emissaries did not receive the expected hospitality in these towns, all of them located close to the northwestern corner of the lake and bordering on the richly fertile Plain of Gennosar, so highly praised by Josephus (*War* 3.516-21). Since these are the only geographic indicators in the Q document, they have received special attention in efforts to identify the location of the presumed Q communities. In particular, Jonathan Reed points to the centrality of Capernaum in the places named in the woes.[25]

---

25. Reed, *Archaeology and the Galilean Jesus,* especially chapter 6, "The Sayings Source Q in Galilee," 170-95. He argues that since Q is a collection of sayings rather than a narrative account, "its textual world closely reflects the Q community's own social map." It is interesting to note that in his later study, *Excavating Q,* Kloppenborg, though initially demurring at

Even if one were to agree with Reed's line of argument on the position of Capernaum in Q's social map, there are further problems with locating the group there or in the immediate environs because of the hostile tone of the woes. The likelihood must be that those responsible for uttering these reproaches had bitter memories of the places in question. In view of the sharpness of the critique of Capernaum in particular, it would seem highly unlikely that the original Q group was still located there when these woes were written. Reed affirms the continued presence of Jesus-followers in the town on the basis of the archaeological evidence from the house of Peter, though this has been called into question.[26] If, in fact, there were Jesus-followers in Capernaum, could it be that the woes were directed against that other group of Jesus-followers, the householders, who may have rejected the radical stance adopted by the Q people? Or was the memory still alive that Jesus had once made Capernaum the center of his actual ministry (Mark 2:1; Q Luke 7:1; Matt 9:1), so that the later non-acceptance there of those who sought to emulate his lifestyle rankled all the more?[27]

In the light of these considerations, I would suggest that, while the Q missionaries may indeed have operated in Lower Galilee and in the region of the lake, they can scarcely have continued in that area, given the stinging condemnation of the three centers that the woes express. Indeed the unfavorable contrast between the Galilean towns and Gentile places, especially the Phoenician cities of Tyre and Sidon, may simply represent "shaming rhetoric" against native Judean locations, as some have claimed. Yet their mention here might represent a consciously positive view of the mission being extended beyond the political borders of Galilee.[28]

Reed's suggestion, eventually accepts it, once he is convinced that Q does indeed read well in a Galilean setting (256 and cf. 171, 174, 204).

26. Both literary and archaeological evidence for a continued Jewish Christian presence in Capernaum is contested. The rabbinic text explicitly referring to *minim* in Capernaum (*Qoheleth Rabba* 1.8) is late and does not identify who these were. Cf. F. Manns, *Essais sur le Judéo-Christianisme* (Jerusalem: Franciscan, 1977), 137-56; For a more critical discussion, cf. S. Mimouni, *Le judéo-christianisme ancient. Essais historiques* (Paris: Cerf, 1998), 397-406. The archaeological evidence for "Peter's House," on which the case has been argued by B. Bagatti and E. Testa, in particular, has been challenged by J. Taylor, *Christians and the Holy Places: The Myth of Jewish-Christian Origins* (Oxford: Clarendon, 1993), 268-94.

27. See U. Luz, *Studies in Matthew* (Grand Rapids: Eerdmans, 2005), 53.

28. W. Arnal, "The Q Document," in M. Jackson-McCabe, ed., *Jewish Christianity Reconsidered: Rethinking Ancient Groups and Texts* (Minneapolis: Fortress, 2007), 119-54, especially 143-45; Kloppenborg, *Excavating Q*, 148.

Fourth-century successor to the synagogue at Capernaum, a town
where Jesus once taught "with authority" but whose continued
relationship with early Jesus-followers is uncertain.
(David Shankbone)

The issue of the language of Q is also relevant in deciding the movement of the Q missionaries. Kloppenborg has insisted that the document
was written in Greek and displays some acquaintance with Hellenistic rhetorical conventions, even at his putative stages one and two. At the same
time, he suggests that it was the work of local village scribes, a rather unlikely scenario, it would seem, on the basis of our current knowledge of the
linguistic and rhetorical competence at this period in Lower Galilee, especially in the villages. Justus of Tiberias was described by Josephus as being
well versed in Greek *paideia* (*Life* 40), but this level of competence was not
likely to be replicated by the lesser village scribes. Justus had attained a high
administrative role in the court of Agrippa II, and, no doubt, the *prōtoi tēs
Galilaias* and the *megistanes* who attended Herod Antipas's banquet (Mark
6:21) would have wanted to know and speak Greek for prestige reasons.[29]

29. S. Porter, "Jesus and the Use of Greek in Galilee," in B. Chilton and C. Evans, eds.,
Studying the Historical Jesus: Evaluations of the State of Current Research (Leiden: Brill, 1994),
123-54, here 129-33.

The evidence from Lower Galilee for Greek, even as a second language within a bilingual situation, is very sketchy to say the least. Mark Chancey's study of the available evidence for linguistic competence is thorough and nuanced, especially his emphasis on the scarcity of evidence for the *first* century. He also highlights the need to attend to the precise provenance of the evidence that is available: Did it come from Lower Galilee itself or from the surrounding regions?[30] Clearly, one cannot dismiss entirely the argument for spoken Greek, especially in commercial and administrative situations, but one must also take account of the fact that Aramaic, and even Phoenician, continued to be in use in the region well after the first century. Much depends on one's overall view of Hellenization and resistance to it, especially by the Judeans who had settled in Galilee since Maccabean times and who may well have felt themselves "encircled" by Greek culture. In other words, language competence and usage has an ideological as well as a prestige or commercial/administrative dimension. One could reasonably suppose that the Jesus movement, in distancing itself from the mores of the Herodian palaces (as expressed in Q Luke 7:25), might have extended its rejection to linguistic practices also. In a word, if we must insist on a Greek Q *ab initio,* my sense is that this was meant for a wider audience than the Jewish villages of Lower Galilee.[31]

Upper Galilee/southern Syria would provide a more suitable location from a linguistic point of view, and there are good reasons why those followers of Jesus who modeled themselves on his life might find this region

30. M. Chancey, *Greco-Roman Culture and the Galilee of Jesus* (SNTSMS 134; Cambridge: Cambridge University Press, 2005), 122-65.

31. The question of an Aramaic source for Q, or Q itself as being originally written in Aramaic, is bound up with earlier attempts to identify Q as the work that Papias (130 C.E.) describes as the *Logia tou Kyriou* ("Sayings of the Lord"), which, he says, Matthew wrote in the Hebrew tongue and which each person translated as they thought appropriate. However, modern Q studies are clear that Q, as it existed prior to its use by Matthew and Luke, was definitely a Greek text, even when some of its idioms may have had Semitic features. Insofar as Q is a source for sayings of the historical Jesus, these sayings would have been originally remembered and passed on in Aramaic. Their translation into Greek has been attributed by Hengel to the Greek-speaking Jesus-followers dispersed throughout Syria-Palestine in the early forties C.E. For a fuller discussion of the issues regarding the Aramaic source, see Tuckett, *Q and the History,* 83-92; Kloppenborg, *Excavating Q,* 328-43; H. Guenther, "The Sayings Gospel Q and the Quest for Aramaic Sources: Rethinking Christian Origins," *Semeia* 55 (1991) 41-76. For a different perspective on the Aramaic background of Q, cf. M. Casey, *An Aramaic Approach to Q: Sources for the Gospels of Matthew and Luke* (SNTSMS 122; Cambridge: Cambridge University Press, 2002).

attractive for their purposes also. Such a situation would resonate with Jewish hopes for restoration in terms of the tribal and land boundaries of the ideal Israel, as discussed earlier.[32] Furthermore, the Q group would not be alone among Palestinian Jesus-followers in having to migrate northward in the context of the internal strife that dominated the Judean ethos leading up to the revolt. The flight to Pella from Jerusalem of the James group in 62 C.E. is indicative of the pressures that Palestinian Jesus-followers must have been experiencing in those years (Eusebius, *H.E.* 3.5.4; cf. Mark 13:14). Perhaps this was the occasion in which the *Gospel of Thomas* also "migrated" to Syria, there, however, to be used in circles that differed socially and theologically from those who were interested in preserving Q by co-opting it into the Matthean milieu, as will be discussed in the next chapter.

Understanding Jesus and His Mission: Three Issues

Discussion of the roles played by these collections of sayings will depend on assessment of their theological contribution to the nascent movement. We have seen in the previous chapter that there were key issues facing all branches of early Christianity, particularly (1) its understanding of Jesus' life and ministry, (2) its relationship with the parent Judaism in its varied forms, and (3) the terms on which Gentiles might be admitted to the messianic community. In all these areas the various sayings collections share a definite horizon with regard to Jesus as the source of wisdom. Yet each took its own distinctive stance, which the later Evangelists could adapt and subsequently include in their gospels. We must outline each of these now.

The Identity of Jesus

Beginning with the first issue, that of the *identity of Jesus*, perhaps the most distinctive aspect is the absence of any explicit reference to his death or res-

---

32. The so-called throne saying, which, in its Matthean form, speaks of the Twelve judging the twelve tribes of Israel, is deemed by many to be the closing statement of the Q document (Q Luke 22:29a, 30/Matt 19:28). It is best understood as a judgment saying against "this generation," yet reflects the notion of restoration of the twelve-tribes structure of all Israel in the background. See D. Zeller, "Jesus, Q und die Zukunft Israels," in A. Lindeman, ed., *The Sayings Source Q and the Historical Jesus* (Leuven: Peeters, 2001), 362-65; cf. J. Verheyden, "Eschatology in Q: The Conclusion of Q 22, 28-30," in Lindeman, ed., 695-718.

urrection. Certainly there is no mention of an "atoning death" as elaborated by Paul in either Q or the *Gospel of Thomas*. Even the *Didache's* account of the eucharistic celebrations has no mention of the sacrificial dimension of the meal as reflected in Paul (1 Cor 11:23-26; *Didache* 9–10). Not that Jesus is just another teacher or prophet in either work. In Q the author(s) clearly believe that Jesus is still active in their ministry of the word: "Whoever listens to you listens to me; and whoever rejects you rejects me and him who sent me" (Q Luke 10:16). It may be that Q Luke 12:10 recognizes a difference between the past of Jesus as the rejected Son of Man and the present of the community where the Spirit is active and alive in his followers: "Whoever speaks a word against the Son of Man will be forgiven; but whoever blasphemes against the Holy Spirit will not be forgiven." Clearly, the Q group acknowledges that its own mission is being performed in the power of the Easter Spirit also.

A distinctive designation for Jesus in Q is "the coming one" (Q Luke 3:16; 7:19-20; 13:35), a designation found in the Hebrew Scriptures for Yahweh's coming to save, but also to judge Israel. However, this description does not suggest that Q is totally oriented to the future role of Jesus — his coming is part of the coming kingdom which he proclaimed and which his followers are now bringing to completion. It was John the Baptist with his urgent call for repentance now who introduced this anonymous figure. He speaks of a "coming one" who will perform judgment, using metaphors of separating good and bad fruit and winnowing of wheat from chaff that would be perfectly familiar to any would-be audience in the Plain of Gennosar, with its lush vegetation (Q Luke 3:7-9, 15-17).[33] At Q Luke 7:19-23/Matt 11:2-6, John sends messengers to enquire as to whether Jesus was in fact "the coming one," only for Jesus to divert the question about his identity by telling the messengers to observe what was occurring now in his ministry, namely, God's saving care for the marginalized, as foretold by Isaiah. The third reference (Q Luke 13:34-35) occurs in Jesus' so-called lament for Jerusalem, when "the coming one" is part of the citation of Ps 118:26a, a scriptural text that Mark also uses for Jesus' actual entry into Jerusalem (Mark 11:9).

The Q lament for Jerusalem was discussed in Chapter 4 (pp. 177-79) regarding the alleged antipathy of Jesus to Jerusalem and its temple.[34] Kloppenborg, Reed, and others are also of the view that Q shared this northern opposition to Jerusalem, but this opinion fails to take account of

33. Freyne, *Jesus, a Jewish Galilean*, 49.

34. S. Freyne, "The Geography of Restoration: Galilee-Jerusalem Relations in Early Jewish and Christian Experience," *NTS* 47 (2001), 308 and notes 58 and 61.

the similarity of this particular saying with the woes against the Galilean towns also.[35] Thus the judgment motif associated with "the coming one" at the outset is maintained here, albeit with a suggestion of future redemption in the not too distant future. Several other sayings on the lips of Q's Jesus emphasize the point that his coming implies separation and judgment: "Be ready, because the Son of Man is *coming* at an hour you will not expect" (Q Luke 12:40); Jesus "has *come* to cast fire on the earth" (Q Luke 12:49) or to cause divisions even in families (Q Luke 12:53; 14:26). Two examples from Israel's epic stories, those of Noah and Lot, are placed before the community, in terms of the urgency of making the right decision and of "being in the right place at the right time to survive," since the sudden *coming* of the Son of Man betokens judgment and separation (Q Luke 17:22-37; esp. vv. 34-35).[36]

A tendency in recent scholarship has been to claim a convergence between the *Gospel of Thomas*'s wisdom and that of the earliest layer of Q (Q1), which, as proposed by Kloppenborg, largely consists of gnomic wisdom. Furthermore, because neither *Thomas* nor Q1 mentions the Son of Man in relation to Jesus, it is assumed that *Thomas* must be assigned to an early date also, since it is only at stage two in Kloppenborg's analysis that the Son of Man figure occurs in Q.[37] However, this argument depends on one's agreement with the three stages of Q's development following Kloppenborg's view, something that not everybody accepts.[38] Against this linking of the two documents at an early stage, the main thrust of the wisdom in the *Gospel of Thomas* is esoteric rather than proverbial, as was noted already, calling for a deeper recognition on the part of the addressees of the sayings. In addition,

35. M. Johnson-Debaufre, *Jesus among Her Children: Q, Eschatology and the Construction of Christian Origins* (Cambridge: Harvard Divinity School, 2005), 111-12.

36. Johnson-Debaufre, *Jesus among Her Children*, 102-8, notes that the image of separating good and bad fruit continues throughout the work and that both Matthew and Luke build on this motif in their instructions about the necessity for the Christian disciple to bring about a correspondence between words and deeds.

37. S. Patterson, "The Gospel of Thomas: An Introduction," in J. Kloppenborg, M. Meyer, S. Patterson, and M. Steinhauser, *Q/Thomas Reader* (Sonoma: Polebridge, 1990), 77-123, here 103-6.

38. D. Zeller, "Jesus, Q und die Zukunft Israels," in Lindemann, ed., *The Sayings Source Q*, 351-70, especially 353-55, discusses the function of the sayings against the Galilean towns within the horizons of both Jesus himself *and* the Q missionaries. They present not just a "last appeal to conversion," but rather "a definite word of judgment," something that the tone of the mission discourse in which they are embedded makes clear. This would entail dating Q somewhat later in the first century, in conjunction with the Jewish War.

the *Gospel of Thomas* does not use any of the usual titles for Jesus — Christ, Son of God, Lord, for example — thus indicating that the absence of the Son of Man designation is not so much due to the gospel possibly sharing an early non-apocalyptic tradition with Q but more probably to *Thomas* essentially seeing Jesus as a revealer figure. He declares: "I took my stand in the midst of the world and in my flesh I appeared to them. I found them all drunk, and I did not find any of them thirsty" (saying 28). Like the Jewish figure of Lady Wisdom (Prov 9:1-6), Jesus invites his hearers to a banquet in order to listen to the esoteric knowledge that his words contain and to apply themselves to their proper interpretation: "When one finds one will be disturbed; when one is disturbed one will marvel and reign over all" (saying 1).[39]

Relations with Parent Judaism

The *second* issue to be discussed has to do with the ways in which the Jesus-followers in the sayings sources related to the parent Judaism. One obvious pointer in Q is the expression "this generation," an expression that occurs five times throughout the collection. But to what does this generalized description refer, the opponents of the Q group only? Or does it include the recipients of the document also? In other words, is Q creating insurmountable barriers between its own group/community and other branches of Judaism, or is the message of judgment addressed to its audience as well so that it is not a question of "them and us," that is, outsiders vs. insiders, but rather of the whole collective entity of Israel, of which the Q group regards itself as representative?[40]

When one examines the occurrences of "this generation" within the structure of Q, it appears in two different blocks of material, Q Luke 7:18-35 (Wisdom is justified by [all] her children) and Q Luke 11:16, 29-32 (seeking a sign). The majority of interpreters understand the expression as a negative judgment by the Q group on other branches of Judaism. While different commentators suggest different nuances, there is general agreement with the suggestion of D. Lührman that use of the term reflects the conflict between the Q community and Israel. Thus, in the earlier of the units, "this generation" is likened to children in the marketplace who cannot agree

---

39. K. King, *What Is Gnosticism?* (Cambridge: Harvard University Press, 2003), 196-200.

40. Johnson-Debaufre, *Jesus among Her Children*, 78-80.

among themselves, accepting neither John nor Jesus despite their differing styles of approach in proclaiming the coming kingdom and the judgment that it will inevitably cause.[41] Likewise, in the second cluster of uses of the expression, the characterization of "this generation" as "evil" (*ponēros*, Q Luke 11:29) and its unfavorable comparison with outsiders such as the Queen of the South and the people of Nineveh suggest a highly negative judgment on those represented by the term.

Contrary to the prevailing trend, Johnson-Debaufre argues for a different and more sympathetic view of the situation. In her estimation many commentators come to the Q text with an already established opinion that its main concern is with the identity of Jesus and John over against "this generation" in the first reference and with a wrong understanding of what is at stake in the request for a sign in the second cluster. Thus, she suggests that in the case of the children in the marketplace, there is "a common identity horizon" between Jesus, John, and "this generation" in that the differences among them is like that of children who will not play together, competing over the rules of the game, when in fact they can all be children of Sophia/Wisdom. Likewise, in the other instance in which "this generation" is compared unfavorably with outsiders, the problem is not that the request for a sign from Jesus is in itself wrong, but rather that they cannot see "what is apparent around them," especially in this instance the presence of God's kingdom in the overthrow of Satan's rule.[42]

This understanding of the use by Q of the term "this generation" is appealing, particularly in view of the fact that it softens considerably the negative opinion of their Jewish contemporaries by the early Jesus-followers. Johnson-Debaufre's overall effort in her study to re-center the issue of the identity of Q independently of the issue of the identity of Jesus is laudable and reflects the efforts of feminist theologian Elisabeth Schüssler Fiorenza to develop a Sophia-centered understanding of Christian identity.[43] However, the final use of "this generation" occurs in what has been described as Q's lampooning of the Pharisees, climaxing with the charge of having rejected Sophia's prophets and the declaration that the punishment for all

41. D. Lührman, *Die Redaktion der Logienquelle* (Neukirchen-Vluyn: Neukirchener Verlag, 1969), 31. Kloppenborg, *Excavating Q,* 192-93; Tuckett, *Q and the History,* 201.

42. In Johnson-Defaufre's view, the description *ponēros* for "this generation" need not be translated as "evil" but rather as "sorry" or "pitiful" (*Jesus among Her Children,* 174-90, here 184-85).

43. E. Schüssler Fiorenza, *Jesus: Miriam's Child, Sophia's Prophet* (New York: Continuum, 1994).

the innocent blood that had been spilled would fall on this generation (Q Luke 11:51/Matt 23:36). In this instance, at least, it would seem to be more difficult to build bridges between the Q group and the Pharisees, a group that also had strong internal boundaries of their own. Q Luke 11:37-44 seeks to ridicule Pharisaic fastidiousness concerning purity (the washing of cups) and tithing of what must have been minuscule amounts of household herbs, while neglecting more important things such as justice and the love of God.

Yet, despite the exaggeration that was essential for the rhetoric of ridicule to function properly, v. 42c — "these you should have done without neglecting the others" — suggests that Q did not totally reject practices such as purity observance and tithing, provided they did not distort the proper response to Sophia's prophets, calling for the core ethical values of the covenant — hesed and ṣedaqah — to be practiced. Blame for the violence against the prophets is laid at the door of the scribes, who represented an elite class, especially in Jerusalem, where they were part of the ruling aristocracy. Q draws from the epic past of Israel ("all the innocent blood shed from Abel to Zechariah") to illustrate the history of callous treatment of "the prophets" by their ancestors, whom they now seek to honor by building their tombs (Q Luke 11:47). The fact that the punishment for this would now be borne by the present generation suggests that perhaps some of Q's own emissaries had suffered at the hands of non-Jesus-believing Judeans, as had others in the Jesus movement, namely, Jesus himself as the proto-martyr but also Stephen, James the son of Zebedee, and no doubt others also.

In contrast to this ongoing struggle with the parent "Judaism" in Q, the *Gospel of Thomas* takes a detached, or better, a distanced view of the relationship. To some extent the dominant viewpoint of the work, namely, searching for and seeking the true interpretation of Jesus' sayings, relativizes traditional religious practices. The attitude to fasting, prayer, almsgiving, and dietary regulations, all of which were part of Jewish piety, is at best ambivalent. The disciples ask Jesus explicitly about these practices (saying 6), and he gives his response in saying 14: "If you fast you will bring sin on yourselves, and if you pray you will be condemned, and if you give alms, you will harm your spirits" (cf. also sayings 27 and 104). The disciples inquire about the usefulness of circumcision, and Jesus replies: "If it were useful their father would produce children already circumcised from their mother. Rather the true circumcision in spirit has become profitable in every respect" (saying 53). This seemingly dismissive attitude to Jewish practices is all the more surprising since the Jewish Christian hero, James the Just, is designated by Jesus as leader after his departure (saying 12). However, as discussed in the previous chapter, this role is consonant with the gnosticizing tendency with regard to James in the Nag Hammadi corpus. It nevertheless points to the probability that the *Gospel of Thomas* had earlier associations with Jewish Christians, even if its target audience had replaced the traditional practices with a search for a higher wisdom.

The *Didache* is quite different from the *Gospel of Thomas* in regard to its Jewish roots and milieu.[44] While there are differing views among the experts on the composition history of this work, there is a general acceptance that at one stage it reflected a Jewish Christian ethos, and these elements are retained, even if the final text reflects "a smooth movement from a Torah-observant Christ-believing congregation toward a 'catholic' Jewish and Gentile Christian church with bishops and deacons."[45] This is represented not just in the opening two ways teaching (1.1–6.2) but also in the eucharistic prayers (chs. 9–10), which are clearly Jewish in wording and inspiration, but with the introduction of a distinctly Christian coloring in the address to God as Father and the reference to Jesus as "the servant." It has been noted that, unlike the early pre-Pauline account of the Christian eucharistic meal (1 Cor 11:23-26), there is no mention of the meal as a remembrance of Jesus' death, but rather thanks is given to God our Father for "the life and knowledge made known to us through Jesus your servant" (*Did.* 9.3).[46]

Inclusion of the Gentiles

The *third* topic to be addressed to the various sayings sources has to do with the inclusion of the Gentiles within the messianic community. Does the translation of the Aramaic sayings of Jesus into Greek suggest a shift of horizons indicating the influence of the *Hellenistai,* as Hengel suggested?[47] In that case, perhaps it is to members of this group of Greek-speaking Jewish Diaspora Jesus-followers, rather than to putative Galilean village scribes,

---

44. M. del Verme, *Didache and Judaism: Jewish Roots of an Ancient Christian-Jewish Work* (London and New York: Clark, 2004). "Living water" for baptism (*Did.* 7.1) and "first-fruits" for the wandering prophet, who "is your High Priest" (13.3), are examples of Jewish rituals being transferred to a Christian setting.

45. K. Syreeni, "The Sermon on the Mount and the Two Ways Teaching of the Didache," in H. van de Sandt, *Matthew and the Didache: Two Documents from the Same Jewish-Christian Milieu?* (Assen: Van Gorcum / Minneapolis: Fortress, 2005), 87-103, here 103.

46. Koester, *From Jesus to the Gospels,* 285-91, here 287-88.

47. See n. 31, p. 257 above, with reference to Acts 8:1 and 11:19-20.

that we should attribute the production of the Greek Q. Q's attitude toward the admission of Gentiles, provided this can be discerned with confidence, should assist in confirming the plausibility or otherwise of these suggestions. However, as Tuckett points out, it should be remembered that "a Gentile mission is not *ipso facto* incompatible with a conservative attitude to the Law."[48]

It is usual to point to Q Luke 13:28-29, the eschatological banquet with the patriarchs Abraham, Isaac, and Jacob, as indicative of Q's openness to outsiders/Gentiles sharing in the messianic blessings. In this Q shared Jesus' own view and that of the *Hebraioi* on the matter of the Gentile presence, as argued in previous chapters. The real issue is whether the Q group envisaged a mission to Gentiles as part of its own outreach in the present. Opinions vary among the scholars. Arnal is the most forceful in his argument against any such development. For him, the shaming element of the threat of Israel being replaced by Gentiles "is only effective on the premise that a Gentile mission is not in the works, is inconceivable."[49] Tuckett, on the other hand, has examined all the possible references to a Gentile mission in Q, including, in particular, the story of Jesus' praise for the faith of the centurion in contrast to anything he had found in Israel (Q Luke 7:9). However, this very positive statement has to be balanced against the quite negative opinion of Gentiles expressed at Q Matt 5:47 and Q Luke 12:30. Tuckett's conclusion is that "any reference to Gentile conversions or Gentile participation in the blessings of the kingdom, are not so much reflection on the missionary activity of Q's Jesus-followers, but are used as part of the document's polemical arsenal in addressing a Jewish audience by intensifying the appeal to other Jews."[50]

In other words, while Q on the whole does not share contemporary Jewish biases about non-Jews, its main focus is clearly on Israel. This emerges also when one examines Q's approach to the Law. As mentioned in n. 19, p. 251, Kloppenborg sees Q Luke 16:17b as a late redaction (stage 3 in his analysis), correcting the earlier (stage 2) statement that the Law was temporary and has been replaced by Jesus' preaching of the kingdom.[51] Tuckett,

---

48. C. M. Tuckett, "Q (Gospel Source)" in Freedman, et al., eds., *Anchor Bible Dictionary*, 5:567-72, here 570.

49. Arnal, "The Q Document," 144.

50. Tuckett, *Q and the History*, 393-404, here 403-4.

51. Kloppenborg, "Literary Convention," 99; *Excavating Q*, attributes v. 17b to the third, late (post-70) stage of redaction; Tuckett, *Q and the History*, 404-9, discusses the difficulty of separating the earlier Q version of the saying from both Matthew's and Luke's later versions and opts for redactional activity "at some stage" to insist that though a new era had dawned, the Law was still operative.

building on the analysis of David Catchpole, argues that the Q group's own self-consciousness, as expressed, for example, in the inaugural sermon (Q Luke 6:20-49), "may have been more of a reform movement working within Israel than a sect separated from its Jewish contemporaries by a rigid line of demarcation." Thus there is nothing in Q that suggests boundary creation, and in this regard there is no reference to the celebration of the Eucharist or other rituals specific to the group. Thus there is little evidence of a specifically Christian community consciousness or social awareness.[52] On balance, therefore, we must say that Q continued to operate more within the horizon of the *Hebraioi* than that of the *Hellenistai,* even though the beginnings of an opening toward the surrounding Gentiles cannot be ruled out.

The views of the *Gospel of Thomas* and the *Didache* on the issue of the Gentiles are difficult to determine in the absence of any explicit remarks on the subject. The latter work warns against the dangers of magic, sorcery, and infanticide, practices associated with Gentiles, especially Gentile women (*Did.* 2.1-2). The author also repeats the negative valuation of Gentile ethical standards, as expressed in Matthew's Sermon on the Mount (Matt 5:44-47; *Did.* 1.3). This may merely be a repetition of a rhetorical shaming ploy that we have encountered more than once in the gospel tradition. However, the dangers of idolatry seem to be quite real and the inference is clear: avoid augury, astrology, or magic since they all lead to idolatry (*Did.* 3.4), and meat sacrificed to idols is to be strictly prohibited (6.3). Clearly this suggests a pagan milieu, not dissimilar to that at Corinth, where the same issue arose (1 Cor 8:1-12). In this case however, the "freedom" that Paul allowed with regard to meat available in the markets during pagan religious festivals is not endorsed by the author of the work, who takes a much stricter view of the matter: "It involves the worship of dead gods." Clearly, contact with pagans is frowned on, and there do not seem to be any Gentile Christ-believers operating in the milieu of the *Didache,* unlike the situation at Corinth. Yet the prayer of thanksgiving after the meal does open up a broader perspective that may well ideally include pagans also: "Just as the broken bread was scattered upon the mountains and then was gathered together and became one, so may your church be gathered together from the ends of the earth into your kingdom; for yours is the glory and the power through Jesus Christ forever" (*Did.* 10.4). Not merely is contact with pagans proscribed in the present, even contact with others of a Jewish background is also excluded.

52. Tuckett, Q *and the History,* 434-35; D. Catchpole, *The Quest for Q* (Edinburgh: Clark, 1993).

The term "hypocrite" occurs in Matthew's gospel in polemical situations involving Jewish practices, suggesting insincerity, self-serving, and dishonesty, especially in religious matters.[53] Its use in the *Didache* would appear to apply to Jews who are non-Christ-believing and who fast on certain days. The Didachist wants the audience to differentiate themselves from these by fasting on different days (*Did.* 8.1), thereby drawing a clear line between the parent and the child, while still recognizing the Jewish background to the practice.

While it is possible to infer the views of the *Didache* with regard to the non-Jewish world from the various exhortations and prohibitions, the *Gospel of Thomas* does not offer any such insights. There is so much stress on becoming "solitary" (in Greek *monachos* = "monk") or "the single one" that it might appear that the work promotes a highly individualistic understanding of Christian existence, and thus ethnic issues were of no importance.[54] It should be noted, however, that the desire for unity that the *Gospel of Thomas* expresses arises from an awareness of a division in the self that requires healing, something that will lead ultimately to rejection of the world as worthless (saying 11). While there may be a suggestion that asceticism, for instance, celibacy, is called for, the main thrust of the message is the need to come to a proper awareness of the true self. Once that enlightenment takes place, the individual has already achieved the kingdom, which is to be construed as neither a place nor an event: "His disciples said to him, 'When will the kingdom come?' It will not come by waiting for it. It will not be said 'Behold here' or 'Behold there.' Rather the kingdom of the Father is spread out upon the earth, and people do not see it" (saying 113). An earlier saying is even more direct: "If your leaders say to you, 'Behold the kingdom is in heaven,' then the birds of heaven will precede you. Rather the kingdom is within you and outside you" (saying 3). To achieve this state is to become like a little child, since they have come forth from the light and are uncontaminated by the world. Saying 22 gives expression to this idea:

> Jesus saw some infants nursing. He said to his disciples, "These nursing infants are like those who enter the kingdom." They said to him, "Then shall we enter the kingdom as infants?" Jesus said to them, "When you

53. In Matthew's gospel it is the constant label of condemnation used against the scribes and Pharisees (Matt 23:13, 14, 15, 23, 25, 27, 29). It also occurs in the Sermon on the Mount in describing those who ostentatiously engage in prayer, fasting, and almsgiving (6:2, 5, 16).

54. *Gospel of Thomas* 4, 11, 16, 22, 23, 49, 75, 106.

make the two into one, and when you make the inner like the outer, and the outer like the inner, and the upper like the lower, and when you make the male and the female into a single one, so that the male will not be male nor the female be female, when you make eyes in the place of an eye, a hand in the place of a hand, a foot in the place of a foot, an image in the place of an image, then you will enter the kingdom."

In light of this presentation of what is involved in achieving the goal of the true life, it is not surprising that there is no explicit discussion in *Thomas* of boundaries as to who is and who is not entitled to enter the kingdom, as defined here. The kingdom is spread out on the earth, and those who wish to seek it will find it in themselves. Jesus has put no limits to his mission, it would seem: "I took my stand in the midst of the world and in flesh I appeared to them, and I did not find any of them thirsty" (saying 28). True, the contours of Jesus' mission as described in the Synoptics can be discerned, but it is very much in the background and does not seem to play any real role in the way the message is delivered.

Some of the sayings that parallel those in Q do indeed appear to have been less embellished, and there is no trace of the allegorizing tendency with regard to the parables that one finds in the Synoptics.[55] However, the overall ethos and tone of the *Thomas* collection as a whole is far removed from the everyday affairs and characters one encounters in the other gospels. The very form of the work, a collection of sayings with no discernible structure, removes it from the immediacy of historical realities and engages the reader at another level. From this point of view, it would be possible to situate this work anywhere in the Mediterranean environment where the search for a higher wisdom in the mystery religions and philosophical speculation was prevalent.

The association of the work with Judas Thomas, who, according to later tradition, was revered in Syria and the East, does point firmly to that general location. However, the fact that it was later translated into Coptic and was used in Egypt indicates that its appeal became much wider. The role of Thomas might appear subordinate to that of James, according to saying 12, but the very next saying (13) indicates that Jesus regards Thomas as already filled with the wisdom that he has to offer, in contrast to both Peter and Matthew. Thomas is taken aside and entrusted with further knowledge that

55. See *Gos. Thom.* 8 (the wise fisherman); 9 (the sower); 65 (the leased vineyard); 76 (the merchant and the pearl); 107 (the lost sheep).

he cannot convey to them. This may well suggest that the *Gospel of Thomas* originated in a group that was in the process of separating itself from the Matthean community, in which the primacy of Peter was recognized.

There are other pointers to a Jewish-Christian background, particularly such practices as circumcision and fasting, as noted previously, but these were no longer regarded as important in the quest for true wisdom. American scholar Ron Cameron has pointed to sayings in which the disciples as a collective ask questions, thus indicating a sense of communal identity. He also points to baptismal imagery in terms of stripping naked as a ritual of entry into the group (*Gos. Thom.* 21.1-2; 22; 37). He also notes passing references to meals (61.1-2; 64), but there is no clear indication that these are anything other than illustrative allusions, and they certainly do not suggest the eucharistic meal of remembrance as described in the *Didache* for example.[56]

What Have We Learned from the Sayings Traditions?

Of the three different saying sources (gospels) that have been examined here, only Q can be positively linked with Galilee, because of the mention of the three Galilean towns beside the Lake. Furthermore, because of its incorporation into Matthew's gospel, we have a *terminus ad quem* dating it to the late first century. A more precise date is dependent on its tradition history as this has been discussed above. Both the *Gospel of Thomas* and the *Didache* can be identified as originating in a Jewish Christian milieu, one that was close to that of Q since both show acquaintance with the sayings tradition of Jesus at a relatively early stage of its development. Yet, as we have seen, each had a different trajectory subsequently. Q with its espousal of radical following of Jesus was incorporated into Matthew's (and later Luke's) narrative account, the relevance of which we shall examine in the next chapter. Insofar as we know, Q did not survive as an independent witness thereafter, nor is there an extant early manuscript of the work.[57]

56. R. Cameron, "The Gospel of Thomas," in Freedman, et al., eds., *Anchor Bible Dictionary*, 6:535-40, here 538-39.

57. The only caveat to this conclusion is the information that Papias of Hierapolis (c. 130) had Matthew writing down "the sayings *(logia)* of the Lord in Hebrew (Aramaic), and each one interpreted them as best they could" (Eusebius, *H.E.* 3.39.16). If this is a reference to the collection that is now identified as Q, it could mean that there was more than one such collection in circulation.

The *Didache* survived as an independent text from antiquity. Even though the manuscript evidence for its distribution in antiquity is not overwhelming — a fragment of a Coptic version has been discovered, as well as a Greek fragment from Oxyrhynchus in Egypt, and some Latin excerpts. The only known full copy of the Greek text was discovered in 1873 in a codex dated to 1056 C.E. and found in the Istanbul library of the Monastery of the Holy Sepulcher of Jerusalem. This codex also contained a number of other early Christian writings. It is unclear what independent impact the *Didache* had on later Christian practice, yet the fact that it was almost totally included in the fourth-century compilation of ecclesiastical law known as the *Apostolic Constitutions* (7.1-32) shows that it continued to be regarded as highly important in defining church order in later centuries. In all probability, it was this circumstance that led to its virtual disappearance as a separate volume until the chance discovery of the work in the Istanbul codex.

A more pressing question for this study is the *Didache*'s influence on the development of early Christian practice. Is it a witness to an independent stream of the Jesus movement at an early stage of its history, or was it derived from other Jewish Christian sources such as Q and Matthew's special material, and thus belongs broadly in the same stream? It certainly reflects a close familiarity with the Jewish religious culture in terms of the ethical demands of the two ways and Jewish fasting practices, washings, and prayers, especially in the context of meals, yet it seeks to draw clear lines between its own adherents and other Jews. The baptismal formula "Father, Son and Holy Spirit" reflects the commission in Matthew to "make disciples of all the nations" (Matt 28:19-20; *Did.* 7.3), and its version of the "Our Father" prayer is Matthean in its wording and number of petitions (Matt 6:9-13; *Did.* 8.2-3). Yet, as we have seen, it has not opened its arms to embrace the Gentiles.

If, as seems likely, the eucharistic prayers in *Didache* 9–10 are reflective of the celebration of the Lord's Supper as practiced by the congregation(s) to which the *Didache* was addressed, it is worth noting that it was the "life and knowledge" that Jesus has made known, rather than his sacrificial death, that is remembered. This conclusion might come as a surprise, even a shock to many modern Christian believers who have been taught that the actual account of the institution is the essential part of the Eucharistic celebration. However, this was by no means standard in the early centuries, as many modern liturgical historians have demonstrated.[58] Accordingly, it

---

58. G. Rouwhorst, "Didache 9-10: A Litmus Test for the Research on Early Christian

would seem that the *Didache* represents a Jewish Christian group differ-ent from the Ebionites and others who were ostracized by the mainstream church and its heresiologists. In the end, its church order was affirmed by being included in the *Apostolic Constitutions*. Presumably that meant that despite its continued adherence to strict Jewish practices, it found ways to include the Gentiles also within its ambit. As we shall see in the next chap-ter, this was the lesson to be learned from Matthew, the scribe who could bring forth from his treasure store the new and the old.

The Coptic *Gospel of Thomas* also belonged to a Jewish Christian mi-lieu, we have argued, on the basis of, among other aspects, the special place among the disciples assigned to James the brother by the Lord. While some scholars have argued for *Thomas* being the earliest independent source of the sayings of Jesus, it must also be acknowledged that at some stage of its development, possibly quite early, this work took on a very different and distinctive direction, usually described as "gnostic," meaning that those who would follow this path would understand the sayings of Jesus as imparting a higher wisdom that went well beyond the often enigmatic and riddle-style sayings that were characteristic of Jesus' speech as this is found in Q and in the other early collections of his sayings, such as the collection of parables in Mark 4. It would go well beyond the bounds of this study to discuss the social and cultural factors that were behind this development. One of the mainline criticisms of the gnostic worldview is that it lacks any clear ethical or social urgency, yet, as we have seen, the *Gospel of Thomas* is countercul-tural in seeing the futility of human endeavors within the world since they block the possibility of finding one's true self. Furthermore, Helmut Koester has pointed to the fact that Paul, in writing to the Corinthians (1 Cor 2:9-10), could speak of esoteric wisdom by citing what he calls "Scripture" in terms virtually identical with saying 13 of the *Gospel of Thomas*. Paul then attributes this understanding, which goes beyond ordinary human percep-tion, to the Spirit that "searches everything, even the depths of God."

The *Gospel of Thomas,* unlike Q and *Didache,* has abandoned its Jew-ish Christian roots for the higher wisdom that Jesus offers. James M. Rob-inson, who, like Helmut Koester, has given his academic life to the study of the sayings traditions, has pointed out that the *Gospel of Thomas* is the only sayings gospel to have survived in later orthodox Christian circles. All the other sayings collections are either embedded in various epistles, or, in the

---

Eucharist," in van de Sandt, ed., *Matthew and the Didache,* 143-56, discusses the issues care-fully and deals with the different opinions on this sensitive topic.

case of Q, in canonical gospels.[59] Likewise the sayings tradition of the two ways in the *Didache* serves as an introduction to the church order, so much so that some have suggested that it represents the pre-baptismal catechesis of the congregations that it served. It, too, was thus "preserved" from the suspicion that was associated with the esoteric speculations of sages, especially in a climate where permanent overseers *(episkopoi)* were edging out the wandering teacher/healers, as can be seen in the *Didache* itself.

By incorporating collections of sayings into a narrative framework, they were insulated from random development that led to wisdom speculation of the genuinely gnostic kind. This consisted in a cosmic dualism and a redeemer myth promising salvation through enlightenment for the initiated from enslavement in an evil world. The *Gospel of Thomas* does not engage in such full-blown gnostic speculation, nor is it developed into the typical gnostic genre of the post-resurrection dialogue with the Savior found in other Nag Hammadi texts. Q had prepared the way for understanding Jesus as Lady Wisdom's envoy (Luke 7:35/Matt 11:19), whose teaching can be presented as esoteric wisdom, revealed to "little ones," but hidden from the wise (Q Luke 10:21/Matt 11:25). The *Gospel of Thomas* is also such a collection of wisdom sayings of Jesus, except that now, without any narrative structure in which to anchor the sayings, their esoteric nature began to be developed in a gnostic direction. Q was saved from this by being incorporated by Matthew into the narrative framework that Mark had provided. *Thomas,* on the other hand, was consigned to the fringes of the emerging great church but cherished by those who shared the lure of esoteric knowledge. Thankfully, the sands of Egypt have preserved it and other documents that suffered a similar fate. These works provide us with windows on the diverse and complex world of the early Christians and the many different paths that were taken on the basis of the memory of Jesus and his ministry.

59. James M. Robinson, "LOGOI SOPHON: On the Gattung of Q," in Robinson and Helmut Koester, *Trajectories through Early Christianity* (Philadelphia: Fortress, 1971), 71-113, especially here 112-13.

CHAPTER SEVEN

Remembering Jesus and Broadening Horizons

II: THE GOSPELS OF MARK AND MATTHEW

In the previous chapter the issue of the emergence of a Galilean Christianity distinct from that in Jerusalem was discussed. The use of the adjective "Galilean" reflected the scholarly tendency to view Roman Galilee as culturally and religiously different from Jerusalem/Judea, leading to the conclusion that both Jesus himself and the movement that arose in his name in Galilee were quite different from, even hostile to, that which obtained in the south. However, it has been one of the major emphases of this study that this is an incorrect inference from the obvious differences in geographical and social realities that did exist between the two regions. In terms of religious affiliation, the evidence from archaeological discoveries in particular but also from literary sources is that loyalty to Jerusalem and its symbolic significance was equally strong among the vast majority of the population of Roman Galilee, who were of Judean extraction.

Nor did the study of the three sayings sources in the previous chapter find evidence to support the assumed polarity. However, by their very nature it is not easy to identify such sources with any particular geographic setting. Yet Q, and by association the other two works, were assumed to have had contacts with the region at some point in their history, even if their tradents were forced to move northward toward Syria and beyond in the wake of the Jewish revolt. The possible tensions that emerged from our investigation referred rather to the different horizons that these documents reflected with regard to the person of Jesus, the relationship of the new movement with the parent "Judaism," and the issue of admission of the Gentiles — in short, the differences previously identified as the contrasting horizons of the *Hebraioi* and the *Hellenistai*.

In this chapter the same set of questions will be put to two of the narrative accounts of Jesus' life, those of Mark and Matthew. They are chosen because they can be shown to belong to the same trajectory as the sayings sources in terms of both the locales where they originated and the issues they sought to address in their representations of the career of Jesus in Galilee and Jerusalem. In brief, the suspicion that both gospels originated in the larger region that can be described as Syria-Palestine will be tested by examining their accounts both against the backdrop of the known political and social factors operating there in the late first century C.E. and in the light of the internal tensions that the Jesus movement was experiencing as it moved to the north and the east out of its originating matrix of Galilee and Jerusalem.

Syria and Palestine in the Late First Century: A Reprise

Before embarking on this project, it may be worthwhile to recall here some of the issues that were covered in earlier chapters, with a specific focus now on the problems likely to have been encountered by Jesus-followers in this region at that time. The province of Syria, which officially included Cilicia until the late first century C.E., was established by Pompey in 62 B.C.E. It replaced the Seleucid kingdom, the dynasty that had held sway in the region since the death of Alexander the Great but had largely self-destructed through internecine rivalries. This had allowed local indigenous kingdoms to emerge, the Hasmoneans and the Itureans in the south being the most important for our study. The Roman province covered a vast area, consisting of a region that extended from the Mediterranean to the Euphrates River on an east-west axis, and from the Orontes Valley in the north, with Antioch as its capital, south beyond the Litani River, which flowed through today's southern Lebanon into the Mediterranean between Sidon and Tyre, the two most important Phoenician cities on the coast.

The governor of Syria had oversight of the Judean procuratorship up to the first revolt in 66 C.E. As part of the post-revolt settlement, Judea became a full-scale province, with a Roman legion located in Jerusalem. After the Bar Kokhba revolt in 135, a second legion was stationed at Kefr Othni (Legio), near the new city Flavia Neapolis, which Vespasian had established in the Jezreel plain as part of the enlarged province of Judea Palestina. This now also included the southern part of Agrippa II's kingdom after his death in 92 C.E. As part of its overall strategy, Rome upped the status of the towns in controlling this rebellious territory, as was discussed earlier with regard to Sepphoris and Tiberias in Galilee. Caesarea Philippi (Banias) and the erstwhile territory of the Itureans, which had also been part of Agrippa II's kingdom, passed to Syria, with Heliopolis (Baalbek) and Chalcis the two major urban centers there.[1]

Damascus, with its oasis Palmyra, an important desert trading post, and Zeugma on the Euphrates were the principal centers in the southeast of the Syrian province. Farther north, apart from Antioch, there were other important cities: Beroea (Aleppo) and Apamea, a Seleucid foundation with significant philosophical credentials, and across the river Edessa and Emessa, both destined to become centers of Syrian Christianity in later centuries. Thus, while Antioch would appear to have been the goal of the Jesus movement from an early stage (Gal 2:11), there were many other cities where it could also have found a home as it moved beyond the confines of political Galilee in the post-70 period. In evaluating the significance of such migration, it should not be forgotten that it was moving into a territory that, as far as Jewish restoration hopes were concerned, belonged to an ideal Israel (Ezek 47:15; Josh 13:2-6; Num 34:7-9).

The urbanization policy of successive Roman emperors was subject to local conditions. Thus, apart from Caesarea Philippi, the territories inherited by Agrippa II (Batanea, Trachonitis, and Auranitis) were largely rural, and hence a policy of administration through local villages *(kōmai)* within a larger regional system was undertaken. The epithet "leading village" *(metrokōmia)* appears on inscriptions for four different villages in Batanea, probably signifying their role as administrative centers within particular districts. West of the Jordan also the term Four Villages *(Tetrakōmia)* was applied to Upper Galilee later.[2] Both regions had been allowed to preserve their village culture, therefore, presumably because of the strong Jewish preference for a village ethos, originating with the Maccabean conquest in the north and continued subsequently by Herod the Great when he introduced both Idumean and Babylonian Jews into the territories he had received from Augustus (*Ant* 16.285; 17.23-31).[3] Two places in Auranitis, Qanatha and Soada/Dionysias, had the Greek title *polis* from early in the second century, the former appearing in some lists of Dekapolis cities.

---

1. A. M. H. Jones, "The Urbanisation of the Iturean Principality," *JRS* 21 (1931), 265-75, here 267; W. Schotroff, "Die Ituräer," *ZDPV* 98 (1982), 137-45.

2. M. Avi-Yonah, *The Holy Land from the Persian to the Arab Conquests (536 B.C. to A.D. 640): A Historical Geography* (Grand Rapids: Baker, 1966), 115, 133.

3. Avi-Yonah, *The Holy Land,* 112.

However, this designation can only have been honorific since a number of these places bearing this designation are only five miles apart, according to Jones.[4]

Jones presents a useful picture of the administrative structure in the villages of Auranitis based on the rich epigraphic evidence from the region. Despite the designation "village" rather than "city," these were not isolated rural hamlets. Indeed their ethos did not differ much from that of a city, as many of them had internal structures similar to those obtaining in cities properly constituted. Thus, technical administrative terms such as "the assembly of the people" crop up, and there is frequent reference to such public buildings as theaters, baths, reservoirs, fountains, temples, and, most interesting of all, inns, which suggest a lively movement of traders and other travelers in the area. The persistence of the separate village culture in the region was due to ethnic differences between the Itureans and the Judeans. The former were originally a nomadic people who roamed the steppe lands of southern Syria, it is assumed,[5] and even after they had adopted a settled way of life, traces of a tribal past can be detected from the inscriptions.[6] This would suggest a greater degree of homogeneity in terms of cultural and social affiliations, presumably.

Josephus and archaeology are helpful with regard to Jewish villages in the region. Thus, the Babylonian Jews whom Herod had planted in this region are described by Josephus as living in "well-stocked villages" at the time of the revolt but choosing to retreat to Gamla because of its defenses against the advancing Romans (*Life* 58). Elsewhere Sepphoris is chided for not supporting the Jewish cause during the revolt, situated as it was in the center of Galilee and surrounded by strong villages (*Life* 346). As previously noted, excavations at Gamla and Yodefat show how self-sufficient larger villages were in terms of installations for local production of pottery, oil, and wine, as well as being able to mount defensive systems. There are occasional signs of decorative elements in a few elite houses as well as public places of worship — synagogues in the case of Jewish villages and small temples in

---

4. Jones, "The Urbanisation of the Iturean Principality," 274.

5. This assumption is not universally accepted today since Josephus and other ancient writers used the name "Arab" in a non-ethnic sense. Thus, Itureans as the inhabitants of Coele-Syria in Roman times may well have Syrian rather than Arabian in background. Cf. E. A. Myers, *The Itureans and the Roman Near East: Reassessing the Sources* (SNTSMS; Cambridge: Cambridge University Press, 2010).

6. Jones, "The Urbanisation of the Iturean Principality," 269-70; W. H. Waddington, *Inscriptions Greques et Latines de la Syrie* (Paris: Didot, 1870), numbers 2393 and 2396.

pagan ones. Presumably these conditions were typical of the larger foundations we hear about in Batanea and Auranitis also.[7]

Genuinely urban settings were more mixed in terms of both social stratification and ethno-cultural allegiances.[8] In assessing the cultural role of cities within a region, it may be useful, therefore, to distinguish between what have been described as "heterogenetic" and "orthogenetic" factors at play in any given situation. The former type introduced elements that were deemed alien to the immediate hinterland in terms of personnel, cultural affiliation, and ways of relating to the countryside, whereas the latter were much more sensitive to local and indigenous concerns. This would explain the Jewish preference for village life, as can be gleaned from archaeological remains and such literary sources as the Mishnah and the Talmud later. When Jews, ever since the beginning of the Hellenistic age, flocked to cities such as Rome, Alexandria, and Antioch, they continued the close-knit pattern of life characteristic of the village by dwelling in particular quarters within the cities. This gave rise to negative stereotypes about their aloofness in refusing to participate in the cosmopolitan atmosphere of the typical Greco-Roman city.[9]

These tensions were not confined to the major cities of the Mediterranean world, since they manifested themselves in Judea also. In the heightened atmosphere leading up to the revolt, there were continued disturbances between Jewish and Syrian inhabitants of Caesarea Maritima on the issue of to whom the city rightly belonged after its adornment by Herod the Great. Josephus identifies the Syrians as Greeks and alleges that they could rely on support from the army since the bulk of the Roman troops in the city were levied in Syria (*War* 2.266-70). Somewhat later he gives an account of a series of attacks by Jews on the inhabitants of all the Greek cities in the periphery of their lands, beginning in Perea and the Dekapolis, moving north to encircle Galilee, before coming south through the coastal towns as far as Gaza. The highly emotive language of the account, the scale of the operation, and the order of the listed cities suggest that this is a lit-

---

7. Jones, "The Urbanisation of the Iturean Principality," 270.

8. S. Freyne, "Urban-Rural Relations in First-Century Galilee: Some Suggestions from the Literary Sources," in Lee I. Levine, ed., *The Galilee in Late Antiquity* (New York: Jewish Theological Seminary of America, 1992), 45-58.

9. Cf. J. Neusner, "The Experience of the City in Late Antique Judaism," in W. Scott Green, ed., *Approaches to Ancient Judaism* (Atlanta: Scholars, 1985), 5:37-52. According to Jewish tradition, cities were viewed as sources of evil, as exemplified in Cain's sin (Gen 4:17; *Ant* 1.60-66).

erary creation intended to enhance the heroic qualities of the Jewish people by the general turned historian (*War* 2.457-60). Nevertheless, there is nothing improbable about the atmosphere of hostility described, especially in view of Greek counter-reprisals against Jews in the various cities in the region, mainly in the north. Significantly, he notes that Antioch, Sidon, and Apamea did not engage in such tactics (*Ant* 2.477-80).[10]

What is noteworthy in these accounts is Josephus's repeated mention of Syria and Syrians in connection with the various recriminations that occurred in this period (*War* 2.266, 461). Most remarkable is the account of the treatment of Jews in Syria itself, where he claims that a reign of terror was conducted by the inhabitants of all the Syrian cities, with a view to getting rid of the Jews, only to find that there were numerous "Judaizers" in their midst, whose loyalty to the Syrian cause was deeply suspect (*War* 2.461-67). A little later a similar situation is reported for Damascus, where many of the women were also Jewish sympathizers and the men were afraid to tell their wives that they had in fact conducted a pogrom against the Jews in that city (*War* 2.560-61; *Life* 27).[11]

Yet Josephus can also claim that Jews and Syrians could live side by side in Philip's territory without any overt animosity (*War* 3.58), and he also reports that somewhat earlier there was rejoicing in Syria when the young Herod the Great got rid of the brigand chief Hezechias, who had terrorized the borderland between Upper Galilee and Syria (*War* 1.205). Furthermore, on the death of Herod a Jewish delegation informed Augustus that they would prefer to have their country united to Syria rather than being ruled over by one of Herod's sons (*Ant* 17.314; 18.2). In fact, ten years later, following the deposition of Archelaus in Judea, their wish was partially realized when Judea was made a Roman procuratorship under the governor of Syria.[12] Despite all the hostility of the pre-revolt period in Palestine, the surrounding areas, and Syria proper, Josephus ends his account of the Jewish War by saying that Jews were particularly numerous

10. S. Freyne, "The Revolt from a Regional Perspective," in A. Berlin and A. Overman, eds., *The First Jewish Revolt: Archaeology, History and Ideology* (London: Routledge, 2002), 47-49.

11. G. Theissen, *The Gospels in Context: Social and Political History in the Synoptic Tradition* (Edinburgh: Clark, 1992), 268-70; M. Hengel and A. M. Schwemer, *Paul between Damascus und Antioch: The Unknown Years* (Louisville: Westminster John Knox, 1997), 61-90.

12. For a full discussion of this nomenclature and the situation in Judea until the time of Agrippa I (41 C.E.), see W. Eck, *Rom und Judaea. Fünf Vorträge zur römischen Herrschaft in Palaestina* (Tübingen: Mohr Siebeck, 2007), 23-45.

in Syria, where by virtue of proximity the two peoples were "intermingling" (*War* 7.43).

A seeming contradiction has emerged, therefore, with regard to Jewish relations with Syria. On the one hand deep-seated animosities of a religio-cultural kind prevailed, and yet there are long-lasting historical and geographical links that brought the two territories and their populations very close. This closeness was not merely a case of geographical proximity but actual intermingling, which, from the Jewish side at least, had deeper roots. Thus, in *Against Apion* Josephus has no difficulty in interpreting Herodotus's claim that "the Syrians of Palestine practice circumcision" as really referring to Jews (1.169, 171). Philo also is aware of the close associations, claiming that Agrippa I was a Syrian and ruled over a large part of Syria (*Flaccus* 39). What is the basis for these Jewish claims that link Jews and Syrians so closely, while at the same time accounting for the deep-seated Syrian animosity toward and suspicion of Jews?

One element of a plausible answer, alluded to previously, is the fact that Jewish claims were based on much older Israelite ideas about the extent of the allotted land, which in later times began to play an important role in Jewish expressions of restoration. Thus according to 2 Sam 8:1-14, David conquered or received submission from all the various kings between Edom and Damascus and as far north as Hamath on the Orontes. These limits of the greater Israel or some variants of them recur in various sections of the Hebrew Bible: the poetic and prophetic literature such as Ps 72:8; Amos 6:14; Ezek 47:15; Zech 9:10; Mic 7:12; in the narrative material Josh 1:4; 13:2-6; Num 34:7-9; 2 Kgs 14:25, 28; Sir 44:21-22.[13] On the other hand, the animosity of the Greek cities toward the Jews described by Josephus has its most likely background in the Maccabean wars of conquest, which were inspired by the ideology of the greater land and the removal or conversion of all non-Jewish peoples from the conquered territories (1 Macc 11:63-74; 15:33; *Ant* 13.257-58, 318-19, 397).

The focus on Syria as the possible reading site for one or both of the texts under consideration has raised a number of important issues that need to be taken into account in any consideration of the first two gospels in their Jewish contexts. Foremost of these is the claim that "Israel" reached into this territory, and therefore all movements of restoration were likely to see this as missionary terrain with regard not just to Gentiles (Syrians), but to

---

13. M. Hengel, "*Judaioi* in der geographischen Liste, Apg 2,2, 9-11 und Syrien als Grossjudäa," *RHPR* 80 (2000), 51-68.

Jews also. In short, there was a geographical as well as temporal dimension to early Christian aspirations on the basis of their Jewish heritage. Another issue that emerges for consideration is the urban-rural divide and how this might have impacted on the Jesus movement. A third factor is the endemic animosity of Syrians toward Jews and how this might play itself out with regard to the Jesus-followers. In the reading exercise that I propose to engage in, these issues will be the main focus of attention. However, in view of the rapidly changing environment of both the Jewish population and the Roman imperial presence, attention to the date of each document will also be crucial to the exercise.

Mark and Galilee: Jesus, Jews, and Gentiles

In his important study of the differing poles of Galilee and Jerusalem within the early Jesus movement, Ernst Lohmeyer developed his argument for a Galilean Christianity on the basis, first of all, of Galilee's precedence over Jerusalem in the earliest post-resurrection account, reported by Mark (16:7).[14] Yet later tradition supports Rome as the place of composition of that gospel, and several modern scholars have defended this position. The so-called "little apocalypse" (Mark 13) is crucial for any attempt to date and locate the gospel. While there is a growing consensus that this chapter reflects the situation surrounding the Jewish War as described by Josephus,[15] a number of influential scholars still prefer Nero's persecution of the Christians in Rome in 64 C.E. as the occasion for the work's composition.[16] This situation, it is claimed, is mirrored in Mark 13:9-13, a passage that deals with the arraignment of the followers of Jesus "before governors and kings." Such a date would also correspond with the tradition reported by the second-century writer Papias, namely, that Mark was Peter's interpreter and that he put Peter's teaching into writing, presumably after the latter's martyrdom in the Neronic persecution.[17]

---

14. E. Lohmeyer, *Galiläa und Jerusalem* (FRLANT 34; Göttingen: Vandenhoeck und Ruprecht, 1937), 13-14.

15. A. Yarbro Collins, *Mark: A Commentary* (Hermeneia; Minneapolis: Fortress, 2007), 7-11; Theissen, *The Gospels in Context*, 236, n. 3.

16. M. Hengel, *Studies in the Gospel of Mark* (London: SCM, 1985).

17. While Theissen (*The Gospels in Context*, 245-49) recognizes the possible Roman coloring of such terms as "Syro-Phoenician" (Mark 7:26) and *Quadrans/kodrantēs* (Mark 12:42), he is able to show that these are quite acceptable usages in the Roman East of the

On the other hand, those who prefer the setting of the Jewish War point to the repeated warnings about false messiahs and false prophets (Mark 13:5-6, 21-22) as indicative of the situation in Judea prior to and during the first revolt. The issue then becomes one of deciding to what precise point in the events of the period the gospel refers. Without going into the details of their arguments, both Joel Markus and Gerd Theissen suggest that Mark's gospel was written immediately after the destruction of the temple, probably in Syria. Both, however, allow for the possibility that a slightly earlier date in 68 C.E. might be contemplated in the light of the Zealot takeover of the temple and the murder of the reigning High Priest (so Markus), or because of the elevation of Vespasian as emperor in 69 (so Theissen).[18]

In arguing for the post-war date, Theissen develops a highly interesting picture of the background to Mark's end-time scenario. On the one hand there was the scene of frightful disorder throughout the cities of Syria because of the persecution of Jews and Jewish sympathizers described by Josephus, thus explaining the warnings about suffering for Jesus-followers that Mark has included in ch. 13 (vv. 9-13; see *War* 2.461-67, 560-61).[19] At the same time, there are indications that rumors of an imminent world-shattering event were circulating in the East and that these were being associated (for propaganda reasons, no doubt) with the arrival of the Flavian emperor, Vespasian, or possibly the return of Nero, who, rumor in Rome had it, was returning to wreak vengeance on his enemies. These speculations would explain why there is an air of anxiety running through Mark 13, a situation which the promise of the return soon of the Son of Man was intended to assuage (v. 26).[20]

Before proceeding to discuss further the date and location of Mark's composition, it is necessary to follow Theissen's advice and ask how well a

---

first century. He also notes "the local Semitic colouring" of such expressions as "the Sea of Galilee"/*Yam ha-Kinneret*, even though the use of the term "sea" for an inland mass of water would have sounded strange to Roman ears (Theissen, 237-38).

18. J. Markus, "The Jewish War and the *Sitz im Leben* of Mark," *JBL* 111 (1992), 441-62; Theissen, *The Gospels in Context*, 258-62.

19. See S. Freyne, "Matthew and Mark: The Jewish Contexts," in E. M. Becker and A. Runesson, eds., *Mark and Matthew I: Comparative Reading: Understanding the Gospels in their First-Century Settings* (WUNT 271; Tübingen: Mohr Siebeck, 2011), 179-203, especially 189-93 dealing with the persecution of Jesus-followers in Mark.

20. Theissen, *The Gospels in Context*, 264-68; See also A. Overman, "The First Revolt and Flavian Politics," in Overman and Berlin, eds., *First Jewish Revolt*, 213-20.

setting during or immediately after the Jewish revolt might assist in interpreting Mark's message more adequately. The questions that a consideration of the early Christian mission have suggested covered a range of issues: the particular understanding of Jesus and his role as portrayed in the gospel, the relationship of the Jesus movement with the parent Judaism in Mark's narrative, and the stance of the work with regard to the admission of the Gentiles to the messianic community. These are broad-ranging questions, discussion of which should provide a more comprehensive understanding of Mark's overall message than consideration of the evidence for Nero's persecution of the Christians in Rome in 64 C.E. alone could offer.

The Markan Jesus and His Activity

Unlike Matthew and Luke, both of whom provide a lead-in to the story of Jesus by presenting diverse accounts of his birth and infancy, Mark puts Jesus on the stage of history without any such introduction. His arrival is connected with John the Baptist's appeal to his contemporaries from both the Judean countryside and from Jerusalem to undergo his rite of baptism in accordance with Isaiah's call to "prepare the way of the Lord in the desert" (Isa 40:3; Mal 3:1). John introduced Jesus to the crowds as "the stronger one" who can baptize with the Spirit, not just water. However, Jesus underwent John's rite, and as he was ascending from the water he had a vision of the Spirit descending like a dove on him, and a voice from heaven addressed him directly: "You are my Son, the beloved, with you I am well pleased" (Mark 1:11). This is a formal enthronement of Jesus as the expected messianic figure in accordance with Ps 2:7, one of the psalms that describes the ideal king of the future as God's son. What is most significant about the scene is the fact that it is Jesus himself who sees the Spirit descending, and he alone hears the heavenly voice. Thus, an aura of secrecy surrounds the person of Jesus from the outset, as far as humans are concerned, giving rise to what has been described as the "messianic secret," a feature of the narrative throughout.[21]

A similar pattern of partial recognition followed by an otherworldly experience recurs at two other key points in the gospel. Thus, at the midpoint in the narrative, Peter, as leader of the chosen group of followers, responds to Jesus' query about his identity with the statement that Jesus is the

---

21. C. Tuckett, ed., *The Messianic Secret* (London: SPCK, 1983).

Christ (Mark 8:29). However, an injunction to silence follows immediately (v. 30), suggesting that such a bald disclosure is premature. Instead Peter and the two sons of Zebedee are privy to the Transfiguration scene, where once again Jesus, this time clothed in otherworldly white and accompanied by two heroes of the Israelite tradition, Moses and Elijah, is presented to the confused disciples by a heavenly voice which declares: "This is my son, the beloved, listen to him" (Mark 9:2-8).

The third instance of this revelatory pattern occurs during the trial and crucifixion scene. This time there is an added element, however. Unwittingly, and probably in mockery, the High Priest puts the correct question to Jesus: "Are you the Messiah, the son of the Blessed One?" To which Jesus replies: "I am, and you shall see the Son of Man seated at the right hand of the Power and coming on the clouds of heaven" (Mark 14:61-62). This time it is Jesus himself, not the voice from heaven, who gives the answer, once more couched in biblical language, which combines two quite separate biblical images, the heavenly Son of Man figure of Daniel (Dan 7:13-14) and the royal Son, seated at God's right hand, as promised in another messianic psalm, Ps 110:1.[22]

This new element in the pattern is a clue to Christian readers, preparing them for, again, the partial yet totally unexpected statement of the Roman centurion at the foot of the cross at the moment Jesus dies: "Truly this man was *a* Son of God" (Mark 15:39). The final disclosure takes place at the tomb when the faithful women encounter "a young man, dressed in *white*" who tells them that Jesus is risen and that they are to tell Peter and the disciples that he will "go before (Greek *proagō*) them to Galilee" as he had promised (Mark 16:7). Again, unlike Matthew and Luke, Mark does not report a vision of the risen Christ reassuring the disciples of his victory over death. Instead they must discover Jesus "going before them" in the journey back to Galilee, no easy challenge in view of their reluctance to follow him as he led the way to Jerusalem earlier when they were expecting a glorious triumph in the holy city (Mark 10:32, again *proagō*).

Mark has thus framed his story of Jesus with these three interlocking revelatory scenes that suggest that the discovery of Jesus' true identity is a gift from on high, not something that can be discovered through human insight, or at least not fully discovered, except through an openness to recognizing God's action in the career of Jesus. The "messianic secret"

---

22. N. Perrin, "Mark XIV.62: The End Product of an Early Christian Pesher Tradition?" *NTS* 13 (1966), 150-55.

is a challenge, not a conundrum, calling on the reader/hearer to recognize God's victory despite human obtuseness and superficiality. It was the genius of Mark to retell the story of Jesus' deeds and words, cloaked with an aura of mystery but accessible to those who have eyes to see and ears to hear. Gerd Theissen describes Mark's literary achievement as follows: "There is no doubt that Mark transfers back into Jesus' life the divine dignity of Jesus, which is in substance grounded in the Easter experience."[23] This strategy does not of course blot out the memory of the historical Jesus, which had come to Mark via various channels, oral and written, going back to Jesus' own contemporaries of the first generation. The issue, rather, is to see how this "new, depth vision" of Jesus' life would lead eventually to a movement in his name, one that would keep alive his memory and yet transform the disciples' understanding of what he was about. It would also enable them to reappraise the values that should henceforth determine their fidelity to Israel's God, especially in the light of the historical experience of the failed revolt and a ruined temple.

The urgency of providing a reassuring account of how God's presence was still operative in the world despite the destruction of the temple, and of the eventual triumph of God's *basileia* was one of Mark's primary objectives in the immediate aftermath of the catastrophe. Unlike Q, where the coming of the Son of Man is described as sudden and for judgment, Mark uses the image to console the elect. The coming of this heavenly figure will be in "power and glory" to gather the elect (Mark 13:26-27). In order to propagate his message of hope in a time of crisis generated by the loss of the temple, Mark chose the Greco-Roman *bios* genre but introduced the apocalyptic message of hope. Presumably, this was because his more literate audience, especially Jewish sympathizers of a Gentile background, were more familiar with such a narrative form and the sense of continuity between past and present that such a genre affirms. Thus much of the material that belonged to the earliest layer of Q, following Kloppenborg's analysis noted in the previous chapter (p. 125), is omitted as of no particular interest to Mark in the situation in which he finds himself. Rather he is keen to present Jesus' career as the manifestation of God's power in the present, not as that of a teacher of deliberative instructions that are to be reflected on and put into practice. To this end, he presents Jesus' deeds within a mythical framework drawn from an apocalyptic worldview that sees the present as

23. G. Theissen, *The Religion of the Earliest Churches: Creating a Symbolic World* (Minneapolis: Fortress, 1999), 172.

Huge stones, each weighing several tons, atop the Herodian street where they fell in C.E. 70 during the Roman destruction of Jerusalem and its temple. (J. Steven Notley, courtesy of JerusalemPerspective.com)

a clash between the forces of good and evil. Several of the miracle stories are cast as exorcisms in which Jesus struggles successfully with the demons and banishes them, thereby displaying his superior power. Indeed he is so successful in this regard that he is accused by the Jerusalem scribes of being in league with Beelzebul, the prince of demons, but he rejects the idea as absurd — "a house divided against itself cannot stand" — and instead attributes his power to the Spirit (or "finger") of God, which makes him the "stronger one" in this life and death struggle (Mark 3:22-27).

Mark is also aware of the other aspect of Jesus' career as a teacher. He repeatedly describes Jesus in introductory statements as engaging in teaching. Jesus' exorcisms are twice described as a "teaching of a different order *(kainē)* with authority," in contrast to that of the scribes (Mark 1:22, 27). Even his townspeople from Nazareth, on hearing of his mighty deeds, inquire about the source of his wisdom *(sophia,* 6:2). Yet, curiously there are no long discourses in Mark's gospel.

The parable chapter (ch. 4) does give some examples of Jesus' teaching. The choice of images, mainly to do with nature and growth, is instructive as to how the Evangelist understands Jesus as teacher, however. There is a hidden, even mysterious quality to the processes of nature that Jesus draws on to illustrate the true meaning of the kingdom as he proclaims it. Indeed he can play on the word *parabolē* to indicate the challenging and enigmatic quality of the message that from death comes life. The corresponding Hebrew word *mashal* has a number of meanings ranging from story to riddle. Mark's Jesus plays on this double entendre by introducing an insider-outsider dynamic. He tells the disciples that "the mystery of the kingdom" has been entrusted to them, but "for those outside everything happens in parables/riddles" (Mark 4:10-12).

On the way to Jerusalem, as the second act of the drama unfolds, Jesus instructs his disciples three times as to what lies in store for him and them. Each time they demonstrate their failure to grasp the message by rejecting the idea of having to suffer for the cause, engaging instead in petty jealousies or seeking special honors. Just as in the parable chapter, there is a subversive and unexpected dimension to Jesus' teaching that defies all human judgment: to save one's life, one must lose it; to be first, one must be last of all and servant of all; to become great, one has to become a slave. These sayings indicate just how countercultural the Markan Jesus expected his group to be in terms of the values that were prized in the honor-shame culture of the Roman world. One way to defeat the enemy is to lampoon its value system.

Retrieving the Jewish Heritage

The Jesus movement was not the only branch of the Jewish heritage that had to reevaluate the meaning of the national tragedy that was unfolding with the destruction of the temple and the cessation of sacrifice. The legend about Johanan ben Zakkai escaping from the ruined city and being allowed to open a school at Jamnia is only one symptom of how the scribal/Pharisaic tradition began to fashion an alternative version that could be lived out in the home and the village. Torah and study would replace temple and sacrifice as the sacred worship of Israel's God.[24] On the other hand an apologist-historian such as Josephus sought to propagate a version of the revolt that placed the blame on small but influential groups of zealots who refused to bow to the inevitable, God-willed power of Rome and so brought destruction on the nation.[25] Later Christian tradition would blame the de-

---

24. J. Neusner, *Development of a Legend: Studies in the Traditions concerning Yohanan ben Zakkai* (Leiden: Brill, 1970); "Studies in the *Taqqanoth* of Yavneh," *HTR* 63 (1970), 183-98.

25. P. Alexander, "What Happened to the Priests after 70?" in Z. Rodgers, et al., eds., *A Wandering Galilean: Essays in Honour of Sean Freyne* (Leiden: Brill, 2009), 5-33.

struction on Jewish rejection of their Messiah Jesus. Mark was at the very beginning of such explanatory/replacement efforts and his way of negotiating the relation between his own group and other branches of the parent religion is, therefore, highly instructive.[26]

There are a number of indications in the text that far from "walking away" from the shared heritage, Mark, building on the example of the historical Jesus, sought to reinterpret it in ways that recognized his and his community's indebtedness to its deep Jewish roots. The success of Paul's Gentile mission was well established by the time Mark came to write his story of Jesus, and certain lines of development were already indicated, even if one does not want to go so far as to suggest that Mark's is simply a Pauline gospel, as some have suggested.

The Jewish symbol system consisted of temple, Torah, and land. The temple represented the continuing divine presence in Israel, the Torah was both the story of God's choice of Israel and the stipulations of the covenant commitment, and the land was the guarantee of God's care and protection for his people. Various institutions, rituals, and personnel had developed around this system over time, and different groups associated themselves with some or all of these. Being Jewish in the Greco-Roman world meant being different. Orthopraxis rather than orthodoxy was the hallmark of a good Jew. How does the Markan Jesus measure up to these standards and where did the emphasis lie in terms of his espousal of his Jewish identity?

Land

Mark's description of the call of the Twelve is highly significant, it would seem: "He went up a mountain and called whom he wished to himself, and he appointed the Twelve to be with him and to be sent to preach and to have authority to cast out demons" (Mark 3:13-15).[27] This account is constructed in such a way as to emphasize the close connection between the group and Jesus. Effectively, they are to continue Jesus' ministry as described by Mark, and that means this was not a temporary arrangement for a once-off sending as noted in Mark 6:7-13. The reason for their appointment must have

26. For an interesting collection of essays dealing with the issues, see D. Schwartz and Z. Weiss, *Was 70 CE a Watershed in Jewish History? On Jews and Judaism before and after the Destruction of the Second Temple* (Leiden: Brill, 2012).

27. S. Freyne, *The Twelve: Disciples and Apostles* (London: Sheed and Ward, 1980).

still been operative when Mark wrote. Thus it is the continuing symbolism attached to the Twelve that is important, since it recalls the ideal Israel of the twelve tribes that had been scattered over the centuries and that were to be reestablished in the messianic age. Not merely did the Twelve recall the tribal arrangement in early Israel, it also had resonances of the territorial dimension of Israel's existence in the land. At a time when Roman rule was about to take over the land of Israel and farm it out to its supporters (*War* 7.216), this was indeed a daring symbolic statement by both Jesus earlier and now by Mark. In other words, Mark had not abandoned hope of Israel's renewal when he wrote, but, as we shall see later, the setting for the account of the call of the Twelve suggests broader horizons than Israel only.

Temple

The situation with regard to the temple was of course extremely sensitive ever since Antiochus Epiphanes' desecration of it over 200 years earlier. Gaius's threat to have his own statue erected there in 41 C.E. was even more relevant in Mark's day, especially if the "abomination of desolation" mentioned in Mark 13:14 actually refers to that incident, as Theissen suggests. Jesus' action in the temple as described by Mark was at least a criticism of existing practice, whether or not one should go farther with E. P. Sanders and see it as a condemnation of the sacrificial system as such.[28] Alone of the Synoptic Gospels, Mark cites Isa 56:7 in full, "my house shall be called a house of prayer *for all the nations,*" suggesting that Jesus is critical of ritual, while reaffirming Isaiah's view of the temple functioning as an inclusive symbolic space for all peoples. At the same time it should be noted that Mark paints an almost nostalgic picture of Jesus in the temple, walking in the temple courts, teaching there, or observing the people making their offerings in the treasury (Mark 11:27; 12:35, 41-44; 13:1). Certainly these glimpses do not indicate any hostility to the temple itself on the part of the Markan Jesus, in contrast to others such as the Zealots who had used its fortifications for their military operations or the Essenes who had abandoned it entirely and constituted an alternative temple community in the desert while they waited for God to build his own temple.

The original Isaian context (Isa 56:1-8) in which the reference to the temple as a house of prayer for all peoples occurs affirms inclusion for the

---

28. E. P. Sanders, *Jesus and Judaism* (London: SCM, 1985), 61-71.

foreigner and the eunuch, individuals who were allowed only partial access to the temple, because of their impurity as Gentiles or their childlessness in the case of eunuchs, who were thus without "monument or name" (v. 5). The only proviso that Isaiah mentions is that they observe the Sabbath and cling to the covenant, elements that can be understood in the light of the creation stories in Genesis rather than the Mosaic dispensation. While the LXX translation suggests that these stipulations only apply to full converts to Judaism, it should be noted that there is no mention of circumcision or the obligation to immerse before entering the holy place, as was the practice in the first century. No distinction is made between prayer and sacrificial offerings, even though the explicit mention of prayer may reflect the beginnings of criticism of animal sacrifice in Judaism.[29] The universalism and inclusivity of the whole passage recalls Isaiah's earlier promise with regard to God's holy mountain, where the eschatological meal will be celebrated with all peoples when the veil of mourning will be removed (Isa 25:6-10).

This Isaian background to Mark's account of access to the temple is in stark contrast to what the contemporary Essenes considered appropriate, according to the Temple Scroll and other texts from Qumran.[30] Of course Mark's notice that with the death of Jesus the temple veil was torn in two from top to bottom (Mark 15:38) makes a more radical symbolic statement. The regulations of access to the sacred space of the temple were now obsolete. The divine presence *(shekinah)* was no longer hidden or restricted but present in the world. This brief declaration meant that for Mark the destruction of the temple was inevitable and indeed had been foretold by Jesus himself (13:1-2). Earlier still, Jesus had used sacrificial language with reference to his own death (10:33-34), thus echoing Paul's theology of expiation as expressed in Rom 3:24-25 and elsewhere in early Christian interpretations of Jesus' death as a sacrifice for sin, for example in the epistle to the Hebrews.

Torah

The Torah was the third element in the Jewish symbolic system, and it was at this point that the deepest divisions occurred between the Markan Jesus

29. S. Freyne, *Jesus, a Jewish Galilean: A New Reading of the Jesus Story* (New York: Continuum, 2005), 162.

30. Freyne, *Jesus, a Jewish Galilean*, 157.

and the Jewish establishment. This may well have resulted from the fact that by the time the gospel was written the scribes and their associates the Pharisees were the one group among the guardians of the symbol system to remain relatively intact, whereas the Zealots who fought for the land and many of the priests who controlled the temple were sold into slavery, captured, or dead. We have already seen that Jerusalem was the center of scribal activity (pp. 108-9), Ben Sira being the prototype of the elite urban scribes whose influence and authority made them dangerous opponents.[31] According to Mark, they had come from Jerusalem, seeking to discredit Jesus with accusations of being in league with the prince of demons (Mark 3:22). Accompanied by local Pharisees, they had come from Jerusalem a second time, clearly spying on Jesus' followers and complaining about their lax attitude toward hand-washing before eating (7:1-2, 5). Again they are found arguing with Jesus' disciples over their failure to complete an exorcism of a possessed boy (9:14).

While the most powerful scribes were located in Jerusalem, there must have been local scribes in Galilee also. The Galilean populace was, according to Mark, at least aware of their instruction and able to compare them unfavorably with Jesus' new and authoritative teaching (Mark 1:22, 27). Jesus' disciples are familiar with their opinion about the coming of Elijah in the end time (8:28), and Jesus himself disputes their claim that the Messiah must be the son of David (12:35-37). On another occasion in Jerusalem, a certain scribe is impressed with Jesus' refutation of the Sadducees' denial of the resurrection from the dead and engages with him on the issue of which is the greatest commandment in the Torah. They concur and Jesus declares that the scribe is not far from the kingdom of God (12:28-34). Despite this one friendly encounter, Jesus' final comment on the scribes is scathing as he warns his disciples about their greed and pretentiousness, "devouring widows' houses, while saying long prayers for appearance' sake" (12:38-40). They continued to wield influence throughout the first century because they were literate and well-versed in Jewish law and customs. They may even have had some judicial functions since they were closely associated with the chief priests and elders in having Jesus executed (14:1, 43, 53; 15:1, 31).

With this profile of sustained opposition and hostility, the scribes rep-

---

31. A. Saldarini, *Pharisees, Scribes and Sadducees in Palestinian* Society (Edinburgh: Clark, 1988), 144-73. See Josephus, *Life* 190, where Simon the son of Gamaliel, a leading scribe, was able to mount an attack on Josephus's role in Galilee in an effort to have him dismissed.

resent the most serious threat from a Jewish perspective to the Jesus movement within the ambit of Mark's gospel. The criticism that the Evangelist places on Jesus' lips suggests that the two groups were bitter rivals, whereas the opposition from the Pharisees was less charged, despite their political links with the Herodians (Mark 3:6; 12:13). In all probability the Pharisees did not have the same political or social influence as the scribes, while sharing the latter's strict observances in the minutiae of the food laws.

The one major dispute the Pharisees (in combination with the Jerusalem scribes) had with Jesus and his disciples occurs in Mark 7, when Jesus defends his own position in ignoring the tradition of the elders and accuses them of "abandoning the commandment of God" while holding on to human traditions. This was a telling distinction, as he instances a situation, one of many, he claims, in which it was possible to avoid one's moral responsibility to one's parents in accordance with the Decalogue by making a vow *(korban)* to God instead (7:8-13). So open is the attack on Jewish tradition here that some have drawn the conclusion that Mark had broken all ties with Jewish practice. The fact that he (or a later interpreter) feels the need to explain customs "of the Pharisees and all the Jews" to his readers with regard to hand-washing and other such practices (vv. 3-4) has convinced some scholars that the gospel is addressed to a purely Gentile audience, one that is ignorant of Jewish practices. However, such a sweeping conclusion seems unwarranted in light of the other evidence in the gospel dealing with the community's indebtedness to its Jewish roots, already discussed.[32]

The Admission of Gentiles

Since the original Markan gospel, unlike those of Matthew and Luke, does not end with a universal commission to preach the good news to all people, we must search elsewhere within the text for its views on a mission to the Gentiles. The women who encountered the heavenly messenger at the tomb on Easter day were told to remind Peter and the disciples of Jesus' promise

---

32. See T. Kazen, *Jesus and Purity Halakah* (Coniectanea Biblica 38; Stockholm: Almqvist and Wiksell, 2002), 60-88. The claim in Mark 7:19c that Jesus declared all foods clean points to the fact that the chapter as a whole had a long tradition history, especially in view of the fact that such a sweeping claim about Jesus' attitude was not alluded to later in debates such as Acts 15:19-21. Matthew, while using Mark as a source here, omits these generalizing statements (Matt 15:1-2, 17).

that he would "go before them to Galilee" (16:7). Since Mark does not report the outcome of this instruction, it is necessary to infer from the narrative as a whole and especially that part dealing with Galilee the views of the Markan community toward a universal mission.

In discussing the election of the Twelve earlier, it was suggested that Mark may be introducing a broader perspective on the event than that of Israel only. The election scene on the mountain is immediately preceded by a typical Markan summary that details Jesus' successes as a healer/exorcist and lists the places from which the crowds following him had come: "Hearing all that he was doing, they came to him in great numbers from Judea, Jerusalem, Idumea, Perea [literally, *beyond* the Jordan], and from Tyre and Sidon" (Mark 3:7-8). This list is followed by an instruction to the disciples to have a boat ready, ostensibly to avoid being crushed by the crowd, but which was used repeatedly afterward for crossing the lake and moving back and forth between Jewish and Gentile territory (4:35; 5:21; 6:53; 8:10, 13). Clearly the boat had a symbolic function, linking two cultural zones, a symbolism that would be exploited later by Matthew and was employed in the patristic age with reference to the church.[33]

Attention should be given to the list of places in Mark 3:7-8: Galilee, Judea (and Jerusalem), Idumea, and Perea appear first, and then Tyre and Sidon are mentioned separately. On closer examination, the first four places are those districts that had been recognized by the Romans as inhabited by Judeans after Pompey's incursion in 63 B.C.E. Subsequently, they retained a certain regional Judean identity, even when they were incorporated into the mixed kingdom of Herod the Great. Tyre and Sidon are added to Mark's list, both of which were important Phoenician coastal cities whose territories bordered Galilee, often encroaching further into the hinterland, as discussed in Chapter 1. They both came within the borders of the ideal Israel, as described more than once in this study, a territory that stretched from "the Great Sea" to the Euphrates (Ezek 47:18-20).

In an earlier chapter it was suggested that the historical Jesus may have been motivated by this ideal map in his journeys outside the political Galilee of his day, seeking to gather "the lost sheep of the House of Israel." For Mark, however, mention of these places in this list is undoubtedly intended to highlight their Gentile character. This emerges clearly later in the narrative when we are told that Jesus visited "the borders of Tyre" and returned from

---

33. G. Bornkamm, *Tradition and Interpretation in Matthew* (London: SCM, 1963), 52-56.

Roman baths and palestra at the al-Mina (or City) site of Tyre, on the
southern part of the former island. Mark records Jesus visiting this Gentile
city which lay beyond the political borders of Galilee.
(A. D. Riddle/BiblePlaces.com)

there via Sidon toward the Sea of Galilee (Mark 7:24, 31). It was while on this
journey that the Markan Jesus encountered the woman of Syro-Phoenician
origin who was culturally Greek (7:24-30), an episode discussed in Chapter 4
(p. 144). The information conveyed about both actors in the mini-drama is so
precise — the woman a Greek with a universalist outlook, and Jesus, a Judean
prophet/healer with ethnocentric tendencies — that Mark clearly wishes to
treat them as typical characters. Their encounter represents the difficulties
that were involved if the Jesus movement was to cross the Jew-Gentile divide,
more especially at that moment in time when a situation of bitter animosity
obtained between both cultures, as described at the outset of this chapter. The
successful healing of the woman's daughter at a distance merely underlines
the heightened miraculous nature of the cultural as well as the physical healing that had taken place. Significantly, the dominant metaphors employed
by both characters had to do with sharing food and table-fellowship, issues
that had created so much friction in the early church, as Mark was well aware
when situating this story in his narrative between the dispute about clean and
unclean food (ch. 7) and the feeding of Gentiles (ch. 8).

This reading of the Markan story suggests that for the author the idea of a restored Israel, represented by the Twelve, must be understood within the broader context of the Gentiles also participating in the messianic community. Mark was well placed at that particular juncture to argue for a broader perspective, especially in view of the loss of the temple and the consequent rearrangement of sacred space that was involved for all, including the Jewish followers of Jesus. The fact that he had to resort to the strategy of creating a symbolic narrative suggests, however, that the situation was fraught with difficulties. Jesus' crossing over to the Dekapolis region in Mark 5, though initially successful in dealing with the demonic possession, did not lead to his conducting a ministry of healing there, since the inhabitants of the region asked him to depart as soon as the exorcism had taken place (Mark 5:17). However, the efforts of the healed man to spread the word about what had happened to him, raised hopes for a future rapprochement between the two regions and their inhabitants (v. 20).

It is no accident that Mark's clearest statement about a mission to the Gentiles occurs in the apocalyptic discourse of ch. 13. As already mentioned, this chapter reflects the turbulent situation in Judea leading up to and including the first revolt, when there was a serious displacement of people in both Galilee and Judea. Borders that heretofore appeared to be set in stone were now being crossed out of necessity, but also out of conviction. If the return of the Son of Man shortly was to bring about the harmony that messianic times envisaged for "the elect" (Mark 13:27), the urge to spread the word became more pressing. Yet in view of what had happened to Jesus' witness, his followers could only expect a similar fate. The witness to the nations that would become in many cases martyrdom had to continue now in the face of opposition from Jews and Gentiles, synagogue and council (vv. 9-13). Clearly, the Markan community had come to understand the meaning of Jesus' going ahead of them in Galilee, as the young man dressed in white had promised the women at the tomb. They followed now with alacrity in the conviction that by their enduring witness to the way of Jesus they would soon enjoy the promised rewards.

Conclusion

At the outset of this chapter it was suggested that a reading of Mark's gospel against the backdrop of the Jewish revolt and the destruction of the temple might assist in giving a more adequate answer to the "when" and "where" questions about the gospel. The end of the Jewish war, rather than Nero's persecution, would seem to be confirmed as the more likely date from a consideration of the argument of the gospel as a whole. In that case, the place of original composition would appear to be resolved, at least in a general way, also: somewhere in Galilee, or its immediate environs! Is it possible to be more precise? Probably not, other than to say that the author would seem to be quite familiar with the political and geographic situation in the region as a whole, and in addition aware of the Galilean social conditions in which Jesus and some of his first followers operated. The village rather than the urban culture of the region, as this has been rediscovered with the aid of archaeology, provided the setting, the images, and the people that make Mark's story thoroughly realistic. The fact that it was written in Greek and that it recognized the importance of Gentiles as well as Jews within the new movement indicates that it belonged to the *Hellenistai* rather than the *Hebraioi* trajectory within earliest Christianity. The next stage of the inquiry will be to assess Matthew's place within this spectrum, especially since he has drawn on both Q and Mark as his sources, thus suggesting a possible synthesis of the two dominant trajectories within the new movement.

Matthew and the Better Righteousness in "All Syria"

When the author of Matthew's gospel writes: "Every scribe who has been trained in the kingdom of heaven can bring forth from his treasure what is new and what is old" (Matt 13:52), he may well be describing the task he has set himself. It is widely, though not universally, accepted that the gospel of Mark has provided Matthew with his basic narrative outline, which he has filled out by including the sayings source Q, with its collection of Jesus' teachings. Thus Matthew has indeed brought forth the old, or at least the already available, for his readers, albeit in a new format. However, because he was faced with a situation very different from that of either the author of Q or Mark, Matthew must also find a new voice in order to address the issues facing the Jesus movement in the late first century. Matthean scholar Ulrich Luz asks, "Is Matthew telling a new Jesus story, or merely editing Mark?" and answers with a resounding affirmation: "Matthew," he writes, "is telling the story of Jesus' fate in Israel, and the story of the separation in Israel because of Jesus," since he has to consider the present rather than the past in addressing a new audience.[34]

34. U. Luz, "The Gospel of Matthew: A New Story of Jesus, or a Rewritten One?" in

What are Matthew's present circumstances and for whom was he writing? It is possible to give a preliminary answer to both questions on the basis of current scholarly opinion. Matthew wrote his gospel, most are agreed, in the late first century, sometime after 80 C.E. when the trauma generated by the destruction of the Jerusalem temple was easing somewhat, as all branches of Judaism were beginning to fashion different versions of the inherited tradition now that temple, sacrifice, and pilgrimage were no more.[35] His was one of several attempts of what has come to be called "formative Judaism" as various pre-70 factions sought to reconstruct systems from the ruins of the past. This was the task facing Matthew also, writing for Christian believers who were also steeped in the Jewish tradition. Indeed the term "Judaization" has been used to describe Matthew's reworking of Mark, meaning that he "engaged in a literary process that involved an increase in the density of explicit and implicit references to the Jewish tradition and the Hebrew Bible."[36]

As regards the place of composition of Matthew's gospel, there have been many different proposals, but Antioch, the capital of the Roman province of Syria and the former center of the Seleucid kingdom, is regarded as the most likely. Internal and external pointers favor this location. In Matthew's rewriting of Mark's list of places Jesus' followers originated from, two changes occur in regard to the non-Jewish sites: the Dekapolis is mentioned, and "all Syria" replaces Tyre and Sidon (Matt 4:23-25; Mark 3:7-8). Furthermore, Ignatius, bishop of Antioch, writing to various churches as he prepares to depart for Rome in the early second century, alludes three times to material only found in Matthew's gospel: Matt 2:1-12 (the Magi story); 3:15; and 10:16b. While the reference to "all Syria" has prompted some scholars to look for a place other than Antioch for Matthew's gospel, the fact that it is written in good Greek, whereas Syriac (a form of the older

---

his *Studies in Matthew* (Grand Rapids: Eerdmans, 2005), 18-38. For an alternative view cf. D. Sim, "Matthew's Use of Mark: Did Matthew Intend to Supplement or to Replace His Primary Source?" *NTS* 57 (2011), 176-92.

35. Several internal indications in the text point to a somewhat later date, certainly later than Mark. In the parable of the wedding feast mention of the king destroying the city of those who refused to attend the banquet is usually seen as a reference to the destruction of Jerusalem (Matt 22:7). Also in the parable of the wise and foolish virgins mention of the bridegroom being delayed (25:5) is seen as an allusion to the delay in the second coming, an issue that came to the fore in the early church later than Mark.

36. A. O'Leary, *Matthew's Judaization of Mark Examined in the Context of the Use of Sources in Greco-Roman Antiquity* (London: Clark-Continuum, 2006), 118, n. 1.

Aramaic language) was almost universally used in the countryside, suggests that the gospel was intended for a Hellenistic rather than Semitic audience. No doubt it was used also in other Greek cities of the province, and so one cannot be definitive about the actual place of composition. Yet, as we shall discuss further below, Matthew's special emphasis on Jewish issues fits rather well with some trends in the Antiochene church known to us from both Paul and Acts.[37]

Since the focus of this study is on the development of the Christian mission in the contexts of both Hellenistic and Hebraic Judaisms, Matthew's gospel is particularly interesting for our investigation. In reworking and combining two separate sources, the one of Hebraic background (the sayings source) and the other Hellenistic (Mark), Matthew was obviously seeking to mediate between different strands of the early Jesus movement just at a time when others were closing ranks and drawing very clear lines of demarcation between themselves and all the alternatives. The manner in which the gospel negotiates the issues that have arisen with regard to Jesus' person and work, the relationship with other Judaisms, and the place of the Gentiles in this new Judaism that he was fashioning in the name of Jesus of Nazareth — the three key issues we have been exploring until now — will tell us much about the prospects of Jewish Christianity going forward as it was called to operate in a totally new and different environment.

The Understanding of Jesus and His Work

Perhaps the most significant change in Matthew's presentation of Jesus in contrast to that of Mark is the removal of the shroud of mystery that the latter places over Jesus' identity. Not only are Markan literary features such as the commands to silence when there is any indication of recognition of who Jesus is and the private meeting places with the disciples to have things explained to the inner circle missing in Matthew's narrative, the first Evangelist gives a formal introduction to the main character in the infancy gospel (Matthew 1–2) that leaves no doubt as to his true identity and mission. Equally, the concluding scene in the gospel, the commissioning of the disciples for the universal mission, is based on the risen Jesus' actual enthronement as the triumphant Son of Man of Dan 7:13, with the formal dec-

---

37. R. E. Brown and J. P. Meier, *Antioch and Rome: New Testament Cradles of Catholic Christianity* (London: Chapman, 1982), 18-27.

laration: "All authority on heaven and on earth has been given to me" (Matt 28:18). Statements such as "I have come" or "I was sent" (5:17; 15:24) give a sense of mission to the Matthean Jesus, especially in relation to his teaching about the Torah and his mission to Israel. It is this assurance of knowing what the Father's will is and that he has been commissioned to realize it that defines the final commissioning of the disciples on the high mountain in Galilee (28:16-20).

In order to validate his claim that he, rather than his competitors, was articulating the proper version of post-destruction Judaism, Matthew needed to ground his story in the past of Israel, thereby reassuring his readers that his interpretation of the divine will is the correct one. In order to achieve this aim he resorts to various rhetorical ploys in his presentation of Jesus. Foremost of these is the repetition of the formula "This was done in order to fulfill the Scripture that said . . ." followed by the application of the biblical text being cited to events occurring in the narrative. It is noteworthy that the majority of these introductory formulas occur in the infancy stories, and they come as "explanatory notes from the author to the reader" identifying who Jesus is (ch. 1) and where he came from (ch. 2).[38]

The account opens in ch. 1 with a genealogy that traces Jesus' line back to Abraham, but he is also of the Davidic house through his father Joseph. Thus from the outset the reader is reassured about the main character's pedigree, one that links him both to the universal promise to Abraham ("in you will all the nations of the earth be blessed," Gen 12:1-3) and the specifically Jewish promise of the Messiah as a "son of David" (2 Sam 7:12-17). Joseph is reassured in a dream that the child that his wife is bearing is of the Holy Spirit, and his name, Jesus, indicates his role as Savior of the people from their sins.

While ch. 1 helps the reader understand the true identity of Jesus as son of Abraham, son of David, and Messiah, ch. 2 addresses the issue of where Jesus is from. To our modern mind this might seem like a marginal issue in identifying the true importance of a person, but for Matthew's readers this was highly significant information. We have already encountered the objection in the Fourth Gospel that being from Galilee disqualified Jesus from any such claims being made about him (John 7:41-42). Matthew has to reassure his readers that Jesus was born in Bethlehem in accordance with the Davidic promise and at the same time explain his presence in Nazareth in Galilee.

38. A. Overman, *Matthew's Gospel and Formative Judaism: The Social World of the Matthean Community* (Minneapolis: Fortress, 1990), 74-78.

It has been noted that each move of Jesus and his parents in this chapter is guided by a scriptural quotation: the wise men who come to visit Jesus are directed to Bethlehem in Judah by Herod and the Jerusalem religious elite, who can cite a passage from the prophet Micah to identify the birthplace of the Messiah (Mic 5:2); when Herod realizes that he has been duped by the wise men, he orders the slaughter of all the young male boys in Judah and Joseph is warned in a dream to take the child and his mother and go to Egypt, again fulfilling a scriptural text from Hosea, "Out of Egypt I have called my son" (Hos 11:1). Finally, after the death of Herod, Joseph is again directed by a dream to go to Galilee, there to avoid the threat of Archelaus, Herod's son. Once more this is seen as a fulfillment of a prophecy from Isaiah that the north too would share in the promised future salvation (Isa 8:23[9:1]).[39] All this shows the continuity of divine purpose associated with Jesus from his birth. The association with Egypt recalls the story of Moses, who like Jesus had to be rescued from an evil king and turns out to be a wise sage and lawgiver for his people, just as the Matthean Jesus will be for his community.[40]

Matthew's infancy story has deep resonances with the Jewish world of the Messiah and his coming, but there are also associations with the Greco-Roman world of miraculous births. Just as Abraham and David can both be forerunners of the Matthean Jesus, likewise Hellenistic and Jewish ideas can assist in presenting Jesus as significant for both the Gentile and the Jewish world. Matthew makes use of the notion of a virgin birth, which involves God's Spirit descending directly on Mary with no human intervention, in order to stress that Jesus is uniquely "of God." The Greek translation of Isa 7:14, "Behold a virgin shall conceive and bring forth a son," is applied as a fulfillment text for Jesus' birth, which Matthew wants to emphasize is of divine origin only. As Gerd Theissen points out, "A group close to Judaism makes use of precisely this un-Jewish notion to express the divine nature of the earthly Jesus," thereby authenticating his teaching as being from God.[41]

The pattern set in the infancy story of citing suitable scriptural texts

---

39. K. Stendahl, "*Quis et Unde?* An Analysis of Mt 1-2," reprinted in G. Stanton, ed., *The Interpretation of Matthew* (Philadelphia: Fortress, 1968), 56-66.

40. R. E. Brown, *The Birth of the* Messiah (Garden City: Doubleday, 1979), 113-15.

41. G. Theissen, *The Religion of the Earliest Churches: Creating a Symbolic World* (Minneapolis, Fortress, 1999), 175. As Theissen notes, the only example in the Bible of divine-human intercourse, occurring when the "sons of God" had intercourse with "the daughters of men" (Gen 6:1-4), unleashes a torrent of evil. This story was used subsequently in *1 Enoch* 15 and elsewhere in Jewish lore to explain the presence of evil in the world.

to orchestrate the movements of Jesus and explain the import of his work continues in the story of the adult Jesus' baptism by John and the beginning of his public ministry (Matt 3:3; 4:15-16). It will recur at later points in the narrative, including the account of his arrest, trial, and crucifixion. Yet this is only one of several indicators of Jesus' true identity and the nature of his work. Matthew, it would seem, has not just included the Q document in his narrative gospel but has taken over the basic theological idea behind Q, namely, Jesus as teacher of his community and his words as a source of life. Thus, even though Matthew has adopted Mark's basic outline for his gospel, he has punctuated it with five major discourses that gather together Jesus' teaching as found in Q and other sayings traditions available to him in order to present Jesus as Wisdom incarnate (11:25-27). That this pattern of five discourses, with its hint of the five books of the Torah, was fully intended by Matthew is obvious from the way in which he signposts the conclusion of each with the repeated formula "When Jesus had finished these sayings" or a slight variant thereof: (a) 7:28, the Sermon on the Mount; (2) 11:1, the mission discourse; (3) 13:53, the parables discourse; (4) 19:1, the community discourse; and (5) 26:1, the eschatological discourse.[42]

Matthew's Jesus and His Jewish Counterparts

The Matthean Jesus is deeply rooted in his own Jewish tradition. The community to which the gospel was addressed was beginning to develop a self-understanding that claimed to be an alternative to other branches of what has come to be called "formative Judaism," and it required a symbolic figure whose life and teaching gave credibility and coherence to such claims. As a skilled member of a Christian scribal school, Matthew was able to weave together an intricate account of Jesus' life and ministry that was grounded in the inherited Scriptures of Judaism. In doing so, he presented a version of Jesus' life that was more compelling than those of Mark and Q to address the new and developing situation. Both those works provided the building blocks for this new edifice, fashioned as they were in the immediate aftermath of the destruction in the case of Mark, or in the period leading up to it in that of Q. However, the changes brought about by the potentially disastrous events of 70 C.E. meant that new visions had to be generated and old hopes had to be

42. J. Robinson, "LOGOI SOPHON," in Robinson and H. Koester, Trajectories through Early Christianity (Philadelphia: Fortress, 1971), 86-87.

adjusted. This applied to all branches of the Jesus movement also, but more especially to those that still remained within the Jewish matrix.

Inevitably this meant that tensions that had existed within the variegated reality of pre-70 Judaism, discussed in earlier chapters, came to the fore in more virulent forms afterward, and these have left their mark on Matthew's text also. Sectarianism can be a loaded word, implying rigid boundaries and vilification of opponents, especially "in-house" ones, with claims of disloyalty, betrayal, and bad faith bandied about among the competing factions.[43] It has been said that in reading Matthew's gospel one is hearing one side of a very intense argument, the other side of which is largely hidden from view. On the whole we are ill-informed about the earliest stages of the rabbinic movement between 70 and 135 C.E.

A clearer picture of the alternative Judaism that would begin to express itself in Galilee and elsewhere emerges only in the post–Bar Kokhba revolt period, leading eventually to the publication of the Mishnah, around 200 C.E. What is noteworthy about the traces of the earlier stages of that development, in which Matthew's circle would have taken part, is how little reference there is to the new movement associated with Yeshua ha-Nozri in the rabbinic traditions. Clearly, the Jewish Christians were under pressure to state their case for Jesus and his movement more forcibly, while the heirs of the scribes and Pharisees continued to build on the foundation of Torah as applied to daily life as though nothing had changed. Today, scholarly opinion is highly dubious about the notion, previously held, of a Council of Yavneh in which a ban on *minim* (heretics) was supposed to have been passed, with special reference to Christian Jews.[44] Undoubtedly there were local disputes within synagogue communities, something attested in the Fourth Gospel as well (John 9:22). Yet the interaction between Christian and non-Christian Jews was to continue for several centuries, and not always in an unfriendly manner, particularly in Antioch. Ignatius, the bishop of that city in the early second century C.E., and John Chrysostom, who held the same role in the fourth, railed against Christians carrying on discussions with Jews or attending the synagogue, thereby indicating that such interaction was continuing to take place.[45]

43. S. Freyne, "Vilifying the Other and Defining the Self: Matthew's and John's Anti-Jewish Polemic in Focus," in J. Neusner and E. Frerichs, eds., *"To See Ourselves as Others See Us": Christians, Jews, "Others" in Antiquity* (Chico: Scholars, 1985), 117-44.

44. S. J. D. Cohen, "Yavneh" in J. J. Collins and D. C. Harlow, eds., *The Eerdmans Dictionary of Early Judaism* (Grand Rapids: Eerdmans, 2010), 1355.

45. W. R. Schoedel, *Ignatius of Antioch* (Hermeneia; Philadelphia: Fortress, 1985) 15-17;

The first of Matthew's five sermons deals directly with the issue of Jesus' teaching, now presented as a renewed and deepened understanding of Torah. The location of the sermon — "on a mountain" — recalls Moses accompanied by the elders of Israel, receiving the Torah from Yahweh on a mountain (Exod 19:20; see also 24:15). After presenting an expanded version of the beatitudes as found in Q to suggest the qualities of the true disciple, Matthew presents potent images of the disciples' role: salt to season the whole, light to indicate their role as guides for others through their good works, and a city on a hill beckoning to Jew and Gentile like Mount Zion as envisaged by Isaiah (Isa 2:2-3).

Once these claims for his community have been set out, Matthew proceeds to relate the new vision with the old wisdom:

> Do not think that I have come to abolish the Law or the Prophets. I have not come to abolish but to fulfill. For I tell you, until heaven and earth pass away, not one letter, not one stroke of a letter, will pass away until all is accomplished. Therefore whoever breaks the least of these commandments and teaches others to do the same will be called least in the kingdom of heaven; but whoever does them and teaches them will be called great in the kingdom of heaven. For I tell you unless your righteousness *(dikaiosynē/sedaqah)* exceeds that of the scribes and Pharisees, you will never enter the kingdom of heaven. (Matt 5:17-20)

This programmatic statement summarizes the Matthean community's commitment both to strict observance of the whole Jewish Torah and to Jesus' radical understanding of what that means. At first reading these might appear to be contradictory demands, accustomed as we are to a Christian replacement theory of Jewish ethics. Yet for Matthew's community there was no such problem. As Overman points out, it is important to distinguish between non-violation of the Law and fulfilling it through a different interpretation of what it really demands.[46] In the course of a later discussion between Jesus and a rich young man it will become clear that "perfection" is attained, not by concentrating on the externals of individual laws of the Decalogue, but by a change of heart that recognizes that following Jesus

---

W. A. Meeks and R. L. Wilken, *Jews and Christians in Antioch in the First Four Centuries of the Common Era* (SBL Source Books 13; Missoula: Scholars, 1978); R. L. Wilken, *John Chrysostom and the Jews: Rhetoric and Reality in the Late 4th Century* (Berkeley: University of California Press, 1983).

46. Overman, *Matthew's Gospel and Formative Judaism*, 86-89.

means letting go of all that humans hold dear (19:16-22). Later still, when the Pharisees ask about the greatest commandment in the Law, Jesus cites the Deuteronomic command "Love the Lord your God with all your heart and with all your soul and with all your mind" as the first and greatest commandment. However, he quickly adds: "And a second is like it: you shall love your neighbor as yourself," concluding with the comment that "On these two commandments hinge/revolve the whole Law and the Prophets" (22:34-40).

The Sermon on the Mount continues to spell out how Jesus' understanding of the Torah operates within a Jewish Christian context. The pattern "You have heard that it was said to them of old," followed by "*but* I say to you," applied to various ethical issues (Matt 5:21-47) is often understood as though Jesus is correcting the older commandment, replacing it with a new one. However, this inference was challenged by a noted rabbinic scholar, David Daube, who claimed that here Jesus is presented as an upholder of the Law, not its destroyer, and in each case his statement should be taken as arising from the earlier meaning and deepening its significance, thereby intensifying the Law's demand as befits an ethical perspective suitable for the messianic age.[47]

The Sermon then proceeds to discuss three different aspects of piety *(dikaiosynē/ṣedaqah)*, namely alms-giving, prayer, and fasting, once again showing how grounded Matthew's community is in its Jewish religious life. In each case it is expected that the Matthean disciples will engage in such practices. What is demanded is that they not imitate the exhibitionist style of the "hypocrites" — a term that occurs in the *Didache* also and is one of Matthew's terms of invective against the scribes and Pharisees, who are accused of not practicing what they preach (Matt 23:3).

At the end of the Sermon on the Mount, Matthew chooses another metaphor for his community, that of the house built on a rock, not on sand. This prepares for a play on the Greek word for rock *(petra)* in the commissioning of Simon, with his new name Peter, who is designated as the rock on which the *ekklēsia* of Jesus is built (Matt 16:16-18). This institution was an alternative to that of the synagogue communities with whom they were in dispute. As he brings closure to this first and most important treatment of Jesus' reinterpretation of Torah, Matthew draws on a rather enigmatic Markan comment, made during Jesus' visit to the synagogue at Capernaum,

---

47. D. Daube, *The New Testament and Rabbinic Judaism* (London: Athlone, 1956), 58-62.

which states that the crowd were "amazed at his teaching, because he taught with authority, not like the scribes" (Mark 1:22). However, Mark has not presented Jesus as a teacher but as an exorcist at that point in his narrative! Matthew now takes this Markan plaudit and applies it to Jesus at the end of the long Sermon, adding the word "their" to "scribes," suggesting a definite separation between the Matthean group and that of their opponents (Matt 7:29).

The same distancing occurs in the way Matthew speaks repeatedly of "their synagogues," an expression which has in the past given rise to a lively debate as to whether the Matthean group had already broken from its Jewish parent organization or was involved in an *intra muros* dispute.[48] However, that discussion was related to the issue of the Jewish ban on the *minim,* which is no longer seen as relevant to Matthew's day by most scholars. The fact that Matthew has appropriated a term more widely used in the Mediterranean world, *ekklēsia,* suggests that he is anxious to differentiate his group from the various Jewish synagogue communities operating in his environment. As Graham Stanton has pointed out, the Matthean *ekklēsia* had its own rites of admission and rules of expulsion (Matt 28:19; 18:17) and could speak of "the Jews" as outsiders (28:15) and present itself as the people *(ethnos)* replacing those who had been entrusted with the vineyard (Israel), but had not honored the trust (21:43).[49]

The dispute that is echoed right through the gospel of Matthew, even when Jesus is instructing his own disciples, is ultimately one of authority: who had the right to declare what God's will for Israel was at a time of deep uncertainty and bitter division, and how could such authority be legitimated? At the close of the gospel, the Matthean Jesus claims that "all authority in heaven and on earth" has been granted to him, and it is on that basis that the disciples are sent "to disciple all the nations, by teaching them to observe all that I have commanded you" (28:18-20).[50] The basis for this claim is the Matthean community's belief that, as the Risen One, Jesus was endowed with universal authority, such as what was envisaged for "one like a son of man" in the book of Daniel (Dan 7:13-14). Earlier in the gospel, Jesus made similar universal claims, this time drawing on the figure of Wis-

48. D. Sim, "Matthew: The Current State of Research," in Becker and Runesson, eds., *Mark and Matthew I,* 33-54. See 36-40 for an overview of the discussion.

49. G. Stanton, *A Gospel for a New People: Studies in Matthew* (Edinburgh: Clark, 1992), 113-30.

50. It is likely that Israel also was included in the phrase "all the nations," at least in Matthew's day. See J. P. Meier, "Nations or Gentiles in Mt 28,19?" *CBQ* 39 (1977), 94-102.

dom, to whom the secrets of the world had been granted and who would impart these to his own, "the little ones," not to "the wise and understanding" — Matthean irony with reference to his opponents (Matt 11:25-27).

In contrast to the community leaders in the Matthean church, who based their claims on revealed Wisdom, the alternative leadership of the scribes and Pharisees sat on "the chair of Moses." Because of this, but also in line with the affirmation of the ongoing validity of the Law and the Prophets by Jesus earlier, their teaching was to be respected, but their leadership was not to be trusted (Matt 23:2-4). Their failure was one of not following their own teaching, imposing heavy burdens on others but not matching their words with their own actions. It is for this reason that they can be repeatedly labeled "hypocrites," that is actors on a stage who seek human adulation but do nothing to earn respect by their performance on the real stage of life. Ch. 23 is the climax of Matthew's attack on the pretentiousness of these alternative authorities, with its series of damning woes on their insincerity and sense of social superiority.

The undermining of these Jewish teachers is not confined to this climactic chapter, however. In fact, it occurs right through the work. A frequent rhetorical ploy for Matthew is the practice of *synkrisis* or unfavorable comparison. Matthew found this strategy already in Q, but he sharpens it considerably, directing it against his main opponents. Thus, the people of Nineveh and the Queen of the South responded more favorably to the preaching of Jonah and the wisdom of Solomon than does this generation to Jesus, even though he embodies both the prophetic and wisdom traditions more fully than any of these scriptural figures (Matt 12:41-42). A Gentile centurion has greater faith than the sons of the kingdom (8:10). Even the tax-collectors and harlots will precede the Jewish leaders into the kingdom because of their genuine repentance (21:31). The image of a "blind guide" is used repeatedly to highlight the actual, but also moral, failure of these leaders. The description is directly related to the opponents' inability to interpret the word of God correctly, since their own halachic interpretations about hand-washing, oath-taking, and the cleansing of utensils and their insistence on the minutiae of the law of tithing result in neglect of the weightier matters of justice, mercy, and faith (15:6; 23:16-25).[51]

---

51. Freyne, "Vilifying the Other," 119-22 and 132-35.

Matthew and the Gentiles

The concentration on the "Jewish question" is so intense in Matthew that one can easily lose sight of the issue of the Gentiles. Yet it is interesting to observe that this topic encloses his whole narrative, appearing already in the infancy stories and bringing closure with the universal commission "to all the nations" in the end. Clearly this was no purely theoretical issue for Matthew and his church. Wherever in Syria we eventually decide to situate the communities for whom this gospel was written, and more especially if Antioch is to be the probable site, the question of the admission of non-Jews into the new movement was a pressing one. The disagreement between Paul and Peter as reflected in Galatians might suggest that Paul's position had prevailed. Yet it is interesting to note that subsequently Antioch was not one of Paul's stomping grounds, and the reference to Peter "going to the circumcised" might be a hint that he, rather than Paul, was the more influential figure among the *Christianoi* or Messiah-followers of Antioch (Gal 2:7; Acts 11:26). Such a supposition would square well with the highly significant though fragile role played by Peter in the Matthean gospel. In this regard also, it is worth noting that the author of Acts uses the figure of Peter as the most appropriate person to initiate the Gentile mission, with the account of the conversion of Cornelius and his household in Caesarea (Acts 10).

Returning to Matthew's account, several aspects of the infancy chapters point the way for what is to follow. As Theissen noted, Matthew's choice of a non-Jewish image, the virgin birth, in his presentation of Jesus was already an opening out to the larger world of Mediterranean mythical thinking. The story of the magi coming "from the East" under the guidance of a star further enlarges the horizons of those for whom the birth of this child was important. Indeed the genealogy of Jesus, tracing his lineage back to Abraham, yet including David also, combines the universal and the particular dimensions of his mission to come. Furthermore, five women are explicitly mentioned in the tightly structured genealogy: Tamar, Rahab, Ruth, the wife of Uriah (Bathsheba), and Mary the mother of Jesus. While the precise symbolic role of these women within a patrilineal account is uncertain, yet the unusual history of the first four in the biblical narrative, who in all probability were understood to be Gentiles, signals the inclusion of "outsiders" in the messianic family. On the other hand, the role of the fifth woman, Mary, breaks the logic of the patrilineal line since Joseph is not the birth father of Jesus but his adoptive father.

It is important to examine the manner in which Matthew will present the mission of the disciples in the subsequent narrative. Unlike Mark, who separates the call and sending of the Twelve (Mark 3:13-19; 6:7-13), Matthew combines the two, suggesting that the Twelve as such have a specific role to play in a mission to Israel only. There is a strict demarcation of the geographic and time limits that Jesus sets: they are to go neither to the Gentiles nor to the Samaritans but only to "the lost sheep of the house of Israel" (Matt 10:5b-6), and they will not have completed all the cities of Israel before the Son of Man comes (v. 23). What precisely Matthew means by the coming of the Son of Man here is unclear, but elsewhere it refers to the judgment, about which Matthew is particularly exercised. This restrictive view of the mission is in line with Jesus' own declaration at 15:24: "I was sent only to the lost sheep of the House of Israel." This connection between the mission of the Twelve and Israel is highlighted also in 19:28, where the Twelve's role of judging the twelve tribes of Israel is highlighted. This will happen in the *palingenesia,* a technical term taken over from Stoicism referring to the rebirth or renewal of all things in a great cosmic upheaval. It thus would seem to correspond with the coming of the Son of Man in judgment depicted elsewhere, when not just Israel but all the nations will be gathered for judgment (25:31-45). Presumably, the role that the Twelve will have in that great assize is based on their having being sent to Israel, despite Israel's refusal to accept them, as stated in 10:18-23.

However, side by side with this view of the mission to Israel, its logic, and its outcome, there are indications that Matthew has gone well beyond that point in his awareness of what was happening in his own day. Already in 10:17-22, the Evangelist indicates broader horizons. Here, persecution not only from Jewish synagogue communities but also from governors and kings is anticipated. This is a clear allusion to the Roman administrative presence, either the provincial government or the local client kings such as the Herods in Judea or the Nabatean royal house in Arabia. Inevitably these conditions will give rise to internal strife and divisions, even within families, but those sent will receive the gift of the Spirit to defend themselves. Thus, their words are a witness *(martyrion)* to both groups (v. 18), and they should rejoice in such persecution, since it is to be understood as a sign of their future blessedness, as this was promised to them in the list of beatitudes (5:11). In 10:24-42 Matthew goes on to give a general instruction on the nature of discipleship and the inevitable disruption in normal relations that conversion to Christianity brings with it. Here Matthew gathers a number of disparate sayings of Jesus within the tradition, thereby showing his awareness of the suffering that people were prepared to undergo and exhorting them to persevere by indicating their place in the long line of those who have suffered before them. Prophets and righteous people are mentioned also, reminding us that the number and background of early Christian missionaries were quite varied. Later Matthew returns again to the theme of persecution, opening another window on the conditions that were likely to have prevailed: "Behold I send you prophets, wise men, and scribes, some of whom you will kill and crucify, and some you will flog in your synagogues and pursue from city to city" (23:34).

While the topic of persecution by synagogue communities is repeatedly mentioned, recalling Paul's fate after his conversion (2 Cor 11:23-27), the provenance and vehemence of Gentile persecution are not so clearly in view in the sources at that point. This has suggested to some that the picture painted in these passages is not so trustworthy after all. However, it should be remembered that in Roman eyes the early Christian movement was an offshoot of Judaism based on the life of a leader who himself had been crucified as a dangerous criminal, thereby setting a pattern for dealing with his followers in local and regional settings, even though there was no empire-wide persecution until the reign of Decius in the late third century.

What about the inner workings of the Jesus movement that would be served by Matthew and his gospel? Where and how might Gentiles be included? Asking such questions is easier than giving definitive answers, however. A number of knotty issues need to be decided. First, how does Matthew regard the Gentiles? One trend in Matthean studies is the claim that, having broken with the parent Judaism, Matthew's gospel was directed solely toward a Gentile mission, on the basis of the final commission.[52] However, a number of passages, especially in the Sermon on the Mount, portray Gentile practices in anything but a favorable light (Matt 5:47; 6:7-8, 31-32; 7:6; 18:17), even if one were to accept the claim that *panta ta ethnē* in 28:19 were to be translated as "all the Gentiles" rather than "all the nations," as some have proposed. Furthermore, it is difficult to see why the Evangelist would have included so much Jewish material and gone to such pains to integrate it into his synthesis of traditions if it was no longer of any interest to his readers/hearers. The suggestion that the concentration of Jewish Chris-

---

52. The discussion is summarized by Sim, "Matthew: The Current State of Research." In addition to Stanton, *A Gospel for a New People*, J. Riches, *Conflicting Mythologies: Identity Formation in the Gospels of Mark and Matthew* (Edinburgh: Clark, 2000), has argued for a separation between the Matthean community and the parent Judaism on the basis that the Evangelist is more interested in the myth of overcoming universal evil than the Jewish restoration myth, thus giving rise to the conflict of myths reflected in the title of his stimulating study.

tian material in the gospel represents a stage in the evolution of the community's development that was now over but that Matthew, as a conservative scribe, did not want to jettison does not in my view explain adequately the importance of this material in the completed work.

An alternative view that has of late gained some traction is the suggestion that both missions, one to Gentiles and one to Jews, continued side by side and are represented now in the two different mission accounts of 10:5-6 and 28:16-20. This view does indeed, in my opinion, reflect the double concern of the Evangelist with regard to an outreach to Jews and Gentiles, and it avoids the claim that the universal mission has replaced the failed mission to Israel.[53] The difficulty is in imagining a situation in which realistically one and the same group might engage in the practice of contact with Gentiles while adhering strictly to the purity laws.[54] If one returns to the situation of Peter and Paul in Antioch as described in Gal 2:11-14, for example, it is difficult to see how either side would have agreed to or been comfortable with a Law-free gospel on the one hand and a circumcision party on the other, sharing common meals and engaging in shared worship. Of course it is possible that Matthew was attempting to promote such an "ecumenical" outlook among various groups operating in the environment to which his gospel was addressed. Indeed, the fact that the later Jewish Christian sects such as the Nazarenes and the Ebionites were located in or near southern Syria, according to later sources, might indicate that in Matthew's gospel we are encountering an earlier phase of those developments.

Another possibility might be to reconsider again the "geography of restoration," which I have touched on more than once in this study. In terms of location, "all Syria" belongs very much within that orbit. Despite the continued political and cultural animosities that had developed between Syria and Judea since Hellenistic times, certain circles within the multi-matrix reality of Judean life continued to keep alive the expectation that found partial expression in hopes for a geographically extended land. This hope was expressed in apocalyptic scenarios, a dimension of Matthew's message that has often been overlooked, despite the images of the banquet with the patriarchs (Matt 8:11-12) and the gathering of all the nations *(panta ta ethnē)* for the great judgment scene in 25:31-45. The ethical focus here is certainly

53. Sim, "Matthew: The Current State of Research," 41-43, helpfully summarizes the various views on this topic, while favoring the view that "all that I have commanded you" in the final commission includes observance of the whole Jewish Law, as 5:17-20 implies.

54. A. Runesson, "Rethinking Early Jewish-Christian Relations: Matthean Community History as Pharisaic Intra-Group Conflict," *JBL* 127 (2008), 95-132.

not on observing the minutiae of Torah as defined by the scribes, but rather on an inclusive justice that cares for "the little ones" who are at the heart of the Matthean community, as this theme was developed already in the "community discourse" of ch. 18.

It should be recalled that the apostle to the Gentiles, Paul, could articulate a strong belief that Israel too would eventually be grafted into the one olive tree in God's time, once the full number of the Gentiles had entered (Rom 11:11-24). There is no reason why Matthew too could not have given expression to such an expectation, given its good biblical warrant from Isaiah and others. However, whereas Paul sees the event as God's doing (v. 23), Matthew, the "scribe discipled in the kingdom" (Matt 13:52), expects an ethical response from "all the nations" — Jew and Gentile alike — who appear before the judgment seat of the Son of Man (25:32). The standards deemed appropriate for entry have nothing to do with ritual concerns, circumcision, food observances, or the like, but rather with the ethical standards that have been articulated throughout the work and are expected to be observed by all disciples of Jesus. Matthew realizes that it is only through such generous acceptance of the deprived others in their midst that the barriers of race and religious culture can be overcome in the new Israel that he is proposing.

Conclusion

This chapter began with the suggestion that the region known as Coele Syria, that is Upper Galilee and southern Syria, was a plausible original reading site for the gospels of Mark and Matthew. The region recommended itself not just because of internal geographic indicators in both gospels but also because it was an area of special interest within Jewish restoration eschatology, which the expanding Jesus movement, especially those from a Jewish background, clearly continued to hope would be realized. It is important to recognize that a case could equally be made for other locations, Rome in the case of Mark and Lower Galilee in the case of Matthew. The value of opting for a definite setting, however, has the double benefit of picking up on some internal geographic indicators as well as clarifying aspects of the texts that might otherwise be taken as generalized statements with no immediate context or audience. The value of a contextual reading of these texts helps to give specificity to the struggle with the hidden others that the Jesus-followers had to contend with in the political and religious maelstrom that was Syria-Palestine of the post-70 period.

Mark's gospel in its present form and with its various emphases certainly seems to address rather well the immediate aftermath of the Jewish revolt and the loss of the temple. Judeans — Jesus-followers and others — needed reassurance that God's presence and power would prevail, despite the calamity that had occurred. Mark's apocalyptically structured narrative combined scenarios of future consolation for the elect with an account of Jesus' career in which he too had to learn to cross boundaries that were both political and cultural. This was the challenge that was now facing the

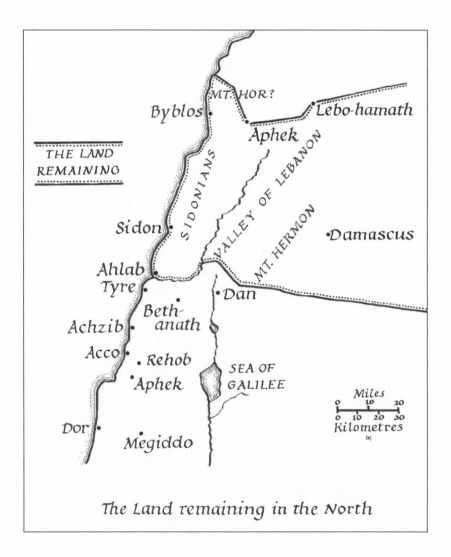

The Land remaining in the North

communities that Mark sought to reassure. Unlike other groups within the Judean family, the Jesus movement lived in the memory of one who had espoused nonviolence, even in the face of unjust power, and who had been crucified as a dangerous criminal by the Roman procurator in Judea.

Matthew, it was argued, was faced with a rather different set of circumstances, some fifteen to twenty years after Mark. He had, therefore, to tell a new story, one that was, however, fashioned out of the building blocks of Q, Mark, and other traditions, either oral or written, that reflected a strongly Jewish ethos of observance and practice. As other branches of formative Judaism began to surface, some possibly in Galilee already, Matthew set about the task of articulating a program of renewal for Israel that was built on the memory and practice of Jesus, the Jewish teacher/healer whose career had come to be understood clearly as that of the messianic ruler, whose reign was intended as "good news" for both Jews and Gentiles according to the prophetic oracles that had been handed down, some of them dating back centuries.

Matthew's vision was for an inclusive Israel, so inclusive indeed that it could also include Syria within its orbit, despite the centuries-old animosities between the two nations. For the project to have any realistic hope of success, Matthew had to bring out of his treasure, things new and old. His vision for the future of this messianic *ekklēsia* was at one level deeply traditional, in terms of the Jewish way of life, yet he had to devise a new configuration by expanding the horizons to embrace others who according to the accepted wisdom of Jews and Syrians alike did not or could not belong.

While Matthew's focus in retelling the story of Jesus was firmly fixed on the debate "within the walls" of the fractured Judean family, he had also to be aware of the Roman presence, particularly because a new dynasty, the Flavians, had come to power and were involved in their exercise of alternative myth-making. By introducing his messianic hero Jesus as a perceived threat to Rome's agent Herod the Great (Matt 2:3), Matthew shows that he is not living in an ivory tower. His story had serious ramifications for those who had overpowered Jerusalem and taken control of the land. He gave the figure of the glorious Son of Man, coming in the clouds and seated on his royal throne, a strong political coloring by drawing on the book of Daniel, where this image has strong political implications for the kingdoms of the world. Yet to achieve his goal of bringing together into one family Jews and Gentiles, Matthew the Evangelist was able to draw on the memory of Jesus and his vision for the poor, the outcast, and the mourners as providing the only way to the harmony that befitted the messianic community of the end time.

CHAPTER EIGHT

Into the Second Century

Up to this point the focus of the second part of this study (Chapters 4-7) has been on the manner in which the Jesus movement expanded and developed within the matrix of the greater Palestinian homeland, beginning in Jerusalem. To this end, the various sayings collections and the gospels of Mark and Matthew have provided trajectories that enabled us to catch glimpses of the difficulties and challenges it encountered, especially during the turbulent period that led up to the first Jewish revolt and its immediate aftermath. It would be possible, but well beyond the limits of this study, to trace the progress of the movement in geographical terms once it had moved beyond the confines of Judea, including Galilee. The development of a thriving Syriac Christianity, the beginnings of which were captured through the lens of Matthew's gospel, would require a book-length study in itself.[1]

There are a number of other trajectories that might be fruitfully traced in the various writings that later came to be part of the New Testament canon. The history of the Johannine and Pauline "schools," as the second and third generations of those belonging to those particular trajectories spread over the whole Mediterranean world, has been plotted by various scholars.[2] In

1. F. Crawford Burkitt, *Early Eastern Christianity: St. Margaret Lectures* (1904, reprinted Piscataway: Gorgias, 2004); R. Murray, *Symbols of Church and Kingdom* (Cambridge: Cambridge University Press, 1975, reprinted Piscataway: Gorgias, 2005); S. Brock, *The Bible in the Syriac Tradition* (Piscataway: Gorgias, 2007).

2. R. E. Brown, *The Community of the Beloved Disciple: The Lives, Loves and Hates of an Individual Church in New Testament Times* (New York: Paulist, 1979); C. E. Hill, *The Johannine Corpus in the Early Church* (Oxford: Oxford University Press, 2004); D. Marguerat, "Paul après Paul. Une histoire de réception," *NTS* 54 (2008), 317-37.

addition, other early Christian writings known collectively as the Apostolic Fathers are important resources for understanding the developments in the early second century.[3] A recent trend, already pioneered by Walter Bauer in his highly acclaimed, if controversial, *Orthodoxy and Heresy in Earliest Christianity*,[4] has been to focus on different locations such as Rome, Ephesus, Corinth, and Egypt in order to chart the development of the movement at key centers and regions, drawing on archaeological as well as literary evidence.[5] The present work is intended as a contribution along similar lines for Syria-Palestine.

Perhaps the most important development of all in terms of our understanding of Christian expansion has been the discovery in 1945 of a collection of Coptic codices at Nag Hammadi in Egypt containing a number of works, including the *Gospel of Thomas* and the *Gospel of Truth*, the existence of which was known, as was mentioned in Chapter 6, through references in various second-century Christian writers such as Irenaeus. The importance of the Nag Hammadi finds consists in the fact that several of the texts of these and other works are now available for study and discussion. While they are written in Coptic, a Greco-Egyptian dialect, several are fourth-century translations of Greek originals. As a result of their discovery, our understanding of trends that in the past were often dismissed as "gnostic" and "heretical" is no longer dependent on the polemics of such Christian defenders of "orthodoxy" as Irenaeus, Tertullian, and Hippolytus. Thanks to the finds, we are now in a position to hear these alternative voices from the second century independently of their detractors, yet mainstream New Testament scholarship has been slow to recognize their importance. However, the work of specialists such as James M. Robinson, Elaine Pagels, Karen L. King, and others is beginning to filter through to those interested

---

3. M. W. Holmes, *The Apostolic Fathers: Greek Text and English Translations* (3rd ed.; Grand Rapids: Baker, 2007) is an excellent edition of the collection with introductory notes and bibliography.

4. Original German edition, *Rechtgläubigkeit und Ketzerei im ältesten Christentum* (2nd ed., ed. G. Strecker; Tübingen: Mohr Siebeck, 1964); trans. R. Kraft, et al. (Philadelphia: Fortress, 1971).

5. For Rome, see P. Lampe, *From Paul to Valentinus: Christians at Rome in the First Two Centuries* (Minneapolis: Fortress, 2003); for Ephesus, see P. Trebilco, *The Early Christians in Ephesus: From Paul to Ignatius* (WUNT 166; Tübingen: Mohr Siebeck, 2004); for Corinth, see J. Murphy-O'Connor, *St. Paul's Corinth: Texts and Archaeology* (Wilmington: Glazier, 1983); for Egypt, see B. Pearson, *Gnosticism, Judaism and Egyptian Christianity* (Minneapolis: Fortress, 2006); W. Pratscher, M. Öhler, and M. Lang, eds., *Das ägyptische Christentum im 2. Jahrhundert* (Vienna: Lit, 2008).

in presenting a fuller account of Christian origins and calls for a reevaluation of the framework within which early Christian diversity should be understood.[6]

The proposal of Karen L. King is highly significant in this regard. In addition to her studies of some of the more important texts, she has also raised significant issues for historians of early Christianity.[7] In particular, she challenges the dominant historical paradigm that had its origins in the work of Ferdinand Christian Baur in the eighteenth century. While Baur's categories of Hellenistic (Pauline) and Jewish (Petrine) Christianities have been critiqued many times, the framework of opposing tendencies within the Jesus movement has remained the dominant one, with that of orthodoxy and heresy as discussed by Walter Bauer being a frequently proposed alternative version of the same opposition. However, from working with the Nag Hammadi materials, King's perspective understands these polarities as too rigid, based as they are on historical and theological categories that do not take account of the flexibility and porosity of the everyday social life of the early Christians. She writes:

> An adequate framework for historical descriptions of early Christian diversity needs to recognize that all religions contain ever-shifting, competing, and contradictory claims, plural possibilities and alternative voices. . . . [Yet] typologies of the varieties of early Christianity instead frequently constitute attempts to define and categorize the unique and essential qualities of distinct theological systems or social groups. Essentializing categories tend to reify the complex, overlapping, multifarious clusters of material that constitute the continually shifting, interactive forms of Christian meaning-making and social belonging into homogenous, stable, well-bounded theological or sociological formations.[8]

6. J. M. Robinson, *The Nag Hammadi Library in English* (New York: Harper and Row, 1977; 3rd ed. 1988), made the texts available to a wider readership. Elaine Pagels, *The Gnostic Gospels* (New York: Random, 1989).

7. K. L. King, *What Is Gnosticism?* (Cambridge: Belknap, 2003); *The Gospel of Mary of Magdala: Jesus and the First Woman Apostle* (Santa Rosa: Polebridge, 2003); *The Secret Revelation of John* (Cambridge: Harvard University Press, 2006); E. Pagels and K. L. King, *Reading Judas: The Gospel of Judas and the Shaping of Christianity* (New York: Viking, 2007).

8. K. L. King, "Which Early Christianity?" in S. Ashbrook Harvey and D. G. Hunter, eds., *The Oxford Handbook of Early Christian Studies* (Oxford: Oxford University Press, 2008), 66-84, here p. 71; "Factions, Variety, Diversity, Multiplicity: Representing Early Christian Differences for the 21st Century," *Method and Theory in the Study of Religion* 23 (2011), 216-37.

The Nag Hammadi material provides the evidence for King's claim that there was a considerable overlap but also a diversity of understandings of how best to remain faithful to the vision of Jesus. In a recent paper she illustrates this point persuasively by showing the different approaches to persecution and martyrdom adopted by different Christian circles in the second century. Thus, Irenaeus, probably influenced by the experience of persecution in his own church in Lyons, saw human suffering in the body as part of God's will and claims that the bodily resurrection of the just must take place in the same created body in order to vindicate God's justice. On the other hand, the *Apocryphon of James* found at Nag Hammadi argues that the true self is not the body but the soul and the spirit. Suffering and death are inevitable consequences for those who confront the evil powers in the world, but it is the example of Jesus that points the way to their true self for his followers. Both are addressing the issue of Roman persecutions and seeking to vindicate God's justice in allowing such things to happen to believers, yet they end up with very different understandings of the significance of the death of Jesus — a necessary sacrifice for sin or an example for faithful Christian discipleship.[9]

Discussion of Christian origins has traditionally been conducted in relation to the documents that make up the New Testament canon. These are for the most part dated to the first century, though of late scholars are prepared to situate writings such as Luke's two-volume work to the second century.[10] Equally, the Johannine writings, especially the epistles, are given a later date also. However, one of the paradigm shifts occurring within the discipline is to broaden the range of writings that should be examined and extend the timeframe to include the multiple receptions that various writings provoked as the new movement began to establish its varied identities in new settings and different circumstances.

To take one example of such a reception process, it was noted in Chapter 7 (pp. 284-85) that Matthew has combined the Q portrait of Jesus as the Son of Man and wisdom teacher with Mark's portrayal of Jesus' violent and unjust death at the hands of Rome, thereby bringing together two quite independent strands of early Christian myth-making. The Markan Jesus

9. K. L. King, "Differences That Make a Difference: Rethinking the Diversity of Early Christianity," Lecture delivered at the 67th General Meeting of SNTS, Leuven 2012, especially 5-14.

10. R. Pervo, *Dating Acts: Between the Evangelists and the Apologists* (Santa Rosa: Polebridge, 2006); J. B. Tyson, *Marcion and Luke-Acts: A Defining Struggle* (Columbia: University of South Carolina Press, 2006).

gives sacrificial significance to Jesus' impending death as "a ransom *(lytron)* for many" (Mark 10:45), whereas Q sees Jesus' death as one in a long line of rejected prophets (Q Luke 11:49-51/Matt 23:34-36) and apparently does not feel the need to narrate the story of Jesus' trial and brutal crucifixion. These two different understandings of Jesus' career are the precursors of the two different understandings that King has identified in the second century: the one will establish itself as the "orthodox" position and the other is rejected as "heretical" or gnostic. Both, however, gave rise to very different forms of Christian praxis and lifestyle, the one glorifying the gaining of the martyr's crown as an act of defiance against unjust power and the other leading to quietism and rejection of the worldly values of the persecutors.

This discussion already introduces two important issues facing all branches of the Jesus movement as it moved farther afield and into the second century, namely, the relationship with imperial power and how internal factionalism will evolve and be dealt with. A third issue is one that we have traced in previous chapters but that continued to be particularly acute in the second century, namely, how the new movement will define itself vis-à-vis the parent Judaism, itself also engaged in an ongoing process of self-definition in the wake of the two revolts against Rome, those of 66-70 and 132-35.

Reception history is indeed crucial for highlighting the issues that did emerge and how these were handled in different groups. It thus sheds light on those aspects of the founding period that would become part of the collective memory as the Christian story developed. From the very beginning, the Jesus movement had to deal with Roman power, the parent Judaism, and internal dissensions, such as those Paul encountered in Corinth as early as 50 C.E. (see 1 Cor 1:10-17). Clearly, Jesus left no single blueprint for his followers in terms of community organization, and it was up to them and their successors to develop structures and strategies to meet the challenges that confronted each generation. The material from Nag Hammadi would also need to be included in a full inventory of second-century Christian literature, and, as we have just seen, some of these writings are on trajectories that originated in the first century. By way of conclusion to this study, therefore, I propose to discuss the three topics just indicated, namely, relations with Rome, separation from the Jewish matrix, and internal dissensions and divisions. It will quickly emerge that all three issues are interconnected within the political, social, cultural, and religious climate of the second century.

Rome and the Christians in the Second Century

There were subtle but real changes in the role of the Roman emperor in the second century in contrast to the situation that obtained in the first century. These changes ranged from close association between the ruler and the Roman army to arrangement for a more orderly transition of power from one emperor to the next. As a result of these developments, the second century has been described as the high-water mark of stability, with the smooth transition of power, good working relations between the various rulers, a Senate that was more representative of provincial interests, and respect for the military achievements of those who came to rule. Emperors such as Trajan, Hadrian, and Antoninus Pius had all seen military service on the frontiers as well as holding various offices in Rome itself. In fairness it should be noted that the Flavians (Vespasian, 69-78, and his sons Titus, 79-81, and Domitian, 81-96) had already set a precedent for this, even though Domitian's reign, after a promising start, ended in his murder. Because of his overbearing attitude in his later years, his memory was erased by a decree of *damnatio memoriae* passed by the Senate, one of only three such condemnations of Roman emperors.[11]

Domitian was replaced by an elderly senator, Nerva, who after a brief reign (96-98) was forced to adopt as his son and heir a successful military general, Trajan, whose rule lasted from 98 to 117. This strategy of the reigning ruler adopting a suitable candidate as his heir was to continue through most of the second century, thus resolving another of the recurring problems of the principate since its inception, namely, an orderly succession of rulers. Thus Hadrian (117-38) had been adopted by Trajan, and he in turn adopted Antoninus (138-61), known as "Pius" because of his loyalty to Hadrian in insisting that his adoptive father be recognized as deified by a reluctant Senate. Antoninus adopted his nephew Marcus Aurelius (161-80) after his natural son, Lucius Verus, had died prematurely. Marcus was known as a philosopher-ruler, and his *Meditations* reveal a sensitive, reflective person-

---

11. Many scholars date the Revelation of John to Domitian's reign on the assumption that he had initiated a persecution of the Christians in Asia Minor. However, there is no direct evidence for such a persecution, even though Domitian had declared himself "Lord and God" *(Dominus et Deus)*, clearly an unacceptable claim to Christian ears and therefore likely to give rise to problems if they were compelled to acknowledge this claim publicly. For a recent discussion of this issue, suggesting the reign of Hadrian as the date for the Apocalypse, see T. Witulski, *Die Johannes Offenbarung und Kaiser Hadrian. Studien zur Datierung der Neutestamentlichen Apokalypse* (Göttingen: Vandenhoeck und Ruprecht, 2007).

ality imbued with Stoic ideals. He, in turn, appointed his son Commodus as co-ruler (177), who then became sole ruler after Marcus's death (180-92). Commodus continued the style of his father's regime at first, but in his later years he became quite deranged and was murdered in 192. The Antonine dynasty was eventually replaced by that of Septimius Severus, a North African who had a successful military career in the West before advancing on Rome, where he was recognized as emperor. He subsequently overcame the claims of the legate of Syria, Piscennius Niger, who was established in the East. The Severans were distinguished throughout the third century, particularly for the development of jurisprudence, and Septimius had extended Roman citizenship to all provincials.

The relative stability that the second-century rulers provided was quite significant from an early Christian perspective. Initially it comes as something of a surprise to find various Christian witnesses mentioning the "good emperors," and in the case of Justin Martyr (d. 165) addressing his *First Apology,* or exposition of the Christian faith, directly to the emperor Antoninus Pius, his son Lucius Verus, and the Senate of Rome (*1 Apol.* 1.1; cf. Eusebius, *H.E.* 4.12). Tertullian (160-220), writing somewhat later, is the most outspoken on the matter of the imperial tolerance: "What sort of laws are these which the impious alone execute against us — and the unjust, the vile, the bloody, the senseless, the insane? Which Trajan to some extent frustrated by forbidding Christians to be sought after; which neither Vespasian, though a subjugator of the Jews, nor a Hadrian, though fond of searching into all things strange and new, nor a Pius, nor a Verus, ever enforced?" (*1 Apol.* 5.7; cf. Eusebius, *H.E.* 4.13). The list is out of chronological order in that Trajan is mentioned first, and the inclusion of Vespasian is somewhat surprising. Nevertheless it reflects what we learn elsewhere about official Roman policy.

Pliny's letter to Trajan and the emperor's reply are the clearest articulation of policy. As governor of the joint provinces of Bithynia and Pontus, situated on the southern shores of the Black Sea, Pliny was confronted with a situation in 112: some Christians refused to acknowledge the emperor's divine status by offering incense to his image. Pliny was not searching for Christians, but he could not ignore such blatant disobedience once it was brought to his attention, albeit anonymously. While he exercised his judgment in letting some go free, either because they claimed that they had never been Christians or had abandoned the faith and were prepared to offer the necessary sacrifices. Others who were more obstinate were either executed or sent to Rome if they were Roman citizens (Pliny, *Letters* 10.96).

Pliny's description gives us a precious picture of the early Christians at worship, gathered for a shared meal and "singing hymns to Christ as to a god," as the movement penetrated the countryside as well as the cities of the region. Yet in terms of official Roman policy it is Trajan's reply to his query as to what the proper procedure for dealing with this "perverse and extravagant superstition" should be that is particularly significant. Pliny has done well in dealing with the matter on a case-by-case basis, Trajan says, but he is not to seek out the Christians, and any anonymous delations are to be ignored, "for they are a very bad example and unworthy of our time" (*Letters* 10.97).[12] According to Eusebius, both Hadrian and Marcus Aurelius repeated this same policy subsequently (*H.E.* 4.9, 13), the former by way of rescript to the proconsul of Asia (c. 125) and the latter to the council of Asia at the behest of Asiatic Christians (c. 161). Marcus claims that several provincial governors had previously written to his "divine father," that is, Antoninus Pius, in the same vein. His decision was that the Christians were not to be interfered with unless "they appeared to be plotting against the Roman government."

Even though Trajan first articulated this Roman policy of limited tolerance of the Christians, it is the reign of Hadrian that is credited with the most positive developments. As a lover of all things Greek *(Philhellene)* he had earned the nickname *Graeculus* or "little Greek" at a young age. As such he was an ardent supporter of the so-called Second Sophistic, a movement that began as a revival of Greek rhetoric and popular education as practiced in Athens by the fifth-century B.C.E. Sophists but in its later incarnation would include a broader cultural agenda. "Greek identity was valued on the Roman imperial market," is a pithy description of the phenomenon by one scholar.[13] As a trend rather than an organized movement, the Second Sophistic can be traced back to the late first century C.E., but it reached its heyday in the second century, the imperial rulers being enthusiastic promoters of *paideia* or Greek learning in all its various facets. This involved an archaizing trend in different fields, literature, philosophy, and religion included, but it also reflected a cultural shift. To some extent it represented a resistance to Roman influences and allowed elites in the cities the freedom

12. For a detailed discussion, see R. L. Wilken, *The Christians as the Romans Saw Them* (New Haven: Yale University Press, 1984), 1-30.

13. L. S. Nashrallah, *Christian Responses to Roman Art and Architecture: The Second-Century Church in the Spaces of Empire* (Cambridge: Cambridge University Press, 2010), 28-30, here 29; M. Rizzi, "Hadrian and the Christians" in Rizzi, ed., *Hadrian and the Christians* (Berlin and New York: de Gruyter, 2010), 9-20, here 10-11.

to develop multiple identities without having to conform to rigid patterns of behavior and manners as defined by Rome.

Thus, Athens became the cultural center again, and Hadrian visited the city several times during his many tours of the empire, East and West. He establishing a recognized *limes,* or border on the northern front, within which the Roman peace was to prevail. Hadrian's wall in Britain was an extension of this separation between Greek and barbarian. On his first visit to Athens in 124, he was inducted into the Eleusinian mysteries and joined in the festival of Demeter and Kore/Persephone called the Thesmophoria. This was an ancient celebration of the annual arrival of spring based on the story of Kore's sojourn in the underworld following her rape by Hades.[14] On a second visit in 128, Hadrian dedicated the temple to the Olympian Zeus, which had remained unfinished previously, commissioning a boundary, Corinthian columns, and a golden roof. A final visit took place in the winter of 131-32 when he dedicated the Zeus temple and established the Panhellenion, a confederation of eastern cities modeled on earlier Greek alliances dating back to the Persian wars in the fifth century B.C.E.[15]

Hadrian's love affair with Athens and its ancient traditions reflected the archaizing tendencies of the period, but the Greek ideal also gave him a more universal outlook, as the "explorer of all things strange" so wryly described by Tertullian in his *Apology,* cited on p. 319. The multiple identities that the prevailing mood of the period fostered allowed for a greater tolerance of difference, within, of course, the limits set by loyalty to Rome. Indeed a later, third-century, work, probably influenced by Christian apologetics, suggests that Hadrian actually contemplated "building a temple to Christ and giving him a place with the gods."[16] The notice goes on to say that Hadrian ordered a temple without an image to be built in every city: "Because these temples are built by him with this intention, so they say, they are dedicated to no particular deity, and they are called today merely Hadrian's temples." In all probability this information relates to various temples built by Hadrian for his own image for the celebration of the imperial cult. Subsequently they could be claimed by the Christians because of the absence of images in the buildings. Yet, in view of the prevailing *Zeitgeist* of

14. A. Galimberti, "Hadrian, Eleusis and the Beginnings of Christian Apologetics," in Rizzi, ed., *Hadrian and the Christians,* 71-87, argues that Hadrian's initiation at Eleusis opened up new perspectives for him with regard to the various cults, including Christianity (p. 73).

15. Nashrallah, *Christian Responses,* 96-104.

16. This information occurs in the *Historia Augusta,* the life of Alexander Severus, 29.2. His reign was a brief one in the early third century after the murder of Caracalla.

Hadrian's reign, there is nothing inherently improbable about the idea of a shift in Roman attitudes. Everything was now linked to the figure and action of the emperor himself, so that a general religious tolerance was replaced by "an active policy of controlled acceptance and integration of the most differentiated cults and doctrines."[17]

Irrespective of whether Hadrian's reign created such a space for second-century Christians to inhabit in a manner that was not previously possible, there can be little doubt that the overall intellectual climate of the Second Sophistic, with its emphasis on Greek *paideia*, was eagerly exploited by Christian apologists of the day. Both Rizzi and Nasrallah are surely correct in emphasizing that the Christian literature usually classified as apologetic should be understood within the broader literary conventions of the period, including the use of parody and satire.[18] Nasrallah points out that there was no genre of *apologia* as such, and hence it is difficult to decide which writings should be considered and who the intended audience was, as distinct from ascribed audience. Eusebius mentions that the two earliest apologists, Quadratus and Aristides, addressed their works directly to Hadrian and indicates that both works were extant in his day, a century and a half later (*H.E.* 4.3). In a similar fashion, Justin Martyr, a native of Neapolis in Palestine, in about 150 addressed his *Apology* in the first instance to the emperor Hadrian, to Verissimus, his son the philosopher (Antoninus Pius), and to Lucius, the lover of instruction, the son by nature of the philosopher emperor. Thereafter the Senate and the Roman people are mentioned. He makes his appeal and petition "on behalf of those of every race who are unjustly hated and abusively threatened, myself being one of them" (*H.E.* 4.12).

This apologetic literature illustrates a confident Christianity, prepared to make its case for equal treatment in the highest court circles, its writers employing the same rhetorical skills as their pagan counterparts, such as Lucian of Samosata or Aelius Aristides. The Christian defense fluctuates between expecting, on the one hand, to be accepted as a distinct *ethnos* within the pluri-ethnic reality that constituted the Roman Empire of the day and, on the other, to be acknowledged as a true *philosophia*, not a *superstitio*, as detractors such as Celsus would continue to maintain.

Furthermore, the appearance in the second century of the martyrological literature recounting the calmness and bravery of people such as

---

17. Rizzi, "Hadrian and the Christians," 14-16, here 16.

18. Nasrallah, *Christian Responses,* 22-50; M. Rizzi, "Multiple Identities in Second Century Christianity," in Rizzi, ed., *Hadrian and the Christians,* 141-51.

Ignatius of Antioch or Polycarp of Smyrna in the face of unjust persecution encouraged a defiant attitude when faced with death for the gospel. Keeping the memory of such heroism alive would encourage others to follow these examples of bravery, and at the same time challenge the self-image of the imperial propaganda associated with the Panhellenion and its philosophy. Toward the end of the second century Tertullian could write as follows:

> Looking up to heaven, the Christians, with hands outspread because inno-cent, with head bare, and without one to give the form of words — for we pray from the heart — we are forever making intercession for all emperors. We pray for them a long life, a secure rule, a safe home, brave armies, a faithful Senate, an honest people, a quiet world, and everything for which a man and a Caesar can pray. All this I cannot ask of any other but only from him from whom I know that I shall receive it. (*Apol.* 30.4-5)

He ends his defense on a positively triumphalist note: "We Christians are but of yesterday, and we have filled everything you have: cities, tenements, forts, towns, exchanges, yes and camps, tribes, palaces, Senate, forum. All we have left you are the temples" (*Apol.* 37.4).

Despite official Roman policy, as endorsed by a number of the second-century emperors, the threat of persecution was never far away for the Christians, as local circumstances determined attitudes. Ironically, however, a very different and potentially more dangerous threat was to come from another quarter entirely. A pagan philosopher, Celsus, probably of middle Platonist persuasion, launched a serious intellectual attack on the new movement. Celsus's work, written probably around 177 C.E. in Rome or possibly in Alexandria, was entitled *The True Doctrine/alēthēs logos,* and was intended to challenge the Christian claim to be a true philosophy. No independent version of the work has survived and we must rely on Origen's refutation in eight books, the *Contra Celsum,* written some seventy years later, where large sections of Celsus's work are cited, in order to re-create the text. Celsus had done his homework well. He was familiar with the gos-pel stories of Jesus' career as well as negative portrayals that were circulat-ing in the second century. He was also well versed in the Hebrew Bible as used by the Christians, and in addition he had a good knowledge of various philosophical traditions — Stoicism, Epicureanism, and, of course, middle Platonism.

The question has been asked as to why Celsus went to such lengths to refute Christian claims. What was it about the new movement that irked him so much, and why was a Christian response so slow in appearing?[19] Several answers to these questions can be suggested on the basis of the various issues he raises and the aspects of the new movement that are particularly targeted. It seems clear that he was upset by the Christians' success in making converts, especially among the intellectual elite, which he saw as a threat to the very fabric of the empire. He mounts a twofold attack, claiming on the one hand that the Christian converts were all from the lowest rung of the social ladder — children, slaves, uneducated women (*Cels.* 3.55; 6.1-2) and on the other that Jesus himself was a deceiver and a magician who had learned magic in Egypt and returned to deceive the gullible with his healings and other deeds. These were achieved through various incantations and spells (6.40), and the Christians have no right to describe him as a son of God (1.38). Christianity was like some other forms of esoteric eastern piety that were long despised in Rome: begging priests of Cybele, soothsayers, and worshipers of Mithras and Sabazius (1.9). Or again they are compared to those who take part in Bacchic orgies (3.17; 4.12).

It is likely that Celsus had read the *Apology* of Justin Martyr, in which the apologist had sought to present Christian beliefs in terms of Greek philosophical ideas, especially the notion taken from the Hebrew Bible that God was one and the ruler of the world. Consequently, Celsus attacks Christian beliefs about the idea of God becoming incarnate in Jesus. God is not that kind of being; he would have to undergo change to live among humans. The idea is ridiculous and Celsus pokes fun at it (*Cels.* 4.3). If Jesus is to be worshiped as God (as Pliny had claimed occurred in the Christian gatherings), then God is no longer one. Celsus was well aware that humans such as Herakles or Orpheus had been elevated to the realm of the gods, but this was quite different to the Christian claims about Jesus (7.3). In Greco-Roman paganism God could be called many names among different peoples and there could be many lesser gods, but Christian claims about Jesus were different, and there could not be two beings who are to be worshipped equally. The story of the virgin birth was a fabrication to disguise the fact that Jesus was the product of an adulterous union between Mary and a Roman soldier named Panthera. Such a claim was circulating in Jewish circles also and Celsus uses it to discredit Christian claims about Jesus' birth (1.32). Likewise the resurrection was a hallucination concocted by a hysterical female (2.55).

Celsus is well aware of the fact that Christianity is a recent offshoot

---

19. B. Aland, *Frühe direkte Auseinandersetzung zwischen Christen, Heiden und Häretiken* (Berlin: de Gruyter, 2005), 5-6.

of Judaism, and he uses this to denigrate Christian claims further. In general, he shares pagan prejudices against Jews, but he is prepared to concede certain points, such as Judaism's relative antiquity (5.25), in order to expose Christian duplicity, claiming that they were the rightful heirs to the Jewish heritage, while they and their founder ignored all the essential elements of Jewish practice (2.1; 7.18) We shall return to this topic in the next section, but here it is important to highlight the audacity and the ingenuity of the Christians in making their claims to be "the true Judaism," given the fact that as far as Roman citizens were concerned they were very recent arrivals on the scene. Jewish Diaspora communities were long established in all the main cities of the empire and had their civic rights acknowledged by successive Roman administrations. Christians threatened this standing by claiming their Jewish heritage while at the same time seeking to establish independent associations within the Roman urban settings. Indeed all Jews were expelled from Rome for a period during the reign of Claudius because of disturbances over Chrestus (Christ?), caused possibly by the arrival of Jewish Christians in the city (Suetonius, *Life of Claudius* 25).

In the second century it was this continued threat to public order that Christians posed — a threat that arose from their theological claims — that troubled the conservative intellectual Celsus most of all. As Wilken has argued persuasively, the idea of only one supreme God had begun to impress many pagan intellectuals as offering a better foundation for political stability than the polytheism of the masses. Basing himself on a citation from Homer, "Let there be one king (i.e., God)," Celsus was aware that Christian factionalism arising from the worship of Jesus as God would lead to social anomie, and the order of the empire, which was meant to replicate the divine world with the emperor as sole ruler, would be reduced to anarchy (*Contra Celsum* 8.68).[20] Celsus was well aware that Christians did not take part in military service or accept public office of any kind and were in danger of becoming a seditious faction in the cities of the empire, refusing to participate in the public festivals or religious rites (8.17). As such they were deemed to be abandoning the ancient *Nomos* or accumulated wisdom, the "true doctrine" that had been handed down by the ancients. In claiming to be a "third nation" but without any land, tradition, or ancient lore, they were breaking the bond of "religion," understood as the synthesis of cult, beliefs, customs, traditions, and peoplehood, a synthesis that was essential, if Roman *Ordo* was to prevail (8.68).

---

20. Wilken, *The Christians as the Romans Saw Them*, 106-8.

Jews and Christians in the Second Century

The Roman settlement of Judean affairs after the first revolt was presented in Chapter 2 (pp. 79-85) and Chapter 7 (pp. 274-75) in discussion of Mark and Matthew. However, it will be useful to recall here the more salient points as we seek to map Jewish-Christian relations in the second century. Rome's settlement of what was now seen as a troublesome region was comprehensive. The destruction of the Jerusalem temple and the dissolution of the Sanhedrin and the priesthood, followed by Titus's triumphant return to Rome with some of the spoils of war, including precious treasures from the temple and many captives to be sold at the slave markets, were measures meant to demoralize Judean resistance. An enlarged Judea was given provincial rather than procuratorial status, and this meant that a legion was located permanently at its center in Jerusalem to deal with any future disturbances. Cities such as Caesarea Maritima, Neapolis, Sepphoris, and somewhat later Tiberias were suitably rewarded for their loyalty with enlarged territories.

There is evidence that some scribes of Pharisaic background who had not supported the revolt were allowed to gather at Jamnia on the coast under the leadership of Yohanan ben Zakkai, there to sow the seeds of an alternative Jewish identity based on the home and the village rather than the temple and its cult. The understanding that this gathering declared a curse on the heretics, that is, all Christians, is now seriously questioned, however. The so-called "parting of the ways," at least in any definitive and universal sense, is seen as involving a much more lengthy process, even if there are examples of local trouble between synagogues and Christian communities from an early stage, as indicated, for example, in John's gospel (9:22; 12:42). When catholic Christianity and rabbinic Judaism had reached something like definitive forms in the fourth century, there were still plenty of grey areas in which various types of interaction continued to take place between the parent and the offspring.[21]

Despite the humiliation of the first revolt and the firm stance adopted by Rome, the Jewish desire for autonomy was undaunted as apocalypses such as *Syrian Baruch* and *4 Ezra* sought to keep hope in a messianic future alive. Their message was that if Israel was prepared to acknowledge that what had befallen the nation was chastisement for its own failures, similar to what had happened in the past during the Babylonian exile, they would

---

21. D. Boyarin, *Border Lines: The Partition of Judaeo-Christianity* (Philadelphia: University of Pennsylvania Press, 2004).

Detail from the Arch
of Titus depicting spoils
taken from the Jerusalem
temple, erected by the
emperor Domitian on
the Via Sacra leading
to the Roman Forum.
(Steerpike)

eventually be vindicated. The order by Vespasian that the half-shekel offering, which formerly was paid for the upkeep of the Jerusalem temple,
should now be sent to Rome for support of Jupiter Capitolinus, was, no
doubt, extremely hurtful and humiliating for many Jews. During the reign
of Domitian the tax was extended further to include Jewish sympathizers,
leading to charges of *maiestas* or treason being made against opponents of
the regime simply on the basis that they were attracted to the Jewish way of
life. Because of these abuses Domitian's successor, Nerva, removed the possibility of such charges being leveled against individuals and issued a coin
with the legend *"fisci Judaici calumnia sublata,"* "The calumny associated
with the *fiscus Judaicus* has been removed."[22]

While the so-called flight to Pella of the Jerusalem Christians seems to
have anticipated the catastrophe, following the advice of Mark 13:14-18/Matt
24:16-20, this does not mean that all Jesus-followers of Jewish background
had departed the land, or at least did not return later, even to Jerusalem,
where access to the temple mount may have been permitted for those who
mourned Zion (Mishnah *Edoyoth* 8.6).[23] Furthermore, Eusebius, relying on
Hegesippus, a second-century Palestinian historian, reports that Vespasian,
Domitian, and Trajan had all sought out Jews of Davidic descent, including
blood relatives of Jesus, in order to obliterate any hopes associated with a
royal Messiah (*H.E.* 3.12.19-20; 3.32.3-4). This suggests that not all Christian
Jews had departed.[24]

22. M. Smallwood, *The Jews under Roman Rule from Pompey to Diocletian* (Leiden:
Brill, 1981), 376-85.
23. K. Clark, "Worship in the Jerusalem Temple after A.D. 70," *NTS* 6 (1970), 269-80;
W. Horbury, "Beginnings of Christianity in the Holy Land," in O. Limor and G. Stroumsa,
eds., *Christians and Christianity in the Holy Land* (Jerusalem: Yad Izhak Ben Zvi, 2006), 7-90,
here 71-74.
24. Horbury, "Beginnings of Christianity," 70.

It is no surprise, however, that the first stirrings of a Jewish revolt took place in the reign of Trajan (115-17), but among the Jews of Egypt, Cyrene, and Cyprus, not in Palestine. A number of papyri, as well as reports by Eusebius (*H.E.* 4.2) and Dio Cassius (*History* 68), make clear that these were no occasional disturbances, but constituted a serious uprising against the Greek population, necessitating the deployment of several legions to restore order. At the same time Trajan himself was engaged in a campaign in Mesopotamia and had to take stringent measures against Jews there who were threatening to cut him off from returning to the West.[25]

Due to discoveries in the Judean desert, we are now equipped to obtain a more detailed picture of the second Jewish revolt under Hadrian (132-35), even though there is still discussion of what the immediate trigger was — a ban on circumcision, as claimed by the *Historia Augusta* (*Hadrian* 14.2), or Dio's claim that Hadrian had plans to build a pagan city with a temple to Jupiter Capitolinus on the site of the Jewish temple (*History* 69.12). In a detailed recent study of the background to these apparently separate, even conflicting, causes, Giovanni Bazzana has convincingly argued that both issues belong together within the Hadrianic policy of, on the one hand, integrating Judea into his wider plans for the empire through benefactions such as giving Jerusalem the status of a Roman *colonia*, while at the same time removing one of the more distinctive signs of Jewish ethnicity in the ancient world, namely circumcision. Not unsurprisingly, each of these aims appealed to different strands of the Jewish people, leading to a very conflicted internal situation, which manifested itself in the bitter and bloody second revolt, which, unlike the first revolt, was confined to southern Judea.[26]

Justin Martyr, writing shortly after the revolt, claims that "Barcochebas, the leader of the Jewish uprising, ordered Christians alone to be led away to terrible punishments if they did not deny Christ and blaspheme"

---

25. E. Schürer, *The History of the Jewish People in the Age of Jesus Christ,* revised edition ed. G. Vermes, F. Millar, and M. Black (Edinburgh: Clark, 1973-84), 1:529-34; Smallwood, *The Jews under Roman Rule,* 389-427.

26. G. Bazzana, "The Bar Kochba Revolt and Hadrian's Religious Policy," in Rizzi, ed., *Hadrian and the Christians,* 85-109. See also P. Schäfer, *Der Bar Kokhba-Aufstand* (TSAJ 1; Tübingen: Mohr Siebeck, 1981); "Hadrian's Policy in Judea and the Bar Kochba Revolt: A Reappraisal," in P. R. Davies and R. T. White, eds., *A Tribute to Geza Vermes: Essays on Jewish and Christian Literature and History* (JSOTSS 100; Sheffield: JSOT, 1990), 281-305. Schäfer does not want to reduce the revolt to a civil war between Hellenized and Law-abiding Jews. Nor was Hadrian involved in "provocative paganising" of Judea. Rather his plan was to establish and secure the borders of the empire.

(*1 Apol.* 31.6; see Eusebius, *H.E.* 4.8.4). While this might appear to be a strange position to have been adopted by somebody leading a revolt against Rome, it becomes perfectly understandable when it is recalled that Bar Kokhba himself was claiming messianic status and was not therefore prepared to tolerate fellow Jews who obeyed another messianic king, namely, Jesus of Nazareth. Since there is no evidence of the revolt having spread beyond southern Judea, this, as Horbury notes, is important additional evidence that some Jewish Christians continued to live in the area of Jerusalem between the two revolts. It also indicates "the attraction exerted by the hopes of the majority Jewish community on the minority of Christian Jews."[27] At the same time, it also highlights the dilemma facing different branches of the Jesus movement at this juncture. We hear, on the one hand, how the two apologists, Aristides and Quadratus, who addressed a defense of the new movement to Hadrian, were well received and, on the other, that there were those whose messianic hopes made them sympathetic to the aims, if not the leadership, of the revolt.[28] No doubt the apologists were able to demonstrate their participation in the cultural ethos of the Second Sophistic, which the emperor was trying to foster, while others found that their ethnic identity was more important.

If the Christian Jews in Palestine were precluded from giving expression to their nationalist aspirations because of their distinctive messianic beliefs, the question arises as to their relationship with other Jesus-followers who did not feel the same attachment to an ethnic identity or with the various other Jewish groupings who eschewed all messianic ideas. In the post-70 period there were several different known groups, and probably others unknown, within Judaism. In the period up to 135 at least, non-Christian Judaism was a variegated phenomenon, with the synagogue and the Beth Midrash representing two different, if not competing, directions in the land of Israel.[29] The former served varied interests, as a village meeting house, a

---

27. Horbury, "Beginnings," 80.

28. A brief letter written in Hebrew and signed by Shimʼon ben Kosiba was found in one of the Judean caves. It threatens with imprisonment the overseer and guards of a prison if they harm in any way the Galileans *(Galilim)* who are in their charge. Various suggestions as to the identity of these Galileans have been made: Jewish Christian followers of Jesus or simply natives of the north who have come to join the campaign. For a discussion, see Schäfer, *Der Bar Kochba–Aufstand,* 116-17.

29. W. Horbury, *Jews and Christians in Contact and Controversy* (Edinburgh: Clark, 1998), 3-14, summarizes the discussion, himself favoring the impulse to unity rather than diversity, stressing the importance of the *Birkath ha-Minim* in this regard.

prayer hall, and a school, whereas the latter was a house of study under the aegis of some important rabbi. Over time, these different functions would merge as the rabbinic movement became more influential in later centuries, forming a power network throughout the land.[30] Gradually too, the synagogue would take the place of the temple as a holy place where the memory of the temple rituals was kept alive through the iconography that began to adorn these buildings. In addition, the situation in the Diaspora varied from place to place.[31] In such a scenario one must avoid giving the impression of a single Judaism, any more than one can or should speak of a single Christianity at this particular juncture in the early second century C.E. It does seem possible, however, to discern two opposing trends in both religions, one based on local autonomy and the other striving to establish a more unified front, especially in dealing with Roman power structures.[32]

Second-century Christianity likewise had several different, even opposing strands, as we saw in Chapter 5 in tracing the three different profiles of James the brother of the Lord that emerged in the second century. These were the proto-orthodox first bishop of Jerusalem (Eusebius), the martyred patron saint of the Jewish Christians (Hegesippus), and the gnostic James who received special revelations from the Risen One (Nag Hammadi). Each group will have negotiated their relationship with the parent Judaism (of whatever hue) in different ways, ranging from Jewish Christians who remained attached to their ethnic identity and sought to remain within the synagogue community while confessing Jesus as Messiah, to Gentile Christians who regarded themselves as the new and replacement Israel, but without adhering to the Jewish way of life. The gnosticizing Christians may well have had counterparts within Judaism also, but the externals of Jewish observance were of little real interest to them.

30. L. Levine, *The Rabbinic Class of Roman Palestine in Late Antiquity* (Jerusalem: Yad Izhak ben Zvi / New York: Jewish Theological Seminary of America, 1985); *Judaism and Hellenism in Antiquity: Conflict or Confluence?* (Peabody: Hendrickson, 1998), especially 139-79 on the ancient synagogue as building and institution.

31. T. Rajak, "Synagogue and Community in the Graeco-Roman Diaspora," in J. R. Bartlett, ed., *Jews in the Hellenistic and Roman Cities* (London: Routledge, 2002), 22-38. A. Runneson, D. Binder, and B. Olsson, eds., *The Ancient Synagogue from Its Origins to 200 C.E.: A Source Book* (Leiden: Brill, 2008), lists as many as forty-five sites where there is literary and/or archaeological evidence for synagogues in the greater Diaspora.

32. As Jewish apologists, both Josephus and Philo present a picture of a unified Jewish belief and practice, stressing the idea of *homophylia* or shared origins as the hallmark of Jewish identity. Both can recognize different philosophies and styles within this common framework.

In mapping Christian diversity in the second century, therefore, the strategies adopted by each of these groupings will be of great interest, now that a clearer picture of the cultural and political circumstances facing both Judaism and Christianity in the second century is in place. To this end, we shall examine three different documents that span the period in order to clarify the different trends and struggles that were in play. The documents are: The *Epistle of Barnabas,* Justin's *Dialogue with Trypho,* and the arguments of Celsus's Jew in Origen's *Contra Celsum.*

The Epistle of Barnabas

According to Horbury, it was from the end of the first century C.E. onward "that signs of an accepted separation from the Jewish community seem clearly detectable." External impulses came from the Jewish community long before the Christians were ready to accept separate existence.[33] The Fourth Gospel expresses anxiety about expulsion from the synagogue (John 9:18-23), and the author of the epistle to the Hebrews is worried about his audience relapsing into Jewish practices (Heb 6:1-6; 10:26-31), despite the sustained argument he has mounted to denigrate the old covenant and highlight the superiority of Christ's once-for-all sacrifice for sin. However, the *Epistle of Barnabas,* a document that is with great probability to be dated to the very end of the first century, is the most sustained and clear response to the issues that have emerged, especially: To whom does the covenant belong — them (the Jews) or us (the Christians)? The author firmly sets his face against any shared view and exhorts his readers not to entertain such ideas, thereby "piling up your sins." The covenant is ours not theirs. They lost it completely almost as soon as Moses received it (*Barn.* 4.6-7; see also 13.1; 14.5).

Stephen Wilson argues that the work is addressed to Gentiles, especially those who are tempted to adopt Jewish customs if the covenant is a shared one, as the passages just cited imply. He therefore poses the important question of "why a group of Gentile Christians (author and readers), living with intense eschatological expectations, with some members lapsing or withdrawing, should be so obsessed with things Jewish."[34]

---

33. Horbury, *Jews and Christians,* 12-13.
34. S. Wilson, *Related Strangers: Jews and Christians 70-170* C.E. (Minneapolis: Fortress, 1995), 128.

While the author does not mention the Jews as such, he does frequently speak of "them" and "us" in order to emphasize the unbridgeable gulf between the two sides (*Barnabas* 3.1, 6; 4.6-8). Just as in the epistle to the Hebrews, there is a danger of some, at least, of the "us," that is, Gentile Christians, being lured into engaging in Jewish practices. The author makes a sharp distinction between "the new law of Jesus Christ that is free from the yoke of compulsion" and the law regarding sacrificial offerings, which are dismissed as "trampling on my courts." What God wants from "us" is "a broken heart; an aroma pleasing to the Lord is a heart that glorifies its Maker" (2.9-10). Fasting, which had become a highly popular form of ascetic practice in Second Temple Judaism and had been adopted by some Jesus-followers also (*Did.* 8.1), can never be pleasing to God, no matter how much it is adorned with rituals such as wearing sackcloth and ashes. Rather the "fast" that pleases God is a passion for justice that cares for the socially oppressed, feeds the hungry, houses the homeless, and does not despise those of low status (*Barn.* 3.1-5). There are clear echoes here of the Sermon on the Mount, seen as the new law of Christ. By observing these standards the addressees will not "shipwreck [themselves] as proselytes to their law" (4.1).

Mention of "proselytes to their law" here is an indication that the author's real target are those who may be thinking of converting to Judaism, not Jewish Christians. It is no accident that the examples of false worship that the author instances are all associated with cultic practice, since it emerges in the closing chapter that, as far as the author is concerned, the immediate historical context of the letter is talk of rebuilding the temple: "Because they went to war, it was torn down by their enemies, and now they and the servants of their enemies will rebuild it" (*Barn.* 16.4). Clearly, there is reference here to the known event of the Roman destruction, not just of the temple but the city, an act that is seen as God's judgment on the people.

However, the reference to its being "rebuilt by the servants of their enemies" is not at all clear, whether it is taken historically or symbolically. One would naturally expect that the reference is to an actual rebuilding of the Jerusalem temple, in line with the mention of the Roman destruction, but the fact that the rebuilding is seen as the fulfillment (*ginnetai nun*) of prophecy, based probably on Isa 49:17, partly cited in v. 3, immediately prior to the reference to rebuilding. This reference may point to a symbolic rather than actual interpretation of the rebuilding.[35] Such an understanding

35. The matter gets even more complicated if one follows the oldest ms. (Sinaiticus),

would point to the identity of the rebuilders as Christians, and the fact that the chapter goes on to develop the idea that the temple which the author has in mind is the new spiritual temple based on various Old Testament allusions might appear to strengthen that interpretation.[36]

However, the text seems to say that the rebuilding is happening now, prompting some people to suggest that Emperor Nerva (96-98) had plans to rebuild the temple since he was well-disposed toward the Jews.[37] Such a date would also concur with the assumed date of the Barnabas letter. Nor would there be a difficulty in including Jews in the rebuilding, since it would be a Jewish temple that would be rebuilt, not a pagan one. The problem with the suggestion, however, is that we have no clear evidence that Nerva ever planned such a project. An alternative would be to relate the rebuilt temple to Hadrian's plans, following Rizzi's and Bazanna's proposal that Hadrian initially wanted to rebuild a Jewish temple on the understanding that it would fit in with his Panhellenion project and the founding of a Roman *colonia* (Aelia Capitolina) in Jerusalem. Again, such a solution would be attractive to some more Hellenized Jews and could be expected to appeal to some Gentile Christians as well, even though it would involve dating the *Epistle* somewhat later than is customary.[38]

Whatever the solution to this interpretative conundrum, it is clear from the letter as a whole that the author is particularly exercised about denigrating all Jewish religious claims. He virtually puts the original Jerusalem temple on a par with pagan temples, claiming that "those wretched people" had set their hopes on the building itself, "as though it were God's house, and not on their God who created them" (*Barn.* 16.1). The notion that circumcision was a sign of divine favor is dismissed. If it were, then the Syrians, the Arabs and the Egyptians should also be seen as belonging to the covenant community, since they too practice it (9.6). However, it is not just the temple that is the object of his attack, but also the rituals that took place there. After the opening salvo in ch. 2, in which, we saw, he attacked the notion of sacrifice as practiced by "them," he returns to the topic in later chapters. Their mistake is that they were led by an evil spirit to understand

---

where a *kai*, "and," is inserted before "the servants," implying that there would be two builders, i.e., "they" (the Jews) *and* the servants of Rome.

36. P. Prigent, *L'Epitre de Barnabe I–XVI et ses sources* (Paris: Cerf, 1981), 75-78.

37. This is the view favored by J. Carlton Paget in his study *The Epistle of Barnabas: Outlook and Background* (Tübingen: Mohr Siebeck, 1994), following the suggestion of M. B. Shukster and P. Richardson, "Barnabas, Nerva and the Yavnean Rabbis," *JTS* 33 (1983), 31-55.

38. Bazzana, "The Bar Kochba Revolt and Hadrian's Religious Policy," 96-100.

the Scriptures in a literal sense (9.4-5). Thus the ceremonies associated with the Day of Atonement (ch. 7), and the red heifer (ch. 8), were intended to refer to the passion of Jesus and his kingdom. The author seems to be familiar with the idea of a second law given by Moses after the Israelites had worshiped the golden calf (Exod 34:1-28), but this was really intended for Christians. The ritual law can continue to have a genuine value since it contains encoded moral instruction which only Christians can understand, a claim already articulated by Paul in 2 Cor 3:12-16.[39]

Justin's Dialogue with Trypho

Even though the *Epistle of Barnabas* articulates a strong rejection of Jewish claims to be the covenant people, it was not the only, or indeed the dominant, Christian viewpoint of the second century. Justin's *Dialogue with Trypho* adopts a quite different stance and is willing to engage in a genuine dialogue. The setting of the work is probably Ephesus, and Trypho is a Jew fleeing from Bar Kokhba's persecution in Palestine. The fact that Justin, himself a convert to Gentile Christianity after having explored various philosophies, is prepared to discuss the issue of Christian Jews (*Dial.* 46-47) is already an indication of a more open position than that of *Barnabas*. While some people have seen Trypho as a "straw man" who does not represent the Jewish position properly, the fact that in the end he is noncommittal with regard to Justin's arguments suggests that, even if he is a fictional character created by Justin, he is realistic in terms of the issues and positions that moderate Jews and Christians would be likely to have debated in the mid–second century.[40]

The main discussion in the earlier part of the *Dialogue* centers around the fact that Christians do not observe the Mosaic law, while claiming to be the true Israel (11.4). Trypho is quite insistent on this point, and Justin

39. For Horbury's highly informative analysis of the theory of Jewish Scriptures propounded by *Barnabas* as the forerunner of later Alexandrian allegorical interpretation in Christian appropriation of the Old Testament, see *Jews and Christians*, 140-46.

40. Wilson, *Related Strangers*, 258-61; T. J. Horne, *Listening to Trypho: Justin Martyr's Dialogue Reconsidered* (Leuven: Peeters, 2001). See, however, T. Rajak, "Talking at Trypho: Christian Apologetic as Anti-Judaism in Justin's Dialogue with Trypho, the Jew," in Rajak, *The Jewish Dialogue with Greece and Rome: Studies in Social and Cultural Interaction* (Leiden: Brill, 2002), 511-33, who stresses the supersessionist polemic of the work and disagrees with those who see this as a realistic account of what such a debate would have been like.

does not come up with an entirely satisfactory answer. He varies his tactics, sometimes appealing to prophetic denouncements of the stipulations of the Old Testament (ch. 27), or again appealing to the idea of a new covenant that is deemed to have abrogated many of the original Mosaic ordinances (chs. 11-12). He can muster historical arguments also, as, for example, the fact that the patriarchs did not undergo circumcision (chs. 19-22), or the more recent history of the destruction of the temple and the expulsion of Jews from Jerusalem, as a sign that God has withdrawn his favor from the Jews and that circumcision is of no avail (chs. 16). What is noteworthy in this opening part of the discussion is the fact that the issue at stake is one of orthopraxis rather than orthodoxy. While Justin does most of the talking, the tone is on the whole different from that of *Barnabas,* even though Justin's views are often more denunciation than dialogue, as Rajak reads the work.

Horbury, on the other hand, describes the difference between the two works as follows: the *Dialogue* breathes a less defensive atmosphere despite the context of bitter rivalry between the two that it documents. Thus, Justin is aware of a corporate Jewish response to the Christian successes, in terms of sending out from Jerusalem chosen men through all the land to tell that the godless heresy of the Christians had sprung up and displaying great zeal in spreading slanderous things about Jesus (*Dial.* 17; see also 108.2). Furthermore, several times he mentions the fact that Christians were cursed in the synagogue (16.4; 46.4; 96.2). Clearly this was a regular ritual, since elsewhere Justin speaks of the rulers of the synagogue *(archisynagōgoi)* reciting "prayers reviling the Son of God and making a mockery of the king of Israel" (137.2; see 35.8; 97.4).[41] In his study of Jewish and Christian relations in antiquity, Daniel Boyarin seeks to minimize these references, which clearly echo the *Birkath ha-Minim* of the rabbinic sources, as being late and legendary. While his point is well taken that the separation was a gradual process rather than a once-for-all decree of expulsion, it is clear from Justin that by the mid–second century a ritual of exclusion had become a fixed element of synagogue worship.[42]

Inevitably, in view of claims being made in certain circles for Bar Kokhba as Messiah, the issue of Jesus' messiahship comes up for discus-

41. Horbury, *Jews and Christians,* 154-61, here 160.

42. Boyarin, *Border Lines,* 67-73. For a detailed discussion of the origins and development of the *Birkath,* see Horbury, *Jews and Christians,* 67-110, who argues that the inclusion of the curse in the *Tefillah* "gave liturgical expression to a separation effected in the second half of the first century through the large group of measures to which it belonged" (p. 110).

sion.[43] Trypho expresses the same argument that was encountered in Celsus's attack, namely, that the claims to divinity for Jesus were a threat to Jewish monotheism. If Jesus is the Messiah, then he is human, not divine, and hence there would appear to be an irreconcilable dilemma for the adherents to both Christian monotheism and messianism (*Dial.* 67-68). Even though the Scriptures speak of two comings of the Messiah, one in lowliness and the other in glory, the idea of a crucified Messiah is not found there (32.6; 85-91; 95-97). This gives rise to a heated discussion about the Scriptures (67-68) in which Justin accuses the Jewish leaders of omitting the phrase "from a tree" in their version of Ps 95(96):10, "The Lord reigns from the tree" — a prooftext for Justin that the crucifixion was indeed foretold in Scripture, even though these words are not found in the LXX translation (*Dial.* 73). Likewise, when Justin appeals to Isa 7:15 (LXX 7:14), Trypho points out that the underlying Hebrew text has no mention of a virgin and does not apply to Christ at all but to King Hezekiah (*Dial.* 43.8; 77).

There is one external issue of concern to both Justin and Trypho, namely, the status of Rome and their respective relationships with it.[44] As mentioned previously, Trypho is in Greece to escape from the Bar Kokhba war, and Justin is on his way to Rome, following the philosopher's path that will eventually lead to his martyrdom, probably in the reign of Antoninus Pius. The topic is not addressed directly, yet the debate between them with regard to the messianic status of Jesus inevitably has the notion of universal rule at its center. They both share a common Jewish expectation of the demise of all earthly kingdoms and the establishment of God's universal reign. Justin is convinced that this will occur with the second coming of Christ in glory and manifest itself in the thousand-year reign in Jerusalem, an image already articulated in the Revelation of John (20:4-6), and alluded to in *Barnabas* (15.5-8).

Already in the *First Apology,* addressed to the emperor, Justin had made a veiled threat: "the Word, than whom after God who begot him, we know there is no ruler more kingly and just," has declared that earthly rulers who seek popularity instead of truth will not prevail (*1 Apol.* 12.7). Elsewhere in the same work he adapted Ps 110:2 (LXX 109:2) to "He shall send to you the rod of power out of Jerusalem," to suggest that nothing Rome

---

43. Schäfer, *Der Bar Kokhba–Aufstand,* 55-67, comments on all the references from rabbinic and early Christian writings dealing with the recognition of Shim'on ben Kosiba as Messiah.

44. Horbury, *Jews and Christians,* 151-54.

can do will block the success of the Christian mission beginning in Jerusalem (*1 Apol.* 45). In the *Dialogue* he cites Daniel 7 at length to include the downfall of the fourth beast (*Dial.* 31-32), clearly intending this to signify the end of Rome. It is against this background that the several references to the thousand-year reign of Christ and his elect in Jerusalem are meant to be understood (40.4; 80-83; 85.7; 138.3; 139.4-5). When one recalls that in the wake of Bar Kokhba's failed messianic war Jerusalem was now a Roman *colonia* from which Jews were excluded, there is a defiant note in Justin's locating the triumphant reign of Christ in the holy city. The fact that some Christians had been executed by Bar Kokhba for refusing to deny Christ and blaspheme (*1 Apol.* 31.6) merely confirms for Justin the certainty of his claim. Thus, the story of God destroying Amalek "with concealed hand" (Exod 17:16 LXX) is applied to "the concealed power of God that was in Christ crucified, before whom demons and all the principalities and powers of the earth tremble" (*Dial.* 49.8).

In view of the supersessionist thrust of Justin's overall argument, which sees Christianity as the replacement of Judaism, it comes as something of a surprise to find that he claims to have adopted a more lenient approach to Christian Jews than several of his contemporaries (*Dial.* 47.1-2). At an early stage in the discussion, baptism is described, in terms borrowed from the mystery religions, as a rite of special initiation (*teleios genomenos,* literally "becoming perfect," 8.2). Christians have a separate identity as an *allo genos,* "another race" that is not defined by the usual ethnic markers (138.2). Trypho, on the other hand, has described himself as a Hebrew, for whom circumcision was at once an ethnic marker and a religious rite, the doorway that leads to the practice enjoined in the Torah of Moses: Sabbath observance, new moon festivals, and ritual washings. In a lengthy discussion, Justin makes an appeal to Trypho and "to those who wish to become proselytes" (i.e., Gentile converts to Judaism) that "the divine message" proclaims that circumcision has been rendered useless by the blood of Christ (23.4).

Later the issue of what elements of Jewish practice can be followed by Christian Jews comes up for greater scrutiny, when Trypho poses the following question: "If some, even now, wish to live in the observance of the institutions given by Moses, and yet believe in this Jesus who was crucified, recognizing him to be the Christ of God, and that it is given to him to be the absolute judge of all, and that his is the everlasting kingdom, can they also be saved?" In reply, Justin adopts a rather paternalistic attitude to this highly orthodox "confession," eliciting a suitable response from Trypho to the counter-question, "Is it possible for one to observe all the Mosaic institutions?" Once again Trypho is the good pupil with an emphatic and correct answer: "No. For we know that, as you said, it is not possible anywhere to sacrifice the lamb of the Passover, or to offer the goats ordered for the fast, or, in short, to present all the other offerings." Justin then invites him to say what is allowed. Trypho replies: "To keep the Sabbath, to be circumcised, to observe months, and to be washed if you touch anything prohibited by Moses, or after sexual intercourse" (*Dial.* 46).[45]

This exchange mirrors perfectly what we know of Jewish Christian practices from other sources. It will be recalled that the *Gospel of the Ebionites* as cited by Epiphanius has Jesus declare: "I have come to abolish sacrifice, and unless you cease from sacrifice the wrath of God will not cease from you."[46] According to Hegesippus, James the Just entered the temple daily, arrayed as the High Priest on the Day of Atonement, but he prayed for the people's sins and did not offer sacrifice. What is significant in Justin's exchange with Trypho is his tolerance of such people, unlike some of his fellow Gentile converts who refused to dine with those who continued to practice aspects of their Jewish heritage, recalling the dispute between Peter and Paul in Antioch over a similar issue a hundred years earlier (Gal 2:11-14). Now however, Justin does set limits: the Jewish Christians are not to insist on new Gentile converts adopting the same practices on joining the Christian family, since such insistence would nullify the orthodox claims of the once-for-all sufficiency of Christ's saving action (*Dial.* 47).

We might well ask why Justin is prepared to allow for such diversity, especially in view of his strong supersessionist position with regard to Christianity's replacement of Judaism, expressed throughout the *Dialogue*, as already mentioned. It should be remembered that Justin was a native of Neapolis in Palestine and was familiar with Samaritans, and perhaps he

---

45. Mention of ritual immersion here as one of the permitted practices raises the question of how such washings relate to Christian baptism. Justin does not deal with the issue, yet it would appear to be as obvious a point of contention as sacrifice. However in the pseudo-Clementine literature the matter is given much more attention, linking the water of baptism and the water of the purification rite with the story of creation in Genesis. See S. Freyne, "Jewish Immersion and Christian Baptism: Continuity at the Margins?" in D. Helholm, et al., eds. *Ablution, Initiation, and Baptism: Late Antiquity, Early Judaism and Early Christianity* (Berlin: de Gruyter, 2011), 1:221-53.

46. *Panarion* 30.16.5-7. The pseudo-Clementine writings, which contain Jewish Christian material, also reflect this ban. Peter says, "The time of sacrifice is over" (*Recognitions* 1.64.1; see also 1.37.1, 39.1-2, 55.3-4).

had also encountered some of the Jewish Christians on the fringes of the rabbinic movement in Galilee that we hear about in later sources. Nevertheless, his tolerance is all the more remarkable when one recalls Paul's strong rhetorical attacks on his "Judaizing" opponents in various epistles. Justin's readiness to tolerate these Jewish Christians is indicative of how things had changed in the intervening century. Paul was in a minority in admitting Gentile converts to what was still perceived as a Jewish sect without insisting on circumcision, and he was under constant surveillance from the Jewish authorities in the Diaspora synagogues. In Justin's day, the Gentile Christian movement initiated by Paul had become the dominant force, and, indeed, Justin himself, in the autobiographical section of the *Dialogue* (1-8), demonstrates that he was quite at home in the world of Greek philosophy, to the point at which he was recognized by Trypho and his companions through his wearing the philosopher's garb.[47]

Clearly, the situation envisaged in this episode of Justin's *Dialogue* is one step closer to a real parting of the ways when the Jewish Christian wing of the movement would be isolated on the margins, becoming more and more fragmented in the process. It is important to realize, however, that our knowledge of the way in which early Christian heresies developed is largely the work of the heresiologists — Irenaeus, Hippolytus, Tertullian, Eusebius, and Epiphanius. In the final section of this chapter we shall return to this phenomenon of the making of heretics as an exercise in promoting orthodoxy. Here it is worth pointing to one trajectory within Jewish Christianity, that associated with Ebion, which would appear to have its roots in the issues that Justin was addressing in chs. 46-47 of the *Dialogue with Trypho*. Irenaeus (c. 170) describes the Ebionites as repudiating Paul as apostate from the Law. They themselves follow the gospel of Matthew, but do not accept the virgin birth. They practice circumcision, follow the customs in accordance with the Law, and follow a Jewish way of life, "even adoring Jerusalem as if it were the house of God" (*Adv. Haer.* 1.26.2).

Epiphanius gives us another account of the Ebionites in the fourth century which combines Irenaeus's description with other elements borrowed from the *Book of Elchasai* and Hellenistic and Samaritan sources (*Pan.* 30).[48] According to this account, the Ebionites could no longer be

---

47. R. M. Thorsteinsson, "By Philosophy Alone: Reassessing Justin's Christianity and His Turn from Platonism," *Early Christianity* 3 (2012), 492-517.

48. G. Luttikhuizen, "Elchasites and Their Book," in A. Marjanen and P. Luomanen, eds., *A Companion to Second-Century Christian "Heretics"* (Leiden: Brill, 2008), 335-64.

regarded as the direct successors of the Jerusalem Jewish Christians.[49] Thus Epiphanius was faced with the task of finding an alternative as part of his efforts to denigrate all Jewish Christian groups, "orthodox" and "heretical" alike. To this end, according to Luomanen, he "invents" the Nazarenes in order to refute an idealized and stereotyped picture of people who try to be "both Jews and Christians" at the same time. In short, his Nazarenes, as described in *Panarion* 29, are a fiction, occupying a position between the Ebionites and the Elchasaites in his grid of Jewish Christian sects and serving as a stereotype of a "pure" Jewish Christianity that can be readily refuted.[50] This was the final stage in the exclusion of the Jewish Christians from the larger Christian family. It reflected the concerns of a developing Christian empire that was recovering from the shock of Emperor Julian's abortive attempt in 351 to restore worship of the sun god, after the Constantinian conversion. In this brave new world there would be little room for either Jews or Jewish Christians.[51]

Celsus's Jew

We must return briefly to Celsus's work, since, as mentioned previously, he employs a Jew as part of his strategy to discredit Christian claims. Doubts about this Jew's authenticity similar to those about Trypho have been raised, and in fact Origen in his reply states that he has often debated with Jewish teachers in Caesarea and that Celsus's Jew bears little or no resemblance to them (*Cels.* 1.49; 2.28, 77; 4.2; 5.6, 8-9). Instead Origen introduces some "genuine" Jewish objections, which he has, he claims, refuted. A typical ex-

49. P. Luomanen, *Recovering Jewish-Christian Sects and Gospels* (Leiden: Brill, 2012), 45-49.

50. P. Luomanen, "Nazarenes," in Marjanen and Luomanen, eds., *A Companion to Second-Century Christian "Heretics,"* 279-314, here 307-12; *Recovering Jewish-Christian Sects,* 77-81. In support of his claim that the Nazarenes of *Panarion* 29 are a fictional creation, Luomanen notes (p. 77, n. 89) that Epiphanius himself describes how he has created the name *Alogi* for those who reject the gospel of John but without claiming that they were a sect (*Pan.* 51). Luomanen also points to Irenaeus's profiling of his gnostic opponents in order to discredit them, a feature of "orthodox" strategies that will be discussed below.

51. See S. Freyne, "Jews in a Christian World: the Fourth Century," in V. McInnes, ed., *New Visions: Historical and Theological Perspectives on the Jewish Christian Dialogue* (New York: Crossroad, 1993), 31-54; R. L. Wilken, *John Chrysostom and the Jews: Rhetoric and Reality in the Late Fourth Century* (Berkeley: University of California Press, 1983); J. Neusner, *Judaism and Christianity in the Age of Constantine* (Chicago: University of Chicago Press), 1987.

ample is the proper translation of the Hebrew word *'almah* in Isa 7:14, as "young woman" or "virgin" in explaining the birth of Jesus. As an outstanding philologist as well as biblical scholar and theologian, Origen was able to engage in learned debates with his peers, and his biblical commentaries display his knowledge of Jewish tradition. Celsus, on the other hand, had no interest in either religion, yet had done his homework well on the Christians and was conscious of the ways in which the figure of a Jew could undermine some of their claims.[52]

Celsus was the first pagan to see the significance of Christianity's relationship with Judaism as a way to denigrate the former. His Jewish interlocutor asks: "Why do you Christians take your origin from our religion, and then, as if you were progressing in knowledge, despise these things, even though you cannot find any other origin for your doctrine than our law?" (*Cels.* 2.4). This is a similar objection to that put by Trypho, namely, that, having claimed a Jewish origin, the Christians ignore the demands of the Torah, the very heart of the Jewish experience (*Dial.* 10). As we saw, Justin was not able to respond with any great conviction to the charge, resorting in the end to pointing to the destruction of Jerusalem as a sign that the Jews had lost God's favor. Origen's reply is more subtle. Christians do indeed base their belief on the teaching of Moses, but unlike the Jews, who continue to see these accounts as mere stories, the Christians seek to progress to a deeper knowledge of what they entail, seeking the mystery that is now manifested by the prophetic utterances and by the appearance of the Lord Jesus Christ.

It should be remembered that Judaism was a recognized ancient religion in the Greco-Roman world. While the Jews' pagan detractors often charged them with being arrogant and separatist, they did have a legal status that was reaffirmed by various Roman rulers. The Christians, on the other hand, had no such ancient pedigree and in fact found that appeal to a Jewish ancestry could be quite advantageous, even though intellectual pagans such as Celsus equally despised Jewish claims to antiquity. Jews were Egyptian by race but left Egypt after revolting against the community there and despising its religious customs (*Cels.* 3.5).

Celsus's Jew asks: "What was wrong with you Christians that you left the law of your fathers and, being deluded by that man Jesus, were ludicrously deceived and have deserted us for another name and another life?"

---

52. N. de Lange, *Origen and the Jews: Studies in Jewish-Christian Relations in Third-Century Palestine* (Cambridge: Cambridge University Press, 1976), 63-73, here 69.

(2.1). Celsus himself sarcastically drives home the point of the inner contradiction of the Christian position: "Did God give contradictory laws to this man from Nazareth, his son? Who is wrong? Moses or Jesus? Or when the Father sent Jesus had he forgotten what commands he gave to Moses? Or did he condemn his own laws and change his mind, and send his messenger for quite the opposite purposes?" (7.18).

Of course, Origen does seek to answer these challenges, using all his skill as a philosopher and exegete and on occasion alluding to different types of discussion he has had with the rabbinic schools in Caesarea. But Celsus's attack had occurred some seventy years earlier and had gone unchallenged in the interim, it would seem. The presence of Jewish communities side by side with Christian ones in the cities of the Roman world was a constant reminder for those who wanted to denigrate the Christians that this new movement was deeply compromised by its claims to a Jewish origin and yet its failure to respect its laws and customs in its own lifestyle and practice. In that respect, the Jewish Christians had chosen the better option, but the increasing Hellenization of the gospel had driven them to the margins, as we shall presently discuss. Another option was to abandon Moses altogether, as Marcion proposed, with his truncated selection of Scriptures that sought to write the Jewish heritage out of the Christian story completely.[53]

Christian Heresies and the Response of Orthodoxy

In the introduction to this chapter we cited Karen L. King's proposal for a discussion of Christian origins, but it is worth repeating it now as we seek to understand Christian diversity in the second century:

53. Marcion was a wealthy merchant from Pontus on the Black Sea who arrived in Rome about 140 and was an active member of one of the several house churches there. He subsequently developed his own ideas, especially with regard to a duality in God. According to Marcion, the Old Testament tells the story of the demiurge or creator, who, because of his harshness and aloofness, could not be the Father of Jesus Christ. Jesus' appearance announced the existence of another, good God, different from the God of the Jews. Accordingly Marcion proposed a Bible that consisted solely of the gospel of Luke and the letters of Paul, shorn of any Old Testament allusions. His movement was highly popular and spread throughout the East and West, surviving in the East well into the Byzantine period. His radical ideas had the effect of hastening the need for the defenders of orthodoxy to develop a canon or list of official books that would include both the Old Testament books, based on the Greek version (LXX), and the fourfold gospel defended by Irenaeus and others. See H. Räisänen, "Marcion," in Marjanen and Luomanen, eds., *A Companion to Second-Century Christian "Heretics,"* 100-124.

An adequate framework for historical descriptions of early Christian diversity needs to recognize that all religions contain ever-shifting, competing, and contradictory claims, plural possibilities and alternative voices. . . . [Yet] typologies of the varieties of early Christianity instead frequently constitute attempts to define and categorize the unique and essential qualities of distinct theological systems or social groups.[54]

King is reacting to the usual reconstruction that operates with the categories of orthodoxy and heresy as the accepted paradigm, following the lead of such ancient writers as Justin and Irenaeus and moderns like Bauer and Harnack. However, the shifting boundaries and plural possibilities of which King speaks are much more characteristic of what we know about second-century Christians on the ground, despite the efforts of heresiologists such as Irenaeus or, two centuries later, Epiphanius to construct heresy as a serious deviation from the true and apostolic faith which was there from the beginning. In discussing the "crossing of the boundaries" between Jews and Christians, Judith Lieu makes a useful distinction between literary discourse about the relationships between groups and the manner in which this was or was not reflective of what happened at the socio-cultural level, which in practice could be quite different.[55]

Even when one is sensitive to the complexity and porosity of religious groups in antiquity, it is difficult to rid oneself fully of the oppositional model of "them and us," even when terms such as "proto-orthodox" and "deviant" seek to indicate that the matter was not so clear-cut from the outset. David Brakke, writing about the "gnostics, so-called," makes a similar point to Lieu when he writes,

Self-differentiation in this period [second century] was always a multilateral affair and resulted in diverse forms of Christian thought and practice. The inclusion of these varied modes of Christian piety in the single category of "orthodoxy" was in fact the achievement of the post-Constantinian imperial church, and even then was never full and complete, but always partial and contested.[56]

54. Cited above, p. 315.

55. J. Lieu, "Self-Definition vis-à-vis the Jewish Matrix," in M. M. Mitchell and F. M. Young, *The Cambridge History of Christianity: Origins to Constantine* (Cambridge: Cambridge University Press, 2006), 214-29, here 218.

56. D. Brakke, "Self-Differentiation among Christian Groups: The Gnostics and Their Opponents," in Mitchell and Young, eds., *The Cambridge History of Christianity*, 245-60, here 246.

From Greek Hairesis to Christian Heresy

Before attempting to delineate how the process of "making heretics" was conducted, it is useful to delineate briefly the way in which the Greek term *hairesis* came to mean "heresy" in second-century Christian parlance.[57] Originally the term had no pejorative overtones, being derived from *hairein,* the Greek verb "to choose." Since philosophy was the search for truth and involved a choice between various opinions, the term was used for "a school of thought," indicating an allegiance to a set of doctrines or an original teacher. As such, it could denote a succession of teachers who passed on and developed the insights of the founding master. Josephus uses the term in describing the Jewish philosophies Pharisees, Sadducees, Essenes, and even the Zealots, with no indication that he finds their multiplicity unacceptable (*Ant* 13.5, 9; 18.1, 2; *War* 2.8, 14). The author of Acts of the Apostles can also use it for both the Jewish groups and the early Christians without any negative overtones (Acts 5:17; 15:5; 24:14; 26:5; 28:22).

It is among Christian writers of the second century that we begin to see the use of the term in an exclusively negative sense. Justin, for example, defends himself against Trypho's charge that he belongs to what the Jews call the "heresy" by professing another God (*Dial.* 62.3). Celsus, too, objects that almost from the beginning the Christians have splintered into many different *haireseis,* an objection that Irenaeus had already countered by claiming that it was only those who had abandoned the true faith who had formed *haireseis* (*Adv. Haer.* 1.9.4; 3.12.7). Origen's reply to Celsus is, as one might expect, more open than that of Irenaeus to the notion that truth has to be researched. He notes that "Any teaching which has had a serious origin, and is beneficial to life, has given rise to different *haireseis*" (*Cels.* 3.12; see also 2.27; 5.61). He instances the numerous medical schools among the Greeks and the barbarians. Thus the existence of Christian *haireseis* is useful and to be expected. The different Christian sects are not at all the result of factions and love of strife, but have emerged because several learned men have made a serious effort to understand Christianity. Like medicine and philosophy, "it was necessary to have looked into the sects of Judaism and Christianity to become a Christian of deep learning" (3.13).

---

57. M. Simon, "From Greek Hairesis to Christian Heresy," in W. R. Schoedel and R. L. Wilken, eds., *Early Christian Literature and the Classical Intellectual Tradition, in Honorem Robert M. Grant* (Paris: Beauchesne, 1979), 101-16.

However, despite Origen's enlightened views, the pejorative connotation of "heresy" was to prevail in Christian discourse. It had not always
been used for what might be regarded as doctrinal aberrations, but could
also be applied to those who are guilty of misdemeanors or moral failings,
such as one finds in the Pastoral Letters (e.g., Tit 2:10; 2 Pet 2:1) and the Apostolic Fathers (Ign. *Eph.* 6.2; Ign. *Trall.* 6.1). However, as we shall presently
see, it was to become a byword for false doctrine from the mid–second
century onward, and as such it became virtually synonymous with another
technical term, *heterodoxia*. This term had a similar history to *hairesis*, with
the root meaning of "mistaking one thing for another." However, within
the Platonic framework, where the first use of the term occurred, it was
easily equated with "false opinion" and as such is found in various Christian writings. It occurs frequently in Eusebius of Caesarea (end of the third
century C.E.), as, for example, when he declares that after the apostolic
generation had passed "godless error appeared through the deceit of false
teachers *(heterodidaskaloi),* who attempted to counter the preaching of the
truth by preaching *the knowledge falsely so called*" (*H.E.* 3.28). The italicized
phrase here echoes the Greek title of Irenaeus's *Adversus Haereses,* which he
called "The Refutation and Overthrow of Knowledge So-Called," according
to Eusebius (*H.E.* 5.7). That work had been written over a hundred years
previously, but such was his influence as champion of orthodoxy that his
work continued to define the issues surrounding heresy and orthodoxy
right up to the Constantinian settlement. Thereafter, Epiphanius of Salamis
(315-403) produced his *Panarion* or "Refutation of All the Heresies," which,
we saw, included Jewish Christian groups also.

Champions of Orthodoxy and the Making of Heretics

One of the important gains from the discovery of the Nag Hammadi library
is that these documents can help us uncover the rhetorical strategies that
the champions of "orthodoxy" deployed against the various "heretics" they
sought to discredit. Heretofore we only had one side of the story, that of the
Christian apologists such as Justin, Irenaeus, Tertullian, and others, and
this was, and still is accepted in some quarters as, the official version of how
the church was saved from the scourge of heterodoxy.

Thanks to the new discoveries, we are now in a position to evaluate
critically the received representation of the various "gnostic" teachers and
recognize the distortions that were perpetrated in the name of preserving

the unity of the church and the integrity of the Christian gospel as defined by one faction. The champions of orthodoxy sought to portray their opponents as outsiders, "heretics" who did not belong, by claiming that they and they alone understood the revelation of Christ and interpreted the Scriptures correctly. The rules of the game in this power struggle were clear and straightforward — then and now. Only one side has the right to decide what is true, and those who propose other ideas are to be banished. Truth is one, error is many, and the fluidity that was characteristic of early Christian praxis on the ground has to be excluded as opening the door to the satanic evil of plurality.

This obsession is not only concerned with banishing internal dissent, but it also involves building walls of exclusion against other "others" — Jews and pagans in particular. Similar rhetorical strategies were at play in defining these relations also, as we have seen in the case of Justin's *Dialogue with Trypho*. But it was a feature of an earlier period also. Thus, for example, Ignatius of Antioch in the early second century describes members of his community who continue with Jewish practices as "poisonous weeds" because their conduct endangers the unity of the community around himself as the bishop. "It is monstrous to talk of Jesus Christ and practice Judaism *(Ioudaizein),*" he declares to the Magnesians (Ign. *Magn.* 10.2), and in a similar vein he indicates to the Philadelphians that he is opposed to those who "interpret Judaism to you," even if they are uncircumcised. This suggests that, in Ignatius's Antiochian experience, Gentiles, probably God-fearers, were interested in discussing Judaism with Christian believers. For him, such an interest in Judaism was of no value to the Christian believer. Yet he is prepared to tolerate circumcised Jews who are prepared to talk about *(hermeneuein)* Christ (Ign. *Phld.* 6.1). Such attitudes make Justin's limited tolerance of Jewish Christians continuing with certain rituals from their Jewish past all the more remarkable (*Dial.* 47). However, that was to change later as various Jewish Christian groups joined the ranks of the heretics in Epiphanius's catalog in the *Panarion*. However, as we saw, he was writing in the context of a Christian empire that merely hastened the process of exclusion of Jews from civic as well as religious life.

The rhetorical devices that the defenders of orthodoxy employ are both obvious and consistent. The basic idea is that the evil of heterodoxy cannot come from the one source of truth, of which they are the sole guardians. Hence a different genealogy has to be created, one in which moral evil prompted by Satan plays a part. For Irenaeus, it comes through Simon Magus, whom we encountered earlier in Samaria as the representation of "the Power of the great God," but who was dismissed by the apostles Peter and John when he sought to purchase their healing powers (Acts 8:9-24). Irenaeus describes him as "one from whom all kinds of heresies derive their origin" and who initiated a sect based on a slave girl, Helena from Tyre, around whom a mythology was developed. Simon's followers practice all kinds of magical arts and lead profligate lives. They are called Simonians, and it is from them that "knowledge, falsely so-called, received its beginning" (*Adv. Haer.* 1.28). Irenaeus then goes on to describe Simon's successors, Menander in Syria and Saturninus and Basilides in Antioch.

In a similar vein, Tertullian (160-220), writing from North Africa, derives heresy from Greek philosophy: Valentinus was a Platonist, Marcion a Stoic, the Epicureans deny the immortality of the soul, and all the philosophers deny the idea of the resurrection. "The same subject matter is discussed over and over again by heretics and philosophers; the same arguments are repeated." Tertullian's advice is to shun pagan culture entirely: "What has Athens to do with Jerusalem? What has the Academy to do with the Church?" (*De Praes.* 7). In short, the only way to deal with the evil of heterodoxy is to build high walls against all outside influences and resist any form of syncretism. All this from a man who himself had imbibed Roman culture, as can be seen in his other writings, which address Roman prefects boldly and confidently!

Another shared aspect of the champions of orthodoxy is their claim that only they can interpret the Scriptures correctly. Even though the canon or official list of books that properly belonged to Scripture was not finally decided until the fourth century, there was a growing consensus regarding the apostolic writings, such as the letters of Paul and the four gospels, though even this was disputed. The Hebrew Scriptures were also a matter of major controversy, especially because of the claim of Marcion (active in Rome c. 160) that they should be excluded altogether because they represented an alien God who was not the Father of Jesus Christ. Marcion's daring and dangerous attempt to produce a Bible consisting only of one gospel (an expurgated version of Luke) and ten of Paul's letters was a huge challenge to the orthodox circles. The unity of the two testaments was particularly important in terms of Christian claims to antiquity, even when it left them vulnerable to the charge of inconsistency in not observing the Mosaic Law, as Trypho, Celsus, and others had rightly pointed out.

We have seen already that the issue of translation of Scripture from Hebrew to Greek was crucial in interpreting its meaning. Justin and Trypho, for example, disagreed as to how '*almah* in Isa 7:14 should be translated into

347

Greek, since an important doctrinal issue hung on the matter, as far as Justin was concerned. For him the claims about Jesus were valid because he fulfilled the Old Testament pattern laid out for the Messiah, whereas for Trypho this was precisely what was in dispute. Celsus was, we saw, aware of a very different story of Jesus' origins and conscious of the fact that there were discrepancies between the different gospels (*Cels.* 2.7). Irenaeus proposes an elaborate scheme as to why there can only be four gospels, based on the cardinal points of the compass, but in fact, there was a practical reason for his wishing to set these limits, since he was aware that the gnostic teacher Valentinus had recently composed a *Gospel of Truth* (*Adv. Haer.* 3.9.11-12). Characteristically, Tertullian is the most forthright. Advising his hearers to avoid discussions about the meaning of the Bible, he sarcastically asks: "What will you accomplish, most learned of biblical scholars, if the other side denies what you affirmed, and affirms what you denied?" (*De Praes.* 17). His advice is that it is better to remain ignorant since it is said that faith, not knowledge, saves: "Faith is established in the Rule. . . . To know nothing against the Rule is to know everything" (14).

Tertullian's reference to the Rule points us to a final aspect of the strategy against the heretics, namely, the external guarantees of the purity of the orthodox position. If the written word of Scripture was open to many different interpretations and different hermeneutical strategies, then the champions of orthodoxy required something more solid, more public, and more certain to uphold their position that they, and they alone, were the repository and guarantors of the true faith. It is to Irenaeus that the development of a definite strategy to deal with the heretics, in terms of what he calls "the rule of faith" or "the rule of truth," must be credited. True, Justin had already developed the idea of constructing a catalog of heretics in order to discredit them in debating with his contemporaries in Rome, Marcion and Valentinus. But as a private philosopher he lacked the authority to insist on his distinction between true and false belief. Irenaeus, on the other hand, was a bishop who was able not only to develop the ideas more fully, but also to convince his audiences of the legitimacy of his claims.

Put simply, Irenaeus believed in the unity of the two testaments and that together they provided an "overarching plotline," not of tragic cosmic failure or duality in the divine, as Valentinus, Marcion, and others held, but rather a coherent story of the one God's concern for his creation, manifested in the sending of his Son as Redeemer and Savior of the human race. This message was given in its fullness to the apostles, who handed it on to the bishops in each local church in an unbroken line of succession to the present day. Because of the unity of the testaments the Scriptures are to be interpreted in accordance with what they teach, taken as a whole, and this cannot be changed no matter what the circumstances in which they are preached. He writes:

> As I have already observed, the church, having received this preaching and this faith, although scattered throughout the whole world, yet, as if occupying but one house, carefully preserves it. She also believes these points [of doctrine] just as if she had but one soul, and one and the same heart, and she proclaims them, and teaches them, and hands them down, with perfect harmony, as if she possessed only one mouth. For, although the languages of the world are dissimilar, yet the import of the tradition is one and the same. (*Adv. Haer.* 1.10)

One further step was required in order to consolidate this structure of an unbroken line of succession from the apostles. The apostle Paul had long before appealed to tradition in authenticating the resurrection experiences in the early church: "I handed on to you what I myself received" (1 Cor 15:3). The witnesses that he lists were all known figures among Jesus' followers, and when he mentions a crowd of five hundred brethren, he adds that "some are still alive" and therefore, presumably, open to being questioned (vv. 2-6). In other words tradition needs to be publicly verifiable if it is to be trusted. Irenaeus is conscious that his opponents are appealing to private revelations, and hence he develops the idea of apostolic succession.

In contrast to this public character of the apostolic witness, the claims of his opponents cannot be verified and are therefore unconvincing. Irenaeus thinks it would be tedious to list the successors of the apostles in all the churches, and so confines himself to the Roman church, where he is certain that there is an unbroken tradition (*Adv. Haer.* 3.3, 2). A hundred years later Eusebius is conscious of the same claims, mentioning the lists of bishops in the Jerusalem church, beginning with James, whose throne was, he claims, still visible in Jerusalem (*H.E.* 2.1-6; 4.5; 7.19). However, one can only be deeply suspicious of the accuracy of these claims by the champions of orthodoxy. True, the Nag Hammadi documents do indeed, for the most part, confine their accounts of the encounters of the disciples with the Savior to post-resurrection appearances, and they are usually private, either to one disciple alone or to a small group. However, given the fact that, as late as the time of Justin, the church in Rome had no figure making claims to apostolic succession against the various "heretical" individuals in that city, one would have to query the trustworthiness of Irenaeus's claim. It was only at his instigation that the then bishop of Rome, Victor (c. 189-99), took measures of exclusion against some Montanist members of his congregation as well as against a Valentinian who was one of his presbyters.[58] One can only wonder what Irenaeus might have thought of the role of women in church leadership, had he known and read the *Gospel of Mary*, where the Savior shows preference for the female disciple Mary of Magdala over the male ones, including Peter, much to their chagrin (*Gos. Mary* 17-18).[59]

58. Brakke, "Self-Differentiation among Christian Groups," 255-56.
59. King, *The Gospel of Mary of Magdala*, especially 170-90.

Epilogue

Exploring the origins of something one holds dear is never an innocent exercise. The story of the search for Christian Origins is no exception. This is all the more true when one is engaged in gathering into one relatively coherent account the many scattered pieces of early Jewish and Christian documentation that I have drawn on for this study. I am deeply conscious of the fact that there are many other items and topics that could have been included but did not fit easily into the trajectory that I wished to follow, namely, that branch of the early Christian expansion that is associated with the non-Pauline mission. Perhaps because of my interest in Galilee over the years, this particular direction seems to have captured my imagination. I can still recall my sense of excitement a number of years ago, as I stood on the rampart of Dura Europus overlooking the Euphrates and wondered how the Jewish and Christian communities that inhabited the areas of the city on either side of the main gate might have related to each other in the early third century C.E.

Traditionally, the search for Christian origins has often devolved into a search for a golden moment where apologetic rather than critical historical interest takes over. This was certainly not my intention in undertaking this study. From the outset it was my presupposition that the rise and expansion of the early Jesus movement was never a linear and neatly organized phenomenon, but involved, rather, a number of often competing factors, social, cultural, economic, and religious, and that consequently the Jesus movement was a multifaceted reality from its very earliest days.

What has been described as "the age of Constantine" is usually seen as the period when Christian diversity was finally banished and the church

351

began to take on aspects of imperial rule that Jesus at least, if not all his first followers, would have abhorred. Whatever one thinks about Constantine's vision of the cross and his "conversion," the manner in which he so readily acquiesced in accepting the imperial honors of the "divine Caesar" suggests that for him personally little had changed. Indeed the image of the sun god Apollo continued to appear on his coins even as late as the 324 (the Council of Nicea). The Edict of Milan, issued together with his coregent Licenius in 313, granted that "no one should be refused complete toleration, who has given up his mind either to the cult of the Christians, or to the religion which he considers best suited to himself." The reason for this tolerance was in order that "the Supreme Divinity, to whose worship we devote ourselves under no compulsion, may continue in all things to grant us his wonted favor and beneficence." At this point Constantine was not prepared to be more precise in naming the deity than to describe it as "whatsoever divinity dwells in heaven."

Subsequently, Constantine was to become sole ruler of the empire, East as well as West, having finally defeated and exiled Licenius in 324 because of the latter's constant persecution of Christians in the East. Thereafter he began to turn his attention to the eastern provinces, where most Christians lived. He founded Constantinople as his new residence and took a much greater interest in the affairs of the church, which was engaged in a bitter doctrinal struggle between the bishops of Antioch and Alexandria and their supporters, dealing with the divinity of Christ. If Constantine was to espouse the Christians as a unifying force within his far-flung territory he could not allow it to be riven by internal disputes. His presence at the Council of Nicea in 325 and his insistence that a suitable formula be produced laid down a clear marker to the assembled bishops as to his intentions and expectations.

In particular his relationship with Eusebius, the bishop of Caesarea in Palestine, was to play an important part in the way Constantine's role as a Christian emperor was understood subsequently. Eusebius wrote his *Ecclesiastical History* with the express intention of giving an account of the church from its foundation to his own day, one that portrays its continuous and changeless character from the beginning. He adopted the idea that the mission of the church and that of imperial Rome were one and the same, and he used this as one of the principles of organization for his history. He thus created the notion of a central, unified orthodoxy, guaranteed by apostolic succession, that ignored all local variations and sharply distinguished orthodoxy from falsehood. With this view of a monochromic Christian history he was well equipped to write the *Vita Constantini,* a work in which the emperor is celebrated as the embodiment of the divine Logos, the guarantor and guardian of the apostolic faith of the church.

It is no accident of history, therefore, that in the last quarter of the fourth century Epiphanius's *Panarion,* or "Medicine Chest," dealing with "remedies" for eighty heresies, real or imagined, appeared (c. 375). As discussed on pp. 342-50, Epiphanius was on a heresy hunt, in some instances drawing on the work of earlier heresiologists such as Irenaeus and Tertullian, and in others describing heresies that never actually existed. This work clearly reflected the growing sense of assurance that the orthodox party was experiencing within the Christian empire and with imperial protection. By the end of the century, the tolerance of the Edict of Milan was still operative with regard to Jews, but not toward the Jewish Christians, it would seem.

Yet, at the same time one begins to notice signs of Jewish unease in the ways in which the rabbis were interpreting their Jewish Scriptures, especially in regard to the figure of the Messiah and the promise of the land. It is altogether likely, as Jacob Neusner has argued, that these exegetical trends were reactions to the appropriation by Christians of the ancient Jewish symbols. In their writings, but also in their building of churches and other monuments within the Jewish homeland, the Christians showed clearly that Christianity had arrived to stay and that Jews were in danger of being pushed to the side, even in their ancestral land.

As the Byzantine age continued, this process was intensified to the point that it was now possible to speak of a "Christian Holy Land." Pilgrims came from all quarters to visit the sites that the Savior had sanctified, especially Bethlehem and Jerusalem. It was somewhat later before the Galilean sites became important, but eventually Nazareth and Capernaum were also recognized as important on the pilgrims' journeys. Epiphanius's account of the permission that Constantine granted to Count Joseph of Scythopolis to build churches at a number of places in Galilee "where no Christians or Samaritans had entered" is at least an indication of the trend by the late fourth century, even if one cannot always be certain of the information coming from that source, as was evident in his somewhat artificial list of heresies.

Under the influence of his mother Helena, Constantine had churches erected at sites such as Bethlehem and Jerusalem. The spatial arrangement of these churches seems to have been based on that of the Jerusalem temple, thereby implicitly at least making a statement of the Christian replacement ideology as far as the "Promised Land" was concerned. Since the destruction of the temple in 70 C.E., Christian apologists had been content to lay claim to being the new, spiritual temple that some Jewish texts had spoken of, and they therefore showed no interest in the application of these texts to the actual Jerusalem and the land. Now, however, the erection of Christian churches was a clear indication that attitudes were changing and that a claim to the city and the land as Christian — "ours, no longer theirs" — was being made. Archaeologists have uncovered the remains of more than three hundred churches from the Byzantine period in Israel, and in addition there are many more from the same period in Jordan.

Eusebius's triumphalist rhetoric on the occasion of the dedication of a church in Tyre may be taken as indicative of Christian attitudes subsequently. The event took place in 336, thirty years after the army's recognition of Constantine as Augustus and Caesar following the death of his father Constantius. After a lengthy paean of praise to God and Jesus Christ for all that was now occurring, especially the fact that the emperor was prepared to show his contempt for the pagan idols, Eusebius described the architecture of the building, calling it "the temple of God." It had a large ceremonial entrance, an atrium open to the air with a fountain, three doors at the main entrance, the center one with bronze embossed fastenings, a spacious nave, and a roof of cedar wood (H.E. 10.4.37-45). The progression from the outer entrance to the highly decorative interior resembled that of the increasing holiness attached to the various courtyards of the Jerusalem temple. While the speech is addressed to Paulinus, the bishop of Tyre, the tone and language strongly suggest that Eusebius had Constantine in mind. He wondered whether one should speak of "a new Bezalel, the architect of a divine tabernacle [in the desert], or Solomon the king of a new and far better Jerusalem, or even a new Zerubbabel, who bestowed on the temple of God that glory which greatly exceeded the former" (10.4.3). Clearly, it is the Jerusalem temple that provides the prototype for the new temple now being formed, which is spiritual but also finds expression in the developing Christian architecture of the new era in Palestine.

In view of this rapid Christianization of the Holy Land, one senses something of the shock that the emperor Julian, the last of the Hellenes, caused when he sought to reverse the whole process only thirty years later. His program of restoring pagan religious practice, especially the worship of Helios the sun god, to its rightful place in the empire was a daring and bold enterprise. As a former Christian himself who had apostatized, he was keenly aware of how important for Christians was the claim that they now had been chosen as the replacement for the disobedient Jews. The fact that the Jerusalem temple still lay in ruins was proof that Jesus' prophecy of its destruction was indeed fulfilled. Julian, therefore, set about having the temple rebuilt, despite his own espousing of Helios. This could only have been to embarrass the Christians, and possibly to give some hope to Jews who still held the temple mount as a holy place. However, the work had only begun when Julian himself was killed in a war against the Persians on the eastern frontier. Christians saw this as the hand of God, and there is mention of an earthquake bringing about cessation of work on the temple. Robert Wilken has noted that it is remarkable how often this episode of Julian's failed attempt to discredit Christian claims was mentioned by later writers, especially by John Chrysostom. It clearly touched the nerve center of Christian claims as these were being formulated now that the favor of the empire seemed to vindicate Christians after three centuries of being on the margins, as far as power and privilege went.

This brief reprise of the Constantinian chapter of Christian history brings us back to where the story began, namely, to the Greek and Roman matrix within which the Jesus movement was spawned. The role of Judaism in determining Christian identity differed considerably at the outset of the process from that of this later juncture. Earliest Christianity was from the beginning thoroughly Jewish, even when it opened its doors to Gentile converts in the Pauline mission. By the beginning of the fourth century, however, those Christians of Jewish disposition who wished to remain loyal to their ancestral heritage were excluded as heretics, and the Christian empire would continue the process of distancing itself further from those to whom it owed its origins and tradition, by turning more and more to the Greeks. From the perspective of the prophet from Nazareth it would seem that much was lost, as power and prestige replaced forgiveness and justice as the weightier matters of the law. A critical retelling of that story will not turn the clock back, but it may, hopefully, assist in underlining the need for an ongoing search for what all religions hold in common, while also discerning those things which can distort their better insights.

Further Reading

Important General Works

Ashbrook, S., D. Harvey, and G. Hunter. *The Oxford Handbook of Early Christian Studies*. Oxford: Oxford University Press, 2008.

Collins, J. J., and D. C. Harlow, eds. *The Eerdmans Dictionary of Early Judaism*. Grand Rapids: Eerdmans, 2010.

Mitchell, Margaret M., and F. Young, eds. *The Cambridge History of Christianity: Origins to Constantine*. Cambridge: Cambridge University Press, 2006.

Roberts, J., ed. *The Oxford Dictionary of the Classical World*. Oxford: Oxford University Press, 2005.

1. "Galilee of the Gentiles?"

Chancey, M. *The Myth of a Gentile Galilee*. SNTSMS 118. Cambridge: Cambridge University Press, 2002.

Collins, J. J., and G. Sterling, eds. *Hellenism in the Land of Israel*. Notre Dame: Notre Dame University Press, 2001.

Freyne, S. *Galilee from Alexander the Great to Hadrian: A Study of Second Temple Judaism*. Notre Dame: Notre Dame University Press / Wilmington: Glazier, 1980. Reprinted Edinburgh: Clark, 2000.

Hengel, M. *Jews, Greeks and Barbarians: Aspects of the Hellenization of Judaism in the Pre-Christian Period*. London: SCM, 1980.

Horsley, R. *Galilee: History, Politics, People*. Valley Forge: Trinity, 1995.

Levine, L. *Judaism and Hellenism in Antiquity: Conflict or Confluence?* Peabody: Hendrickson, 1998.

Mendels, D. *The Rise and Fall of Jewish Nationalism: Jewish and Christian Ethnicity in Ancient Palestine.* New York: Doubleday, 1992.

Meyers, E., ed. *Galilee through the Centuries: Confluence of Cultures.* Winona Lake: Eisenbrauns, 1999.

Rajak, T. *The Jewish Dialogue with Greece and Rome: Studies in Cultural and Social Interaction.* Leiden: Brill, 2002.

Zangenberg, J., H. Attridge, and D. Martin, eds. *Religion, Ethnicity and Identity in Ancient Galilee.* WUNT 210. Tübingen: Mohr Siebeck, 2007.

2. The Roman Presence

Alcock, S., ed. *The Early Roman Empire in the East.* Oxbrow Monographs 95. Oxford: Oxbrow Books, 1997.

Berlin, A., and A. Overman, eds. *The First Jewish Revolt: Archaeology, History, Ideology.* New York and London: Routledge, 2002.

Brodd, J., and J. Reed. *Rome and Religion: A Cross-Disciplinary Dialogue on the Imperial Cult.* Atlanta: Society of Biblical Literature, 2011.

Chancey, M. *Greco-Roman Culture and the Galilee of Jesus.* SNTSMS 134. Cambridge: Cambridge University Press, 2005.

Goodman, M. *The Ruling Class of Judea and the First Revolt.* Cambridge: Cambridge University Press, 1987.

Levine, L. *The Rabbinic Class of Roman Palestine.* Jerusalem: Yad Ishak Ben-Zvi, 1989.

————, ed. *The Galilee in Late Antiquity.* New York: The Jewish Theological Seminary of America, 1992.

Millar, F. *The Roman Near East 31 B.C.–A.D. 33.* Cambridge: Harvard University Press, 1993.

Netzer, E. *The Architecture of Herod, the Great Builder.* Grand Rapids: Baker, 2008.

Richardson, P. *Herod King of the Jews and Friend of the Romans.* Columbia: South Carolina University Press, 1996.

3. Palestinian Society and Economy

Edwards, D. R., ed. *Religion and Society in Roman Palestine: Old Questions and New Approaches*. New York and London: Routledge, 2004.

Esler, P., ed. *Modelling Early Christianity: Social Scientific Studies of the New Testament in Context*. London and New York: Routledge, 1995.

Freyne, S. *Galilee, Jesus and the Gospels: Literary Approaches and Historical Investigations*. Dublin: Gill & Macmillan / Philadelphia: Fortress, 1988.

————. *Galilee and Gospel: Collected Essays*. WUNT 125. Tübingen: Mohr Siebeck, 2000.

Hanson, K. C., and D. Oakman. *Palestine in the Time of Jesus: Social Structures and Social Conflicts*. Minneapolis: Fortress, 1998.

Hørning Jensen, M. *Herod Antipas in Galilee*. WUNT 215. Tübingen: Mohr Siebeck, 2006.

Horsley, R. *Sociology and the Jesus Movement*. New York: Crossroads, 1989.

Reed, J. *Archaeology and the Galilean Jesus: A Reexamination of the Evidence*. Harrisburg: Trinity, 2000.

Rocca, S. *Herod's Judaea: A Mediterranean State in the Classical World*. Tübingen: Mohr Siebeck, 2008.

Theissen, G. *The Gospels in Context: Social and Political History in the Synoptic Tradition*. Edinburgh: Clark, 1992.

4. Situating Jesus

Alison, D. C. *Jesus of Nazareth: Millenarian Prophet*. Minneapolis: Augsburg Fortress, 1998.

Charlesworth, J. H., ed. *Jesus and Archaeology*. Grand Rapids: Eerdmans, 2006.

Chilton, B., and C. Evans, eds. *Studying the Historical Jesus: Evaluations of the State of Current Research*. Leiden: Brill, 1994.

Crossan, J. D. *The Historical Jesus: The Life of a Mediterranean Jewish Peasant*. New York: HarperCollins, 1992.

Fiensy, D. *Jesus the Galilean: Soundings in a First Century Life*. Piscataway: Gorgias, 2007.

Freyne, S. *Jesus a Jewish Galilean: A New Reading of the Jesus Story*. Edinburgh: Clark, 2005.

Heschel, S. *The Aryan Jesus: Christian Theologians and the Bible in Nazi Germany*. Princeton: Princeton University Press, 2007.

Keener, C. S. *The Historical Jesus of the Gospels*. Grand Rapids: Eerdmans, 2009.

Keith, C. *Jesus' Literacy: Scribal Culture and the Teacher from Galilee.* New York and London: Clark, 2011.

Meyer, B. *The Aims of Jesus.* London: SCM, 1979.

Moxnes, H. *Jesus and the Rise of Nationalism: A New Quest for the Nineteenth-Century Historical Jesus.* London and New York: Tauris, 2012.

————. *Putting Jesus in His Place: A Radical Vision of Household and Kingdom.* Louisville: Westminster John Knox, 2003.

Sanders, E. P. *Jesus and Judaism.* London: SCM, 1986.

Schüssler Fiorenza, E. *Jesus: Miriam's Child, Sophia's Prophet.* New York: Continuum, 1994.

Theissen, G., and A. Merz. *The Historical Jesus: A Comprehensive Guide.* London, SCM, 1996.

Vermes, G. *Jesus the Jew.* London: Collins, 1973.

5. The Jesus Movement in Jerusalem and Its Later History

Chilton, B., and C. Evans, eds. *James the Just and Christian Origins.* NovT Supplements. Leiden: Brill, 1999.

Dodd, C. H. *The Apostolic Preaching and Its Development* London: Hodder and Stoughton, 1936.

Elliott-Binns, L. E. *Galilean Christianity.* Studies in Biblical Theology 16. London: SCM, 1956.

Evans, C. F. *Resurrection and the New Testament.* London: SCM, 1970.

Hengel, M. *Acts and the History of Earliest Christianity.* Trans. J. Bowden. London: SCM / Philadelphia: Fortress, 1979.

————, *Between Jesus and Paul: Studies in the Earliest History of Christianity.* Trans. J. Bowden. London: SCM / Philadelphia: Fortress, 1983.

Hengel, M., and A. Schwemer. *Paul between Damascus and Antioch: The Unknown Years.* Trans. J. Bowden. London: SCM, 1997.

————. *Paulus und Jakobus. Kleine Schriften III.* WUNT 141. Tübingen: Mohr Siebeck, 2002.

Hill, C. *Hellenists and Hebrews: Reappraising Division within the Earliest Church.* Minneapolis: Fortress, 1992.

Jackson-McCabe, M., ed. *Jewish Christianity Reconsidered.* Minneapolis: Augsburg Fortress, 2007.

Lüdemann, G. *The Resurrection of Jesus.* London: SCM / Philadelphia: Fortress, 1994.

Meyer, B. *The Early Christians: Their World Mission and Self-Discovery.* Wilmington: Glazier, 1986.

Moule, C. F. D., ed. *The Significance of the Message of the Resurrection for Faith in Jesus Christ.* London: SCM, 1968.

Nickelsburg, G. *Ancient Judaism and Christian Origins: Diversity, Continuity and Transformation.* Minneapolis: Fortress, 2003.

O'Mahony, K., ed. *Christian Origins: Worship, Belief and Society.* JSNTSS 241. Sheffield: Sheffield Academic, 2003.

Painter, J. *Just James: The Brother of Jesus in History and Tradition.* Columbia: University of South Carolina Press, 1997.

Penner, T. *In Praise of Christian Origins: Stephen and the Hellenists in Lukan Apologetic Historiography.* Emory Studies in Early Christianity. New York and London: Clark, 2004.

Taylor, J. *Where Did Christianity Come From?* Collegeville: Liturgical, 2001.

6. Remembering Jesus and Broadening Horizons
I: The Sayings Sources

Cameron, R. *The Other Gospels: Non-Canonical Gospel Texts.* Philadelphia: Westminster, 1982.

Casey, M. *An Aramaic Approach to Q.* SNTSMS 122. Cambridge: Cambridge University Press, 2002.

Del Verme, M. *Didache and Judaism: Jewish Roots of an Ancient Christian Jewish Work.* London and New York: Clark, 2004.

Johnson-Debaufre, M. *Jesus among Her Children: Q, Eschatology and the Construction of Christian Origins.* Harvard Theological Studies 55. Cambridge: Harvard University Press, 2005.

Kloppenborg, J. *Q Parallels: Synopsis, Critical Notes, Concordance.* Sonoma: Polebridge, 1988.

Kloppenborg, J., M. Meyer, S. Patterson, and M. Steinhauser, eds. *Q, Thomas Reader.* Sonoma: Polebridge, 1990.

Kloppenborg-Verbin, J. *Excavating Q.* Edinburgh: Clark, 2000.

Koester, H. *Ancient Christian Gospels: Their History and Development.* London: SCM / Philadelphia: Trinity, 1990.

———. *From Jesus to the Gospels: Interpreting the New Testament in Its Context.* Minneapolis: Fortress, 2007.

Milavec, A. *The Didache: Text, Translation, Analysis and Commentary.* Collegeville, Minn.: The Liturgical Press, 2003.

O'Loughlin, T. *The Didache: A Window on the Earliest Christians.* London: SPCK, 2010.

Patterson, S. J. *The Gospel of Thomas and Jesus.* Sonoma: Polebridge, 1993.

Robinson, J., and H. Koester. *Trajectories through Early Christianity.* Philadelphia: Fortress, 1971.

Theissen, G. *Sociology of Early Palestinian Christianity.* Trans. J. Bowman. London: SCM, 1978.

Tuckett, C. *Q and the History of Early Christianity.* Edinburgh: Clark, 1996.

7. Remembering Jesus and Broadening Horizons II: The Gospels of Mark and Matthew

Aune, D., ed. *The Gospel of Matthew in Current Study.* Grand Rapids: Eerdmans, 2001.

Becker E.-M., and A. Runesson, eds. *Mark and Matthew I.* WUNT 271. Tübingen: Mohr Siebeck, 2011.

Brown, R., and J. Meier. *Antioch and Rome: New Testament Cradles of Catholic Christianity.* London: Chapman, 1982.

Hengel, M. *Studies in the Gospel of Mark.* Trans. J. Bowden. London: SCM, 1985.

Luz, U. *Studies in Matthew.* Grand Rapids: Eerdmans, 2005.

Overman, J. A. *Matthew's Gospel and Formative Judaism: The Social World of the Matthean Community.* Minneapolis: Fortress, 1990.

Riches, J. K. *Conflicting Mythologies: Identity Formation in the Gospels of Mark and Matthew.* Edinburgh: Clark, 2000.

Saldarini, A. *Matthew's Christian-Jewish Community.* Chicago: University of Chicago Press, 1994.

Sim, D. *The Gospel of Matthew and Christian Judaism: The History and Social Setting of the Matthean Community.* Edinburgh: Clark, 1998.

Stanton, G. *A Gospel for a New People.* Edinburgh: Clark, 1992.

———, ed. *The Interpretation of Matthew.* London: SPCK / Philadelphia: Fortress, 1983.

Telford, W., ed. *The Interpretation of Mark.* 2nd ed. Edinburgh: Clark, 1995.

Tolbert, M. A. *Sowing the Gospel: Mark's World in Literary-Historical Perspective.* Minneapolis: Fortress, 1989.

Tuckett, C., ed. *The Messianic Secret.* London: SPCK / Philadelphia: Fortress, 1983.

Yarbro Collins, A. *The Gospel of Mark.* Hermeneia. Philadelphia: Fortress, 2007.

Zetterholm, M. *The Formation of Christianity in Antioch.* London and New York: Routledge, 2003.

8. Into the Second Century

Bartlett, J. R., ed. *Jews in the Hellenistic and Roman Cities.* London: Routledge, 2002.

Bauer, W. *Orthodoxy and Heresy in Earliest Christianity.* Trans. R. Kraft, et al. Philadelphia: Fortress, 1971.

Boyarin, D. *Borderlines: The Partition of Judaeo-Christianity.* Philadelphia: University of Pennsylvania Press, 2004.

Buell, D. K. *Why This New Race? Ethnic Reasoning in Early Christianity.* New York: Columbia University Press, 2005.

Chadwick, H. *Early Christian Thought and the Classical Tradition.* Oxford: Clarendon, 1966.

————. *Origen: Contra Celsum.* Cambridge: Cambridge University Press, 1953.

Helholm, D., et al., eds. *Ablution, Initiation, and Baptism: Late Antiquity, Early Judaism and Early Christianity.* 3 vols. Berlin: de Gruyter, 2011.

Holmes, M. W., *The Apostolic Fathers: Greek Text and English Translations.* 3rd ed. Grand Rapids: Baker, 2007.

Horbury, W. *Jews and Christians in Contact and Controversy.* Edinburgh: Clark, 1998.

King, K. L. *The Gospel of Mary of Magdala: Jesus and the First Woman Apostle.* Santa Rosa: Polebridge, 2003.

————. *The Secret Revelation of John.* Cambridge: Harvard University Press, 2006.

————. *What Is Gnosticism?* Cambridge: Belknap, 2003.

Limor, O., and G. Stroumsa, eds. *Christians and Christianity in the Holy Land.* Jerusalem: Yad Izhak Ben Zvi, 2006.

Luomanen, P. *Recovering Jewish-Christian Sects and Gospels.* Leiden and Boston: Brill, 2012.

Marjanen, A., and P. Luomanen, eds. *A Companion to Second-Century Christian "Heretics."* Leiden: Brill, 2008.

Nashrallah, L. *Christian Responses to Roman Art and Architecture: The Second-Century Church in the Spaces of Empire.* Cambridge: Cambridge University Press, 2010.

Pagels E., and K. L. King. *Reading Judas: The Gospel of Judas and the Shaping of Christianity.* New York: Viking, 2007.

Pervo, R. *Dating Acts: Between the Evangelists and the Apologists.* Santa Rosa: Polebridge, 2006.

Rizzi, M., ed. *Hadrian and the Christians.* Berlin and New York: de Gruyter, 2010.

Robinson, J. M. *The Nag Hammadi Library in English.* New York: Harper and Row, 1977. 3rd ed. 1988.

Runneson, A., D. Binder, and B. Olsson, eds. *The Ancient Synagogue from Its Origins to 200 C.E.: A Source Book.* Leiden: Brill, 2008.

Schäfer, P. *Der Bar Kokhba-Aufstand.* TSAJ 1. Mohr Siebeck: Tübingen, 1981.

Schoedel, W., and R. Wilken, eds. *Early Christian Literature and the Classical Intellectual Tradition in Honorem Robert M. Grant.* Paris: Beauchesne, 1979.

Smallwood, M. *The Jews under Roman Rule from Pompey to Diocletian.* Leiden: Brill, 1981.

Tyson, J. B. *Marcion and Luke-Acts: A Defining Struggle.* Columbia: University of South Carolina Press, 2006.

Wilken, R. L. *The Christians as the Romans Saw Them.* New Haven: Yale University Press, 1984.

————. *John Chrysostom and the Jews.* Berkeley: University of California Press, 1983.

————. *The Land Called Holy: Palestine in Christian History and Thought.* New Haven: Yale University Press, 1992.

Wilson, S. *Related Strangers: Jews and Christians 70-170 C.E.* Minneapolis: Fortress, 1995.

Index of Modern Authors

Index of Subjects

Acco. *See* Ptolemaios/Acco
Agriculture in Galilee, 102-3
Agrippa I. *See* Herod Agrippa I
Agrippa II. *See* Herod Agrippa II
Alexander Jannaeus, 99-100, 101, 103, 104, 105
Am ha-aretz, 133-34, 156
Antioch, 66, 72, 78, 87, 205, 208, 222-23, 226-27, 228, 240, 274, 275, 278, 296-97, 301, 306, 309, 347
Antiochus Epiphanes, 13-14, 15, 39, 67, 97, 150, 171, 172-73, 204, 288
Antipas, tetrarch. *See* Herod Antipas
Antipater. *See* Herod Antipater
Apocalyptic worldview, 151, 157-59, 165-76, 199-200, 284-85, 309-10, 311, 326-27
Apologetic literature, 319, 321, 322, 329, 345
Apostles, the. *See* Twelve, the
Apostolic succession, 348-49, 352-53
Archelaus, tetrarch. *See* Herod Archelaus
Asklepius, 36-37
Augustus/Octavian, 47, 52-53, 73, 79, 112-13, 119, 163

Bacchae (Euripides), 40-41
Banias. *See* Caesarea Philippi/Banias
Baptism, 338
Barnabas, Epistle of, 331-34

Basileia, rule (of God), 158, 160, 163, 172, 175, 284
Beroea/Aleppo, 245, 275
Bethsaida, 63-64, 166, 213, 250, 254
Bethshan. *See* Scythopolis/Bethshan
Birkath-ha-Minim, 329, 335

Caesarea Maritima, 23-25, 55, 57, 58, 114-15, 277, 326
Caesarea Philippi/Banias, 23, 24, 26, 55, 57, 63, 68, 72-73, 81-82, 143, 146, 275
Caligula, emperor. *See* Gaius Caligula
Canon, biblical, 9, 342, 347, 348
Capernaum, 129, 166, 244, 250, 254-56
Celsus, 322, 323-25, 336, 340-42, 344, 348
Ceramic remains. *See* Pottery finds
Cerinthus, 234
Chorazin, 166, 250, 254
Christians (as a designation), 205
Church/*ekklēsia,* 303-4, 312
Circumcision, 225-26, 228, 263, 279, 289, 328, 333, 335, 337-39, 346
Claudius, emperor, 66, 67
Coinage, 4, 17, 60-63, 67, 68, 71-72, 80-81, 86, 90, 98, 116, 123, 127, 129, 130-31, 163, 327
Constantine, the age of, 351-55
Council of Jerusalem, 77, 223, 224, 228

Index of Ancient Sources